T0373886

DEVELOPING CRITICAL CONSCIOUSNESS IN YOUTH

Critical consciousness is the ability to critically analyze societal inequities and to develop the motivation and agency to promote social change. While there has been a proliferation of empirical work on critical consciousness over the last two decades, this is the first volume to consider how we can support youth's critical consciousness development – their ability to recognize and fight injustice. Leading scholars address some of the field's most urgent questions: How does critical consciousness develop? What are the key developmental settings (homes, schools, community programs) and societal experiences (racism, police brutality, immigration, political turmoil) that inform critical consciousness development among youth? Providing novel insights into key school-based, out-of-school, and societal contexts that propel youth to greater critical reflection and action, this book will benefit scholars and students in developmental, educational, and community psychology, as well as practitioners working in schools, community-based organizations, and other youth settings.

Erin B. Godfrey is Associate Professor of Applied Psychology in the Steinhardt School of Culture, Education, and Human Development at New York University. She is coeditor of *Critical Consciousness: Expanding Theory and Measurement* (2023) and an editorial board member for the *Journal of Youth and Adolescence*. She won NYU Steinhardt's W. Gabriel Carras Research Award in 2013 and NYU Steinhardt's Griffiths Research Award in 2018.

Luke J. Rapa is Assistant Professor in the Department of Education and Human Development at Clemson University, USA. He is coeditor of *Critical Consciousness: Expanding Theory and Measurement* (2023) and *Disproportionality and Social Justice in Education* (2022). He was Clemson University's College of Education Junior Researcher of the Year in 2022.

Contemporary Social Issues Series

General Editor: Brian D. Christens,

Vanderbilt University

Contemporary Social Issues is the official book series of the Society for the Psychological Study of Social Issues (SPSSI). Since its founding in 1936, SPSSI has addressed the social issues of the times. Central to these efforts has been the Lewinian tradition of action-oriented research, in which psychological theories and methods guide research and action addressed to important societal problems. Grounded in their authors' programmes of research, works in this series focus on social issues facing individuals, groups, communities, and/or society at large, with each volume written to speak to scholars, students, practitioners, and policymakers.

Other Books in the Series

Developing Critical Consciousness in Youth: Contexts and Settings
Erin Godfrey and Luke Rapa, editors

Critical Consciousness: Expanding Theory and Measurement
Luke Rapa and Erin Godfrey, editors

Developing Critical Consciousness in Youth

Contexts and Settings

Edited by

Erin B. Godfrey

New York University

Luke J. Rapa

Clemson University

CAMBRIDGE
UNIVERSITY PRESS

Shaftesbury Road, Cambridge CB2 8EA, United Kingdom

One Liberty Plaza, 20th Floor, New York, NY 10006, USA

477 Williamstown Road, Port Melbourne, VIC 3207, Australia

314–321, 3rd Floor, Plot 3, Splendor Forum, Jasola District Centre,
New Delhi – 110025, India

103 Penang Road, #05–06/07, Visioncrest Commercial, Singapore 238467

Cambridge University Press is part of Cambridge University Press & Assessment,
a department of the University of Cambridge.

We share the University's mission to contribute to society through the pursuit of
education, learning and research at the highest international levels of excellence.

www.cambridge.org
Information on this title: www.cambridge.org/9781009153836

DOI: 10.1017/9781009153843

First published 2023

A catalogue record for this publication is available from the British Library.

Library of Congress Cataloging-in-Publication Data
NAMES: Godfrey, Erin B., editor. | Rapa, Luke J., editor.
TITLE: Developing critical consciousness in youth : contexts and settings / edited by Erin B.
Godfrey, New York University, Luke J. Rapa, Clemson University, South Carolina.
DESCRIPTION: Cambridge, United Kingdom ; New York, NY : Cambridge University Press, 2023.
| Series: Contemporary social issues series | Includes bibliographical references and index.
IDENTIFIERS: LCCN 2022057081 | ISBN 9781009153836 (hardback) | ISBN 9781009153829 (paper-
back) | ISBN 9781009153843 (ebook)
SUBJECTS: LCSH: Social justice – Study and teaching (Secondary) – United States. |
Youth – United States – Attitudes. | Critical pedagogy – United States. | Mindfulness
(Psychology) – United States.
CLASSIFICATION: LCC HM671 .D426 2023 | DDC 303.3/720973–dc23/eng/20230110
LC record available at https://lccn.loc.gov/2022057081

ISBN 978-1-009-15383-6 Hardback
ISBN 978-1-009-15382-9 Paperback

Cambridge University Press & Assessment has no responsibility for the persistence
or accuracy of URLs for external or third-party internet websites referred to in this
publication and does not guarantee that any content on such websites is, or will
remain, accurate or appropriate.

For Sonny – you teach me every day what it means to truly live what you believe. Thank you for showing me how to walk alongside someone else in true partnership in this world.

EBG

For Jonah, Adelyn, and Sylvia – and all the children of your generation – that you might come to know and experience a more loving, equitable, and just world.

LJR

CONTENTS

FIGURES

TABLES

CONTRIBUTORS

CARLOS AGUILAR, University of Pennsylvania, USA

ADRIANA ALDANA, PHD, California State University, Dominguez Hills, USA

ANITRA R. ALEXANDER, North Carolina State University, USA

MARIA ALEJANDRA ARCE, PHD, Georgia State University, USA

PARISSA J. BALLARD, PHD, Wake Forest School of Medicine, USA

JOSEFINA BAÑALES, PHD, University of Illinois at Chicago, USA

CANDICE W. BOLDING, Clemson University, USA

EDMOND P. BOWERS, PHD, Clemson University, USA

ALEXIS S. BRIGGS, North Carolina State University, USA

GERMÁN A. CADENAS, PHD, Lehigh University, USA

BRIAN D. CHRISTENS, PHD, Vanderbilt University, USA

ALISON K. COHEN, PHD, University of California, San Francisco, USA

CLAUDIA A. DELBASSO, Georgia State University, USA

CHRISTINA DUCAT, University of Baltimore, USA

AALIYAH EL-AMIN, EDD, Harvard Graduate School of Education, USA

ERIN B. GODFREY, PHD, New York University, USA

DAREN GRAVES, EDD, Simmons University, USA

ELAN C. HOPE, PHD, North Carolina State University, USA

DEANNA IBRAHIM, New York University, USA

SHABNAM JAVDANI, PHD, New York University, USA

SELIMA JUMARALI, University of Baltimore, USA

JULIANA E. KARRAS, PHD, San Francisco State University, USA

GABRIEL P. KUPERMINC, PHD, Georgia State University, USA

ELENA MAKER CASTRO, University of California, Los Angeles, USA

RAFAEL MARTINEZ OROZCO, PHD, Arizona State University, USA

CHANNING J. MATHEWS, PHD, North Carolina State University, USA

LIDIA Y. MONJARAS-GAYTAN, DePaul University, USA

KATHRYN Y. MORGAN, Vanderbilt University, USA

ANDREW NALANI, New York University, USA

LUKE J. RAPA, PHD, Clemson University, USA

BERNADETTE SÁNCHEZ, PHD, University of Illinois at Chicago, USA

SCOTT SEIDER, PHD, Boston College, USA

SCOTT WARREN, SNF Agora Institute, Johns Hopkins University, USA

ACKNOWLEDGMENTS

A project like this cannot materialize without the contributions of so many people. We are grateful to all who supported this work – in big and small ways, and in seen and unseen ways.

To all who contributed chapters to this volume, thank you for engaging with us in this project and for trusting us with your ideas and your scholarship. Your contributions truly are the sine qua non of this work; without your commitment to participate in conversations, writing groups, idea exchanges, and peer review processes – not to mention doing the hard work of writing and revising your own chapters – this volume would not be what it is today. We are eternally grateful for your participation in this project and we are honored to be a part of a scholarly community with you, sharing in your intellectual, academic, and critically reflective spaces.

To colleagues who offered guidance, support, and encouragement along the way, thank you for your commitment to us and for your care about our work, our ideas, and our successes.

To our families, thank you for your love, encouragement, patience, and support. We are only able to do what we do because of you.

To Luke, I (Erin) cannot express how thankful I am – and how deeply lucky I feel – to have had the opportunity to join you in this undertaking. Our collaboration has been a light in dark times and one of the most rewarding and enriching projects in my career. Your passion, intellect, and perspective inspire me in my work and your friendship lifts me up in my life. Thank you for choosing me to go on this journey with you.

Dr. Brian Christens, we offer you our most sincere gratitude for your assistance and your guidance over the course of this project. We appreciate the trust and confidence you placed in us, and your willingness to allow us to engage in this work as we did. The volume would surely not be what it is today without your support of the vision we had for this book.

Janka Romero and Rowan Groat, at Cambridge University Press, thank you for your expert hands in guiding us through the process, from initial proposal development through manuscript completion. Your insights and care were invaluable to us, and this volume could not have come to fruition without you. Your patience and your speedy replies to our queries are greatly appreciated.

This project was funded in part by Clemson University's R-Initiative Program. We are grateful to the Clemson University Division of Research for the generous funding provided to support a portion of Luke's work on this volume. This project was also funded in part by NYU's University Research Challenge Fund and the NYU Steinhardt School of Culture, Education and Human Development Faculty Challenge Grant. We thank NYU and NYU Steinhardt for their generous support of this scholarship.

We dedicate this book to the young people everywhere, and to those who love, teach, support, guide, and learn with, from, and alongside them. Your activism, creativity, passion, and strength inspire us to try every day to make the world we live in worthy of you.

Introduction

Introducing the Contexts and Settings of Youth's Critical Consciousness Development

ERIN B. GODFREY AND LUKE J. RAPA

Structural oppression and systemic inequity are interwoven into the fabric of American society. One need only reflect on the past decade to see the continued pernicious influence of racism, sexism, classism, ableism, nativism, heterosexism, transphobia, and multiple other forms of marginalization on the rights, freedoms, and humanity of large segments of our society. We live in a system of white supremacy and patriarchy that patterns not only our history but our current society, institutions, interactions, and beliefs about each other and ourselves (Bonilla-Silva, 2006). To be Black, Brown, Indigenous, immigrant, differently-abled, gay, gender-expansive, female-identified – among many other identities – means being subjected to systems and structures that, at best, limit access to the resources and privileges others take for granted and, at worst, take away fundamental rights to life, liberty, and choice. To be white, straight, able-bodied, male-identified, and more (e.g., Christian Protestant) means wielding privilege one may or may not know one has, but that contributes to the maintenance of these inequities. These unfair, unjust, and inequitable social conditions shape all our lives in multiple seen and unseen ways and have effects across all developmental domains (Brown et al., 2019; Ruck et al., 2019).

Social scientists have amassed considerable evidence on how oppressive systems shape people's development, adaptive functioning, and general well-being (Heberle et al., 2020), showing deleterious effects on multiple life outcomes across multiple populations. It is only relatively recently, however, that scholars have begun to consider people's own beliefs and actions regarding the fairness and legitimacy of the systems in which they live. This shift in perspective recognizes that individuals can be formidable assets in the fight against injustice, and treats them as active agents in the construal and transformation of systems of oppression. Central to this area of inquiry is critical consciousness (Freire, 1968/2000; Watts et al., 2011), which relates to how individuals critically "read" social conditions, feel empowered to change those conditions, and engage in action toward that goal. Alongside allied perspectives such as sociopolitical development, culturally relevant pedagogy, critical theory, and antiracist perspectives, critical consciousness theory has emerged as a particularly useful framework for interrogating how people understand, navigate, and resist social injustice and inequity.

WHAT IS CRITICAL CONSCIOUSNESS AND WHY DOES IT MATTER?

Critical consciousness was originally conceptualized by Paulo Freire (1921–1997) as a pedagogical method to foster the ability of marginalized people to analyze the economic, political, historical, and social forces that contribute to inequitable social conditions and become empowered to change these conditions (Freire, 1973, 1968/2000). Freire termed this process *"conscientização"* – translated into English as "conscientization" – and described it as a dialectical process of reflection and action in which people engage with others about their experiences of oppression and marginalization and attend to their historical, social, and economic sources. Through discussion and dialogue – core elements of Freirean pedagogy – people become critically aware of the causes of their marginalization at the hands of historical and societal forces, take action to address this marginalization, and further deepen their understanding of the causes of oppression based on this experience.

Critical consciousness is considered to be especially potent for those who experience marginalization and structural oppression firsthand, in their daily lives and across their lived environments. It has even been called the "antidote to oppression" (Watts et al., 1999) because of its ability to arm marginalized youth with the insight, agency, and engagement needed to navigate and change oppressive systems (Watts et al., 2011). Yet, critical consciousness is also important for those experiencing relative privilege, as they work to understand systems of power, and their own power and privilege within those systems, and ally with others to bring about social change.

Building on Freire's theory of conscientization, and his pedagogical approach, developmental scientists typically conceptualize critical consciousness as three distinct, but overlapping components (e.g., Diemer et al., 2015; Watts et al., 2011). The first component, critical reflection, refers to an individual's ability to analyze current social realities critically, and recognize how historical, social, economic, and political conditions limit access to opportunity and perpetuate injustice. The second component, critical motivation (also referred to as sociopolitical or political efficacy), encompasses an individual's motivation and perceived ability to act to change these social, economic, and political conditions. The third component, critical action, is the extent to which individuals participate in action, individually or collectively, to resist, challenge, or disrupt social inequity. While the first component concerns increased awareness of and deepening reflection on unjust circumstances and their causes, the latter two involve the translation of this critical reflection into behaviors and action. The process of gaining critical awareness and acting to change conditions is self-perpetuating and reciprocal. That is, scholars conceptualize critical reflection as leading directly to action, but they also see critical action as reinforcing and deepening critical reflection and analysis, creating a virtuous cycle starting from either reflection or action. The role of critical motivation in this cycle is the subject of continued conceptual (i.e., theoretical) and empirical debate, but it is often thought of as a mediator through which reflection is linked to action or as a moderator that changes the way reflection and action influence each other or interrelate (e.g., Diemer & Rapa, 2016). Scholars are just beginning to delve more deeply into how these components interact and/or pattern together to characterize different types, levels, and/or processes of critical consciousness development (Christens, et al., 2013; Diemer & Rapa, 2016; Godfrey et al., 2019). This is the case, at least in part, because measures incorporating all three dimensions of critical consciousness are just emerging (e.g., Diemer et al., 2022; Rapa et al., 2020a; see also Rapa & Godfrey, in press[a]).

Critical consciousness is important from a societal perspective as it can play a central role in addressing unjust systems, challenging marginalization in society, and promoting positive community development. It is also an extremely important developmental competency for individuals, as it promotes positive growth and development. As mentioned earlier, it can function as an "antidote to oppression" or a form of "psychological armor" (Watts et al., 1999) for individuals experiencing and navigating oppressive systems. Indeed, we now have considerable evidence, primarily for Black, Brown, and low-socioeconomic status (SES) youth, that higher critical consciousness is connected to better educational outcomes (e.g., Seider et al., 2020), higher occupational aspirations and attainment (e.g., Rapa et al., 2018), greater political, civic and community participation (e.g., Bañales et al., 2020; Diemer & Rapa, 2016; Tyler et al., 2020), and enhanced well-being across a range of dimensions (e.g., Godfrey et al., 2019; Zimmerman et al., 1999) (for excellent reviews, see Diemer et al., 2016; Heberle et al., 2020; Maker Castro et al., 2022). Although less scholarship to date has examined critical consciousness among individuals holding ethnic/racial, class, and/or other forms of privilege, developing a critical stance toward the status quo is also important – and doing so should not be the sole responsibility of those who are marginalized or oppressed. As many authors in this volume argue, it is also important for those who hold power and privilege to recognize it, and then to use that power and privilege to engage in efforts to dismantle systems that reify, uphold, or perpetuate injustice and inequity. Indeed, recognizing privilege and its sources, and learning how to work in allyship and solidarity with those individuals and groups experiencing oppression, is a critical developmental competency for those who hold more privilege as well (Spanierman & Smith, 2017).

THE ROLE OF CONTEXTS AND SETTINGS AND THE
ORGANIZATION OF THIS VOLUME

It is clear that fostering critical consciousness has considerable value – both for society as a whole and for individuals themselves. Yet, important questions remain about how to foster this fundamental competency, particularly during adolescence and young adulthood, which are especially sensitive developmental periods during which youth are uniquely enabled and motivated to think and act critically about societal fairness and social injustice (Brown & Larson, 2009; Erikson, 1968; Lerner & Steinberg, 2009; Quintana, 1999). While the field has matured in recent years (Heberle et al., 2020), until now no authoritative, contemporary volume has existed that brings together leading scholars to address some of the field's most urgent questions: How does critical consciousness develop? What are the key settings (e.g., homes, schools, community programs) and societal contexts (e.g., racism, immigration) that inform critical consciousness development among youth? These questions are of utmost importance to deepen our understanding of youth development and societal change. Answering them is more urgent than ever given the current sociopolitical moment – a moment in which longstanding racial inequity, bias, discrimination, and competing ideologies are not only evident, but amplified.

Developing Critical Consciousness in Youth: Contexts and Settings addresses these questions and more. This edited volume – along with the complementary volume *Critical Consciousness: Expanding Theory and Measurement* (Rapa & Godfrey, in press[b]) – stems from our engagement with leading scholars in the field to identify topics and content considered most necessary to meaningfully advance critical consciousness scholarship. The chapters in this volume represent the most cutting-edge work by scholars to understand the key contexts and settings that contribute to critical consciousness development in youth. Following Heberle et al. (2020) and Watts et al. (1999), we explore key contexts and settings of youth's lives relevant for critical consciousness development, introducing new perspectives and empirical data regarding the features of these contexts and settings that play a consciousness-raising role. In the remainder of this introduction, we review what answers the literature has provided so far regarding the contexts and settings of youth development and then describe how the chapters in this volume seek to add to this growing understanding. We focus on three areas that are predominant in shaping youth's lives and lived experiences: (1) pedagogical, curricular, and school-based contexts; (2) extracurricular contexts; and (3) societal contexts.

Part I: Pedagogical, Curricular, and School-Based Contexts

Summary of Current Knowledge Parental and peer socialization and the contexts of classrooms and schools have arguably received the most attention from scholars to date as primary settings of critical consciousness development, and for good reason (e.g., Heberle et al., 2020). Central to Friere's (1973) pedagogy was the concept of open dialogue and problem-posing approaches. He argued that critical consciousness develops through a process of open dialogue with others, in which people discuss divergent and convergent experiences with societal inequity and opinions about its sources. The available evidence suggests that opportunities and support for this kind of dialogue may indeed be a key contributor to youth's critical consciousness. Critical consciousness (especially reflection and motivation) tends to be higher for youth whose parents and/or peers engage with them in discussions about social issues, support critical perspectives on injustice, and stress the importance of standing up for one's beliefs (Bañales et al., 2020, Diemer et al., 2006, 2009; Diemer & Hsieh, 2008; Diemer & Li, 2011; Heberle et al., 2020). Alongside parents and peers, schools and classrooms are another important setting for critical consciousness development. School and classroom climates that support open, critical, and respectful dialogue about political and social issues foster critical consciousness among their students, particularly their critical reflection skills (Heberle et al., 2020). This support can occur at multiple levels through multiple mechanisms, including the overall educational model in place in the school (e.g., progressive schools vs. no excuse schools; e.g., Seider et al., 2016), support from teachers and principals (e.g., Diemer et al., 2009), encouragement and presence of critical educational opportunities (e.g., Clark & Seider, 2017), and the climate in the classroom itself (e.g., Godfrey & Grayman, 2014; Rapa et al., 2020b).

For example, in their groundbreaking mixed-methods study of five schools grounded in five different pedagogical models (problem-posing, expeditionary, habits of mind, action civics, and no excuses), Seider and Graves (2020) found that no one model was "best" at fostering overall critical consciousness. Instead, models were more or less effective at promoting different components of it. A common set of features characterized effective teaching for critical consciousness development across these differing pedagogical models. These "teaching tools for critical consciousness" included: (1) introducing theoretical frameworks that unpack and name aspects of oppression; (2) engaging youth themselves to teach others about experiences of injustice; (3) creating opportunities for social action to challenge inequities within youth's own school community; (4) developing real-world assignments that push youth to exert influence on the world outside school walls; and (5) having teachers' share their own personal experiences with forces of oppression. These teaching tools were successfully employed across a variety of contexts and settings within each school, including the core academic curriculum and elective courses, along with extracurricular programs, clubs, and events, and school community assemblies and gatherings.

In addition to the climate and overall pedagogical approach of the school and classroom as a whole, qualitative work has described how specific curricular interventions foster youth critical consciousness, again with particular influence on critical reflection (Heberle et al., 2020). The specific focus of the curricular intervention – whether literature and the arts, science, social science and ethnic studies, civic education, sex education, or cross-curricular – does not seem to matter as much as its inherent pedagogical processes. As Heberle and colleagues note, dialogic instruction that is developmentally appropriate, connects information to students' lived experiences of injustice, encourages dialogue and critique through open-ended questioning, and challenges bias is the critical ingredient that seems particularly effective in promoting critical consciousness development. Similarly, culturally-responsive pedagogy and ethnic studies programs that emphasize critical thinking, feature the historical, literary, and social contributions of marginalized groups, and tackle controversial topics such as race, discrimination, and socioeconomic inequality through a critical lens have strong potential to foster critical consciousness in youth. They have been shown to boost academic achievement as well (an excellent example is the now banned Mexican American Studies program in Tucson, Arizona; Cabrera, et al., 2014).

The Chapters in Part I School-based settings (and their pedagogical features) clearly function as centrally important contexts in youth's critical consciousness development, and are especially relevant given the salience of school itself as a primary context and setting of youth development. In Part I of this volume, we present three chapters that extend and enhance our understanding of school-based pedagogical tools and curricular programs and their role in fostering critical consciousness. Building off prior knowledge in this area, they introduce new perspectives on the ways school-based contexts inform critical consciousness. In Chapter 1, Daren Graves, Aaliyah El-Amin, and Scott Seider delve more deeply into the notion of teaching tools for critical consciousness. Overlaying Picower's (2009) "tools of whiteness" framework on observational data from a handful of teachers, they detail the traps and pitfalls that even well-meaning and critically conscious white teachers fall into when seeking to support the critical consciousness development of their Black and Brown students. They then provide examples of how white teachers – who make up 79% of the United States teaching force (Pew Research Center, 2021) – can overcome these barriers and create counter-spaces of liberation. Chapters 2 and 3 shift the focus from teacher practices to curricular programs, delving into two specific widespread civics approaches that may be relevant for critical consciousness development. They draw important theoretical and empirical links between more broadly implemented school-based civics interventions and critical consciousness development. In Chapter 2, Parissa Ballard, Elena Maker Castro, Julianna Karras, Scott Warren, and Alison Cohen describe the action civics program Generation Citizen. Using the program's theory of change and products from youth participants, they compare programmatic elements of Generation Citizen against core elements of critical consciousness development to elucidate how this program, and others like it, may support youth's critical consciousness. Finally, in Chapter 3, Kathryn Morgan and Brian Christens build on the conceptual connections between action civics programs and critical consciousness described in Chapter 2. They use quantitative and qualitative data to empirically demonstrate that participation in Design Your Neighborhood, another action civics program emphasizing local and community embeddedness, can promote youth critical consciousness, in nuanced ways.

Part II: Extracurricular Contexts

Summary of Current Knowledge We focus next on intervention programs and other extracurricular contexts that can foster critical consciousness. Extracurricular interventions specifically designed to promote youth's critical consciousness are also fairly prevalent in the current literature. Whether they occur during the school day or as out-of-school-time programs, these are stand-alone programs targeting critical consciousness that take place outside of school's core instructional activities. These programs leverage approaches such as critical media pedagogy, ethnic studies, youth participatory action research (YPAR), theater and the arts, and service learning and often use similar dialogic approaches to the ones described earlier to help youth notice, critically reflect upon, and challenge injustice (Heberle et al., 2020). In their review, Watts and Hipólito-Delgado (2015) identified three types of activities as central to efforts to raise critical consciousness in these kinds of interventions: (1) fostering awareness and reflection of sociopolitical circumstances through small group discussion (with critically conscious group leaders) (see also Ginwright & James, 2002; Youniss & Yates, 1997); (2) encouraging critical questioning; and (3) promoting collective identity. However, Watts and Hipólito-Delgado (2015) also identified an important gap in this work so far: that much less attention has been paid to actually engaging in critical action as a means to foster critical consciousness development. They thus identified youth community organizing – where young people come together to identify and discuss common interests, mobilize their peers, and engage in action to address school and community-based quality of life and social justice issues (Kirshner & Ginwright, 2012) – as a promising strategy to bridge the gap between critical reflection and action.

The Chapters in Part II Based on the above, it is safe to say that most programs designed specifically to foster critical consciousness are more or less successful at doing so, particularly when it comes to critical reflection. The three chapters in Part II of this volume are devoted to understanding what happens in the context of extracurricular programs that are not necessarily designed with critical consciousness goals in mind. The chapters in this section explore if, when, and how more general types of extracurricular programming may also serve as settings for critical consciousness development. This is critically important as we seek to develop consciousness-raising systems (Heberle et al., 2020) and expand opportunities for youth to grow this important developmental and societal competency. In Chapter 4, Edmond Bowers, Candice Bolding, Lidia Monjaras-Gaytan, and Bernadette Sánchez re-envision the "Big Three" model of effective out-of-school time programming (positive and sustained relationships, activities to develop and practice life skills, and meaningful opportunities for youth) in light of social justice youth development principles (Ginwright & James, 2002) and critical consciousness theory. They offer a synthesized model through which out-of-school programs can scaffold youth of color to recognize and challenge oppression, and sound a call to action for practitioners, policy makers, and scholars. In Chapter 5, Deanna Ibrahim, Andrew Nalani, and Erin Godfrey zero in on participation in the arts and arts programming as a potentially relevant and under-tapped setting of critical consciousness development. They draw conceptual links between arts participation and critical consciousness skills and components, detailing how and why arts participation of various kinds may support youth's critical consciousness development and then use survey data to provide empirical evidence of these associations among youth of color. Finally, in Chapter 6, Shabnam Javdani, Erin Godfrey, Christina Ducat, and Selima Jumarali examine the potential role of service-learning approaches as a context of critical consciousness development, an area that has received limited attention in the critical consciousness literature. They articulate distinctions between service-learning and *critical* service-learning approaches and describe one such critical approach, the Resilience, Opportunity, Safety, Education, and Strength (ROSES) community-based advocacy program. They specify how particular features of ROSES are likely to promote each component of critical consciousness among educationally privileged university students. Using pre–post survey data, they find that ROSES is connected to noteworthy shifts in student's critical reflection, motivation, and action.

Part III: Societal Contexts

Summary of Current Knowledge Finally, we turn to a consideration of how broader societal contexts, particularly those of marginalization and oppression, can influence youth's critical consciousness development. In recent years, scholars have begun to unpack the relationship between critical consciousness development and societal contexts of ethnic and racial marginalization, oppression, and identity development (Cervantes-Soon, 2012; Diemer & Li, 2011; Kelly, 2018; Roy et al., 2019). This research generally supports the notion that critical consciousness is higher among youth with personal exposure to oppressive systems, including personal experiences of racial prejudice and discrimination, racial microaggressions, exclusionary school disciplinary practices, and police and community violence. Scholars have also begun to conceptually and empirically explore connections between critical consciousness development, ethnic/racial identity development, and ethnic-racial socialization (Bañales et al., 2020, 2021; Mathews et al., 2020). This is an exciting new area of growth for critical consciousness scholarship and one that can be meaningfully expanded to include additional contexts of marginalization and oppression (e.g., nativism, heterosexim, ableism, classism) and their intersections (Godfrey & Burson, 2018).

The Chapters in Part III In Part III, we share four chapters that build on this nascent work to more deeply consider how specific societal contexts, such as race, racism, nativism, and immigration, inform youth's critical consciousness development. Although these contexts are foundational to the critical consciousness perspective, surprisingly little work conceptualizes or delineates how specific systems of marginalization and privilege might uniquely shape critical consciousness development for youth. Thus, important questions remain about the extent to which critical consciousness develops differently for youth facing different contexts and intersections of marginalization (e.g., Godfrey & Burson, 2018) and whether it develops in domain-specific or domain-general ways (e.g., Diemer et al., 2015, 2016; see also Rapa & Godfrey, in press[b]). In Chapter 7, Joesfina Bañales, Adriana Aldana, and Elan Hope focus specifically on the context of race. They share their newly developed model of critical race consciousness, detailing the specific processes through which Black, Brown, and white youth come to critically reflect on race as a unique system of oppression and challenge its manifestations. Their model is rooted in critical consciousness and sociopolitical development perspectives, but delineates different processes and pathways that better describe the work of reflecting on and resisting *racism* per se. In Chapter 8, Elan Hope, Channing Mathews, Alexis Briggs, and Anitra Alexander further take up the societal context of race, focusing on experiences of racism and their connection to critical action. Reminding us that racism is a system of oppression that manifests through culture, institutions, and individuals and creates acute and chronic stress responses, they recast critical action as an adaptive coping response to racist experiences, broaden its conceptualization, and provide a systematic review of research on racism and critical action among racially marginalized youth.

Chapters 9 and 10 invoke a societal context of marginalization that has received considerably less attention in critical consciousness scholarship to date: that of nativism, immigration, and documentation. In Chapter 9, Germán Cadenas, Rafael Martinez Orozco, and Carlos Aguilar review the ways in which immigration and documentation status uniquely intersect with daily contexts of school, work, family, and community to create uniquely marginalizing – but also critical consciousness-promoting – experiences for undocumented immigrants. They also draw on historical perspectives to craft a critical review of immigration policy as a specific and intentional context of marginalization immigrants must navigate. Finally, in Chapter 10, Maria Alejandra Arce, Claudia Delbasso, and Gabriel Kuperminc conceptualize processes of critical consciousness development unique to the context of immigration. They describe how certain features of the immigrant experience, particularly sense of social responsibility, immigrant bargain, and immigrant optimism, interplay with experiences of marginalization and contribute in unique and unexplored ways to immigrant youth's critical consciousness development.

IN SUMMARY AND SOLIDARITY

Youth today face a sociopolitical moment in which the systems of oppression that have long patterned American society are in bold relief. Critical consciousness is fundamental to helping youth navigate and resist these oppressions, and in contributing to the fight for justice and liberation. Amidst this landscape, the chapters in this volume expand our understanding of the settings and contexts of youth's critical consciousness development. They provide new perspectives on how the major contexts of youth's lives can function to support and enhance critical consciousness, and form a blueprint for future scholarship. We invite you to engage with these ideas. We hope they open up new ways of thinking and novel intervention possibilities, stimulate the imagination, and add to the growing scholarly and practical knowledge needed to understand and promote this important developmental and societal competency.

REFERENCES

Bañales, J., Hoffman, A. J., Rivas-Drake, D., & Jagers, R. J. (2020). The development of ethnic-racial identity process and its relation to civic beliefs among Latinx and Black American adolescents. *Journal of Youth and Adolescence*, 49(12), 2495–2508.

Bañales, J., Lozada, F. T., Channey, J., & Jagers, R. J. (2021). Relating through oppression: Longitudinal relations between parental racial socialization, school racial climate, oppressed minority ideology, and empathy in Black male adolescents' prosocial development. *American Journal of Community Psychology*, 68(1–2), 88–99.

Bonilla-Silva, E. (2006). *Racism without racists: Color-blind racism and the persistence of racial inequality in the United States*. Rowman & Littlefield Publishers.

Brown, B. B., & Larson, J. (2009). Peer relationships in adolescence. In R. M. Lerner & L. Steinberg (Eds.), *Handbook of adolescent psychology: Contextual influences on adolescent development* (pp. 74–103). John Wiley & Sons.

Brown, C. S., Mistry, R. S., & Yip, T. (2019). Moving from the margins to the mainstream: Equity and justice as key considerations for developmental science. *Child Development Perspectives*, *13*(4), 235–240. https://doi.org/10.1111/cdep.12340.

Cabrera, N. L., Milem, J. F., Jaquette, O., & Marx, R. W. (2014). Missing the (student achievement) forest for all the (political) trees: Empiricism and the Mexican American studies controversy in Tucson. *American Educational Research Journal*, *51*(6), 1084–1118.

Cervantes-Soon, C. G. (2012). Testimonios of life and learning in the borderlands: Subaltern Juárez girls speak. *Equity & Excellence in Education*, *45*(3), 373–391.

Christens, B. D., Collura, J. J., & Tahir, F. (2013). Critical hopefulness: A person-centered analysis of the intersection of cognitive and emotional empowerment. *American Journal of Community Psychology*, *52*(1), 170–184.

Clark, S., & Seider, S. (2017). Developing critical curiosity in adolescents. *Equity & Excellence in Education*, *50*(2), 125–141.

Diemer, M. A., Frisby, M. B., Pinedo, A. et al. (2022). Development of the Short Critical Consciousness Scale (ShoCCS). *Applied Developmental Science*, *26*(3), 409–425. https://doi.org/10.1080/10888691.2020.1834394.

Diemer, M. A., & Hsieh, C. A. (2008). Sociopolitical development and vocational expectations among lower socioeconomic status adolescents of color. *The Career Development Quarterly*, *56*(3), 257–267.

Diemer, M. A., Hsieh, C. A., & Pan, T. (2009). School and parental influences on sociopolitical development among poor adolescents of color. *The Counseling Psychologist*, *37*(2), 317–344.

Diemer, M. A., Kauffman, A., Koenig, N., Trahan, E., & Hsieh, C. A. (2006). Challenging racism, sexism, and social injustice: Support for urban adolescents' critical consciousness development. *Cultural Diversity and Ethnic Minority Psychology*, *12*(3), 444–460.

Diemer, M. A., & Li, C. H. (2011). Critical consciousness development and political participation among marginalized youth. *Child Development*, *82*(6), 1815–1833.

Diemer, M. A., McWhirter, E. H., Ozer, E. J., & Rapa, L. J. (2015). Advances in the conceptualization and measurement of critical consciousness. *The Urban Review*, *47*(5), 809–823.

Diemer, M. A., & Rapa, L. J. (2016). Unraveling the complexity of critical consciousness, political efficacy, and political action among marginalized adolescents. *Child Development*, *87*(1), 221–238.

Diemer, M. A., Rapa, L. J., Voight, A. M., & McWhirter, E. H. (2016). Critical consciousness: A developmental approach to addressing marginalization and oppression. *Child Development Perspectives*, *10*(4), 216–221.

Erikson, E. H. (1968). *Identity: Youth in crisis*. W. W. Norton and Co.

Freire, P. (1968/2000). *Pedagogy of the oppressed*. Continuum.

Freire, P. (1973). *Education for critical consciousness* (Vol. 1). Bloomsbury Publishing.

Ginwright, S., & James, T. (2002). From assets to agents of change: Social justice, organizing, and youth development. *New Directions for Youth Development, 2002* (96), 27–46.

Godfrey, E. B., & Burson, E. (2018). Interrogating the intersections: How intersectional perspectives can inform developmental scholarship on critical consciousness. *New Directions for Child and Adolescent Development, 2018*(161), 17–38.

Godfrey, E. B., Burson, E. L., Yanisch, T. M., Hughes, D., & Way, N. (2019). A bitter pill to swallow? Patterns of critical consciousness and socioemotional and academic well-being in early adolescence. *Developmental Psychology, 55*(3), 525–537.

Godfrey, E. B., & Grayman, J. K. (2014). Teaching citizens: The role of open classroom climate in fostering critical consciousness among youth. *Journal of Youth and Adolescence, 43*(11), 1801–1817.

Heberle, A. E., Rapa, L. J., & Farago, F. (2020). Critical consciousness in children and adolescents: A systematic review, critical assessment, and recommendations for future research. *Psychological Bulletin, 146*(6), 525–551. https://doi.org/10.1037 /bul0000230.

Kelly, L. L. (2018). A snapchat story: How Black girls develop strategies for critical resistance in school. *Learning, Media and Technology, 43*(4), 374–389.

Kirshner, B., & Ginwright, S. (2012). Youth organizing as a developmental context for African American and Latino adolescents. *Child Development Perspectives, 6*(3), 288–294.

Lerner, R. M., & Steinberg, L. (2009). *Handbook of adolescent psychology: Individual bases of adolescent development* (Vol. 1). John Wiley & Sons.

Maker Castro, E., Wray-Lake, L., & Cohen, A. K. (2022). Critical consciousness and wellbeing in adolescents and young adults: A systematic review. *Adolescent Research Review*, 1–24.

Mathews, C. J., Medina, M. A., Bañales, J. et al. (2020). Mapping the intersections of adolescents' ethnic-racial identity and critical consciousness. *Adolescent Research Review, 5*(4), 363–379.

Pew Research Center (2021, December 10). America's public school teachers are far less racially and ethnically diverse than their students. www.pewresearch.org /fact-tank/2021/12/10/americas-public-school-teachers-are-far-less-racially-and- ethnically-diverse-than-their-students/.

Picower, B. (2009). The unexamined whiteness of teaching: How white teachers maintain and enact dominant racial ideologies. *Race Ethnicity and Education, 12*(2), 197–215.

Quintana, S. M. (1999). Children's developmental understanding of ethnicity and race. *Applied and Preventive Psychology, 7*(1), 27–45.

Rapa, L. J., Bolding, C. W., & Jamil, F. M. (2020a). Development and initial validation of the short critical consciousness scale (CCS-S). *Journal of Applied Developmental Psychology, 70*, 101164. https://doi.org/10.1016/j.appdev.2020.101164.

Rapa, L. J., Bolding, C. W., & Jamil, F. M. (2020b). (Re)Examining the effects of open classroom climate on the critical consciousness of preadolescent and adolescent youth. *Applied Developmental Science*. Advance online publication. https://doi .org/10.1080/10888691.2020.1861946.

Rapa, L. J., Diemer, M. A., & Bañales, J. (2018). Critical action as a pathway to social mobility among marginalized youth. *Developmental Psychology, 54*(1), 127–137. https://doi.org/10.1037/dev0000414.

Rapa, L. J., & Godfrey, E. B. (in press[a]). Critical consciousness theory and measurement: Mapping the complex terrain. In L. J. Rapa and E. B. Godfrey (Eds). *Critical consciousness: Expanding theory and measurement.* Cambridge University Press.

Rapa, L. J., & Godfrey, E. B. (Eds.) (in press[b]). *Critical consciousness: Expanding theory and measurement.* Cambridge University Press.

Roy, A. L., Raver, C. C., Masucci, M. D., & DeJoseph, M. (2019). "If they focus on giving us a chance in life we can actually do something in this world": Poverty, inequality, and youths' critical consciousness. *Developmental Psychology, 55*(3), 550–561.

Ruck, M. D., Mistry, R. S., & Flanagan, C. A. (2019). Children's and adolescents' understanding and experiences of economic inequality: An introduction to the special section. *Developmental Psychology, 55*, 449–456. https://doi.org/10.1037/dev0000694.

Seider, S., Clark, S., & Graves, D. (2020). The development of critical consciousness and its relation to academic achievement in adolescents of color. *Child Development, 91*(2), e451–e474. https://doi.org/10.1111/cdev.13262.

Seider, S., & Graves, D. (2020). *Schooling for critical consciousness: Engaging Black and Latinx youth in analyzing, navigating, and challenging racial injustice.* Harvard Education Press.

Seider, S., Graves, D., El-Amin, A. et al. (2016). Preparing adolescents attending progressive and no-excuses urban charter schools to analyze, navigate, and challenge race and class inequality. *Teachers College Record, 118*(12), 1–54.

Spanierman, L. B., & Smith, L. (2017). Roles and responsibilities of white allies: Implications for research, teaching, and practice. *The Counseling Psychologist, 45*(5), 606–617. https://doi.org/10.1177/0011000017717712.

Tyler, C. P., Olsen, S. G., Geldhof, G. J., & Bowers, E. P. (2020). Critical consciousness in late adolescence: Understanding if, how, and why youth act. *Journal of Applied Developmental Psychology, 70*, 101165. https://doi.org/10.1016/j.appdev.2020.101165.

Watts, R. J., Diemer, M. A., & Voight, A. M. (2011). Critical consciousness: Current status and future directions. *New Directions for Child and Adolescent Development, 2011*(134), 43–57. https://doi.org/10.1002/cd.310.

Watts, R. J., Griffith, D. M., & Abdul-Adil, J. (1999). Sociopolitical development as an antidote for oppression – theory and action. *American Journal of Community Psychology, 27*(2), 255–271.

Watts, R. J., & Hipólito-Delgado, C. P. (2015). Thinking ourselves to liberation?: Advancing sociopolitical action in critical consciousness. *The Urban Review, 47* (5), 847–867.

Youniss, J., & Yates, M. (1997). *Community service and social responsibility in youth.* University of Chicago Press.

Zimmerman, M. A., Ramirez-Valles, J., & Maton, K. I. (1999). Resilience among urban African American male adolescents: A study of the protective effects of sociopolitical control on their mental health. *American Journal of Community Psychology, 27*(6), 733–751.

PART I

PEDAGOGICAL, CURRICULAR,
AND SCHOOL-BASED CONTEXTS

1

Tools of Whiteness and Teaching for Critical Consciousness

DAREN GRAVES, AALIYAH EL-AMIN, AND SCOTT SEIDER

As the United States has been going through its latest iterations of racial reckonings in the wake of murders and violence against children, women, and men of color, there has been increasing attention to the roles that educators have played or can play in either reproducing or disrupting racism in educational spaces. While powerful socializing forces such as families and media certainly contribute to these phenomena, schools are also being recognized as key socializing levers that influence how students of all races come to understand what race is and how racism works in overt and covert ways.

For example, educators have the potential to ignore reckoning with the ways that racism manifests in the lives of students inside and outside of school and let the powerful ideas that underpin racism go unchallenged. In so doing, educators facilitate a process for white students and students of color to take on the trappings of internalized racism. Under these circumstances, the problematic ideas and oppressive outcomes that disproportionately and detrimentally impact people of color may come to be seen by students as natural, normal, or deserved. At best in this scenario, both white students and students of color grow into adults who do not question or challenge the racist conditions evident in our society. At worst, white students grow up to actively perpetrate violence against people of color at interpersonal, institutional, and ideological levels. This dynamic is even more fraught – and reflective of the power of racism – in the context of a teaching force that is predominantly composed of white people, especially in schools and districts serving predominantly students of color.

In our own work (e.g., El-Amin et al., 2017; Seider & Graves, 2020), we have intentionally sought to research and report on the work of educators and schools who do seek to engage their students in recognizing, understanding, and resisting racism. Specifically, we conducted a longitudinal research project in high schools intentionally engaged in developing Black and Latinx students' critical consciousness. By *critical consciousness* we refer to the skills and motivation necessary to analyze and challenge oppressive social forces such as racism.

Following students from the class of 2017 in participating high schools in five different northeastern cities from their first day of school through their high school graduations, we collected five waves of quantitative data in the form of surveys measuring students' (n = 643) critical consciousness development over four years. We also conducted interviews each year with a subset of students (n = 60) from each of the participating high schools to hear how students were making sense of their critical consciousness and how they felt their schools were contributing to it. Lastly, we conducted more than 300 day-long observations across all the schools to document how the participating high schools helped develop their students' critical consciousness. In so doing, we have identified numerous curricular, pedagogical, and relational practices through which educators can support Black and Latinx youth's developing critical consciousness of race and racism (Seider & Graves, 2020).

Broadly, our research suggests that schools are an essential site for nurturing critical consciousness about race and racism with youth of color (El-Amin et al., 2017; Seider & Graves, 2020). Yet, limited research has taken up how this work can be carried out with a primarily white teaching force. Additionally, while it is extensively documented that white educators frequently resist teaching about race and racism, oddly we know far less about the classroom practices of white educators who are motivated to engage their students of color in learning about racism. Essentially, we lack insight into the contexts and pedagogical moves that help white teachers (in their racial identity) effectively support the critical consciousness development of their students of color.

Early literature about white teachers teaching about race and racism focused predominantly on the tendency of white teachers to avoid, minimize, and resist conversations about race and learning about racism, both during preservice training and as full-time classroom teachers (e.g., Hytten & Warren, 2003; Lewis, 2001; McIntyre, 1997; Sleeter, 1993). This research also revealed the large numbers of white teachers who lack knowledge about the complexities of structural racism and lack reflective stances about their white identity. More recent research about white teachers teaching about race – often referred to as second-wave white teacher identity studies – nuances this narrative and highlights white teachers who are race-aware (Segal & Garrett, 2013; Ullucci, 2011), who understand the relationship between race, teaching, and learning (Ukpokodu, 2011), and who attempt to teach in culturally responsive ways in predominantly schools of color (Hyland, 2009). Notably, a few recent studies found that some white teachers have high levels of racial awareness and can intellectually describe the importance of developing the critical race consciousness of students of color. However, many of these same white teachers lack the confidence to actually embed topics of race and racism in their teaching practice (Segall & Garrett, 2013).

Very few studies explore what white teachers do when they have the confidence to teach about race and racism and attempt to do so. What pedagogical approaches do they try? How do these approaches land with students? Where do white teachers experience challenges, and what are the roots of these challenges?

Our goal in this chapter is to begin to explore some of these questions. Drawing on our observational data, we look closely at lessons taught by three white educators as they earnestly attempt to teach about race and racism. Ultimately, we conclude that these white teachers used meaningful, thoughtful, and rigorous curricular resources to support their students' developing critical consciousness about race and racism, yet they encountered several pedagogical challenges that may be rooted in their socialization into whiteness. Our findings have implications for white teacher preparation and support, and they offer practical insights for white teachers who are actively seeking to foster critical race consciousness with their students. We describe several key theoretical frameworks that we drew upon in investigating and making sense of these lessons by white educators about race and racism.

CRITICAL CONSCIOUSNESS

The term "critical consciousness" comes from Brazilian philosopher-educator Paulo Freire (1970), who defined critical consciousness as the ability to recognize and understand oppressive social forces such as racism as well as to resist and challenge these forces. From his work as a literacy teacher in rural Brazil, Freire came to believe that fostering critical consciousness should be the primary goal of education, particularly for individuals from oppressed and marginalized groups.

Building on Freire's foundational work, Watts et al. (2011) have conceptualized critical consciousness as consisting of three distinct but related components: critical reflection or social analysis, political self-efficacy, and critical action. *Critical reflection* refers to the ability to name and analyze forces of inequality. *Political self-efficacy* (sometimes referred to as a sense of agency or critical motivation) is the internal belief that one is capable of, and has the capacity and desire to effect, social change. Finally, *critical action* refers to an individual's actual engagement in events and activities intended to challenge oppressive forces and structures and the unequal conditions they perpetuate. The combination of these three components is what Freire calls *praxis*, and he posited that critical consciousness should be understood as the integration of all three components: critical reflection, political self-efficacy, and critical action.

In terms of how to foster critical consciousness, Freire (1970) characterized traditional approaches to education as a "banking model" in which the teacher serves as an all-knowing authority figure depositing knowledge into students. Freire critiqued this banking model as antithetical to nurturing critical consciousness in students from oppressed groups because this approach teaches students to adapt to their conditions rather than learning to challenge the social forces that oppress them. Rather, Freire wrote, critical consciousness must be nurtured through a "problem-posing education" in which the educators and students work together as partners to investigate real-world problems facing their community. Through this problem-posing approach, students are able to see their community and society as capable of transformation and are able to recognize themselves as capable of contributing to such transformation.

Freire's foundational writings have served as a guide for numerous contemporary approaches in education for supporting young people's developing critical consciousness of oppressive forces. These approaches include critical literacy (Kincheloe, 2008; Lee, 2007), critical media literacy (Kelly, 2013; Morrell, 2002), participatory action research (Duncan-Andrade & Morrell, 2008; Fine, 2008), critical civic inquiry (Kirshner, 2015), and ethnic studies (Cabrera et al., 2014; Cammarota, 2007). Other scholars and educators have reported on specific classroom-based practices that can contribute to students' critical consciousness development. These classroom-based practices include "open classrooms" that foster free and respectful exchanges of ideas (Campbell, 2008; Godfrey & Grayman, 2014), debate of controversial public issues (Hess, 2002), and experiential and project-based learning (Flanagan & Christens, 2011; Kahne & Westheimer, 2003). A number of the studies reporting on these approaches and practices for students' critical consciousness development hold useful insights for considering the teacher practices featured in this chapter.

COLORBLIND RACISM

Also relevant to the present study is scholarship that explores white teachers' resistance to teaching about race (e.g., Amos, 2011; LaDuke, 2009; Segall & Garrett, 2013). Although this chapter focuses on teachers who are motivated to deepen their students' critical race consciousness, theories of resistance that explicate how white racial socialization and white dominant culture can unconsciously live in the practices of white teachers are useful because they explain why the white teachers we observed still faced pedagogical challenges. In sum, white teachers can have high literacy about whiteness (i.e., white privilege or white dominant culture) and still lean into these constructs in their practice.

Putting aside the possibility that some white teachers adopt explicitly racist ideas and/or are actively enacting racist behaviors or dispositions, the potential of white teachers to ignore how racism impacts the lives and schooling of students of color can be informed by Bonilla-Silva's (2006) colorblind racism framework. Colorblind racism,[1] according to Bonilla-Silva, is defined as an ideology that "explains contemporary racial inequality as the outcome of nonracial dynamics" (p. 2). White people who subscribe to colorblind racism believe that wide-scale racism has been overcome in the United States and that existing racial disparities can be attributed to the choice and efforts of people of color rather than any overarching racially oppressive ideologies or practices. The result of this mistaken "colorblind" ideology is a further reproduction of racism, as white people will not see race as a useful lens through which to analyze racial disparities, much less to analyze their own roles in reproducing and perpetuating these disparities.

According to Bonilla-Silva (2006), the foundation for the multiple frames of colorblind racism is abstract liberalism. Abstract liberalism is described as "using ideas associated with political liberalism (e.g., 'equal opportunity,' the idea that force should not be used to achieve social policy) and economic liberalism (e.g., choice, individualism) in an abstract manner to explain racial matters" (p. 56). In this regard, people applying abstract liberalism tend to foreground an individual's choices and effort and minimize or deny the effects of the structural forces that inform and constrain the choices of people of color. In the realm of teaching and pedagogy, abstract liberalism can take many forms, including teachers focusing on the achievements or behaviors of people of color (whether in their curriculum, or even students in their classes) while obscuring or ignoring the role of racism or other dynamics of oppression in informing their behaviors or achievements.

Bonilla-Silva (2006) describes a number of different ways that colorblind racism can manifest. One particular manifestation that can occur as white people actively or passively refuse to reckon with race is in the form of *minimization*. Minimization is described as a semantic move or ideology characterized by a sense that racial discrimination "is no longer a central factor in affecting [people of colors'] life chances" (p. 57). Operating under this frame, white people may not discount the notion of individually experiencing discrimination but will attribute the discrimination to causes other than race or racism. At worst, white people operating under this frame will accuse

---

[1] While Bonilla-Silva's concept of "colorblind racism" makes an important contribution to the research literature, we also believe the term itself has several shortcomings. First, the term "colorblind" can lead people to believe that race is equated with skin color while we understand skin color to be just one of many markers of race. Second, the term "colorblind" can be confused with the biological condition that impacts people's abilities to perceive color. Lastly, the biological form of "colorblindness" has some ableist connotations in the label itself (i.e., someone being defined by their lack of ability). Accordingly, our preference is to use the term "race evasiveness" in its place.

people of color of being oversensitive to how and when racism is operating. In the realm of schooling, white teachers employing the minimization frame downplay or obscure the ways that their students of color articulate how race and racism are impacting their lived experiences inside and/or outside of school (Picower & Kohli, 2017).

TOOLS OF WHITENESS

As highly publicized events and phenomena informed by racism have made it more difficult for white educators to comfortably apply the minimization frame to their analysis of the lives of their students of color, there have been calls for white educators to authentically confront the ways racism has informed their own ideologies as teachers as well as the lives of their students of color (DiAngelo, 2018; Love, 2019; Picower, 2021). Calls from the public sector and the research realms have put schools and educators in positions where they are expected to reckon with racism and help their students of color better understand and resist racism. At the same time, researchers have been documenting how white teachers have much work to do to teach about race and in racism in ways that do not do further harm to their students of color. In *Reading, writing, and racism: Disrupting whiteness in teacher education and the classroom*, Picower (2021) documents numerous ways in which white teachers, through unreflective training and practice, enact pedagogies or implement curricula that "socialize students to internalize existing racial ideologies, ensuring that racial hierarchies are maintained through the education system" (p. 26). Picower refers to these practices as "tools of whiteness." In this regard, tools of whiteness represent moves made by educators that facilitate a lack of awareness and/or critical analysis of how racism impacts students' lives inside and out of school – and how the ideology of whiteness will reproduce racism in the absence of intentional efforts to disrupt it. Picower is clear that white people and whiteness are not to be equated. Whiteness, according to Picower is, "the way in which people . . . enact racism in ways that consciously and unconsciously maintain [a] broader system of white supremacy" (p. 6). Although people of color can participate in whiteness, according to Picower it is generally white people who participate in it, and who are the only ones who would benefit from this participation. Two particular tools of whiteness that are relevant in our research project are the "Not That Bad" and "White Gaze" tools.

The "Not That Bad" tool is characterized by teachers who "downplay the horrific nature of past oppressions by promoting a sanitized picture of history, thereby maintaining 'white innocence'" (Picower, 2021, p. 35). In conversation with Bonilla-Silva's (2006) minimization frame, teachers employing this tool do students of color a disservice by minimizing the oppression that their ancestors (or even closer family relations) faced in the past and "mask children's ability to understand current inequality" (Picower, 2021, p. 35). Although teachers' intentions may be grounded in notions of developmental appropriateness or desires not to traumatize students, Picower argues that this tool will undermine the well-being of students of color by skewing their senses of what challenges their communities have faced and what their communities have done (or can do) to resist racism.

The "White Gaze" tool is characterized by "attempting to collapse everyone into seeing the world through ... the perspective of white people ... [and teaching] students to think like those in power, in turn preparing students to empathize with oppressors rather than those marginalized by power" (Picower, 2021, p. 43). Again, this tool has the very real potential of having white students and students of color internalizing racist ideologies, even if the teacher has the intention of shedding light on or problematizing circumstances where racism is actively occurring. In considering the ethnographic field notes we collected from the classrooms of white teachers as part of our Schooling for Critical Consciousness project, we found that the practices described by Bonilla-Silva (2006) and Picower (2021) were manifest in different ways in the work of a number of these educators, even as these educators actively engaged youth of color in analyses of racism and other forms of oppression.

TRANSGRESSIVE AND NEGOTIATED WHITE RACIAL KNOWLEDGE

Research by Crowley (2016) offers an additional lens for considering the ways in which white teachers who do not resist opportunities to talk and teach about race can still struggle with their own roles or complicity with reproducing racism. Specifically, in his study of preservice white teachers, Crowley reported on a distinction between, on the one hand, white teachers' willingness to critique larger structural and ideological issues that impact students of color and, on the other hand, an unwillingness to examine their own racialized behaviors and teaching choices. Drawing on work by Leonardo (2009), Crowley (2016) characterized the former occurrences as white teachers displaying *transgressive white racial knowledge*, which Leonardo describes as occurring when "white individuals engage in race discourse that runs counter to established norms of white racial knowledge" (p. 1019). However, Crowley observed that, in instances where the white preservice teachers were prodded to examine their own behaviors and teaching choices, they were more likely to engage in *negotiated white racial knowledge*, which occurs when white people make "connections between critical understandings of race and their own lives [and then draw] conclusions that [allow] for a measure of comfort and distance from the implications of racism" (p. 1022). In other words, Crowley's work illustrates ways that despite white educators' abilities to critique systems such as colorblind racism or meritocracy writ large, they may still struggle to see, articulate, or act on the ways that they themselves might be reproducing racism with their own teaching choices and behaviors.

FALSE HOPE AND CRITICAL HOPE

There can also be profoundly negative consequences for students of color if educators teach sanitized or magical narratives about how communities of color have displayed resilience in the face of oppression (Clay, 2019). If students of color are taught narratives that portray the racism that people of color face(d) as normalized and the ways they resist(ed) as the acts of brave individuals, these lessons can actually counteract their will to analyze racism and take action against it. Clay (2019) asserts that students of color need to be taught about how communities of color escaped from racism in its various and dehumanizing forms, and how communities (i.e., not individuals) came together to organize against racism and other systems of oppression in acts of what Clay calls "organized deviance" (p. 105). Framing racism as an explicitly dehumanizing system that should never be normalized will help students reject its current pervasiveness. Foregrounding the collective actions that communities have taken to resist racism, according to Clay, will facilitate the will of students of color to resist racism themselves. In the absence of the approach Clay calls for, students of color may develop a sense of "false hope" (Duncan-Andrade, 2009), wherein young people embrace an unfettered sense of future possibility that leaves them unprepared to cope with the racism that they are likely to encounter. To counter false hope, Duncan-Andrade argues that educators need to help students of color develop a sense of "critical hope," wherein they recognize opportunities for individual and collective socioeconomic mobility in the face of racist structures and practices and are, consequently, empowered to see resisting racism as possible and necessary.

While work that outlines the traps and pitfalls white teachers make while teaching about race tends to foreground curricular choices or struggles, our observations led us to notice how white teachers can also err in their pedagogical choices intended to nurture their students' developing critical consciousness about race and racism. Most of the white teachers in our study used curricular materials written by authors of color or rigorous curricular resources that actively engaged structural racism. Yet, even with robust source materials, white teachers faced several challenges as they tried to facilitate critical race analysis with their students.

THREE TEACHING VIGNETTES REPRODUCING WHITENESS DESPITE GOOD INTENTIONS

We turn now to the presentation of three key teaching vignettes that we drew from the field notes and interviews from our Schooling for Critical Consciousness study. These vignettes illustrate how well-intentioned white educators can unwittingly replicate patterns of whiteness, as described herein, that can have deleterious effects on Black and Latinx students' skills and will to resist racism. There were other teachers we observed who engaged in actions similar to those portrayed in the vignettes presented here, but our goal in sharing these vignettes is less to claim that such specific pedagogical moves are pervasive and more to offer them as teachable moments for white teachers committed to antiracism work in their own classrooms. All teachers, students, and schools in the vignettes are pseudonymous.

"I'm Going to Switch You to More AP Language"

In an eleventh-grade Advanced Placement English course at Baker High School, Ms. Jamie Beckham, a white teacher in her forties, introduced her class of predominantly Black students to a personal essay by *New York Times* journalist Brent Staples (2007): "Just walk on by: A Black man ponders his power to alter public space." In this powerful essay, Staples describes numerous strategies he employs as a Black man during late-night walks through his city to avoid appearing threatening to white passersby and police officers. For example, he describes whistling melodies from classical composers such as Beethoven and Vivaldi as the "equivalent of the cowbell that hikers wear when they know they are in bear country." Staples confesses to the reader that adopting such tactics has required him to "smother the rage I felt at so often being taken for a criminal."

After students pulled out the copies of this essay, which they had read the previous night for homework, Ms. Beckham began the class discussion by asking them "What was our main idea for this essay?"

One young woman raised her hand to speak: "Stereotypes can cause harm for innocent victims."

"I'm writing that down," Ms. Beckham said. "Then I'm putting a semicolon here to add to the main idea. And I want to go stronger than 'to cause harm.'"

The same young woman continued: "They can become dangerous."

"Good," Ms. Beckham said. "What about the cowbell reference?"

A young man raised his hand. "I thought the cowbell was like a warning signal because I looked at the paragraph. He compared bear country to white society, and the cowbell to his whistling Vivaldi that he's coming."

"I'm going to switch you to more AP language," Ms. Beckham told him. "The word is *analogous*. In the same way he whistles to calm the society who think he's a criminal, a hiker uses a cowbell to warn the bears he is coming. Now let's go back to the paragraph structure. What was going on prior to that sentence?"

Another student volunteered to answer this question: "He is writing about how no mugger would be whistling Vivaldi's *Four Seasons*."

Ms. Beckham nodded affirmatively: "What is Staples' ultimate message that he says is happening at the end of this?"

"I think he's saying despite all his actions, danger still exists," a young woman asserted.

A classmate offered a different perspective: "I thought he was saying that there are dangers, but he is lessening them and changing them. He is changing himself to be more accepted by the society."

"Great!" Ms. Beckham said enthusiastically. "We have an argument here, which we love. So let's capture our two arguments." She jotted down both students' perspectives on the white board and then shifted the discussion back toward the essay's diction related to music.

In observing this lesson and then discussing our field notes after the fact, several key impressions emerged from this lesson. First, Ms. Beckham used Staples's essay to great effect in supporting her students' development of technical skills related to identifying the main idea and analyzing paragraph structure and diction. Second, Ms. Beckham's choice of this essay introduced her students to the writing of Brent Staples, a journalist of color and editor at *The New York Times* who is a Pulitzer Prize recipient. But, third, the class discussion that Ms. Beckham led and moderated only lightly alluded to the fact that the focus of Staples's essay was the pernicious ways in which his movement through the world is shaped by racism, discrimination, and stereotyping – and the corresponding pain and rage this reality causes the author. Put another way, Ms. Beckham pushed her class to focus more intensively on Staples's rhetorical use of analogies than on his description of the ways he had to appeal to the sensibilities of white people so as to avoid the very real possibility that their lack of critical reflection about his race could lead to emotional if not physical violence.

The focus Ms. Beckham puts on the technical aspects of Staples's writing, at the expense of the substantive issues he raises about navigating racism, represents a subtle version of Bonilla-Silva's (2006) minimization frame of colorblind racism. Bonilla-Silva's presentation of minimization involved ways that some white people will try to downplay or refute when people of color say that they have experienced racism. In this particular case, Ms. Beckham does not deny the ways that race and racism contextualize what Staples is describing, but she does not take the time to have her students reflect on the substance of Staples's piece. The concern is that Ms. Beckham's focus on the technical aspects of Staples's writing may obscure or downplay the role that racism has in Staples's life and (perhaps by extension) in the lives of her Black and Latinx students. As her students describe how Staples employs strategies to avoid the mental and physical violence informed by racism, Ms. Beckham uses the lesson as an opportunity to focus on teaching AP-level vocabulary words and lauds her students for developing a clear argument. In this regard, Ms. Beckham ignores the likelihood that her own students have to navigate the same high-stakes dynamics that Staples describes. This teaching move has the potential for sending the message to her students that the racism that they navigate is not worthy of attention or analysis.

This teaching move also reflects some measure of Picower's (2021) "Not That Bad" tool of whiteness. While the examples of the "Not That Bad" tool that Picower presents tend to focus on teachers downplaying the horrific and dehumanizing nature of historical iterations of racism, we see ways that the essence of this tool can apply to contemporary iterations as well. In this case, Staples reflects on how Black men can be criminalized while engaging in mundane activities such as walking down the street. Importantly, our society is rife with examples of the types of violence enacted against Black men while engaging in such mundane activities. Accordingly, the dynamics that Staples describes having to navigate can have life-and-death implications for him and other people of color in similar situations. While acknowledging the role of stereotypes in this situation, Ms. Beckham's teaching of Staples's piece places little to no focus on the grim implications for Black men and other people of color in similar situations. Looking through the lens of the "Not That Bad" tool, the potential result of this teaching move could be to inadvertently send the message to students that the racism navigated and endured by people of color is unremarkable and part of what society should expect for people of color. A metaphor that illuminates the danger of this approach would be to analyze the swimming patterns of a fish in a pond without acknowledging that the pond is polluted and could ultimately kill the fish no matter where or how it swims. Ultimately, normalizing the racism that people of color navigate and endure (with potentially deadly consequences) can, as Clay (2019) describes, socialize students of color not to feel that racism is a pernicious system that needs to be dismantled. In addition, it may reduce their sense of hope or agency to engage in a process of resisting racism.

There is no one right way that Ms. Beckham should have approached this lesson to facilitate students' critical consciousness development about race. Arguably, Ms. Beckham's opening question about the article's main idea was an excellent foundation. Yet, for this question to have motivated the deep racial literacy that critical social analysis involves, Ms. Beckham needed to allow students to sit with the specific racial context and racial themes in the text, putting race on the table as the primary analytic lens. For example, consider the first student's response: "Stereotypes can cause harm for inno-cent victims." Here, Ms. Beckham could have said something like "Yes, and in this article, who is the author foregrounding in their discussion about how stereotypes harm?" This question may have created space for the class to explore the intersection of race and gender implicated in the article, and to analyze the distinct experience of being a Black male in the United States. Ms. Beckham could also have asked students to unpack the stereotypes Staples described and to discuss their own experiences with racial stereotypes. This conversation might have allowed students to generate a social analysis motivated not only by the essay's narrative but also by their own experiences. Lastly, Ms. Beckham could have pushed students to think about the relationship between racism and critical action and led students to analyze the strategies that Staples described as mechanisms for his survival. Why did he feel that whistling songs from white composers would provide him cover or safety? What are the implications of that reality, if it is one? What experiences did students have with similar or different strategies for resisting or surviving racism? Do these strategies change the underlying structures of power that lead to pervasive stereotypes to begin with? Any of these conversation strands would have provided a more robust pathway to students' critical consciousness development and still facilitated opportunities to build technical skills related to diction, mechanics, and literary analysis.

"You Need to Let us Linger There More"

In the twelfth-grade African American Literature course at Baker High School, we observed one of Ms. Beckham's colleagues, Mr. Henry, enact another of the tools of whiteness. Mr. Henry – a white teacher in his mid-thirties – was leading his students in a discussion of James Baldwin's 1962 novel, *Another Country*, which focused on interracial relationships during a time period when such relationships were not only taboo but illegal in many parts of the United States. In one class discussion of *Another Country*, Mr. Henry and his students considered Baldwin's claim that the blues represent a lever for transforming racial injustice in America. First, Mr. Henry played his students a blues standard, "Trouble in Mind," that Baldwin explicitly references in the novel:

> Trouble in mind, I'm blue,
> But I won't be blue always.
> 'Cause I know the sun's gonna shine in my back door someday.

When the song ended, Mr. Henry asked his students: "Why in this song is the sun going to come in the back door?"

"The back door represents Black history," a young woman said.

"Black history will shed light on what America is," another young woman explained.

Mr. Henry nodded enthusiastically. "Yes. If the house is America, what does the darkness represent?"

"Ignorance?" asked a young man.

Another young man jumped in. "So the house represents America, and it's filled with darkness, which is ignorance. And Black people will open the back door to bring the truth."

"Yes!" Mr. Henry told his students. "Baldwin believes the blues will bring the truth about the Black experience in America." He pointed to his well-worn copy of Baldwin's novel. "And how do the blues help lead Black and white people to another country without actually leaving America?"

"The other country is when both Black and white people understand each other," a student suggested.

"Yes!" Mr. Henry said. His enthusiasm at his students' reading of Baldwin's work was palpable.

This lesson was an engaging and intellectual one, and Mr. Henry was one of the most impressive teachers we observed across all of the schools in our *Schooling for Critical Consciousness* study. Importantly, however, midway through their study of *Another Country*, a group of students requested a meeting with Mr. Henry to express some concerns about their learning. As Mr. Henry explained in an interview, his students were concerned that he "was guiding the [class's] conversations to optimistic outcomes." In other words, Mr. Henry was focusing the class's discussions on Baldwin's prescriptions for overcoming white supremacy rather than on Baldwin's descriptions of "Black suffering and Black pain and the experience of living under white supremacy." According to Mr. Henry, the students told him "You need to let us linger there more."

Our observations of Mr. Henry's classroom point to both similarities to and differences from the vignette of Ms. Beckham's class described earlier. Similar to Ms. Beckham, Mr. Henry provided students with a rigorous text by a writer of color and effectively taught students a technical skill using the text – in this case, the ability to decode a metaphor. Mr. Henry also made a similar misstep in failing to create space for students to discuss the connections of the text to their material and embodied experiences *as* people of color. Unlike Ms. Beckham, Mr. Henry foregrounded issues of race and racism in his lessons, but he did so by focusing primarily on the novel's hopeful sentiments.

Importantly, Mr. Henry may have chosen this approach because he felt that optimism was important for students against the backdrop of sweeping national racial unrest at the time of his lesson. He may have also believed that highlighting Baldwin's strategies for countering white supremacy would help students connect to strategies of resistance in their own lives. While these goals are understandable and admirable, Mr. Henry's intentions fell short precisely because they were not coupled with opportunities for students to authentically contend with the painful realities of structural racism. As a result, even though Mr. Henry was urging his students to focus on "hopeful" moments in the text and actively working to facilitate hope, ironically he was simultaneously failing to foster the kind of hope that research suggests is most beneficial to his students as people of color.

Recall from this chapter's introduction that scholar Jeffrey Duncan-Andrade (2009) characterizes critical hope as the ability to assess one's lived experience realistically and authentically through a justice-based lens while also envisioning the possibility of a better future. In schools, critical hope is facilitated when teachers and students *painfully examine* their lives in an unjust society alongside discussions of prescriptions for change. In other words, facilitating critical hope requires teachers to not only make room for pain in classroom discussion and analysis but to honor that pain itself may pave the path to justice. In essence, Mr. Henry's students asked their teacher to adopt a pedagogy of critical hope when they requested more time and space to contend with and linger in Black suffering before moving forward into offering strategies for change.

In lieu of critical hope, Mr. Henry was facilitating what Duncan-Andrade (2009) refers to as "false hope" or "hokey hope," which seeks to deepen young people's feelings of optimism and possibility without acknowledging the presence of oppressive forces in their lives. Whether intentionally or unintentionally, false hope minimizes the severe impact of inequities on students' lives. Duncan-Andrade (2009) suggests that such false hope is most often facilitated by "spectators": those on the outside of the deleterious impacts of injustice who instead experience systemic privilege (p. 183). By offering his students an analysis of Baldwin's novel that focused on reasons for optimism about race relations in the United States, Mr. Henry used a framework of the world likely generated by his status as a white man and inadvertently imposed this lens on his students. In so doing, he effectively silenced the connections students wanted to draw from their lived experiences to the experiences of racial mourning described in the novel. Additionally, by creating classroom conditions wherein Black and Latinx students had to avoid the dehumanizing realities of racism and focus almost exclusively on the spaces of possibility in conversations about race, Mr. Henry was also socializing students to approach critical racial analysis with this same white ideological worldview.

As described in the introduction to this chapter, Picower (2021) refers to the intentional or unintentional socialization of students of color into white ideologies on the part of white teachers as "White Gaze." While Picower suggests that white teachers ask students to take on a white ideological worldview through their white-washed curricular content, Mr. Henry's lesson suggests that white teachers can also enact the White Gaze even as they engage a text written by an author of color. As we saw with Mr. Henry, this enactment of White Gaze involved selectively determining the aspects of a text that should have salience in the classroom and making those selections based on his white racial point of view. In this case, the passages Mr. Henry elevated provided a pathway to "rosier" conversations about racism. His enactment of White Gaze also included signaling his desire for optimistic responses through overt enthusiasm when students' answers contained a hopeful glimmer.

Notably, Mr. Henry's students were not receptive to this socialization and exercised their agency to resist his pedagogical approach and speak up about their concerns. They provided clear guidance about what they wanted and needed from their teacher: the opportunity to contend with their feelings and pain as students of color in the United States. Importantly, Mr. Henry responded gratefully and positively to students' feedback. His response serves as a model for current and future teachers. He told the class what he had heard from them and acknowledged that his positionality as a white man prevented him from seeing the text as his students did and also shaped his pedagogical choices and analysis. Mr. Henry also followed this acknowledgment with material changes. He began to restrain his participation in class discussions, minimizing the impact of his whiteness, and invited students to identify readings and topics to incorporate into the course's syllabus. Further, he began to share power with students, asking them to serve as discussion leaders in future race-based discussions. All of these moves contributed to Mr. Henry's students praising his abilities as a teacher and the influence of this African American Literature course on their developing critical consciousness in interviews with our research team.

"Are We Going to Be the Only Black Kids There?"

At Legacy Academy, Ms. Michaela Todd, a white social studies teacher in her early forties, sought to prepare the predominantly Black and Latinx students in her eleventh-grade history class for a mock presidential debate with other local high schools. Ms. Todd's class had participated in this event in previous years, and she had observed that the other high schools participating in the mock debate were from affluent suburban communities comprised predominantly of white students. From these past experiences, Ms. Todd had concerns about how her students might be perceived or treated by these other students. In this lesson, Ms. Todd sought to prepare her students for encountering these peers. The school's principal, Mr. David Johnson, observed the lesson from the back of the room.

The lesson began with a "Quick Write" in which Ms. Todd explained "At our debate tomorrow, it is possible that we will hear things that feel offensive or hurtful to us, our families, and our communities. I want to take some time today to think about how we will respond." She asked her students to write silently for five minutes in response to the following prompts: Think about a time when someone said something to you that you found especially offensive or hurtful. What did they say? How did it make you feel, and how did you respond? Looking back now, would you change anything about your response?

Then several students shared what they had written. One student shared an incident with a racist bus driver. Another described a recent experience in a store and explained that her strategy was to smile sarcastically and incorporate the person's response into whatever she said next. Other students shared that, when they are insulted, they respond by laughing, insulting the other person, and making skeptical facial expressions. Another student loudly sucked on his teeth to illustrate his response to hearing an insulting comment.

Ms. Todd picked up on this last example. "Some of the other kids tomorrow won't know what that [teeth-sucking] means."

"Are we going to be the only Black kids there?" a young woman in the class asked immediately.

Ms. Todd acknowledged that there were likely to be just a few other Black students participating in the event, and she shifted the discussion to offering several "self-care" strategies that her students could utilize if they heard something offensive or hurtful from other participants. She shared a slide on the class's white board that included "talk to someone you trust," "breathe," "take a break/step out," and "sit next to/look at your people."

"Isn't that racist?" one student asked, in response to the last point about seeking out allies.

Ms. Todd shook her head. "It's a reminder to support each other and to speak up when you hear things you disagree with."

A young woman raised her hand. "So, basically what I'm getting from this is that we need to watch out because we're Black?"

Principal Johnson spoke up in response to this last comment. He rejected the idea that the students had to watch out because they were Black: "This is about holding your stance and your values." There was a low rumble of discontent across the classroom in response to this explanation, and the class period ended shortly thereafter.

Interestingly, interviews with Legacy Academy students following this lesson suggested that their frustration with the lesson had to do with perceiving Ms. Todd to be raising the specter of racism or racial prejudice in ways that did not name race explicitly, and doing so in a way that left them feeling less motivated to engage in the mock debate. While it seems clear that Ms. Todd had laudable intentions to prepare her students for the racial prejudice they might face at the debate and to think about strategies for how to navigate these potential situations, we can see in her instructional choices that she failed to name race explicitly, a fact her students found puzzling and frustrating. They repeatedly tried to clarify Ms. Todd's intentions. One student asked whether they would be the only Black students there after Ms. Todd expressed a vague sense of concern about whether white students would understand some of her students' potential responses to insensitive comments or behaviors. A second student asked if it would be "racist" to take Ms. Todd's race-evasive suggestion that the students look to each other for support if they encountered any racial prejudice. A third student asserted "So, basically, what I'm getting from this is that we need to watch out because we're Black" after yet another response from Ms. Todd that failed to mention race specifically. Her students gave Ms. Todd three opportunities to name race in explaining the dynamics about which she was concerned. However, Ms. Todd never named race explicitly, and the conversation ended with the principal stating that the students did not need to think about their perceived behaviors through the lens of their identities as Black and Latinx young adults.

Ms. Todd's goal of helping students modulate their behaviors because of potential racial prejudice without explicitly naming race represented an honest attempt to help her students navigate racism that backfired. The impetus for the conversation was Ms. Todd's concern for how her students might be treated and viewed by white people in ways that reflected racial prejudice. Furthermore, she attempted to guide her students to (re)act in ways that she felt would not reflect poorly in the eyes of potentially prejudiced white people, but without explicitly naming this racial dynamic. Ms. Todd's seeming reluctance to name the dynamics of whiteness explicitly resembles Crowley's (2016) notion of enacting a form of *negotiated white racial knowledge*. Her reticence in specifying whiteness and her focus on helping her students focus on their own behaviors in a potentially racist context gave Ms. Todd an opportunity to distance herself from whiteness and some of the advantages she and other white people receive. Furthermore, the way Ms. Todd framed the issue implicitly asked her Black and Latinx students to sympathize with and/or not challenge the perspectives of potentially prejudiced white peers they encountered at the mock debate. Rather she seemed to ask her students to respond to these potentially problematic perceptions held by their white peers by acting in ways that would not further fuel these perceptions. This type of approach has the potential to teach students to sympathize with racist ideologies or behaviors rather than to challenge them or see them as problematic.

Ms. Todd might have facilitated this conversation to greater impact if she simply stated to students that she wanted to have a conversation about race and racism ahead of the scheduled debate. She could have framed it as an honest conversation with her students about the racial dynamics she anticipated they were going to face because of her own experiences of and socialization with whiteness. Ms. Todd could have also talked about the ways that she, herself, was still learning how to enact *transgressive racial knowledge* in her own teaching practices and asked her students to share more of their own thinking about the racial dynamics – and effective responses to these dynamics – in predominantly white spaces (Crowley, 2016). In this regard, rather than trying to distance herself from whiteness, she could have framed her proximity to whiteness and her desire to disrupt it as uniquely positioning her to work with her Black and Latinx students to navigate or disrupt the racial dynamics with a critical eye.

DISCUSSION

Recall from the chapter introduction that we ground our understanding of critical consciousness in Watts, Diemer, and Voight's (2011) model that describes critical consciousness as the praxis of social analysis, social action, and political agency (Seider & Graves, 2020). What emerges in the vignettes featured in this chapter are examples of well-meaning and engaged white teachers seeking to nurture the critical consciousness of their students of color but inadvertently employing pedagogical tools of whiteness that subvert their best intentions. In so doing, these educators hampered their students' opportunities to engage in social analysis of oppressive forces such as racism and/or weakened their will and skill to challenge such forces.

In the first vignette, for example, Ms. Beckham committed the error of focusing her teaching on the technical aspect of Brent Staples's (2007) "Whistling Vivaldi" essay at the expense of addressing the ways in which Staples's essay illustrated the persistent and pernicious nature of racism. In so doing, Ms. Beckham applied a "Not That Bad" frame that limited her students' opportunity to use Staples's work for reflecting upon experiences with racism – and how to navigate such racism – in their own lives (Picower, 2021). In the second vignette, Mr. Henry's students demanded that their teacher apply a less optimistic (perhaps even naively informed) analysis of Baldwin's (1962) novel *Another Country* because doing so denied them the opportunity to engage in deeper social analysis of Baldwin's writing and to reflect on its relevance to their own lives. In this regard, Mr. Henry's error was to facilitate an investigation of Baldwin's work dominated by his own "White Gaze" (Picower, 2021). Similar to Ms. Beckham, Mr. Henry's enactment of one of the tools of whiteness limited his students' opportunities to engage in a more critical analysis of Baldwin's work (until his students intervened). It is instructive that both Ms. Beckham and Mr. Henry selected texts for their respective courses that could be characterized as culturally relevant or culturally responsive due to their potential resonances with their students' backgrounds and experiences. Nonetheless, both educators made pedagogical choices that limited their students' opportunities to engage in meaningful social analysis of these texts' content and contexts.

The third vignette featured in this chapter is fascinating. The teacher, Ms. Todd, seemed invested in helping her students develop a sense of political agency to challenge racism and to nurture social action skills, but she sought to do so without offering her students an authentic opportunity to engage in social analysis about race and racism. Because Ms. Todd wanted her students to be prepared for the likelihood that they would experience some measure of racism in their upcoming debate competition, she engaged them in a conversation about brainstorming strategies they might employ if they encountered racism. The problem was that Ms. Todd failed to explicitly name racism as the social force they needed to analyze and subsequently challenge. Over the course of this vignette, Ms. Todd's students engaged in three separate attempts to nudge their teacher to name racism explicitly, so as to contextualize and make relevant the actions and strategies she had instructed them to brainstorm. In the absence of this context, Ms. Todd's students expressed discontent and a lowered motivation to participate in the mock debate at all. As described earlier, Ms. Todd's race evasiveness, reluctance to speak explicitly about racism and whiteness, and encouragement of her students to focus on their own behaviors in a potentially racist context seemed to emerge from Ms. Todd's own negotiated white racial knowledge (Crowley, 2016). Put another way, Ms. Todd's enactment of another tool of whiteness led students to lose their motivation to compete in the debate competition at all because she pushed them to engage in social action without adequate social analysis of the context into which they were walking.

Our multiple years conducting research at these educators' respective schools informs our sense that these educators were actively and earnestly committed to nurturing their students' critical consciousness. However, building on the work of Bonilla-Silva (2006) and Picower (2021), our analysis also revealed that white educators who are not sufficiently reflective about how they center whiteness in their pedagogical choices can reproduce racism or other oppressive systems. This leaves Black and Latinx students without the skills or motivation to challenge racism. White teachers' positionalities often give them privilege over students of color on the basis of teacher–student, adult–youth, and racial dynamics. This gives white teachers an extraordinary amount of power to shape teaching and learning, especially as it pertains to race. With these power dynamics in mind, it becomes even more important for white teachers to reflect on the kind(s) of authority they exercise over students of color whose critical consciousness they are trying to develop.

White teachers who rely on a banking model of teaching, where the teacher is seen as the ultimate possessor of information, are more likely to reproduce racism because whiteness is so powerful and often invisible to those who benefit from it (DiAngelo, 2018; McIntosh, 1988). Freire's (1970) notion of a more reciprocal, problem-posing relationship between teacher and students better positions white teachers to disrupt whiteness in their teaching because they are engaging with students of color as teaching and learning partners while still honoring the fact that their primary role is to facilitate learning for their students. For Ms. Beckham, that would entail having students engage in a social analysis of key texts, rather than merely technical analyses. For Mr. Henry, that would entail decentering whiteness and, instead, engaging his Black and Latinx students in analyses of key texts that feel authentic to their lived experiences as people of color. For Ms. Todd, that would mean naming race and racism explicitly as she prepared her students to navigate and challenge the racism she anticipated they would face. Importantly, Mr. Henry exemplified such reciprocity at the end of his vignette by engaging his students as teaching and learning partners, putting himself in a position to receive critical feedback from them and pivoting his teaching as a result. This is the kind of partnership that more white educators would do well to cultivate with their students of color. Such partnerships allow students' perspectives to hold value in the teaching and learning process and therefore to center perspectives of peoples of color in the teaching and learning process. Moreover, decentering perspectives informed by whiteness will better position students of color to build the skills, motivation, and agency to further develop critical consciousness.

IMPLICATIONS

Schools have the potential to be important sites for the critical consciousness development of youth of color, yet there is a need for more research and scholarship on how this work can be carried out with a primarily white teaching force. Our study begins to fill this knowledge gap. Importantly, our analysis underscores that a desire to nurture critical consciousness about race is not sufficient for effectively doing so. Even when white educators are deeply committed to critical consciousness development with their students of color, they face numerous challenges. The teachers in our study experienced challenges that move beyond the curriculum and push us to think not only about what teachers teach but about how teachers teach. The white teachers in our study all had access to high-quality materials that had the potential to deepen students' critical consciousness about race, but they lacked the full range of pedagogical techniques that would allow them best to develop their students' critical racial analysis, agency, and commitment to social action. To advance critical consciousness development in schools, we need to think carefully about the opportunities teachers have to deepen their instructional repertoire with respect to teaching about racism. In classrooms with students of color, teachers may also need support navigating and holding the complexity and range of emotions that accompanies learning about lived experience in a marginalized identity as a part of classroom content.

Overall, we should not underestimate the complex pedagogical questions involved in developing critical consciousness about race and racism. For example, how should educators balance creating space for the raw and painful emotions that emerge from learning about racism with the goal of developing the sense of agency and possibility required to complete the critical consciousness cycle? How should educators facilitate conversations about historical texts and literary works in ways that allow students ample space to elevate their everyday experiences alongside historical narratives? How can educators leverage a text containing visceral racial content to teach technical skills (i.e., literary devices) without minimizing or diminishing either of these domains?

One possible space of intervention is to provide all teachers with professional development as a part of preservice and in-service training, wherein they can both discuss and practice instructional moves that effectively create a container for racial dialogue. Given the demographics of our current teaching force, it is also critical that we begin to ensure educators have access to differentiated professional development based on their identities. Even with the best intentions, white teachers in our study frequently made pedagogical decisions rooted in their racial socialization as white people and their positionality as racially privileged. To effectively support the critical consciousness development of their students of color, white teachers need opportunities to consistently analyze how their whiteness can influence their instructional choices to the detriment of critical consciousness development and, in some cases, increased harm for students.

As for what such professional development might look like in schools, one approach that we are currently exploring is a professional learning community. A professional learning community is a collaborative space that offers sustained support for educators to critically analyze their practice and learn from one another (Dobbs et al., 2017). In our approach, middle school educators lead advisories in their respective schools. These advisories meet monthly for approximately an hour and a half to work collaboratively to plan, try out, and reflect upon practices for nurturing students' critical consciousness of race and racism. We are serving as participants and facilitators in these professional learning communities. Although these professional learning communities are not designed specifically for white educators invested in supporting their students' critical consciousness development, many of the participating educators are white. In the role of facilitator within these professional learning communities, we *do not* position ourselves as experts capable of offering answers about how to strengthen students' critical consciousness. As described herein, such a banking approach to education is at odds with the concept of critical consciousness, and, moreover, schools and classrooms are such context-specific places that impactful curriculum and practices in one school or classroom might be received very differently in another schooling context. However, the professional learning communities *do* offer educators the time and space to engage in deep and collaborative reflection upon curricula and practices they are contemplating sharing with their students, to solicit and wisdom feedback from colleagues that allows for refinement and improvement, and to debrief and discuss afterward how particular lessons or activities landed.

Our interest in deepening educators' capacity to do critical consciousness work via professional learning communities emerged, in part, out of the recognition that the white educators profiled in this chapter are genuinely committed to supporting their students' developing critical consciousness of race and racism. The challenges or missteps we profiled were often the result of insufficient opportunities for feedback, collaboration, and coaching. In-school professional learning communities might be one route to creating such feedback, collaboration, coaching, and space for self-reflection for educators invested in this work.

To be clear, we believe it is incredibly important for educators to learn, think, and reflect upon the ways in which race and racism impact their own lives and those of their students, but it is also the case that this is a continuous, lifelong process. These topics are both complex and dynamic. There is no "end zone" or "finish line" at which point educators know enough to lead lessons on race and racism without error. What this means is that educators have to be willing to position themselves as learners alongside their colleagues in spaces such as professional learning communities and alongside their students in academic courses, advisories, and extracurricular activities. Think back to the vignette of Mr. Henry featured earlier in this chapter in which his students respectfully but forcefully rejected his positioning of himself as an expert on the ideas about race and racism offered by Baldwin in *Another Country*. What Mr. Henry's students pushed for, instead, was for their teacher to position himself as a coteacher and colearner alongside them, working collaboratively to decipher Baldwin's ideas. When Mr. Henry learned to embrace this role, the learning experience for all involved became deeper, richer, and far less fraught.

REFERENCES

Amos, Y. T. (2011). Teacher dispositions for cultural competence: How should we prepare white teacher candidates for moral responsibility? *Action in Teacher Education, 33*(5–6), 481–492. https://doi.org/10.1080/01626620.2011.627037.

Baldwin, J. (1962/2013). *Another country*. Vintage.

Bonilla-Silva, E. (2006). *Racism without racists: Color-blind racism and the persistence of racial inequality in the United States*. Rowman & Littlefield Publishers.

Cabrera, N., Milem, J., Jaquette, O., & Marx, R. (2014). Missing the (student achievement) forest for all the (political) trees: Empiricism and the Mexican American studies controversy in Tuscon. *American Educational Research Journal, 51*(6), 1084–1118. https://doi.org/10.3102/0002831214553705.

Cammarota, J. (2007). A social justice approach to achievement: Guiding Latina/o students toward educational attainment with a challenging, socially relevant curriculum. *Equity & Excellence in Education, 40*, 87–96. https://doi.org/10.1080/1066 5680601015153.

Campbell, D. (2008). Voice in the classroom: How an open classroom climate fosters political engagement among adolescents. *Political Behavior, 30*(4), 437–454.

Clay, K. L. (2019). "Despite the odds": Unpacking the politics of Black resilience neoliberalism. *American Educational Research Journal, 56*(1), 75–110. https://doi .org/10.3102/0002831218790214.

Crowley, R. M. (2016). Transgressive and negotiated white racial knowledge. *International Journal of Qualitative Studies in Education, 29*(8), 1016–1029. https://doi.org/10.1080/09518398.2016.1174901.

DiAngelo, R. (2018). *White fragility: Why it's so hard for white people to talk about racism.* Beacon Press.

Dobbs, C. L., Ippolito, J., & Charner-Laird, M. (2017). Scaling up professional learning: Technical expectations and adaptive challenges. *Professional Development in Education, 43*(5), 729–748. https://doi.org/10.1080/19415257.2016.1238834.

Duncan-Andrade, J. (2009). Note to educators: Hope required when growing roses in concrete. *Harvard Educational Review, 79*(2), 181–194. https://doi.org/10.17763/haer.79.2.nu3436017730384w.

Duncan-Andrade, J., & Morrell, E. (2008). *The art of critical pedagogy: Possibilities for moving from theory to practice in urban schools.* Peter Lang Publishing.

El-Amin, A., Seider, S., Graves, D. et al. (2017). Critical consciousness: A key to student achievement. *Phi Delta Kappan, 98*(5), 18–23. https://doi.org/10.1177/00317 21717690360.

Fine, M. (2008). An epilogue of sorts. In J. Cammarota and M. Fine (Eds.), *Revolutionizing education: Youth participatory action research in motion* (pp. 213–234). Routledge.

Flanagan, C. A., & Christens, B. D. (2011). Youth civic development: Historical context and emerging issues. *New Directions for Child and Adolescent Development, 134,* 1–9. https://doi.org/10.1002/cd.307.

Freire, P. (1970). *Pedagogy of the oppressed.* Continuum.

Godfrey, E. B., & Grayman, J. K. (2014). Teaching citizens: The role of open classroom climate in fostering critical consciousness among Youth. *Journal of Youth Adolescence, 43,* 1801–1817. https://doi.org/10.1007/s10964-013-0084-5.

Hess, D. (2002). Discussing controversial public issues in secondary social studies classrooms: Learning from skilled teachers. *Theory and Research in Social Education, 30*(1), 10–41. https://doi.org/10.1080/00933104.2002.10473177.

Hyland, N. E. (2009). One white teacher's struggle for culturally relevant pedagogy: The problem of the community. *The New Educator, 5*(2), 95–112. https://doi.org/10.1080/1547688X.2009.10399567.

Hytten, K., & Warren, J. (2003). Engaging whiteness: How racial power gets reified in education. *International Journal of Qualitative Studies in Education, 16*(1), 65–89. https://doi.org/10.1080/0951839032000033509a.

Kahne, J., & Westheimer, J. (2003). Teaching democracy: What schools need to do. *Phi Delta Kappan, 85*(1), 34–67.

Kelly, L. (2013). Hip-hop literature: The politics, poetics, and power of hip-hop in the English classroom. *English Journal, 102*(5), 50–55.

Kincheloe, J. L. (2008). *Critical pedagogy primer* (Vol. 1). Peter Lang.

Kirshner, B. (2015). *Youth activism in an era of education inequality.* New York University Press.

LaDuke, A. E. (2009). Resistance and renegotiation: Preservice teacher interactions with and reactions to multicultural education course content. *Multicultural Education, 16*(3), 37–44.

Lee, C. D. (2007). *Culture, literacy, and learning: Taking bloom in the midst of the whirlwind.* Teachers College Press.

Leonardo, Z. (2009). *Race, whiteness, and education.* Routledge.

Lewis, A. E. (2001). There is no "race" in the schoolyard: Color-blind ideology in an (almost) all-white school. *American Educational Research Journal, 38*(4), 781–811. https://doi.org/10.3102/00028312038004781.

Love, B. L. (2019). *We want to do more than survive: Abolitionist teaching and the pursuit of educational freedom.* Beacon Press.

McIntosh, P. (1988). White privilege: Unpacking the invisible knapsack. *Race, class, and gender,* 95–105.

McIntyre, A. (1997). Constructing an image of a white teacher. *Teachers College Record, 98*(4), 653–681.

Morrell, E. (2002). Toward a critical pedagogy of popular culture: Literacy development among urban youth. *Journal of Adolescent & Adult Literacy, 46*(1), 72–77.

Picower, B. (2021). *Reading, writing, and racism: Disrupting whiteness in teacher education and in the classroom.* Beacon Press.

Picower, B., & Kohli, R. (2017). *Confronting racism in teacher education.* Routledge.

Segall, A., & Garrett, J. (2013). White teachers talking race. *Teaching Education, 24*(3), 265–291. https://doi.org/10.1080/10476210.2012.704509.

Seider, S., & Graves, D. (2020). *Schooling for critical consciousness: Engaging Black and Latinx youth in analyzing, navigating, and challenging racial injustice.* Harvard Education Press.

Sleeter, C. E. (1993). How white teachers construct race. In G. Ladson-Billings & D. Gillborn (Eds.), *The Routledge Falmer reader in multicultural education* (pp. 163–178). RoutledgeFalmer.

Staples, B. (2007). Just walk on by: A Black man ponders his power to alter public space. In M. Mitrašinović & V. Mehta (Eds.) (2021). *Public Space Reader* (1st ed.) (pp. 186–189). Routledge. https://doi.org/10.4324/9781351202558.

Ukpokodu, O. (2011). Developing teachers' cultural competence: One teacher educator's practice of unpacking student culturelessness. *Action in Teacher Education, 33*(5–6), 432–454. https://doi.org/10.1080/01626620.2011.627033.

Ullucci, K. (2011). Learning to see: The development of race and class consciousness in white teachers. *Race Ethnicity and Education, 14*(4), 561–577. https://doi.org/10.1080/13613324.2010.519982.

Watts, R. J., Diemer, M. A., & Voight, A. M. (2011). Critical consciousness: Current status and future directions. *New Directions for Child and Adolescent Development, 2011*(134), 43–57. https://doi.org/10.1002/cd.310.

2

Critical Consciousness Development in the Context of a School-Based Action Civics Intervention

PARISSA J. BALLARD, ELENA MAKER CASTRO, JULIANA E. KARRAS, SCOTT WARREN, AND ALISON K. COHEN

The idea of critical consciousness (CC) is rooted in theories and practice related to sociopolitical actions of groups facing oppression (Friere, 2000; Watts et al., 1999). CC scholarship is often based on Paulo Friere's theory and teaching focused on "marginalized or oppressed people's analysis of societal inequities and their motivation and actions to redress such inequities" (Diemer et al., 2016, p. 216). Modern conceptualizations of CC focus on the development of three core elements: critical social analysis and reflection, critical motivation (or efficacy), and critical action (Diemer et al., 2020; Rapa et al., 2020; Seider & Graves, 2020). Recently, scholars and practitioners have focused efforts on understanding and designing interventions to support the development of CC, especially in classroom contexts (e.g., Seider & Graves, 2020). It is a complex endeavor. Although many educators support the goals of CC development, which are rooted in critical thinking, the contexts of traditional schooling are often not set up to encourage students to challenge the systems and conditions of their schools, communities, and society more broadly. In this chapter, we present school-based action civics interventions as a setting for CC development. Action civics overlaps with other participatory approaches such as youth participatory action research (e.g., Ballard et al., 2019), which is defined as "a form of CBPR [community-based participatory research] that engages young people in identifying problems that they want to improve, conducting research to understand the nature of the problems, and advocating for changes based on research evidence" (Ozer et al., 2013, p. 13). However, the action civics curricular structure, uniformity of approach, and adult-initiated framework renders it distinct from youth participatory action research (YPAR). We highlight one action civics program, Generation Citizen (GC), and overlay its programmatic components with the core elements of CC. We elucidate how action civics may support CC development and where the constraints may be with regards to CC development. We use images of youth-generated action civics presentation posters to illustrate aspects of CC. Finally, we offer next steps to bridge CC and action civics theory, research, and practice. In Chapter 3, Morgan and Christens explore links between CC and another action civics program.

ACTION CIVICS AND CRITICAL CONSCIOUSNESS

In this section, we consider how school-based action civics programs relate to CC. Action civics programs guide students to take collective action to address locally relevant civic issues within a context that promotes reflection and skills development (Pope et al., 2011). Through student-driven projects, youth learn how to civically engage to solve community problems through a process of: (a) community analysis, (b) issue selection, (c) issue research, (d) planning for action, (e) taking action, and (f) reflection (Fitzgerald, 2017). This process expands the ecology of learning beyond the classroom walls (Fitzgerald & Andes, 2012). There are various action civics models, including semester-long programs implemented by trained classroom teachers (Cohen et al., 2018; Morgan et al., 2022) as well as summer camp programs (LeCompte & Blevins, 2015; LeCompte et al., 2020). Studies suggest that action civics positively relates with civic knowledge (Cohen et al., 2018), civic self-efficacy (Ballard et al., 2016), and civic skills (LeCompte et al., 2020). Action civics programs typically focus on middle and high school students and allow flexibility for teachers or other action civics leaders to tailor the programs to the developmental stage, abilities, and interests of their student population. This is important because the action civics process is meant to be broadly applicable; however, high school seniors might be further along in their critical thinking and possess more advanced civic skills – and thus might choose different types of classroom projects compared to, for example, eighth grade students.

GENERATION CITIZEN

This chapter highlights the approach of one action civics nonprofit organization, Generation Citizen (GC), to propose features of an action civics program that align with CC development. Although action civics has gained more traction across the country in recent years, GC is one of the oldest and largest action civics organizations and has national reach, currently implemented in ten states and regions throughout the United States. GC delivers action civics programming to middle and high school students primarily through a school-based action civics curriculum taught over the course of a semester. Like other action civics programs, classes in GC collectively assess community issues and teach and practice civic strategies and skills via taking civic action on a specific local issue the class collectively selects (Pope et al., 2011). GC's theory of change is guided by the Advocacy Hourglass, which is GC's framework for action that depicts the process that students learn and practice (Generation Citizen, n.d.). The Advocacy Hourglass is introduced at the beginning of the action civics semester and guides the action process over the course of the semester. The hourglass shape is intentional: students begin by brainstorming potential community issues and then collectively narrow down to one issue and determine its root cause and a specific goal. They then utilize many tactics to take action. Recently, GC has moved exclusively to a teacher-led model in which the curriculum is delivered by trained classroom teachers – a shift from the original model which relied on partnerships between college volunteers (called democracy coaches) and trained classroom teachers. This shift was predicated on a recognition that the most effective and scalable iteration of the program is one that helps educators master the pedagogical components rather than focusing on implementing a curriculum.

The culmination of the semester-long GC experience is Civics Day. On Civics Day, all participating classroom in a region come together to showcase their class projects using a format in which students make presentations to judges alongside posters they created. GC organizes local community members to serve as judges who rate the quality of the action civics projects. Civics Day is an opportunity for students to showcase what they learned, take action toward their chosen issue, and connect with community members and peers from other schools. The poster that each class creates is an important part of their GC experience because it reflects students' semester-long journey.

It is important to note that many action civics programs, including GC, were not explicitly developed as CC interventions. However, in practice, action civics programs use processes that align with CC development. Indeed, GC notes "building CC" as one of their effective qualities (Generation Citizen, 2019, p. 14). Although we use GC as a case example, many other action civics models may share these features and may have additional features that support CC.

FEATURES OF GENERATION CITIZEN THAT ALIGN WITH CRITICAL CONSCIOUSNESS

In this section, we describe four features of GC that, based on our analysis, might effectively scaffold aspects of CC. The features of GC that we propose align with CC development are: placing action at the center of the program, fostering critical social analysis and reflection, valuing children's right to participation, and focusing on skill-building (see Table 2.1). To illustrate these four features, we use pictures of Civics Day posters from a subset of action civics projects from middle and high school classes in public schools in the San Francisco Bay Area who participated in GC in the fall of 2017. We blurred some portions of the posters to deidentify the classes and we point out in the text the specific features illustrated in the action civics posters.

TABLE 2.1 Four key features of Generation Citizen's action civics curriculum that align with critical consciousness

Key Feature	How It Is Related to CC	Example of How It Is Applied in GC
Action	Action is a central aspect of CC; recent scholarship has called to recenter action.	Action is infused into the goals, process, and outcomes of the curriculum.
Critical social analysis and reflection	How people come to see and call out systems of oppression is a core component of CC.	Curriculum is focused on understanding root causes of issues in local community. Students reflect on local issues (via the Advocacy Hourglass framework) and formally reflect at the end of the action civics program about the process, what they learned, and next steps.
Children's right to participation	CC honors children's and adolescents' right to participate and highlights the importance of opportunities to address social inequities.	Students participate in projects about issues that affect their lives.
Skill-building	Skill-building is key to CC development and liberation.	Students learn skills through practice, for example, organizing skills such as writing a petition and persuading others about issues and solutions.

Action

As one of the core components of CC, critical action describes individual and collective actions aimed at challenging and changing systems and conditions that maintain inequity (e.g., Diemer, 2020; Heberle et al., 2020). GC has action at the center of the program. In contrast to many other school-based civic curricula, action is built into the goals, processes, and outcomes of the curriculum. From the start, it is clear that action is part of the *goal*, which contrasts with many traditional civics classes wherein gaining knowledge and preparing for civic participation are the goals. Here, we see a clear parallel to Freire's original conceptualization of CC as a process that refutes "banking" methods of education that position education as a process of feeding information into otherwise empty minds (Watts et al., 2011). Rather, true to CC theory, GC builds on students' lived experiences and upon "problematizing" societal issues (Watts &

Hipólito-Delgado, 2015). In GC, action is conceptualized as a context for developing civic knowledge and skills and thus action is a main feature of the process as well as part of the goal; for example, students take action by assessing the needs and assets in the local community. In this way, GC aligns with CC scholars (e.g., Watts & Hipólito-Delgado, 2015) who challenge the idea that critical action occurs after critical reflection and analysis. Rather, GC's context of action facilitates ongoing analysis and reflection, creating a reciprocal process reflective of ways in which CC dimensions inform one another (Rapa et al., 2020; Watts et al., 2011). At the same time, action is a major *outcome* of the program, as seen in the culmination activities of the program wherein students participate in Civics Day to showcase what they have learned and inform local leaders about their findings and proposed solutions. Although the outcomes of the action are not the focus per se, action is the context for student development. Again, GC's emphasis on action prompts critical analysis and reflection, as students' learning processes occur within an action-based context, wherein critical analysis and reflection can then prompt further action (Watts et al., 2011). In addition, GC's approach to assessing critical action through the sharing of posters at Civics Day allows for students to make meaning of their action, a potential advancement from the way critical action is typically assessed using quantitative measures of frequency of participation (Watts et al., 2011; see also Diemer et al., 2020; Rapa et al., 2020). GC's action-focused model aligns with recent calls to recenter action in CC (Diemer et al., 2020; Watts et al., 2011) and parallels evolving definitions of critical action that include antiracist actions (e.g., Aldana et al., 2019; McWhirter & McWhirter, 2016). Coupled with GC's emphasis on critical social analysis and reflection (see the following section), the ultimate actions that students take are intended to be critical in that they are aimed at challenging or raising awareness about root causes of community issues. Importantly, however, students are free to choose what issues to address as a class and may not always choose issues meant to redress inequalities as CC frameworks would imply.

The poster presented in Figure 2.1 showcases a range of actions that young people took over the course of their project. For example, students conducted a survey (bottom of left panel), wrote an email to their school about their issue, and conducted a social media campaign to raise awareness (bottom of right panel). In this context, it is not clear how much these actions represent critical actions, as students are constrained by the options available to them inside the structured school setting (McAvoy & Hess, 2013; Ozer et al., 2013). In addition, action Civics Day is itself also an "action" that provides the opportunity for students to present their work to local stakeholders and to advocate for solutions to the issues they identified in their communities.

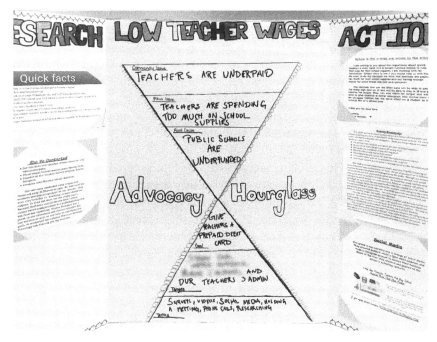

FIGURE 2.1 Civics Day poster illustrating action.

Critical Social Analysis and Reflection

A second feature of GC that aligns with CC is that GC scaffolds the practice of critical social analysis and reflection. Consistent with CC development, the curriculum is focused on understanding root causes of local community issues (Freire, 1973; Watts & Hipólito-Delgado, 2015). This is a departure from other action-focused school-based civic programs, such as service-learning programs. Service-learning programs are similar in some ways to action civics, in particular in their focus on action, encouraging students to participate in the local community, and having students drive choices about project participation. However, service learning tends to be focused on helping others through direct service as opposed to being politically oriented toward understanding and changing systems (e.g., Walker, 2000, 2002).

Action civics programs such as GC are focused on understanding root causes – a system-oriented rather than individual-oriented approach – and advocating for changing the underlying systems that lead to issues, thus emphasizing both participation and a justice-oriented approach (Westheimer & Kahne, 2004). GC also encourages students to consider who within the system may be responsible for creating change as they consider who their action should target (e.g., a mayor, peers within a school). Grappling with how individuals may be complicit in perpetuating systemic inequities aligns with a definition of critical analysis that includes understanding the roots of inequality alongside considerations for social responsibility (Hope & Bañales, 2019). More broadly, GC's approach aligns with CC's main premise: emphasizing how people come to see, call out, and change systems of oppression (Watts et al., 2011), which relies on both developing a critical lens for analysis of social issues and developing the capacities to enact change.

GC also incorporates reflection as an important and repeated part of the action civics process that happens at multiple timepoints across the curriculum and is incorporated in various ways. The Advocacy Hourglass structures reflection so that students first reflect on general issues in their community, then focus on more specific and local issues, and finally specify their potential root causes and solutions. This scaffolds a process whereby students ask "why" questions throughout the action civics curriculum, digging deeper with each question to guide their actions (Watts & Hipólito-Delgado, 2015; Watts et al., 2002). Ideally, the questioning process prompts critical curiosity, a potential precursor of CC development wherein students develop curiosity about the state of society around them (Clark & Seider, 2017, 2020). This curiosity then feeds the analysis process as questions help to elucidate the systems ungirding societal inequities (Clark & Seider, 2017).

As students analyze the conditions around them, they may then be compelled to act (Diemer et al., 2016; Freire, 1973; Jemal, 2017). The reflection that occurs through critical social analysis may guard against a natural tendency of students to jump to action without full understanding and reflection on the existing landscape. At the same time, students' subsequent action may further inform their critical social analysis as they analyze and reflect on the change-making process, thus nurturing the reciprocal nature of CC development. Students also formally reflect at the end of the action civics program about the process, what they learned, and any next steps.

Critical social analysis and reflection is evident across many action civics projects. For example, the poster presented in Figure 2.2 showcases a critical orientation to root causes and solutions to the issue of homelessness. Students could have focused on the issue of homelessness and come up with a solution that involved handing out hygiene kits for homeless youth. This could be seen as a more individual and service-oriented approach to the same issue. However, likely due to their critical social analysis emphasizing individual- versus systemic-level root causes, paired with the reflection process involved in GC, this project tackles homelessness from a critical approach and identifies the root cause of it as unaffordable housing. In a less critical approach, youth may consider providing unhoused individuals with food or clothing. While meaningful, this type of action does not critically question why certain individuals cannot access what they need for daily living. The proposed solution of advocating for changes in housing policy illustrates a systemic view of the problem. This example illustrates how GC students practice social analysis and reflection and develop a critical orientation through their action civics projects.

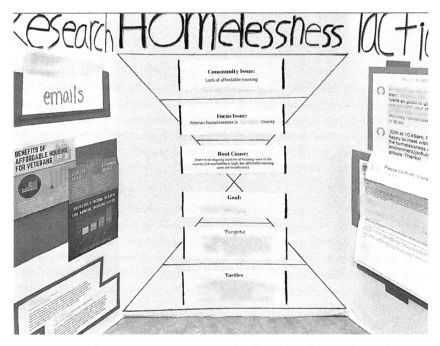

FIGURE 2.2 Civics Day poster illustrating critical social analysis and reflection.

Participation as a Right

Another feature of GC is the notion that children have the right to active participation in their lives and communities and a right to high-quality civics education. This is central to the children's rights framework (CRC; UN General Assembly, 1989) but often missing from schools and youth programs. As young people learn how to collectively mobilize on social issues that matter to them and their communities through GC, they are invited to exercise their right to participate in society, whereas they are traditionally left out of these processes (Kosher & Ben-Arieh, 2017). Developmentally, the right to active participation in society is understood as both empowering for young people (Ruck et al., 2014) and instrumental in providing learning opportunities to cultivate skills and dispositions that positively contribute to their own and broader societal well-being (Helwig et al., 2014; Wray-Lake & Syversten, 2011). By creating opportunities for all young people, including those who have faced systemic oppression and marginalization, to participate in society via action civics, GC both honors children's and adolescents' right to participate and potentially builds opportunities to disrupt social inequities. Both of these are central to CC (Karras et al., 2022).

Action civics programs do not necessarily use the framework of children's rights, but we believe that GC honors children's right to participate in society by preparing them to critically engage with social issues and providing them with opportunities to do so (Karras et al., 2022; Ruck et al., 2014). The opportunity for children to exercise their participation rights by taking action in their community supports CC development by structuring critical social analysis and reflection informed by their own lived experience. This scaffolds their agency and self-efficacy, which in turn engenders their motivation to act and empowers them to take critical action (Karras et al., 2022). The right to participation aspect is the least evident in posters, perhaps because it is not a focal point of action civics, and perhaps because students do not necessarily see participation as a right they can claim. However, given that GC presents the opportunity to learn about rights, it is interesting to observe that some projects do feature students grappling with, and claiming, personal rights. For example, the poster presented in Figure 2.3 showcases a classroom project that took on the topic of sexual violence against adolescents. This illustrates two aspects of students noticing violations of their rights. First, the poster includes information about "your body, your rights" (the Healthy Me flyer, bottom right in the middle panel) in the context of sharing information about sexual assault.

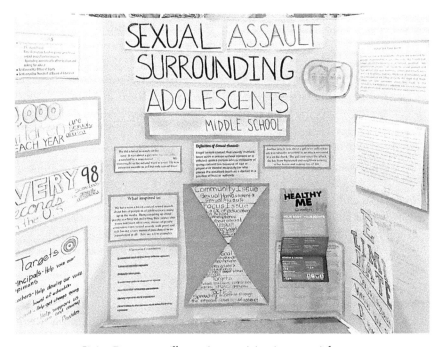

FIGURE 2.3 Civics Day poster illustrating participation as a right.

In addition, the poster emphasizes "voice" through a focus on targeting teachers to help students develop their voice and targeting principals to help students voice their opinions (Targets section, bottom of left panel); this can be seen as an example of these middle school students claiming the right to participate and be heard.

Skill-Building

Finally, GC builds a diverse set of skills relevant for civic engagement. Part of Freire's original conception of CC was building literacy skills among oppressed people as key to fostering their liberation. GC is not only about building civic skills such as a sense of efficacy in civic life, it is also about building the tangible skills and networks to help young people participate in civic life. Through providing the opportunity to practice, the GC curriculum helps students learn research skills through a focus on understanding the local landscape before proposing action. GC also builds civic communication skills, such as writing letters and emails to political officials and making phone calls to gather support for chosen strategies. Through GC, students might practice organizing skills, such as instigating a petition and persuading others about issues and solutions. The focus on acquiring skills through practice aligns with the original conception of CC as a vehicle for empowerment (Friere, 2000). Building tangible skills may also increase a sense of efficacy to join with others to create changes in one's community; this sense of efficacy is considered a central aspect of CC development.

GC focuses on experiential learning; pursuing action civics projects requires students to learn skills that they are likely not afforded the chance to learn in many educational settings. The poster shown in Figure 2.4 illustrates students practicing skills they gained through their action civics project. They used several tactics that rely on communication skills, many of which were likely new to students (described in the Tactics section, bottom of right panel). For example, students report that they developed an argument based on their applied research, lobbied decision makers (for example, by making phone calls), and organized others (through petitions and flyers). Developing such skills that may transfer to other domains of life is a benefit of experiential learning and is aligned with the empowering focus of CC development.

THEMES ACROSS POSTERS

Looking across this set of action civics posters, some additional themes are noteworthy. First, the Advocacy Hourglass is used to frame every poster. This may stem from encouragement from GC leaders or from the students' own initiative, but it showcases how central the framework is to action civics

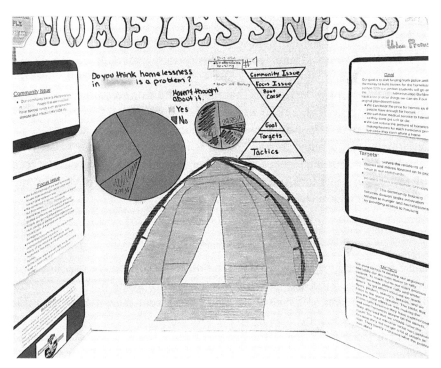

FIGURE 2.4 Civics Day poster illustrating skills.

projects. This illustrates the idea that GC classrooms share a common approach and language around which to build their civic actions. This type of "group-based belief system" has been discussed as a characteristic of empowering community settings (Maton, 2008; Morgan & Ballard, in press). In addition, the Advocacy Hourglass framework has a critical orientation that narrows down to an analysis of root causes of focal issues. The framework itself can be seen as scaffolding a developmental CC process from social analysis to critical action.

Second, it is evident when looking across the set of posters that the process of CC development is messy as it plays out "in real life." For example, some posters exemplify a strong critical analysis of root causes of local issues, but ultimately select an individual-level tactic or solution rather than one that tackles the root causes identified. This reflects a common tendency toward more sanitized or palatable solutions and highlights the challenge of identifying more structural levers of change (Watts & Hipólito-Delgado, 2015). These individually oriented solutions may reflect the developmental stage of students who may be learning about systemic issues for the first time. Or, they may reflect the limitations of more systemic solutions within settings where students likely experience "bounded empowerment" (Larson et al., 2005;

Larson & Walker, 2010; Ozer et al., 2013) with regards to what they can really propose and achieve.

Third, many classrooms chose similar topics. In this set of posters, the topics of homelessness and food insecurity were especially salient. While a systematic examination of the topics frequently addressed is beyond the scope of the chapter, we do note that manifestations of economic inequality are especially prevalent. This focus across classrooms may reflect the students' experiences in a famously expensive region. Or, students may be more developmentally attuned to, and able to rally around, economic issues. The theme of economic inequality across this set of posters illustrates how GC can offer an opportunity for students to develop a critical analysis of an issue and take action at a local level.

WHERE GC AND CC MAY NOT ALIGN

There are several ways in which GC's action civics curriculum may not align with CC theory. First, CC generally centers on critiquing one's own conditions of oppression, although there have been recent calls, including in this volume, to broaden this lens to youth with more privilege. GC operates in a range of schools where some students may experience various forms of oppression and other students may not. For example, a project geared toward antiracism may cultivate different experiences and skills among white youth who have not experienced racism (e.g., allyship, understanding personal experiences with white privilege) than among students of color, whose learning may be more focused on contextualizing and resisting racism in their everyday lives. Similarly, addressing the nation's current housing crisis is a recurring theme among GC projects; based on their proximity to the issue, a student currently experiencing housing instability may relate differently to such a project compared to students not experiencing housing instability. While CC may be fostered among students across both action civics projects, the pathways and outcomes may be distinct.

Second, action civics projects are not always focused on conditions of oppression. Students have the mandate to study and choose social issues relevant to their lives; these sometimes center on oppression but many times do not. Despite a programmatic focus on critically analyzing the root causes of social issues that aligns with analyzing oppression, because action civics projects are chosen by students they deal with a range of social issues. Even when issues are chosen that relate to oppression, ultimately students may propose actions to address the issue that are focused on individual-level solutions. GC is currently working to encourage systemic solutions and focus on equity more explicitly through changes to the curriculum and training procedures (Generation Citizen, n.d.). Some action civics projects address topics important to students' lives, such as better mental health support or issues with the quality of school lunch; these issues may or may not be framed in relation to oppression.

Further, contemporary CC conceptualization and measurement is focused on the individual as the unit of analysis (Diemer, 2020; Rapa et al., 2020). While Freire's foundational work considered how marginalized individuals work collectively for social change, more recent work has focused on individual-level CC. For example, widely used critical action measures focus on what an individual does (e.g., "contact an elected official" or "participate in a civil rights organization") without assessing when, how, and under what conditions an individual collaborates with others on these actions. Some recent work extends this individual-level focus by examining how individuals operate and develop within the broader contexts of schools and classrooms (e.g., Seider & Graves, 2020). GC projects are executed by an entire class of students; thus, action civics projects are the outcome of an entire group. It may be difficult to disentangle the role each individual student played, and how each student may or may not have developed CC in the process. While it is possible to measure the impact of GC on individual students' CC development, it is important to note that GC is a group process. Indeed, this chapter examines how CC is reflected in the product of GC, which is constructed by groups of students together.

Additionally, CC is often conceived and measured to assess students' CC regarding a variety of marginalizing forces (e.g., racism, sexism, poverty; Diemer et al., 2016, 2020; Shin et al., 2016). Meanwhile, students' experiences in GC are often very domain specific. By nature of the program, students may focus, for example, specifically on environmental justice or a local unhoused population. GC may thus foster CC in one area, which may or may not encourage CC growth in other areas. This may be particularly true when considering the intersectional nature of oppressions, such that students may focus their semester on anti-Black racism without considering the ways in which anti-Blackness intersects with sexism and homophobia to create further experiences with marginalization.

Finally, while all GC students are exposed to a curriculum that encourages critical reflection and action, experiences with critical motivation may be more varied by nature of classroom dynamics and the project selection process. Students get to choose projects after assessing community needs. This may center students' critical motivation, yet it is important to acknowledge that, in any given classroom, there are many interpersonal dynamics at play. These dynamics can dramatically influence the course of any lesson or unit. While GC teachers are supposed to be responsive to students' experiences and interests, there may be some classroom voices that drown out other perspectives or even instances of interpersonal discrimination that surface. Some students may end up highly engaged in the action civics project and consequently may build a strong sense of efficacy that they can indeed enact change, while other students may lose critical motivation if they feel as though their experiences and interests were not incorporated into the class project. GC works to instill democratic decision-making throughout the action process so as to ward off, as much as possible, unequal power dynamics in any particular class. However, GC, and action civics more broadly, may herein be departing from traditional CC conceptualizations, given that these programs are not exclusively focused on people from marginalized backgrounds coming together specifically because of a shared experience with marginalization.

NEXT STEPS TO BRIDGE CRITICAL CONSCIOUSNESS AND ACTION CIVICS THEORY, RESEARCH, AND PRACTICE

Here, we consider how action civics practice may benefit from more explicitly drawing on CC, how CC theory and interventions might benefit from action civics practices, and how future research can specify and extend the promise of both CC and action civics.

While this chapter considers the ways that GC aligns with CC theory, we also underscore that GC was not explicitly developed as a CC intervention and therefore does not necessarily target every aspect of CC development. Action civics practices can benefit from further integrating aspects of CC theory and the evidence of practices that support CC development (Seider & Graves, 2020). For example, GC might potentially emphasize redressing inequality more, even as they retain a focus on students' freedom to collectively choose an issue of interest for their action civics project. GC might more explicitly teach about privilege and systems of oppression affecting people with various identities. Additionally, GC, and action civics programs more broadly, could consider how they support sustained CC development beyond a specific program. CC development is found to progress through adolescence (Seider et al., 2020). Youth may make important advances in their CC capacities through GC programming; determining how to further support CC through extended programming and school-based opportunities for collective change could further instill a CC lens and further support a more just and equitable society. Finally, GC can consider advancing more explicitly the process of healing that is embedded in CC development (Prilleltensky, 2008; Sánchez Carmen et al., 2015). Given that experiences with marginalization and oppression can cause harm to both individuals and communities, it is important that addressing sources of harm includes space for self- and community care.

At the same time, CC theory and interventions could benefit from integrating some of the promising practices that GC and action civics intervention include. For example, GC uses a collective action approach which aligns with original conceptualizations of CC but departs in some ways from a modern focus on individual actions. As the CC field continues to evolve, researchers and practitioners can consider how to account for group-level CC development. Questions such as "What does it mean to measure collective action?" and "How can we account for the ways in which students' various sources of critical knowledge and skills intersect in the classroom?" can be further explored. In pursuing such questions, GC and action civics programs can serve as models or "test sites" for what this type of collective action and shared pool of knowledge and skills looks like as it unfolds across a particular project. Project outcomes such as Civics Day posters, as examined here, could serve as data for systematic analysis of CC.

Furthermore, research can help bridge CC theory and practice. First, future research can use rigorous designs, such as randomized-controlled trial (RCT) methods, to explicitly test whether GC and other action civics interventions affect CC outcomes such as critical reflection, motivation, and action. In one large study led by Ballard and Cohen, the research team is applying RCT methods to examine the impacts of action civics on youth development. The I-ACTED Study (Investigating Action Civics Training through an Experimental Design) is a new project employing a cluster randomized trial to understand whether, and how, action civics programming affects aspects of students' civic development and well-being. Advances in evaluating civic interventions with rigorous methodology approaches holds promise both for building effective civic practice and for building theory.

Second, CC develops differently for people depending on their experiences of oppression, marginalization, and privilege. Many scholars are exploring what CC means for people at the intersection of different identities and experiences with oppression and privilege (Godfrey & Burson, 2018; Hazelbaker et al., 2021; Hershberg & Johnson, 2019). While research often focuses on one form of oppression or privilege at a time, researchers are moving toward more nuanced consideration of intersectionality and multiple systems of oppression (e.g., Godfrey & Burson, 2018). Action civics classrooms are a potentially rich context for future research studying how CC development unfolds in settings where people come from different backgrounds and occupy many different social identities, both within individuals and across groups. Such research could illuminate how best to support CC development in classrooms with students holding diverse experiences with oppression and privilege while at the same time extending our knowledge about CC development in classroom contexts for young people.

Finally, it would be beneficial to both CC theory and action civics practice to closely examine processes happening "in vivo" within classrooms. For example, systematically examining democratic classroom practices and the processes by which classes make decisions about focal issues in their action civics project would shed light on CC as a collective process while also presenting the opportunity to understand how individuals, perhaps at different points in developing CC, function and grow within the class context. In addition, GC and other action civics programs continue to refine and adapt their curricula. GC is currently focused on centering equity throughout its programming; this shift may provide further opportunities for CC development. As GC has moved to a model wherein teachers implement the action civics curriculum, more research on teacher CC would be very valuable. For example, teachers' own critical orientation would likely affect their skills and preparation to enact curricular teaching critical reflection and orientation (Heberle et al., 2020; Seider & Graves, 2020).

CONCLUSION

Action civics programs provide a valuable school-based model for developing CC, even if not originally conceptualized as a CC intervention using the CC framework. This chapter introduced readers to action civics programs in general and GC in particular; presented programmatic features of GC that align with CC scholarship; provided evidence of these features as seen through student projects; considered implications for theory, practice, and research; and proposed future directions for linking action civics with CC.

REFERENCES

Aldana, A., Bañales, J., & Richards-Schuster, K. (2019). Youth anti-racist engagement: Conceptualization, development, and validation of an anti-racism action scale. *Adolescent Research Review, 4*(4), 369–381.

Ballard, P. J., Cohen, A. K., & Littenberg-Tobias, J. (2016). Action civics for promoting civic development: Main effects of program participation and differences by project characteristics. *American Journal of Community Psychology, 58*(3–4), 377–390.

Ballard P. J., Suleiman A. B., Hoyt L. T. et al. (2019). Participatory approaches to youth civic interventions in multicultural societies. In P. F. Titzmann & P. Jugert (Eds). *Youth in Superdiverse Societies* (pp. 251–267). Routledge.

Blevins, B., LeCompte, K. N., Riggers-Piehl, T., Scholten, N., & Magill, K. R. (2020). The impact of an action civics program on the community & political engagement of youth. *The Social Studies, 112*(3), 146–160. https://doi.org/10.1080/00377996.2020.1854163.

Clark, S., & Seider, S. (2017). Developing critical curiosity in adolescents. *Equity & Excellence in Education, 50*(2), 125–141. https://doi.org/10.1080/10665684.2017.1301835.

Clark, S., & Seider, S. (2020). The role of curiosity in the sociopolitical development of Black and Latinx adolescents. *Journal of Research on Adolescence, 30*(1), 189–202. https://doi.org/10.1111/jora.12511.

Cohen, A. K., Littenberg-Tobias, J., Ridley-Kerr, A. et al. (2018). Action civics education and civic outcomes for urban youth: An evaluation of the impact of Generation Citizen. *Citizenship Teaching & Learning, 13*(3), 351–368.

Diemer, M. A. (2020). Pushing the envelope: The who, what, when, and why of critical consciousness. *Journal of Applied Developmental Psychology, 70*, 1–4. https://doi .org/10.1016/j.appdev.2020.101192.

Diemer, M. A., Rapa, L. J., Voight, A. M., & McWhirter, E. H. (2016). Critical consciousness: A developmental approach to addressing marginalization and oppression. *Child Development Perspectives, 10*(4), 216–221.

Fitzgerald, J. (2017). Pre-planning civic action: An analysis of civic leaders' problem solving strategies. *Journal of International Social Studies, 6*(2), 58–83.

Fitzgerald, J. C., & Andes, S. (2012). Preparing active citizens: Exploring ethical issues of providing educative civic experiences for youth. *Issues in Engaged Scholarship, 2*, 4–14.

Freire, P. (1973). *Education for critical consciousness.* Seabury Press.

Freire, P. (2000). *Pedagogy of the oppressed (30th anniversary ed).* (M. Bergman Ramos, Trans.). Continuum.

Freire, P. (2021). *Education for critical consciousness.* Bloomsbury Publishing.

Generation Citizen. (n.d.) Everyday Equity. https://generationcitizen.org/everydaye quity/.

Generation Citizen. (n.d.) Framework for Action. https://generationcitizen.org/our-approach/framework-for-action/.

Generation Citizen (2019). 360 Civic Learning. https://generationcitizen.org/wp-content/uploads/2019/08/360-Civic-Learning-updated-8.12.19.pdf.

Godfrey, E. B., & Burson, E. (2018). Interrogating the intersections: How intersectional perspectives can inform developmental scholarship on critical consciousness. *New Directions for Child and Adolescent Development, 2018* (161), 17–38.

Hazelbaker, T., Brown, C. S., Nenadal, L., & Mistry, R. (2021). Raising white resisters: Studying the development of anti-racist white children and youth [preprint]. https://doi.org/10.31234/osf.io/ej9a5.

Heberle, A. E., Rapa, L. J., & Farago, F. (2020). Critical consciousness in children and adolescents: A systematic review, critical assessment, and recommendations for future research. *Psychological Bulletin, 146*(6), 525–551. https://doi.org/10.1037 /bul0000230.

Helwig, C. C., Ruck, M. D., & Peterson-Badali, M. (2014). Rights, civil liberties, and democracy across cultures. In M. Killen & J. Smetana (Eds.), *Handbook of moral development* (pp. 46–69). Psychology Press. https://doi.org/10.4324/97802 03581957.ch3.

Hershberg, R. M., & Johnson, S. K. (2019). Critical reflection about socioeconomic inequalities among White young men from poor and working-class backgrounds. *Developmental Psychology, 55*(3), 562–573. https://doi.org/10.1037 /dev0000587.

Hope, E. C., & Bañales, J. (2019). Black early adolescent critical reflection of inequit-able sociopolitical conditions: A qualitative investigation. *Journal of Adolescent Research, 34*(2), 167–200. https://doi.org/10.1177/0743558418756360.

Jemal, A. (2017). Critical consciousness: A critique and critical analysis of the literature. *The Urban Review, 49*(4), 602–626.

Karras, J., Ruck, M. D., Peterson-Badali, M., & Emuka, C. (2022). Being and becoming: Centering the morality of social responsibility through children's right to participate in society. In M. Killen & J. Smetana (Eds.), *Handbook of moral development* (3rd ed.) (pp. 118–132). Routledge.

Kosher, H., & Ben-Arieh, A. (2017). What children think about their rights and their well-being: A cross-national comparison. *American Journal of Orthopsychiatry*, *87*(3), 256–273. https://doi.org/10.1037/ort0000222.

Larson, R., & Walker, K. C. (2010). Dilemmas of practice: Challenges to program quality encountered by youth program leaders. *American Journal of Community Psychology*, *45*(3–4), 338–349. https://doi.org/10.1007/s10464-010-9307-z.

Larson, R., Walker, K., & Pearce, N. (2005). A comparison of youth-driven and adult-driven youth programs: Balancing inputs from youth and adults. *Journal of Community Psychology*, *33*(1), 57–74.

LeCompte, K., & Blevins, B. (2015). Building civic bridges: Community-centered action civics. *The Social Studies*, *106*(5), 209–217.

LeCompte, K., Blevins, B., & Riggers-Piehl, T. (2020). Developing civic competence through action civics: A longitudinal look at the data. *The Journal of Social Studies Research*, *44*(1), 127–137.

Maton, K. I. (2008). Empowering community settings: Agents of individual development, community betterment, and positive social change. *American Journal of Community Psychology*, *41*(1–2), 4–21.

McAvoy, P., & Hess, D. (2013). Classroom deliberation in an era of political polarization. *Curriculum Inquiry*, *43*(1), 14–47.

McWhirter, E. H., & McWhirter, B. T. (2016). Critical consciousness and vocational development among Latina/o high school youth: Initial development and testing of a measure. *Journal of Career Assessment*, *24*(3), 543–558. https://doi.org/10.1177/1069072715599535.

Morgan, K. Y., & Ballard, P. J. (in press). Action civics. In B. D. Christens (Ed.), *The Cambridge handbook of community empowerment*. Cambridge University Press.

Morgan, K. Y., Christens, B. D., & Gibson, M. (2022). Design your neighborhood: The evolution of a city-wide urban design learning initiative in Nashville, Tennessee. In R. Stoecker & A. Falcón (Eds.), *Handbook on participatory action research and community development*. Edward Elgar.

Ozer, E. J., Newlan, S., Douglas, L., & Hubbard, E. (2013). "Bounded" empowerment: Analyzing tensions in the practice of youth-led participatory research in urban public schools. *American Journal of Community Psychology*, *52*(1), 13–26.

Pope, A., Stolte, L., & Cohen, A. (2011). Closing the civic engagement gap: The potential of action civics. *Social Education*, *75*(5), 265–268.

Prilleltensky, I. (2008). The role of power in wellness, oppression, and liberation: The promise of psychopolitical validity. *Journal of Community Psychology*, *36*(2), 116–136

Rapa, L. J., Bolding, C. W., & Jamil, F. M. (2020). Development and initial validation of the short critical consciousness scale (CCS-S). *Journal of Applied Developmental Psychology*, *70*, 101–164.

Ruck, M. D., Keating, D. P., Saewyc, E. M., Earls, F., & Ben-Arieh, A. (2014). The United Nations Convention on the rights of the child: Its relevance for adolescents. *Journal of Research on Adolescence*, *26*(1), 16–29. https://doi.org/10.1111/jora.12172.

Sánchez Carmen, S. A., Domínguez, M., Greene, A. C. et al. (2015). Revisiting the collective in critical consciousness: Diverse sociopolitical wisdoms and onto-logical healing in sociopolitical development. *The Urban Review*, 47(5), 824–846. https://doi.org/10.1007/.

Seider, S., Clark, S., & Graves, D. (2020). The development of critical consciousness and its relation to academic achievement in adolescents of color. *Child Development*, 91(2), e451–e474. https://doi.org/10.1111/cdev.13262.

Seider, S., & Graves, D. (2020). *Schooling for critical consciousness. Engaging Black and Latinx youth in analyzing, navigating, and challenging racial inequality*. Harvard Education Press.

Shin, R. Q., Ezeofor, I., Smith, L. C., Welch, J. C., & Goldrich, K. M. (2016). The development and validation of the contemporary critical consciousness measure. *Journal of Counseling Psychology*, 63(2), 210–223.

United Nations General Assembly. (1989, November 17). Adoption of a convention on the rights of the child. http://wunrn.org/reference/pdf/Convention_Rights_Child.PDF.

Walker, T. (2000). The service/politics split: Rethinking service to teach political engagement. *PS: Political Science and Politics*, 33(3), 647–649.

Walker, T. (2002). Service as a pathway to political participation: What research tells us. *Applied Developmental Science*, 6(4), 183–188.

Watts, R. J., Abdul-Adil, J. K., & Pratt, T. (2002). Enhancing critical consciousness in young African American men: A psychoeducational approach. *Psychology of Men & Masculinity*, 3(1), 41–50. https://doi.org/10.1037/1524-9220.3.1.41.

Watts, R. J., Diemer, M. A., & Voight, A. M. (2011). Critical consciousness: Current status and future directions. *New Directions for Child and Adolescent Development*, 2011(134), 43–57. https://doi.org/10.1002/cd.310.

Watts, R. J., Griffith, D. M., & Abdul-Adil, J. (1999). Sociopolitical development as an antidote for oppression – Theory and action. *American Journal of Community Psychology*, 27, 255–271. https://doi.org/10.1023/A:1022839818873.

Watts, R. J., & Hipólito-Delgado, C. (2015). Thinking ourselves to liberation? Advancing sociopolitical action in critical consciousness. *Urban Review*, 47, 847–867. https://doi.org/10.1007/s11256-015-0341.

Westheimer, J., & Kahne, J. (2004). What kind of citizen? The politics of educating for democracy. *American Educational Research Journal*, 41(2), 237–269.

Wray-Lake, L., & Syvertsen, A. (2011). The developmental roots of social responsibility in childhood and adolescence. In C. A. Flanagan & B. D. Christens (Eds.), Youth civic development: Work at the cutting edge. *New Directions for Child and Adolescent Development*, 2011(134), 11–25. https://doi.org/10.1002/cd.308.

3

Critical Consciousness Development in Place-Based Action Civics

KATHRYN Y. MORGAN AND BRIAN D. CHRISTENS

Critical consciousness (CC) – the ability to recognize and analyze inequitable social conditions and act to change those conditions – is a construct with transformative potential for youth and learning contexts (Freire, 1973; Watts et al., 2011). The development of CC is characterized by the interplay of three components: *critical reflection, critical motivation,* and *critical action* (Diemer et al., 2017; Rapa & Geldhof, 2020; Watts & Flanagan, 2007). Critical reflection involves developing an awareness of inequitable social conditions and endorsing equality as a moral ideal. Critical motivation, sometimes referred to as sociopolitical efficacy, involves a commitment to and belief in one's ability to create change. Critical action involves working to change these inequitable conditions.

Although scholarship is converging around the major components of CC, evidence is still emerging about the developmental pathways and contexts that promote them. CC has sometimes been theorized as a sequential process in which youth move from critical reflection to motivation to action in stages (e.g., Heberle et al., 2020; Watts et al., 2011; Jemal, 2017). Movement across these stages may be reinforced through continued engagement in collective action. Some studies point to a reciprocal process in which each domain develops through ongoing cycles of action and reflection (e.g., Christens & Dolan, 2011; Diemer et al., 2016). Still other accounts emphasize contextual influences (e.g., Tyler et al., 2020). Regardless, engaging in these processes and developing CC has consistently been found to be associated with a range of positive outcomes for youth, especially minoritized youth (see Cammarota, 2007; Diemer & Blunstein, 2006; Ginwright, 2010). Those seeking to promote positive youth development are increasingly attending to the ways that they can support students' CC development through participatory approaches, including youth organizing and youth participatory action research (YPAR). These common participatory approaches have substantial evidence linking youth engagement with CC development (Cammarota, 2016;

Christens et al., 2016, 2021; Diemer et al., 2016; Heberle et al., 2020; Kennedy et al., 2020; Watts et al., 2011).

Comparatively less is known about CC development within school-based youth participatory approaches like action civics education (Ballard et al., 2016; Morgan & Ballard, in press, but see Ballard et al., Chapter 2 [this volume]) and place-based education (Delia & Krasny, 2018; Smith, 2007). *Action civics education* is an emerging field that is centrally concerned with engaging youth "in a cycle of research, action, and reflection about problems they care about personally while learning about deeper principles of effective civic, and especially political, action" (Levinson, 2012, p. 224). Action civics is distinguished as an approach to civic education in the ways that it values youth voice and experience, promotes collective action to address inequity, and creates spaces for youth to reflect on issues relevant to their lives and their roles in civic processes (Gingold, 2013; National Action Civics Collaborative, 2014). *Place-based education* similarly positions youth as key actors in, and assets to, the well-being of their communities (McInerney et al., 2011). Place-based education links learning to relevant community issues through local inquiry in which students come to know, value, critique, and engage in the place they live (Demarest, 2014; Smith & Gruenewald, 2007).

At the intersection of these emerging fields is *place-based action civics*, an experiential learning approach in which youth learn about and collectively address sociopolitical issues in their cities and communities. Place-based action civics shares many core commitments with YPAR and youth organizing. All three approaches offer a space for students to deconstruct existing power dynamics and destabilize systems of oppression at work in society (Westheimer & Kahne, 2004) through exploring locally relevant issues in communities, researching the root causes and impacts of these issues, and engaging in policy and advocacy strategies to address the issues collectively (Christens & Kirshner, 2011). Due to these shared commitments, place-based action civics education is positioned as a context that may support CC development among youth. By exploring power structures and root causes of injustice, place-based action civics engages youth in the Freirean process of "reflection and action on the world in order to transform it" (Freire, 2000, p. 51), a driver of CC development.

CC (a theorized psychological construct) and place-based action civics (an engaged approach to civic education) are both centrally concerned with root cause analysis. CC refers to students' understanding of how marginalizing systems perpetuate inequity (Godfrey & Burson, 2018), and place-based action civics scaffolds students as they analyze these marginalizing systems in their local contexts. Both the theory of CC and the practice of place-based action civics are concerned with how systems of oppression have developed, how they intersect, and how they are rooted in privilege and power (Montero, 2009). Both support examining structural causes of racial, socioeconomic, gender, and other identity-centered disparities that perpetuate systemic issues in students' communities (Watts & Hipolito-Delgado, 2015). In short, the underlying goals of the scholarship on CC development and the practice of place-based action civics are consonant, making CC an ideal framework for examining youth civic development within place-based civic education efforts.

Pedagogical approaches to place-based action civics are also well aligned with CC development. For both CC development and place-based action civics, the aim of participation is social change as well as learning (Watts et al., 2011). In school contexts, this requires an open classroom climate in which youth can discuss complex topics relevant to their communities (Godfrey & Grayman, 2014; Hess, 2009). Teachers and facilitators must subvert adultist paradigms through structuring learning communities that encourage active participation, youth leadership, and a colearning, nonhierarchical power structure (Freire, 2000; Montero, 2009; Watts & Hipolito-Delgado, 2015). Like other approaches to CC development, place-based action civics draws on experiential and progressive pedagogies to promote opportunities for youth to learn through social change by having a voice in collective decision-making, educating others about an issue, and getting involved in local political processes. Finally, place-based action civics builds on culturally responsive and humanizing pedagogies, which aim to connect what students learn in the classroom to their lived experiences (del Carmen Salazar, 2013; Heberle et al., 2020) and reframe students' roles in social change efforts from being targets of adult-led interventions to active agents in addressing issues relevant to their lives (Camino, 2000; Watts & Flanagan, 2007). Because these features of place-based action civics reflect so much of what is known about CC development, we expect that place-based action civics contexts promote CC development, although no research to date has specifically examined this hypothesis.

Middle school is a rich developmental context for employing place-based action civics to enhance CC development. As students and teachers work collaboratively to implement participatory curricula, individual and institutional factors converge to impact student learning. Participatory approaches challenge white, middle-class norms entrenched in traditional curricula (Voight & Velez, 2018), allowing students to exercise their agency to advocate for themselves and critique social injustices while deepening academic skills (Edirmanasignhe, 2020; Morales et al., 2017; Mediratta et al., 2008). However, place-based action civics is not a "homogenous intervention" (Ballard et al., 2016, p. 378), and the literature points to a range of factors that impact students' educational outcomes, including variation in implementation techniques, instructional techniques, curricular innovations, and classroom climate (Andolina & Conklin, 2020; LeCompte & Blevins, 2015; Morales et al., 2017; Walsh, 2018).

Additionally, the benefits of engaging with place-based action civics in middle school may be particularly pronounced for youth who are marginalized by systemic inequities rooted in race and socioeconomic status (Butler, 2017; Christens & Kirshner, 2011; Conner & Slattery, 2014; Kornbluh et al., 2015; Voight & Velez, 2018). While evidence of these effects is still limited in the action civics literature, it is well-documented in the school-based youth organizing and YPAR literature, particularly among first- and second-generation immigrant students (Walsh, 2018), low-income students (Means et al., 2021), and Latinx students (Edirmanasignhe, 2020; Morales et al., 2017).

THE CURRENT STUDY

In this mixed-methods study, we consider the effects of engaging with a place-based action civics curriculum on middle school students' CC development. Place-based action civics is not yet widespread as a type of learning context, and thus CC development has not been empirically explored within it, prompting the following research questions: Is participation in place-based action civics associated with increased CC among middle school students, and, if so, what do students' narratives convey about the nature of their CC development?

Study Context

Nashville is the capitol of the US state of Tennessee. Nashville–Davidson County is a consolidated city-county government with 689,447 residents (US Census Bureau, 2020) anchoring a metropolitan area of approximately 2 million residents. Over the last several decades, Nashville has experienced rapid growth and change in its built environment, and this trend has accelerated due to increasing prominence as a tourist destination and relocation site for corporations (Plazas, 2018). This growth has driven real estate investment, development, and speculation, ultimately contributing to gentrification and displacement of residents in many formerly affordable neighborhoods (Plazas, 2018). The city's investments in affordable housing, public transportation, and other resident-focused infrastructure (e.g., schools, parks) have significantly lagged the pace of growth.

The Metro Nashville Public School (MNPS) District currently serves more than 86,000 students across 550 square miles throughout Nashville–Davidson County. The district serves a high-poverty population, with 71.4% of students considered economically disadvantaged. MNPS is highly diverse, with students representing nearly 140 countries and speaking more than 120 different languages (Gonzalez, 2015). The school district faces many obstacles rooted in the historical legacies of inequitable urban planning and policy, from the long-term impacts of school and neighborhood segregation to the out-migration of affluent, white students to neighboring school districts (Erickson, 2016).

MNPS is surrounded by suburban school districts that are generally better resourced and have higher average scores on standardized measures of student achievement. Thus, MNPS faces legacies of race and class inequities that continue to negatively impact students and schools. Teacher shortages in the district have grown substantially in the past five years, with many teachers citing disproportionately low wages and diminishing morale as their catalyst for leaving the district or the profession (Garcia & Weiss, 2019). Teachers who remain increasingly struggle to afford housing in the city where they teach. Despite the systemic nature of these problems and their profound impact on the educational landscape in the city, attempts to remedy these issues often ignore the underlying systems that created these inequitable conditions (Nation et al., 2020).

Design Your Neighborhood

Design Your Neighborhood (DYN) is a place-based action civics curriculum that is currently being offered in partnership with the MNPS District (Morgan et al., 2022). DYN engages students in addressing disparities in the city's built environment and explores how Nashville's urban planning has impacted community members. Nashville has a robust history of grassroots community organizing that has worked to mitigate these issues, particularly in addressing disparities in access to affordable housing and transit. However, there are few opportunities for youth engagement or leadership in these efforts. To combat this lack of youth voice, the Civic Design Center, a participatory community development nonprofit organization in Nashville, set out to integrate the *Plan of Nashville* (Gaston & Kreyling, 2015; Kreyling, 2005), a participatory guide to enacting equitable design and development decisions in the city, into the public school system through a middle school action civics curriculum.

To launch DYN, the Civic Design Center assembled a team of local teachers interested in engaging their students in social justice–oriented education to build the curriculum. These teachers worked closely with community-development and urban-planning professionals from the Civic Design Center to learn about Nashville's built environment and the principles of equitable design outlined in the Civic Design Center's books on *The Plan of Nashville*. This curriculum development team created action civics units that function independently within each content area but are combined to offer an interdisciplinary exploration of locally specific urban design issues that have exacerbated inequality in Nashville. Middle school teachers opt in to adopt DYN's 15-hour project-based learning units. These units are cross-curricular, design-oriented lessons on the built environment that fit into existing seventh and eighth grade coursework and allow students the opportunity to apply the MNPS curriculum to real-world challenges facing Nashville (Morgan et al., 2022).

The DYN curriculum introduces students to structural issues facing Nashville's residents, including Nashville's history of neighborhood displacement, blockbusting, systemic disinvestment in public transit, highway construction, and school busing policies (Erickson, 2016). DYN then offers a brief urban design education that introduces important factors for a healthy built environment (e.g., active transit, parks and open spaces, affordable housing). This urban design education becomes a lens through which youth can address structural issues entrenched in Nashville's built environment.

Through DYN, students learn about community-driven responses, such as community organizing and action research, that could increase equity in Nashville's built environment. They also learn about common change-making strategies in the field of urban design, including tactical urbanism interventions, in which low-cost, temporary installations provide evidence for permanent design solutions, and placekeeping projects, in which community members generate long-term, flexible plans for the management of public spaces such as parks and community centers to ensure they can be enjoyed by all.

They then take part in a collaborative project aimed at decreasing disparities in the city's urban policies, systems, and environments. Each subject area selects a collaborative project appropriate to the subject's learning standards. For example, art classes have created functional art pieces that promote connectivity in the school's neighborhood, English classes have created podcasts that advocate for active transit options, and social studies classes have created comprehensive advocacy plans to convince city leaders to support affordable housing development. Volunteer design professionals from the Nashville community assist with project development in middle school classrooms, consulting with students and teachers during the intensive design portions of the projects. Students' projects are showcased at the end of the school year at a citywide exhibition. Students invite community stakeholders (e.g., city council members, business leaders, school officials, design professionals) to attend and engage them in addressing Nashville's issues through youth-led urban design. At the exhibition, students set up stations to share their final projects with attendees and lead panel discussions to address topics relevant to the curriculum. Attendees move between groups of students to learn about their projects, offer feedback and next steps for their work, and support students' ongoing efforts toward improving Nashville's built environment.

Conceptual Framework

Our mixed-methods analysis is rooted in the three-component conceptualization of CC described in the introduction to this chapter, which attends to critical reflection, critical motivation, and critical action (Diemer et al., 2015;

Watts et al., 2011). To assess the extent to which DYN contributed to students' *critical reflection*, we compare pre- and post-curricular assessments of the egalitarianism domain of the Short Critical Consciousness Scale (CCC-S; Rapa et al., 2020). This scale assesses students' burgeoning commitment to egalitarianism as a subcomponent of critical reflection over the course of their experience with DYN. These findings are enriched by student's retrospective qualitative accounts of a deepened understanding of local social issues, their reanalysis of past experiences, and their endorsement of more egalitarian futures for the city. *Critical motivation* is similarly assessed both quantitatively and qualitatively. We use pre- and post-intervention measures of the Sociopolitical Control Scale for Youth (Lardier et al., 2018) as a proxy for understanding students' feelings of agency in addressing injustice (Christens et al., 2015; Diemer et al., 2015). To contextualize findings related to critical motivation, we draw on focus group data that recount students' perceptions of how the curriculum enhanced their motivation to teach adults about injustice in the city and to shape the city for future generations. Finally, we draw exclusively on the qualitative focus group data to assess critical action, as this behavioral rather than psychological element of CC can be assessed through students' descriptions of how the curriculum has shaped their current participation in civic life (Diemer et al., 2015).

METHODS

Participants and Procedures

DYN was implemented in 18 of 33 middle schools in Nashville during the 2018–2019 academic year. Ultimately, 31 teachers across these partner schools taught the curriculum to more than 2,000 seventh and eighth grade students. Sample recruitment took place in three stages. First, seventh and eighth grade teachers from across the district were invited to incorporate the place-based action civics curriculum in their classroom. Teachers in the same school who did not elect to teach DYN were recruited as a quasi-control group (teacher $n = 18$ treatment, $n = 12$ control). All students with teachers who opted in to implement the DYN curriculum or take part in the control group were included in the initial sampling frame. Students could then opt in to participate in the study by providing parental informed consent and student assent. Students in classrooms where teachers opted in to use DYN engaged with the curriculum regardless of their participation in the research. Students in control group classrooms could similarly opt in to take part in the research by providing parental informed consent and student assent, but did not engage with the DYN curriculum. Students were recruited from the classes of all teachers who elected to either incorporate the curriculum or participate in the control group. From this group, all students whose guardians provided consent to participate and who completed surveys at both timepoints of data collection were included in the sample (student n = 620 treatment, n = 255 control). Participants are diverse in terms of gender and race/ethnicity, as shown in Table 3.1.

Finally, eight classrooms from the treatment group were selected as the site of focus groups. Focus groups were designed to yield insights into the experience of DYN as a context for the development of CC. The research team used a purposive sampling method (Patton, 1990) for focus group site selection to capture the experiences of students in schools that are diverse based on neighborhood characteristics. Twelve students from DYN classrooms were randomly selected to participate in a focus group at each of the eight schools in the focus group sample (N = 96). Table 3.2 provides contextual, occupational, and demographic characteristics of the teachers and classrooms included in the focus group sample.

Focus groups took place at the end of the DYN curriculum. Focus groups were particularly well suited for the evaluation of place-based action civics as a collective learning process, as they allowed participants to build upon or

TABLE 3.1 Demographic characteristics of the sample

	Treatment		Control		Total	
	n	%	n	%	N	%
Gender						
Male	258	41%	101	40%	359	41%
Female	328	54%	136	54%	464	53%
Nonbinary	13	2%	4	2%	17	2%
Prefer not to answer	21	3%	10	4%	31	4%
Race/ethnicity						
American Indian/Alaskan Native	34	5%	6	2%	40	5%
Asian	65	10%	17	7%	82	9%
Black/African American	274	44%	119	47%	393	45%
Hispanic/Latino	141	23%	47	19%	188	22%
Middle Eastern/North African	28	5%	9	4%	37	4%
Native Hawaiian/Pacific Islander	13	2%	2	1%	15	2%
White	208	34%	62	25%	270	31%
Prefer not to answer	40	6%	13	5%	53	6%
Grade						
Seventh	154	25%	154	61%	308	35%
Eighth	466	75%	97	38%	563	65%

TABLE 3.2 Characteristics of focus group classrooms and teachers

School	Grade	Subject	Teacher Certification	Years Teaching	Gender	Race/ Ethnicity
OMS	8	English	Undergraduate	23	F	White
PMS	8	Social Studies	Graduate	22	F	Black
SMS	8	Art	Graduate	3	F	White
MMS	8	Social Studies	Alternate Route	2	M	White
CMS	7	English	Graduate	13	F	Black
BMS	7	English	Graduate	7	F	Latinx
PiMS	7	Art	Undergraduate	14	F	Latinx
WMS	7	Social Studies	Undergraduate	3	F	Latinx

Note. All school names are pseudonyms.

interrogate one another's ideas (Stewart & Shamdasani, 2014) regarding civic participation (e.g., "If you were the president of your neighborhood association, what would be your top three priorities, and why?") and equity in the built environment (e.g., "What does it mean for a community to be healthy?") presented in the curriculum. The complete focus group protocol is included in Appendix A.

Survey Data and Analysis

Survey data were collected from students in treatment and control groups across two grade levels. Sixty-question self-report surveys were administered at two timepoints during the academic year. Presurveys took place during the term preceding DYN, and postsurveys took place immediately after the project exhibition. The survey instrument was designed to capture civic and education-related outcomes, as well as covariates. Two measures from the study were included in this analysis: egalitarianism and sociopolitical control.

The egalitarianism domain of the Short Critical Consciousness Scale (CCC-S) was used as a measure of critical reflection (Rapa et al., 2020). The CCC-S measures the degree to which students endorse equality and a belief that all people should be treated equally (e.g., "group equality should be our ideal"). The 5-item egalitarianism domain uses a 5-point Likert scale ordered *from strongly disagree to strongly agree* without a neutral response, instead utilizing *slightly disagree* as a midpoint. Responses were averaged to create a composite score. For this sample, the mean baseline score for treatment group egalitarianism was 4.04 (SD = 0.60; α = 0.78). Table 3.3 includes means and standard deviations at each timepoint across both groups.

TABLE 3.3 Means and standard deviations of treatment and control group pre- and postsurvey scores

	Pretreatment		Posttreatment		Precontrol		Postcontrol	
	M	SD	M	SD	M	SD	M	SD
Sociopolitical Control	58.52	15.60	61.37	15.70	61.21	14.45	61.15	14.50
Leadership Competence	63.48	17.80	67.72	17.83	66.42	17.77	66.62	17.57
Policy Control	53.50	19.74	54.99	19.38	57.00	18.03	56.57	17.39
Egalitarianism	4.04	0.60	4.01	0.59	4.10	0.57	4.07	0.61

The abbreviated Sociopolitical Control Scale for Youth (SPCS-Y) (Lardier et al., 2018) was used to assess sociopolitical control, a construct conceptually related to critical motivation (Christens et al., 2015). SPCS-Y measures youth's perceived ability to contribute to social change via political participation and social action, making it a useful indicator of students' political efficacy and critical motivation. The 8-item SPCS-Y used 1–100 scale responses ordered from disagreement to agreement. Sociopolitical control is considered to be a bidimensional construct consisting of leadership competence (e.g., "I am often a leader in groups") and policy control (e.g., "There are plenty of ways for youth like me to have a say in what our community or school does") (Peterson et al., 2011). The mean score for leadership competence was 63.48 (SD = 17.80; α = 0.78), the mean score for policy control was 53.50 (SD = 19.74; α = 0.76), and the overall scale had a mean of 58.52 (SD = 15.60; α = 0.72). In our analysis, we explore changes between pre- and postsurvey scores for the overall scale and its subscales. This is consistent with previous studies which illustrate that community-based interventions may differentially cultivate youth's civic participation skills via leadership competence and civic participation expectations via policy control (Peterson et al., 2011).

Quantitative data were first analyzed using descriptive statistics (see Table 3.2). Normality of the data was assessed for each group using the Shapiro–Wilk test, and the condition of equal variance was verified using Levene's test. Independent samples t-tests were then used to compare mean difference scores for egalitarianism and sociopolitical control between the treatment and control groups. Finally, paired samples t-tests were used to compare mean scores for egalitarianism and sociopolitical control from pretest to posttest among students in the treatment and control groups.

Qualitative Data and Analysis

Qualitative descriptive data were collected through semistructured focus groups that lasted between sixty and ninety minutes. Focus groups took place on school campuses during school hours within a two-week period after classes completed the DYN curriculum. We conducted a thematic analysis of the qualitative data (Braun & Clarke, 2012) by drawing on the semistructured interview prompts to develop initial thematic domains. Data were analyzed in NVivo (QSR International, Version 12, 2018) to generate an iterative codebook by applying codes to all the transcribed data based on initial thematic domains represented in the semistructured focus group protocol. To do so, the first author reviewed all transcripts in NVivo to assign participant responses to themes that aligned with these deductive thematic categories derived from the focus group protocol and then worked with the second author to refine the codes until agreement was reached.

The codebook was then revised from the broad, initial thematic coding domains derived from the protocol questions into themes that fell within our concept of interest for this analysis: students' CC development. Because there were no direct questions in the focus group protocol in which students reflected on their CC development, we reviewed all the initial thematic domains to cross-classify coded text into instances in which students were describing one or more dimensions of CC development: *critical reflection, critical motivation,* and/or *critical action.* Given that youth were coconstructing these themes collectively during the focus groups, coded data were chunked to include multiple consecutive turns of talk that related to a given theme (Stewart & Shamdasani, 2014). The resultant coding categories were created by the first author and reviewed by the second author. Variation in the authors' assessment of coded text was discussed until agreement was reached. The first author then further defined subcodes within each of the three categories of the thematic frame, with particular attention to the way that qualitative data might support or complicate our quantitative findings. The coded data and codebook which explained our conceptualization of the three components of CC development were then deidentified and shared with our community partner at the Civic Design Center, who served as a critical friend (Kember et. al, 1997). We integrated their reflections and contextual knowledge to enhance the trustworthiness of the data and enrich our findings about CC development in place-based action civics (Lincoln & Guba, 1985).

RESULTS

Quantitative Findings

We used both independent samples and paired samples t-tests to compare scores across variables and groups within our sample. First, independent samples t-tests were conducted to compare scores for egalitarianism and sociopolitical control by calculating the mean difference in scores for students in the treatment and control groups (see Table 3.4). There was no significant difference in mean scores for egalitarianism between the two

TABLE 3.4 Results of independent samples t-tests

	Mean Diff	SE Diff	t	df	p
Sociopolitical Control	−2.75	1.27	−2.16	868	0.031
Leadership Competence	−3.837	1.457	−2.63	867	0.009
Policy Control	−1.779	1.671	−1.06	867	0.287
Egalitarianism	−0.011	0.058	−0.243	852	0.808

groups, $t(852) = -0.243$, $p = 0.808$. There was, however, a significant difference in students' overall sociopolitical control between treatment and control groups, $t(868) = -2.16$, $p = 0.031$. Cohen's d was estimated at 0.162, indicating a small effect size. This suggests that students in the treatment group experienced statistically larger gains in sociopolitical control than their peers in the control group. The bidimensional constructs that make up sociopolitical control, leadership competence, and policy control were then considered separately to account for mean score differences in each subdomain between treatment and control groups. There was a significant difference in students' leadership development between the treatment and control groups, $t(867) = -0.263$, $p = 0.009$. However, there was no evidence of a significant difference in mean scores for policy control, $t(867) = -0.106$, $p = 0.287$. This suggests that students in the treatment group experienced gains in their self-perceived skills and abilities necessary for leading a group in comparison to their peers in the control group, but their scores for self-perceived ability to exert influence on policy decisions were not significantly different from that of control group members. These quantitative findings suggested that qualitative accounts of the impact of curricular participation on sociopolitical control may illuminate students' perceptions of the practical significance of their participation in DYN.

Next, paired samples t-tests were conducted to compare changes in sociopolitical control and egalitarianism from presurvey to postsurvey separately for students in the treatment vs. control groups (Table 3.5). There was no significant difference in students' egalitarianism between the presurvey and postsurvey among students in either the treatment or the control groups. High average scores at both timepoints across both conditions suggest that students have, on average, high and relatively stable endorsements of the idea that all people should be treated equally. This finding is aligned with other research that suggests dispositions aligned with CC and civic development may be highest during adolescence and decline in adulthood (Christens et al., 2018).

Although no significant changes were observed in sociopolitical control scores among students in the control group, there was a significant increase in treatment group students' overall sociopolitical control between the presurvey

TABLE 3.5 Results of paired samples t-tests

	Treatment				Control			
	Change	Pre	Post	*p*	Change	Pre	Post	*p*
Sociopolitical Control	2.85	58.52	61.37	<0.001	−0.06	61.21	61.15	0.95
Leadership Competence	4.24	63.48	67.72	<0.001	0.20	66.42	66.62	0.87
Policy Control	1.49	53.50	54.99	0.099	−0.43	57.00	56.57	0.76
Egalitarianism	−0.03	4.04	4.01	0.331	−0.03	4.10	4.07	0.45

and postsurvey, $t = 4.16$, $p < 0.001$, suggesting that students' beliefs about their perceived ability to contribute to social change significantly increased during the DYN curriculum to a greater degree than it would have if students were not participating in DYN. However, examining the subconstructs of sociopolitical control separately reveals that DYN students only exhibit statistically significant gains in the leadership competence domain between the presurvey and post-survey, $t = -4.18$, $p < 0.001$. This suggests that students' skill and confidence in exercising leadership in local community and organizational processes increased over the course of the curriculum, but their self-perceptions of competence in influencing decisions in community contexts remained unchanged.

Qualitative Findings

Next, we examined focus group data to contextualize students' experiences with the DYN curriculum. This is consistent with calls in the CC literature to "allow youth to expand upon their reflection, motivation, and the targets of their stated efficacy and action in more detail" (Godfrey & Burson, 2018, p. 33). Three themes related to CC development were observed in the focus groups. First, many youth shared how place-based action civics cultivated their *critical reflection*, or awareness of local issues that are rooted in structural inequality. Second, youth described feeling *critical motivation* to address injustices in their communities but indicated few avenues for channeling their motivation toward social change. Their critical motivation was limited to educating those who they perceive to hold positions of relative authority about the root causes of these injustices. Third, youth struggled to see themselves as personally or collectively capable of addressing the injustices they see in their communities through direct *critical action*. Taken together, these findings suggest that place-based action civics curricula may be better suited to fostering critical reflection and motivation, the psychological processes related to CC (Watts & Flanagan, 2007), than supporting youth action toward improving material conditions in their communities.

In what follows, we describe each of the three themes that emerged from the data. We outline the prevalence of these themes across focus groups through noting the number of focus groups in which each theme was raised. For instance, themes such as critical reflection and critical action were ubiquitous in our data, with each of the eight focus group classrooms addressing the theme at some point in their discussion. Alternatively, critical motivation was only discussed in seven focus groups, and many subthemes were similarly not present in certain focus groups. To further contextualize the prevalence of a given theme or subtheme in the data, we note the number of conversations in which each theme arose. Conversations related to critical reflection, critical motivation, and critical action occurred sixty-six times across eight focus groups. In many focus group classrooms, a theme was raised in more than one conversation over the course of the focus group. Noting both the number of classrooms and the number of conversations in which a given theme arose in the data supports a nuanced interpretation of the prevalence of each theme both within and across focus groups.

Critical Reflection

Instances in which students or groups of students demonstrated increased critical reflection that they linked to key learning from the DYN curriculum occurred thirty times across all eight focus group classes. Students described three pathways for demonstrating critical reflection: through reflecting on local issues, past experiences, and egalitarianism.

Reflecting on Local Issues Across fifteen conversations in seven classrooms, youth described aspects of the DYN curriculum that increased their awareness of local issues that are rooted in structural inequality. For example, students often mentioned an exercise in the curriculum that challenged them to find housing in their communities when given profiles of families with differing wants, needs, and financial circumstances. One student reflected on the unique struggles faced by "a family with an unemployment crisis," describing the experience as "eye-opening for me, since I don't face that struggle. It was hard to fathom how people get housing when [my neighborhood] is so overrated in cost." The curriculum also includes community surveying and neighborhood audits that created space to "get our neighbors' perspective" and "step back ... look around and think about what we want Nashville to be like." One student noticed that DYN "put words to what I see every day," while another described that it "opened my eyes to what's happening behind the scenes ... that there is a reason for the struggles people face to find a house they can afford or the struggle between traffic and people, and people made these problems."

Reflecting on Past Experiences Ten discussions in five classrooms included youth reinterpreting personal experiences with injustice and inequity in Nashville through a new, more critical lens. Some described experiencing relatives, friends, and their own families being pushed out of their neighborhoods, noticing that "it wasn't until this project that I learned this happens every day in Nashville; kids just don't talk about it." One group collectively described the harmful impacts of residential displacement driven by Nashville's unregulated growth through connecting their experiences to structural oppression stemming from racism and classism:

STUDENT 1:   So higher-income people and white Americans are changing the way that Nashville is – and making us move to like, Clarksville and La Vergne [suburbs of Nashville] and stuff.

STUDENT 2:   Yeah, making people live further out, gentrification.

STUDENT 1:   And I feel like higher-income people aren't really thinking about the low-income people's lives after their neighborhood has been gentrified.

STUDENT 3:   They're not thinking about what the effects of them living in that neighborhood is . . .

STUDENT 2:   Like "I'm about to build a bigger house," not thinking "hope it doesn't affect you." They don't even think about it, even though there is ways to go about it to where it doesn't have to affect us so much.

Here, students articulate their frustration with the status quo, referencing alternative ways of "go[ing] about it" as Nashville adds new residents that could mitigate the impact of displacement they have seen in their communities. Another group of students who lived in a public housing complex slated for redevelopment similarly described a shared awareness that interlocking forms of oppression in their community were linked to larger oppressive forces:

STUDENT 1:   History is starting to repeat itself.

STUDENT 2:   I feel like it's worse since Trump moved in the White House, building that wall and stuff. Everything has a backframe to it. Him building that wall has a backframe on [our housing complex], on our community, getting destroyed . . . but we can't go into the White House and mess it up, we can't build a wall around his house.

In this quote, students are reflecting on the impending displacement they face when the city transitions their housing complex to a mixed-income development, linking their experience to broader forms of displacement and forced separation perpetrated by the Trump administration through border wall mandates. In doing so, they demonstrate an understanding of how legacies of oppression are linked through a *backframe*, or a sociohistorical legacy of similarly unjust practices, and how these injustices drive structural inequity in society.

Reflecting on Egalitarianism Finally, students articulated egalitarian visions for the future of the city in five discussions during five focus groups. In doing so, many framed the need to engage in equitable development as a moral imperative. For example, one student described the need for Nashville to temper its rapid growth through valuing people over development:

> I wish Nashville would slow down and think about everything before just making changes and getting rid of the culture. So I wish they would recognize the fact that we lose so much culture and diversity in Nashville when we get rid of houses and restaurants and businesses just 'cause they are a little old. It's the people that create the culture and diversity, so I just want people besides just us to care instead of just plowing over them.

Given the high and relatively stable levels of egalitarianism outlined in the quantitative findings, DYN likely does not develop students' desire for greater equality in Nashville. However, qualitative findings suggest that DYN may offer a starting point for youth to critically reflect on inequitable systems in their local communities, articulating an understanding of perceived injustice in the city and a desire to create more equitable futures for themselves and their communities.

Critical Motivation

Students described a new or renewed commitment to and belief in their ability to create change and promote equitable social conditions in fifteen conversations across seven focus groups.

Motivation to Teach Adults Ten groups of students across five focus groups expressed motivation to educate others, particularly adults who they perceive to have more decision-making power, about what they learned through DYN. Most students who described this motivation alluded to a sense that their political efficacy was limited due to their age, but that their unique insights were important for adults to engage with. For example, one student shared a desire to "teach [adults] about what's really going on in Nashville and why. They wouldn't expect it from someone younger. So that if you say something they might think, wow, you're so mature, maybe we should like, consider this now." Another student shared a commitment to making change through "present[ing] what we were learning about and show[ing] them we actually know what we're talking about when it comes to making Nashville a good place. And we're not just like, researching stuff that's not even important." Others reflected on a developing sense of responsibility to educate adults about current local issues manifested in the built environment. For example, one student reflected on how the process of creating a podcast about residential displacement in her neighborhood catalyzed a desire to educate adults who may not share a salient connection to place with the students they teach.

I think we should teach more people about how affordable housing is a major issue, because when we were doing the podcast, we interviewed people to learn how it was impacting them. We were interviewing teachers, and quite a few of them didn't even know what gentrification was. Like our history teacher, I started the interview and asked him how he defined gentrification, and he was like, "I prefer not to answer," which basically meant "I have no idea what you're talking about, go away." And it wasn't just him, a few other people didn't know anything about it, or knew that there was a lot of new houses coming in but didn't know anything about what that means for people who live in our neighborhoods.

This student frames themselves as a teacher of their own teachers, particularly those who are not yet critically reflective. This quote demonstrates that youth view working to cultivate critical reflection among other people, particularly adults who youth see as having more decision-making power, as a generative approach to creating change.

Motivation to Shape the Future In three classrooms, five discussions occurred in which youth attributed their critical motivation to the stake they have in ensuring Nashville develops into an equitable city because they "want to create a city we can stay in," making it "worth it for us to struggle." One student described youth's stake in addressing structural issues now as a matter of necessity, as they will ultimately inherit the decisions of previous generations of Nashville's leadership: "Youth also care more because we're the ones that are facing these problems. And we're the ones who are going to be left with the problems. So we're fixing it now . . . reducing kind of the issue that's at hand." This sense of youth's collective stake in supporting an equitable city was also shared as a reason to educate adults as a social change mechanism. Some youth framed their desire to educate adults through appealing to a shared interest in youth thriving. For example, one student shared the importance of "tell[ing] adults about what we learned, especially if they are only worried about their families and their neighborhoods, [so] they'll not only start thinking about their future, but their child's future, and it'll motivate them to make a change." Students shared a unique vision of how they could best invest their time in supporting adults' critical reflection in order to make change that could benefit youth collectively. Their motivation to educate others with more influence demonstrates an understanding of collective, relational forms of power as crucial to making change.

Ultimately, students' discussions of avenues for channeling their critical motivation toward social change were limited to educating those with more power to act on their behalf. This limited pathway to action reflects students' quantitative increase in the leadership competence subscale of Sociopolitical

Control, which manifests here in their desire to lead adults in considering inequity in the built environment, and their unchanged scores on Policy Control, which manifests in students' inability to envision themselves as actors with political power.

Critical Action

Although twenty-one conversations across eight focus groups discussed the degree to which youth felt prepared to take action to change inequitable conditions in their communities, their approaches to action and perceptions of power varied.

Despite their critical reflection and critical motivation, youth struggled to situate themselves as agents capable of addressing the root causes of social issues. For some students, their perceptions of the sources and nature of social power and the role of youth in local power dynamics exclude youth voice. For example, when asked about which issue in Nashville should be the top priority for city planners and government officials, one group of students responded in this way:

STUDENT 1:   Well, do you think like city planners will actually listen?
STUDENT 2:   I think, honestly, no.
STUDENT 3:   Probably like, if we all like, walk around and pick up trash.
STUDENT 2:   Yeah, that helps our community.
STUDENT 1:   Yeah, we can like, help our own community. Because I think adults are not gonna listen to us because we're kids, but like, we can help like our own community. We can like, pick up trash or like, plant trees.
STUDENT 2:   Or make a garden.
STUDENT 3:   Or we can help like, give money towards like a community center.
STUDENT 2:   We can like set up different things that are meant for kids.

As demonstrated here, students eschew the idea of city leaders seriously considering youth priorities for Nashville. Instead, this conversation and six others in three focus groups offered ideas for how they could enact changes in their neighborhood that are limited to "things meant for kids" that do not require adult support. These suggested changes often did not address the root causes of the injustices that were discussed at other points in the focus group.

In fourteen conversations across six focus groups, students described feeling structurally limited in their ability to make change because of the limitations on civic engagement imposed by their age. These limitations are coupled with students' awareness of normative power dynamics that exist between youth and adults which limit youth agency:

Adults have the whole thing of like, children should be seen and not heard, which I think is complete trash. And like what we think is important, like, because we're not able to vote, and they're just like, you're, you're little, you know, you don't understand this, and this, and this, when I'm very political. We're treated like we are not mature.

Many students expressed awareness of a disconnect between their self-perception as being informed civic agents and dominant narratives of youth as precitizens without rights to participate in issues that impact them. Another group similarly addressed the ways that disenfranchisement limits youth's ability to engage in critical action while attending to interlocking forms of marginalization that shape their experiences:

STUDENT 1:   They won't take us serious.
STUDENT 2:   I agree, they won't take us serious.
INTERVIEWER: What do you think it would make them take you seriously?
STUDENT 2:   If we was big. If we was older they might listen.
STUDENT 1:   It's your sense of authority. Like if we was a police officer, a teacher, if we could vote, then it would feel like they would listen. But since we kids, I don't think they would listen.
STUDENT 3:   And I don't really wanna say this but a lot of impact is on our skin color, because our skin color has gone through a lot and we've got a lot of history. And I just feel like it's coming back. That's just how I feel.

Here, students point to both racist and adultist narratives that contribute to their silencing on issues that leave them without a "sense of authority" in community decisions. Through connecting the interlocking systems that limit their critical action, youth are engaged in critical reflection. Still, without avenues for action, particularly given that they are excluded from formal political processes like voting, students struggled to identify avenues to meaningfully participate in social change efforts.

DISCUSSION

Taken together, these mixed-methods data offer insights into features unique to DYN that may foster dimensions of CC among youth. Qualitative findings contextualize the variability in the quantitative data, illuminating how critical reflection, critical motivation, and critical action may be differentially facilitated through participation in place-based action civics.

Critical Reflection

Students' critical reflections help them understand root causes of injustice in their communities and are linked to positive psychological outcomes (Watts & Hipolito-Delgado, 2015). Our quantitative findings suggest that students have a high and relatively stable self-reported egalitarianism – a domain of critical reflection – irrespective of participation in place-based action civics. These quantitative findings are consistent with previous research that suggests critical reflection may be highest during adolescence and decline into adulthood (Christens et al., 2018), and are consistent with measurement studies (e.g., Diemer et al., 2017; Rapa et al., 2020) that suggest egalitarianism is a distinct construct from perceptions of inequality. The DYN curriculum offers opportunities for youth to reflect on the importance of an egalitarian society through teaching them about systemic barriers to equitable built environments (i.e., redlining, blockbusting, and urban disinvestment). It also introduces avenues for creating a more equal society (i.e., considering housing as a human right). The adolescents in our study entered their experiences of the curriculum already espousing a commitment to equality, and therefore our quantitative data do not reveal growth happening in students' critical reflection. However, qualitative findings further elucidate students' perceptions of inequality, in particular their sense of intersectional consciousness (Godfrey & Burson, 2018) about the interlocking sources of inequity present in their communities. Through focus groups, students described how the DYN curriculum offered a shared language for understanding disparities in the built environment, helped them to connect their neighborhood experiences with structural inequity in Nashville, and provided outlets for sharing their voice outside the classroom, demonstrating how these issues are reflected in their worldviews (Roy et al., 2019). Therefore, while our quantitative findings demonstrate students' consistent belief in equality in the abstract, focus group data illustrate students' evolving reflection on structural breaches to an ideal egalitarian society present in their neighborhoods and in Nashville.

Place-based interventions such as DYN may not be well suited for supporting change in students' universal appraisals of equity. Our null quantitative findings paired with rich qualitative accounts of growth in reflection on local issues and past experiences suggest that place-based action civics interventions may support students' reflection on structural and historical inequities in the settings and contexts that matter most to them. Current quantitative measures of CC do not capture students' critical reflection on their own lived experiences and local realities. To address this, quantitative measures could be derived to assess the extent to which participation in locally relevant interventions increase students' CC at a local scale.

Critical Motivation

The sociopolitical constructs of Leadership Competence and Policy Control were assessed as a quantitative proxy for understanding students' critical motivation to address injustice (Christens, et al., 2015; Diemer et al., 2015). While leadership competence was statistically higher among DYN students than among their peers in the control group and increased from presurvey to postsurvey, policy control remained stable across both groups. This finding suggests that while DYN supports students' perceptions of efficacy in leading a group, it may not impact students' perceived ability to exert influence on policy decisions in community and organizational settings. Although sociopolitical control is a bidimensional construct, previous studies have found only small proportions of samples of youth reporting diminished policy control and elevated leadership competence (Christens et al., 2015), making this an unusual finding. Most studies of youth sociopolitical control, however, have been among older (high-school aged) youth, so this suggests a future direction for research on civic development.

The discrepancy between DYN students' sense of leadership competence and their perceived policy control is illustrated qualitatively through students' suggested strategies for harnessing their critical motivation to educate adult change agents. Qualitative data offered insights into the discrepancies between youths' sense of their internal political efficacy, or perceived capacity for political participation, and external political efficacy, or beliefs that those with power will be responsive to ones' political interests (Watts et al., 2011). Participation in the curriculum quantitatively increased students' leadership competence, and they described feeling committed to social change, which suggests high internal efficacy. However, they did not feel that their voice would be heard or respected by adults in positions of power, which is reflected in their stable self-reported policy control and suggests low external efficacy.

To navigate this tension, students' primary approach for channeling their critical motivation was through positioning themselves as teachers. Drawing on what they learned from DYN and their leadership skills, they expressed a commitment to teaching adults about systemic injustices in Nashville. Students may feel limited to teaching those with greater power than they perceive themselves to have about inequitable systems in hopes that they will act to change these systems. This may be in part because DYN is nested in schools and not inherently connected to ongoing community-based social change efforts where students can take on scaffolded roles that help them translate their motivation into action. The opportunity to reflect on injustices in Nashville's built environment without sustained opportunities to act may be hindering students' critical motivation (Christens et al., 2013; Watts & Hipolito-Delgado, 2015).

Taken together, our quantitative and qualitative findings suggest that Sociopolitical Control is a useful proxy for assessing critical motivation in place-based action civics. Qualitative accounts of increased readiness to educate others substantiate quantitative growth in Leadership Competence. In addition, the limited avenues for direct engagement in the civic realm that youth described in the focus groups are aligned with their unchanged expectations for civic participation, measured quantitatively through Policy Control.

Critical Action

Despite findings suggesting that place-based action civics supports critical reflection and some aspects of critical motivation, youth overwhelmingly described feeling stalled in critical action despite their commitment to creating a better city. Youth largely attributed this inability to a lack of power exacerbated by their position within interlocking systems of marginalization.

As a classroom intervention, place-based action civics courses such as DYN face several barriers to supporting critical action and resultant social change (Morgan & Ballard, in press). For example, youth–adult power dynamics are difficult to flatten within the often-rigid hierarchy of schools. This might exacerbate students' feelings that adults will not value them as civic agents. Additionally, while place-based action civics curricula are less prescriptive than traditional forms of civic education, DYN still assumes a sequential developmental process in which students progress from critical reflection through learning about the root causes of injustice in their neighborhood to critical action through engaging in a student-initiated project to subvert inequity. This progression occurs in discreet stages in accordance with a school-based curricular unit plan, rather than reciprocal processes in which students' CC develops through engagement in cycles of reflection and action (Christens et al., 2021; Freire, 1968).

Our qualitative findings suggest students struggled to see themselves as change agents despite being informed civic agents educating others about issues in their city. This discrepancy points to a need for a more expansive understanding of the ways youth engage in critical action. Emerging research on critical and antiracist action has illustrated the importance of everyday acts of resistance in social change efforts (Goessling, 2020; Nah et al., 2021; Wright, 2020). Youth engage in these expressive forms of critical action through arts-based processes that center digital media and seek to foster conversation about local community issues. These forms of everyday resistance mirror expressive media creation in place-based action civics curricula like DYN, including the creation of podcasts, infographics, maps, and other forms of digital media that seek to elicit community conversations about built environment equity in Nashville. Ultimately, students did not perceive these forms of action to be viable strategies for enacting social change, although emerging literature suggests they may be. To address this discrepancy, place-based action civics might benefit from adopting a broader definition of what constitutes critical action. Doing so may support youth in recognizing the potential of expressive forms of civic action to support social change.

Limitations and Future Directions

This study illuminates potential directions for future research and practice in CC development through place-based action civics education. However, findings should be interpreted with consideration of the limitations of this data. Survey data in this study were only collected at two timepoints. To support place-based action civics curriculum improvement, future research could follow youth longitudinally to understand developmental trajectories of key indicators, such as CC. Similarly, focus group data were only collected after students had completed DYN, and therefore is limited to students' retrospective accounts of their own group and development. We also did not directly ask students to reflect on their CC development over time, and instead gleaned insights presented here from our interpretation of students' reflections. Findings are also constrained by the age of the youth in the sample. Few studies of CC focus on early adolescents, who are "just beginning to grapple with a more complex systemic understanding of societal inequality and to identify their place in the system and ideological stance" (Godfrey et al., 2019, p. 584). As middle school students like those in our sample gain autonomy, they may have more opportunities to participate in critical action. This could be understood longitudinally in light of their early experiences with DYN.

IMPLICATIONS FOR PRACTICE

This study points to place-based action civics as a generative starting point for youth CC development. Stakeholders and practitioners who seek to foster CC development in ways that embrace youth's lived experience and local ways of knowing should consider extending classroom interventions into empowering community settings to support critical action and fostering long-term youth–adult partnerships to enhance critical motivation.

Empowering Community Settings

As the primary context for youth learning, developing students' CC within schools is crucial for ensuring equitable access. However, social change does not follow the academic calendar, and out-of-school positive youth development settings may offer less prescriptive, bounded, and adult-centric opportunities for meaningful engagement. To address these limitations to school-based social change, some place-based action civics programs are transitioning to long-term models of engagement that extend the in-school action civics curriculum and further students' opportunities for CC development (Morgan & Ballard, in press). Findings from this study illustrate that the boundedness of the academic calendar may be an especially limiting factor in students' ability to engage in critical action. Students struggled to identify avenues to meaningfully participate in social change efforts happening in their communities within the confines of the classroom. To build on CC development catalyzed through classroom experiences, links between place-based action civics in schools and positive youth development settings in communities are needed to support youth in becoming active agents in local social change efforts.

Youth–Adult Partnerships

Youth–adult partnerships offer avenues for youth to foster collaborative relationships with adults as they work to address locally relevant issues. Place-based action civics educators and practitioners should seek to support youth–adult partnerships within schools that disrupt adultism and help youth imagine pathways to social change beyond convincing adults to act on their behalf. These relationships can be initiated through classroom interventions and carry on as youth transition from classroom to community settings. In their qualitative accounts, youth illustrated skepticism about their ability to influence adults, who they perceived to be the only group with power and influence to enact change in Nashville. Simultaneously, they described a deep motivation to educate adults about issues in their community. The tensions students articulate between their perceptions of adults and their desire to support adult learning may be a generative space for fostering youth–adult partnerships. These partnerships could allow youth to share their immense knowledge of local issues with receptive, caring adults and dismantle students' deeply held assumptions that adults will not be responsive to their attempts to enact power in the civic sphere.

APPENDIX A
Design Your Neighborhood Focus Group Protocol

PART 1: GENERAL PROGRAM QUESTIONS

In this focus group, I'll ask you about your thoughts on what you've been learning in class during the Design Your Neighborhood unit. If you change your mind about participating at any time during our talk, that's fine. I like to audio-record focus groups so that I don't miss any of your feedback. I'm the only person who will hear your recording, and I'll delete the recording as soon as possible. Is it okay for me to audio-record this focus group? Any questions before we begin?

Questions	Probes
1. What is your idea of a perfect neighborhood?	Walk me through what a day in a perfect neighborhood would be like.
2. What does it mean for a community to be healthy?	Make sure they discuss physical health of community members?
3. What do you know about Nashville beyond your neighborhood?	What do you know about the different people and cultures that make up Davidson County beyond your neighborhood? What do you know about issues in other parts of the city?

PART 2: CONTENT-FOCUSED QUESTIONS

Now we are going to talk about some of the things you learned about during the unit. These questions are mostly about how you would improve your community. There are no right or wrong answers; I just want to hear your opinion. Any questions?

Questions	Probes
4. How does the neighborhood that a person lives in impact their quality of life?	Probe with domains of wellness.
5. You are writing a letter to your council member about [class issue] in your neighborhood. What would you recommend, and why?	
6. A group of city planners have asked for your input [class issue]. What would you say, and why?	
7. Do the [class issue] options in your neighborhood fit the needs of the people? Why or why not?	
8. What are some ways that you can be involved in making decisions in your community?	In your school community?
9. What do you know about the decision makers and leaders in your community?	How are they chosen? How do community members communicate with them to make change?
10. If you were the president of your neighborhood association, what would be your top three priorities, and why?	
11. What are some ways that designers can get input from the public before they start designing?	What is the process of getting public input?
12. What are some careers that help build healthy communities?	Ask student to summarize job description.
13. What did you like about the Design Your Neighborhood Project? What did you dislike?	

REFERENCES

Andolina, M. W., & Conklin, H. G. (2020). Fostering democratic and social-emotional learning in action civics programming: Factors that shape students' learning from Project Soapbox. *American Educational Research Journal, 57*(3), 1203–1240. https://doi.org/10.3102/0002831219869599.

Ballard, P. J., Cohen, A. K., & Littenberg-Tobias, J. (2016). Action civics for promoting civic development: Main effects of program participation and differences by project characteristics. *American Journal of Community Psychology, 58*(3–4), 377–390. https://doi.org/10.1002/ajcp.12103.

Braun, V., & Clarke, V. (2012). Thematic analysis. In H. Cooper, P. M. Camic, D. L. Long, et al. (Eds.), *APA handbook of research methods in psychology, Vol. 2* (pp. 57–71). American Psychological Association. https://doi.org/10.1037/13620-004.

Butler, T. (2017). "We need a song": Sustaining critical youth organizing literacies through world humanities. *Equity & Excellence in Education, 50*(1), 84–95. https://doi.org/10.1080/10665684.2016.1250233.

Camino, L. A. (2000). Youth-adult partnerships: Entering new territory in community work and research. *Applied Developmental Science, 4*(S1), 11–20. https://doi.org/10.1207/S1532480XADS04Suppl_2.

Cammarota, J. (2007). A social justice approach to achievement: Guiding Latina/o students toward educational attainment with a challenging, socially relevant curriculum. *Equity & Excellence in Education, 40*(1), 87–96. https://doi.org/10.1080/10665680601015153.

Cammarota, J. (2016). The praxis of ethnic studies: Transforming second sight into critical consciousness. *Race Ethnicity and Education, 19*(2), 233–251. https://doi.org/10.1080/13613324.2015.1041486.

Christens, B. D., Byrd, K., Peterson, N. A., & Lardier, D. T. (2018). Critical hopefulness among urban high school students. *Journal of Youth and Adolescence, 47*(8), 1649–1662. https://doi.org/10.1007/s10964-018-0889-3.

Christens, B. D., Collura, J. J., & Tahir, F. (2013). Critical hopefulness: A person-centered analysis of the intersection of cognitive and emotional empowerment. *American Journal of Community Psychology, 52*(1–2), 170–184. https://doi.org/10.1007/s10464-013-9586-2.

Christens, B. D., & Dolan, T. (2011). Interweaving youth development, community development, and social change through youth organizing. *Youth & Society, 43*(2), 528–548. https://doi.org/10.1177/0044118X10383647.

Christens, B. D., & Kirshner, B. (2011). Taking stock of youth organizing: An interdisciplinary perspective. *New Directions for Child and Adolescent Development, 134*, 27–41. https://doi.org/10.1002/cd.309.

Christens, B. D., Morgan, K. Y., Ruiz, E. Aguayo, A., & Dolan, T. (2021). Critical reflection and cognitive empowerment among youth involved in community organizing. *Journal of Adolescent Research, 38*(1). https://doi.org/10.1177/07435584211062112.

Christens, B. D., Peterson, N. A., Reid, R., & Garcia-Reid, P. (2015). Adolescents' perceived control in the sociopolitical domain: A latent class analysis. *Youth & Society, 47*(4), 443–461. https://doi.org/10.1177/0044118X12467656.

Christens, B. D., Winn, L. T., & Duke, A. M. (2016). Empowerment and critical consciousness: A conceptual cross-fertilization. *Adolescent Research Review, 1* (1), 15–27. https://doi.org/10.1007/s40894-015-0019-3.

Conner, J., & Slattery, A. (2014). New media and the power of youth organizing: Minding the gaps. *Equity & Excellence in Education, 47*(1), 14–30. https://doi.org /10.1080/10665684.2014.866868.

del Carmen Salazar, M. (2013). A humanizing pedagogy: Reinventing the principles and practice of education as a journey toward liberation. *Review of Research in Education, 37*(1), 121–148. http://dx.doi.org/10.3102/0091732X12464032.

Delia, J., & Krasny, M. E. (2018). Cultivating positive youth development, critical consciousness, and authentic care in urban environmental education. *Frontiers in Psychology, 8*, 1–14. https://doi.org/10.3389/fpsyg.2017.02340.

Demarest, A. B. (2014). *Place-based curriculum design: Exceeding standards through local investigations.* Routledge.

Diemer, M. A., & Blunstein, D. L. (2006). Critical consciousness and career development among urban youth. *Journal of Vocational Behavior, 68*, 220–232. http://dx .doi.org/10.1016/j.jvb.2005.07.001.

Diemer, M. A., McWhirter, E. H., Ozer, E. J., & Rapa, L. J. (2015). Advances in the conceptualization and measurement of critical consciousness. *The Urban Review, 47*(5), 809–823.

Diemer, M. A., Rapa, L. J., Park, C. J., & Perry, J. C. (2017). Development and validation of the critical consciousness scale. *Youth & Society, 49*, 461–483. http://dx.doi.org/10.1177/0044118X14538289.

Diemer, M. A., Rapa, L. J., Voight, A. M., & McWhirter, E. H. (2016). Critical consciousness: A developmental approach to addressing marginalization and oppression. *Child Development Perspectives, 10*(4), 216–221. https://doi.org/10.1111 /cdep.12193.

Edirmanasinghe, N. (2020). Using youth participatory action research to promote self-efficacy in math and science. *Professional School Counseling, 24*(1), 1–12. https://doi.org/10.1177/2156759X20970500.

Erickson, A. T. (2016). *Making the unequal metropolis: School desegregation and its limits.* University of Chicago Press.

Freire, P. (1973). *Education for critical consciousness.* Continuum.

Freire, P. (1968/2000). *Pedagogy of the oppressed.* Continuum.

García, E., & Weiss, E. (2019). The teacher shortage is real, large and growing, and worse than we thought. First report in "The Perfect Storm in the Teacher Labor Market" Series. *Economic Policy Institute.*

Gaston, G., & Kreyling, K. (2015). *Shaping the healthy community: The Nashville plan.* Vanderbilt University Press.

Gingold, J. (2013). *Building an evidence-based practice of action civics: The current state of assessments and recommendations for the future.* The Center for Information and Research on Civic Learning and Engagement.

Ginwright, S. A. (2010). *Black youth rising: Activism and radical healing in urban America.* Teachers College Press.

Godfrey, E. B., & Burson, E. (2018). Interrogating the intersections: How intersectional perspectives can inform developmental scholarship on critical consciousness.

New Directions for Child and Adolescent Development, 161, 17–38. https://doi.org/10.1002/cad.20246

Godfrey, E. B., Burson, E. L., Yanisch, T. M., Hughes, D., & Way, N. (2019). A bitter pill to swallow? Patterns of critical consciousness and socioemotional and academic well-being in early adolescence. *Developmental Psychology, 55*(3), 525. https://doi.org/10.1037/dev0000558.

Godfrey, E. B., & Grayman, J. K. (2014). Teaching citizens: The role of open classroom climate in fostering critical consciousness among youth. *Journal of Youth and Adolescence, 43*(11), 1801–1817. https://doi.org/10.1007/s10964-013-0084-5.

Goessling, K. P. (2020). Youth participatory action research, trauma, and the arts: designing youthspaces for equity and healing. *International Journal of Qualitative Studies in Education, 33*(1), 12–31. https://doi.org/10.1016/j.appdev.2020.101164.

Gonzales, J. (2015, November 13). Nashville schools have more than 120 languages. *The Tennessean.* https://eu.tennessean.com/picture-gallery/news/2015/11/13/nashville-schools-have-more-than-120-languages/75664508/.

Heberle, A. E., Rapa, L. J., & Farago, F. (2020). Critical consciousness in children and adolescents: A systematic review, critical assessment, and recommendations for future research. *Psychological Bulletin, 146*(6), 525–551. https://doi.org/10.1037/bul0000230.

Hess, D. E. (2009). *Controversy in the classroom: The democratic power of discussion.* Routledge.

Jemal, A. (2017). Critical consciousness: A critique and critical analysis of the literature. *The Urban Review, 49*(4), 602–626. https://doi.org/10.1007/s11256-017-0411-3.

Kember, D., Ha, T. S., Lam, B. H. et al. (1997). The diverse role of the critical friend in supporting educational action research projects. *Educational Action Research, 5* (3), 463–481.

Kennedy, H., Matyasic, S., Schofield Clark, L. et al. (2020). Early adolescent critical consciousness development in the age of Trump. *Journal of Adolescent Research, 35*(3), 279–308. https://doi.org/10.1177/0743558419852055.

Kornbluh, M., Ozer, E., Allen, C., & Kirshner, B. (2015). Youth participatory action research as an approach to sociopolitical development and the new academic standards: Considerations for educators. *The Urban Review, 47*(5), 868–892. http://dx.doi.org/10.1007/s11256-015-0337-6.

Kreyling, K. (Ed.) (2005). *The plan of Nashville: Avenues to a great city.* Vanderbilt University Press.

Lardier, D. T., Reid, R. J., & Garcia-Reid, P. (2018). Validation of an abbreviated Sociopolitical Control Scale for Youth among a sample of underresourced urban youth of color. *Journal of Community Psychology, 46*(8), 996–1009. https://doi.org/10.1002/jcop.22087.

LeCompte, K., & Blevins, B. (2015). Building civic bridges: Community-centered action civics. *The Social Studies, 106*(5), 209–217.

Levinson, M. (2012). *No citizen left behind.* Harvard University Press.

Lincoln, Y. S., & Guba, E. G. (1985). *Naturalistic inquiry.* Sage.

McInerney, P., Smyth, J., & Down, B. (2011). 'Coming to a place near you?' The politics and possibilities of a critical pedagogy of place-based education. *Asia-Pacific*

Journal of Teacher Education, 39(1), 3–16. https://doi.org/10.1080/1359866X
.2010.540894.

Mediratta, K., Shah, S., & McAlister, S. (2008). *Organized communities, stronger schools.* Annenberg Institute for School Reform at Brown University.

Means, D., Blackmon, S., Drake, E. et al. (2021). We have something to say: Youth participatory action research as a promising practice to address problems of practice in rural schools. *The Rural Educator, 41*(3). https://doi.org/10.35608 /ruraled.v41i3.1074.

Montero, M. (2009). Methods for liberation: Critical consciousness in action. In M. Montero & C. Sonn (Eds.), *Psychology of liberation* (pp. 73–91). Springer.

Morales, D., Bettencourt, G., Green, K., & George Mwangi, C. (2017). "I want to know about everything that's happening in the world": Enhancing critical awareness through a youth participatory action research project with Latinx Youths. *The Educational Forum, 81*(4), 404–417. https://doi.org/10.1080 /00131725.2017.1350236.

Morgan, K. Y., & Ballard, P. J. (in press). Action civics. In B. D. Christens (Ed.), *The Cambridge handbook of community empowerment.* Cambridge University Press.

Morgan, K. Y., Christens, B. D., & Gibson, M. (2022). Design your Neighborhood: The evolution of a city-wide urban design learning initiative in Nashville, Tennessee. In R. Stoecker & A. Falcón (Eds.), *Handbook on Participatory Action Research and Community Development* (pp. 281–300). Edward Elgar.

Nah, S., Lee, S., & Liu, W. (2021). Community storytelling network, expressive digital media use, and civic engagement. *Communication Research, 49*(3), 327–352. https://doi.org/10.1177/00936502211019677.

Nation, M., Christens, B. D., Bess, K. D. et al. (2020). Addressing the problems of urban education: An ecological systems perspective. *Journal of Urban Affairs, 42* (5), 715–730. https://doi.org/10.1080/07352166.2019.1705847.

National Action Civics Collaborative. (2014). *Action civics framework.* https://action civicscollaborative.org/why-action-civics/framework/.

Patton, M. Q. (1990). *Qualitative evaluation and research methods.* Sage.

Peterson, N. A., Peterson, C. H., Agre, L., Christens, B. D., & Morton, C. M. (2011). Measuring youth empowerment: Validation of a sociopolitical control scale for youth in an urban community context. *Journal of Community Psychology, 39*(5), 592–605. https://doi.org/10.1002/jcop.20456.

Plazas, D. (2018). The costs of growth and change in Nashville. *The Tennessean.* www .tennessean.com/story/opinion/columnists/david-plazas/2017/01/29/costs-growth-and-change-nashville/97064252/.

QSR International Pty Ltd. (2018) NVivo qualitative data analysis. Version 12 [software]. https://support.qsrinternational.com/nvivo/s/.

Rapa, L. J., Bolding, C. W., & Jamil, F. M. (2020). Development and initial validation of the short critical consciousness scale (CCS-S). *Journal of Applied Developmental Psychology, 70*, 101–164. https://doi.org/10.1016/j.appdev.2020.101164.

Rapa, L. J., & Geldhof, G. J. (2020). Critical consciousness: New directions for understanding its development during adolescence. *Journal of Applied Developmental Psychology, 70*, 101187. https://doi.org/10.1016/j.appdev.2020.101187.

Roy, A., Raver, C., Masucci, M., & DeJoseph, M. (2019). "If they focus on giving us a chance in life we can actually do something in this world": Poverty, inequality, and youths' critical consciousness. *Developmental Psychology*, *55*(3), 550–561. https://doi.org/10.1037/dev0000586.

Smith, D. A., & Gruenewald, G. A. (Eds.) (2007). *Place-based education in the global age: Local diversity*. Routledge.

Smith, G. A. (2007). Place-based education: Breaking through the constraining regularities of public school. *Environmental Education Research*, *13*, 189–207. https://doi.org/10.1080/13504620701285180.

Stewart, D. W., & Shamdasani, P. N. (2014). *Focus groups: Theory and practice* (Vol. 20). Sage Publications.

Tyler, C. P., Olsen, S. G., Geldhof, G. J., & Bowers, E. P. (2020). Critical consciousness in late adolescence: Understanding if, how, and why youth act. *Journal of Applied Developmental Psychology*, *70*, 101165. https://doi.org/10.1016/j.appdev.2020.101165.

US Census Bureau (2020). Quick facts – Davidson County, TN. www.census.gov/quickfacts/davidsoncountytennessee.

Voight, A., & Velez, V. (2018). Youth participatory action research in the high school curriculum: Education outcomes for student participants in a district-wide initiative. *Journal of Research on Educational Effectiveness*, *11*(3), 433–451. https://doi.org/10.1080/19345747.2018.1431345.

Walsh, D. (2018). Youth participatory action research as culturally sustaining pedagogy. *Theory into Practice*, *57*(2), 127–136. https://doi.org/10.1080/00405841.2018.1433939.

Watts, R. J., Diemer, M. A., & Voight, A. M. (2011). Critical consciousness: Current status and future directions. *New Directions for Child and Adolescent Development*, *2011*(134), 43–57. https://doi.org/10.1002/cd.310.

Watts, R. J., & Flanagan, C. (2007). Pushing the envelope on youth civic engagement: A developmental and liberation psychology perspective. *Journal of Community Psychology*, *35*(6), 779–792. https://doi.org/10.1002/jcop.20178.

Watts, R. J., & Hipolito-Delgado, C. P. (2015). Thinking ourselves to liberation? Advancing sociopolitical action in critical consciousness. *The Urban Review*, *47* (5), 847–867. https://doi.org/10.1007/s11256-015-0341-x.

Westheimer, J., & Kahne, J. (2004). What kind of citizen? The politics of educating for democracy. *American Educational Research Journal*, *41*(2), 237–269.

Wright, D. E. (2020). Imagining a more just world: Critical arts pedagogy and youth participatory action research. *International Journal of Qualitative Studies in Education*, *33*(1), 32–49. https://doi.org/10.1080/09518398.2019.1678784.

PART II

EXTRACURRICULAR CONTEXTS

4

Re-envisioning the "Big Three" of Out-of-School Time Programs to Promote Critical Consciousness Development in Youth of Color

EDMOND P. BOWERS, CANDICE W. BOLDING, LIDIA Y. MONJARAS-GAYTAN, AND BERNADETTE SÁNCHEZ

The many structural and social inequities that youth of color face often constrain development and hamper thriving (García Coll et al., 1996). Youth of color in the United States live within marginalizing systems (Causadias & Umaña-Taylor, 2018; Godfrey & Burson, 2018) and as a result experience inequitable access to quality housing, education, and economic opportunities (Duncan & Murnane, 2011; Ushomirsky & Williams, 2015). Rates of poverty disproportionately include youth of color (Cabrera, 2013; US Department of Commerce, 2017), and these youth are also more likely to live in racially segregated neighborhoods and attend high-poverty schools with limited resources (Ushomirsky & Williams, 2015).

Solely focusing on the restricted resources or adverse contexts in which youth of color are embedded and the associated negative outcomes, however, provides a greatly limited view of these youth (Spencer & Spencer, 2014; Travis & Leech, 2014). Strengths-based, positive youth development (PYD) approaches posit that the development of all young people, no matter the circumstances, can be optimized by aligning their individual strengths (e.g., intentional self-regulation) and the resources in their sociocultural contexts (e.g., families, schools, out-of-school time programs; Lerner et al., 2015; Osher et al., 2020). The potential for PYD approaches to promote well-being even in the face of institutional and systemic racism has been recognized. For example, Barbarin and colleagues (2020) explain that "PYD suggests that children growing up in harsh environments acquire psychosocial competence that enables them to avoid the adverse effects of racism, racial denigration, resource insufficiency, and inequality" (p. 201).

A socially just approach to PYD requires attending to the culturally and contextually relevant strengths of youth of color (Bowers et al., 2020). There are many examples in which youth have utilized their strengths and resources to transform communities and nations. Among the relevant strengths that have received both scholarly and practical attention is critical consciousness (CC): the capacity to reflect on, navigate, and challenge the injustices of marginalizing and oppressive systems in society in promoting healthy and positive development in youth of color (Diemer et al., 2015; Freire, 1973).

A growing body of evidence points to the influence of sociocultural contexts on the development of CC, but there is a need for greater understanding of how key youth contexts, such as out-of-school-time (OST) settings, can promote critical consciousness in youth of color (Heberle et al., 2020). Therefore, in this chapter we review the existing evidence linking OST program participation to CC development in youth of color. We review findings derived from various contexts – including after-school programs, formal mentoring programs, and informal mentoring relationships – with several aims in mind. First, we synthesize the evidence on characteristics and practices of OST programs that promote CC by leveraging a well-recognized frame for quality OST programming: the "Big Three." However, we draw on both social justice youth development (SJYD; e.g., Ginwright & James, 2002) principles and current literature on OST to recast the "Big Three" from the standpoint of youth of color as participants in OST programs and CC as an outcome. That is, how might each of the "Big Three" be reimagined to promote CC among youth of color? Finally, based on the literature review, we provide implications for scholars, practitioners, and policy makers who aim to foster CC in youth of color through OST programs.

CRITICAL CONSCIOUSNESS AND POSITIVE YOUTH DEVELOPMENT

Recent theoretical work has adapted existing PYD models to enhance their applicability to the diverse experiences and contexts in which youth of color develop (e.g., Case, 2017; Clonan-Roy et al., 2016; Gonzalez et al., 2020; Travis & Leech, 2014). Each of these adapted models points to the importance of CC in promoting thriving among youth who live in marginalizing systems. For example, Travis and Leech (2014) proposed an empowerment-based identity- and relationships-driven model to identify culturally specific strengths of African American youth, emphasizing the processes by which youth develop the "consciousness, skills, and power" (Travis & Leech, 2014, p. 102) to engage the social context critically to promote their own healthy development and the health of their community.

Emerging from the work of esteemed Brazilian educator and activist Paulo Freire (1921–1997), critical consciousness, or *conscientização*, comprises three mutually influential components: (a) critical reflection, which is the critical analysis of inequitable social conditions; (b) critical motivation (also referred to as political efficacy), which is the desire and agency one has to correct societal inequities; and (c) critical action, which is the production of or participation in activities focused on promoting societal change (Diemer et al., 2016; Freire, 1970, 1973; Watts et al., 2011). A body of evidence indicates that CC serves as a developmental asset (Diemer et al., 2016) to mitigate the impact of inequities and promote markers of thriving, such as better health, academic, career, and civic outcomes, in marginalized youth (Heberle et al., 2020). These dimensions of CC have been linked to domains of positive development in youth of color (see Heberle et al., 2020 for a full review) including self-esteem (Zimmerman et al., 1999) and sense of self (Luginbuhl et al., 2016); academic engagement and success (Cabrera et al., 2014; Ramos-Zayas, 2003); resilience (Ginwright, 2010) and PYD (Bowers et al., 2020; Clonan-Roy et al., 2016); civic engagement and contribution (Bowers et al., 2021; Diemer & Li, 2011; Diemer & Rapa, 2016; Ginwright & Cammarota, 2007); and career development (Diemer & Blustein, 2006) and occupational attainment (Diemer, 2009).

A comprehensive understanding of how youth settings promote CC is needed (Heberle et al., 2020). OST programs can be an exemplary setting for facilitating CC. Youth spend about 80% of their waking time outside formal class settings (Lopez & Caspe, 2014) as youth have about 5.5 hours per day of free time (US Bureau of Labor Statistics, 2018). OST programs are particularly important developmental contexts for marginalized youth to engage in during this free time (Deutsch, 2008; Williams & Deutsch, 2016). In addition, unlike schools, OST programs are not limited by an emphasis on state-based benchmarks and guidelines and standardized testing, and they often offer opportunities unavailable in schools because OST programs have the flexibility to implement practices that touch on the social issues that affect youth more readily (Murray & Milner, 2015).

OUT-OF-SCHOOL TIME SETTINGS AS A CONTEXT FOR CRITICAL CONSCIOUSNESS DEVELOPMENT

An extensive body of evidence points to the influence of structured OST experiences on PYD outcomes (Mahoney et al., 2009; Vandell et al., 2015), but the links between these OST experiences and CC are just emerging (Heberle et al., 2020). In a systematic review of sixty-seven studies of CC in children and adolescents, Heberle and colleagues (2020) identified ten studies aimed at promoting CC development through OST programs. Participating in these programs generally benefited CC; however, a comprehensive understanding of how OST youth settings – and the relationships youth form within these settings – influence CC is warranted.

We organize this work by utilizing the key features identified in the "Big Three" model of effective OST programs (Lerner, 2004; Lerner et al., 2011). Lerner (2004) indicated that participation in OST programs was optimally linked to PYD outcomes when they are marked by three key features: positive and sustained relationships between youth and adults, activities to develop and practice life skills, and meaningful opportunities for youth contribution and leadership. In this chapter, we will present research reflecting the importance of each of these three components for strengthening the three dimensions of CC in young people: reflection, motivation, and action. However, Simpkins and colleagues (2017) pointed out the limitations of universal approaches, such as the "Big Three," when organizing OST programs to promote PYD within culturally diverse youth. The operationalization of the "Big Three" and associated practices may differ due to a host of individual and contextual factors, including the context of racial, social, and historical inequities experienced by youth of color as well the targeted outcomes of the program, such as CC. Thus, we reframe each aspect of the model from a SJYD lens (Ginwright & Cammarota, 2002, 2007; Ginwright & James, 2002) in order to identify ways that each aspect might promote CC in youth of color participating in OST programs. Leveraging a social justice–oriented "Big Three" framework provides a way to organize a multidisciplinary and diverse literature to identify promising practices and implications for research, practice, and policy aimed at promoting CC development in youth of color through OST programming.

RECASTING THE "BIG THREE" OF EFFECTIVE OST PROGRAMS FROM A SOCIAL JUSTICE YOUTH DEVELOPMENT PERSPECTIVE

Proponents of an SJYD approach to OST programs believe that marginalized youth, such as youth of color, may feel a lack of agency and limited ability to effect change in their lives due to marginalizing systems (Ginwright & Cammarota, 2002, 2007; Ginwright & James, 2002). An SJYD approach aims to promote young people's self-efficacy to be change agents within their communities through their reflection on the injustices suffered by themselves, their families, and their communities and by understanding more fully how power operates within society. As youth become more adept at critical reflection, they develop skills essential to taking critical action, such as youth organizing and activism. The SJYD approach is structured by five principles – analyzing power in social relationships, making identity central, promoting systemic social change, encouraging collective action, and embracing youth culture – and associated practices and outcomes (Ginwright & James, 2002). With the support of peers and adult allies within OST programs, the principles are intended to organize and mobilize youth to contribute to their communities through social justice activities. Reflecting on these principles is useful to re-envision how the "Big Three" might be conceptualized or operationalized within OST programs to promote critical reflection, critical motivation, and critical action among youth of color.

The first component of the "Big Three" framework is sustained caring relationships with adults. Relationships with committed, caring adults are consistently identified as the key asset for promoting PYD and mitigating youth risk behaviors across youth settings (Bowers et al., 2015). Youth–adult relationships have been shown to be effective in improving outcomes in youth across behavioral, social, emotional, and academic domains (Bowers et al., 2015; DuBois et al., 2011; Van Dam et al., 2018). In youth development programs, these adults are often instructors, advocates, and role models, and they can serve as contextual resources that can contribute to thriving. Therefore, it is important for scholars and practitioners to understand how these relationships promote CC and associative outcomes in youth of color. Indeed, evidence indicates that care and concern from adults is not enough to promote CC (Bowers et al., 2020; Krauss et al., 2014). However, in OST programs framed by SJYD principles, positive and caring youth–adult relationships take the form of youth–adult partnerships (Zeldin et al., 2005), in which youth are empowered to work collaboratively with adults, and youth and adults learn from each other and jointly contribute to program decisions. These positive youth–adult relationships provide a foundation for the other components of the "Big Three."

Quality OST programs also engage young people in activities to develop and build key life skills, such as goal setting, responsible decision-making, communication, cooperation, critical thinking, and leadership (Bean et al., 2017; Durlak et al., 2010; Mueller et al., 2011). Durlak and colleagues (2010) indicated that activities are more likely to promote important life skills when they are intentionally planned and well integrated into the overall program, and when youth are actively engaged in the activities, practicing the skills in real-world and hands-on experiences (e.g., role plays or service-learning opportunities). When identifying key life skills for youth of color, it is essential to consider their cultural and contextual relevance for targeted youth (Simpkins et al., 2017). By identifying key skills from the cultural perspectives of youth of color, activities become more meaningful and engaging. For example, during adolescence, skills related to exploring and forming one's identity are a key developmental task for youth (Erikson, 1968; Xing et al., 2015). For youth of color, however, issues of race, ethnicity, and culture may become particularly significant (Umaña-Taylor et al., 2014). In addition, life skills such as goal setting, communication, cooperation, and critical thinking are essential to the promotion of CC (Ginwright & James, 2002); however, for programs aiming to promote CC among youth, these skill-building activities must be in service of changing inequities and injustices in the local community (Ginwright & Cammarotta, 2002, 2007). In SJYD-framed programs, youth are provided with the life skills to analyze, reflect on, and challenge the systems of power that surround them (Ginwright & Cammarota, 2002), and, in turn, they take leadership roles to contribute to their communities and society.

In the final component of the "Big Three," program staff provide opportunities for youth to take on leadership roles in valued community activities, which may strengthen youth's purpose and guide young people to set meaningful goals that actively contribute to their families, schools, communities, or society. These leadership opportunities are a key means by which youth can apply the life skills they develop within OST programs under the guidance of caring adults to serve their families, schools, or communities as empowered and agentic individuals. OST programs can help youth to foster leadership and take responsibility when they allow youth to make meaningful decisions about the issues important to them (Agans et al., 2015). From an SJYD perspective, the key predictors of contribution in youth of color and the ways these youth might contribute to their contexts must also be understood in light of historical and social inequities (Hershberg et al., 2015). The opportunities for youth of color to contribute in meaningful ways must be relevant and reflective of their own lives. To promote CC in youth of color, opportunities for contribution must involve youth taking the lead in designing and implementing action plans to address local inequities and injustices through organizing and activism (Ginwright & James, 2002).

Although the "Big Three" features of effective OST programs are differentiated in this review, the dimensions mutually influence each other to promote CC and related outcomes; these three components need to be present and integrated for PYD outcomes, such as CC, to be promoted (Lerner, 2004). In many instances, programs that are highlighted as exemplars of one of the features (e.g., skill-building activities) also include the other two features (positive youth–adult relationships and opportunities to lead and contribute). In addition, we do not present the research reviewed in this chapter as an exhaustive or all-inclusive list, as our goal was not to provide an extensive review but to highlight evidence in support of recasting the "Big Three" in light of SJYD principles and possible implications based on this evidence for practice, policy, and research. We have familiarity with the work of scholars from the fields of mentoring and OST programs who take a social justice or culturally-responsive lens to their work to promote positive outcomes in youth of color. Therefore, our initial search was based on these readings. In addition to reviewing the work of these scholars, we also conducted forward and backward searches to find additional articles. For the backward search, we carefully examined the reference sections of these initial articles, including recent review articles on CC (e.g., Heberle et al., 2020). For the forward search, we reviewed studies that cited the papers in our initial body of evidence using the "cited by" feature in Google Scholar and PsychInfo. Studies included in our review met the following criteria: (a) they examined organized OST programs, mentoring programs, or informal mentoring relationships; (b) they included an outcome that explored at least one aspect of critical reflection, motivation, or action; (c) they included a description of one dimension of the "Big Three"; (d) participating youth were primarily youth of color; and (e) participants were youth primarily between the ages of ten and twenty-one.

YOUTH–ADULT RELATIONSHIPS AND CRITICAL CONSCIOUSNESS DEVELOPMENT

A key feature of OST settings that promote CC is positive and sustained adult–youth relationships. Youth may see nonparental adults as individuals who they can turn to and talk to about societal power structures and the ways in which they can challenge systemic injustices. Youth become critically conscious through their experiences and interactions with others over time. Researchers have found that youth's socialization within their family, school, community, and neighborhood influences their CC (Heberle et al., 2020; Tyler et al., 2020; Watts et al., 2003). At the same time, youth may reach out to others as they become aware of injustices and/or engage in critical action in order to process their own views and experiences (Harro, 2000). Thus, as young people develop their CC, they may interact with and have conversations with nonparental adults who help them make sense of sociopolitical issues around them (Albright et al., 2017). Researchers have recently begun to examine the role of nonparental adults in youth's CC.

The mere presence of a supportive nonparental adult or the quality of the youth–adult relationship is insufficient in influencing youth's CC (Bowers et al., 2020; Krauss et al., 2014). For example, it was found that the presence of supportive adult relationships within 299 Malaysian adolescents' communities was not significantly associated with participants' sociopolitical efficacy (Krauss et al., 2014). Another investigation found that the association between overall quality of natural mentoring relationships with after-school program staff and youth critical reflection was not significant in a sample of high-achieving, low-income, high school students (mostly Black or Latinx; Bowers et al., 2020). It may be that nonparental adults need to play a more targeted role in order to promote youth's CC.

Research reveals that adult support for challenging racism, the presence of adults who are engaged in social action, discussions with natural mentors about social justice issues, and youth voice in OST programming are significantly related to CC (e.g., Diemer et al., 2006; Godfrey & Grayman, 2014; Monjaras-Gaytan et al., 2021). An ethnographic study showed that intergenerational networks of caring adults and youth who were working toward social change in their community played a positive role in the critical civic praxis (i.e., elevated CC, capacities for activism, and civic engagement) of urban African American and Latinx adolescents (Ginwright & Cammarota, 2007). Similarly, a study examined how adolescent–staff relationships at a community-based organization helped youth develop as social activists (O'Donoghue & Strobel, 2007). Results showed that not only were the relationships supportive and egalitarian (nonhierarchical, democratic, collaborative, youth-centered, and reciprocal), but they were also embedded in public action. That is, adults and adolescents engaged in meaningful public action projects together, which played an important role in youth's development as activists (O'Donoghue & Strobel, 2007). Another investigation of 145 racially/ ethnically diverse college students found that having more frequent conversations on social justice issues with natural mentors (i.e., nonparental adults who provided support and guidance to participants) was significantly associated with participants' critical reflection and action (Monjaras-Gaytan et al., 2021). Finally, more youth voice in program decision-making was significantly associated with more sociopolitical control in Malaysian adolescents in OST programs, above and beyond demographic characteristics, school connectedness, religious community involvement, family cohesion, and parental monitoring (Krauss et al., 2014). These findings are consistent with a youth–adult partnership approach in OST (Zeldin et al., 2005) and critical mentoring approaches (Liang et al., 2013; Weiston-Serdan, 2017).

Researchers suggest that CC develops when youth are provided support and guidance to reflect upon and challenge social injustices (Diemer & Li, 2011). A mixed-methods study provided an in-depth view of how natural mentors support college students' CC (Monjaras-Gaytan et al., 2021). Qualitative interviews of students revealed that mentors support their CC via dialoguing and reflecting about social issues, current events, and shared interests and experiences; sharing information and resources about social issues and opportunities for involvement; engaging in nonjudgmental, comfortable conversations about social issues; and serving as role models by engaging in social action and community work (Monjaras-Gaytan et al., 2021). Thus, in addition to critical dialogue with mentors to help young people make sense of sociopolitical issues (Albright et al., 2017), there are other ways that adults help to promote youth CC that should be utilized in OST settings.

Although most research has been focused on the role of nonparental adults in youth's sociopolitical development, it might be that youth seek out the support of nonparental adults as they engage in critical reflection and action because of the cyclical process of CC (Watts et al., 2011). In other words, CC may lead to interactions with and the support of nonparental adults in order to help young people make sense of the world. For example, it was found that engaging in more critical action and higher critical reflection about societal inequalities was significantly related to more frequent conversations about social justice issues with natural mentors approximately one year later among college students (Monjaras-Gaytan et al., 2021). Further, higher critical action and critical reflection about perceived inequalities were indirectly and longitudinally associated with critical reflection about perceived inequalities and critical action via higher sociopolitical efficacy and more frequent mentoring conversations (Monjaras-Gaytan et al., 2021). These findings have implications for OST settings. OST programs that offer opportunities for engaging in social action projects and reflection about societal inequality may lead youth to turn to adults in these settings for their support. Further, partnering with youth offers opportunities for dialogue and reflection while youth and adults engage in social action projects together. These opportunities allow for youth to immediately turn to an adult while they reflect about what they are learning. Because of the cyclical process of CC, youth may engage in further critical action after they dialogue and reflect with nonparental adults (Watts et al., 2011).

SKILL-BUILDING ACTIVITIES AND CRITICAL CONSCIOUSNESS DEVELOPMENT

The second of the "Big Three" features of effective OST programs is youth engagement in life-skill-building activities. In many youth programs, these life skills have included goal setting, communication, critical thinking, decision-making, self-responsibility, and teamwork, among others (e.g., Duerden et al., 2012). Ginwright and James (2002) indicated that OST programs framed by SJYD principles promoted a similar set of life skills essential to the development of CC among "fully developed" youth (Ginwright & James, 2002, p. 40). These skills include sociopolitical development and analysis, critical thinking, self-understanding and awareness of one's identity, empathy, decision-making, goal setting, teamwork, and social and community problem-solving. To promote CC development among youth of color, however, practitioners must be intentional in designing and implementing skill-building activities in two primary ways. First, the skills must be embedded within culturally and contextually relevant practices (Ngo, 2017; Simpkins et al., 2017). Providing skill-building activities in a culturally relevant and meaningful way empowers young people, as these efforts communicate to youth that that their culture, background, and experiences are important (Simpkins et al., 2017). In addition, although several life skills (e.g., critical thinking, teamwork) are essential to dimensions of CC development (e.g., critical reflection, critical action), if skill-building activities are to promote CC, they must focus on changing inequities and injustices in the local community (as identified by youth). From an SJYD perspective, youth of color need to participate in skill-building activities that help them to analyze how power operates within the systems that marginalize them, and take action to contribute to changing those systems (Ginwright & Cammarota, 2002).

Therefore, central to programs that aim to support CC development is the promotion of sociopolitical development in youth (Brown et al., 2018; Delia & Krasny, 2018; Fegley et al., 2006; Foster-Fishman et al., 2010; Groves Price & Mencke, 2013; Harper et al., 2017; Ngo, 2017; Nguyen & Quinn, 2018). Sociopolitical development is grounded on several life skills, such as critical and creative thinking as well as decision-making (Watts et al., 1999). Programs successful in promoting sociopolitical development in youth of color have been designed to be culturally responsive. For example, Brown and colleagues

(2018) conducted a multicase study to explore how sociopolitical development was supported in three culture-specific programs designed to promote CC among Black youth. Findings indicated that each site was guided by a philosophy rooted in Pan-Africanism or Afrocentrism, guiding the development and implementation of program curriculum. All sites incorporated historical and contemporary texts, films, and artifacts on the Black experience. One program used the history of the African Diaspora to build critical thinking and reflection skills as youth came to know the history of people of African descent, to understand their connection to that history, and to spur their agency to impact the future (Brown et al., 2018).

In addition, programs that promote sociopolitical development engage youth in addressing inequities and injustices in the local community. Foster-Fishman and colleagues (2010) conducted a youth participatory action research (YPAR) photovoice project with twenty middle school students who were primarily youth of color to learn about how youth can become involved in their community and how the community can support them. Through this project, youth developed critical reflection around why community issues exist and the impact of these issues on community members. As a YPAR project, youth were engaged in the continuum of research activities, including a photovoice project, qualitative data analysis, feedback and community dialogue, and the creation of a guidebook. The active engagement of youth in the data analysis was key to fostering CC by promoting skills fundamental to CC, including problem identification, critical thinking, and decision making (Foster-Fishman et al., 2010).

Programs aiming to promote CC also implement activities that strengthen self-awareness in youth of color to foster positive identities (Brown et al., 2018; Delia & Krasny, 2018; Groves Price & Mencke, 2013; Ngo, 2017; Nguyen & Quinn, 2018). This emphasis on identity development is seen as the starting point for youth taking critical action (Ginwright & James, 2002) as they become aware of how social forces influence how they are perceived. The importance of self-understanding and awareness in relation to the larger social context is particularly important for marginalized youth, who are often expected to navigate multiple worlds in which power and privilege operate. Culturally responsive OST programs allow youth of color to feel comfortable exploring and expressing their hybrid identities (Ngo, 2017; Simpkins et al., 2017) as they develop pride in their identity and become motivated to take action. For example, Ngo (2017) conducted an ethnographic study of an OST theater program within a Hmong arts organization to explore how the program promoted CC among a group of nine second-generation Hmong immigrant youth aged 16–19 from low-income backgrounds. The program engaged youth in a mix of arts-based activities throughout the year, but the primary activity was a theater project on their Hmong heritage and identity. Ngo (2017) found that the program provided opportunities for youth to "name their world" (p. 41) by critically examining their experiences of marginalization and engaging in creative processes that strengthened their agency to enact change. They had to be able to "manage a split world between their Hmong families and schools" (p. 46). In exploring how they managed and navigated these worlds and the associated intra- and intergroup struggles, participants were able to construct a positive bicultural Hmong Americans identity. These youth were able to "rescript" their own life stories to grow in agency to name, critique, and challenge injustices.

Through the process of bicultural identity development, youth of color become more adept at critically reflecting on the inequities of the social context, and they grow in pride and motivation to address those inequities. The skills that come with having a positive bicultural identity were evident in many of the OST programs reviewed. Groves Price, Mencke, and partners from a Native American tribe (2013) created a week-long residential summer camp experience for youth between the ages of 13–17 living on or near a local reservation. The camp was framed around a problem-posing approach to learning to support youth identity development and CC. Problem-posing approaches provide for shared power, allow for diverse perspectives, and recognize that both youth and adults are capable of generating critical questions and solutions as they coconstruct knowledge. Freire (1970) indicated that through "problem-posing education, people develop their power to perceive critically *the way they exist* in the world *with which* and *in which* they find themselves" (p. 64). As part of a YPAR project at the camp, youth engaged in a digital storytelling workshop, in which many youth stories reflected the negotiation of their identity in "multiple worlds" (Groves Price & Menke, 2013, p. 88). These Native American youth negotiated the worlds of reservation and nonreservation, home and school, Native American and white. The youth became critically reflective of the differences across contexts but also recognized the strengths that came with these experiences. The authors also suggested that the act of "doing" throughout the project was fundamental. Youth were more likely to see themselves as active agents of change because of their active project engagement.

Within these programs, youth of color also build awareness and knowing of others who also struggle against oppressive forces. In connecting with others, youth are encouraged to build solidarity among marginalized groups and take collective action (Burson & Godfrey, 2020). Therefore, OST programs based on Freirean principles have been linked to increased perspective-taking abilities and empathy, helping youth to understand the perspectives of other community members and to put themselves in their shoes (Foster-Fishman et al., 2010; Harper et al., 2017; Quinn & Nguyen, 2017). These programs often explicitly teach about culture, race, and ethnicity, which in turn can strengthen perspective taking, empathy, and teamwork (Ginwright, 2005). For example, in response to tensions between Vietnamese and African American youth in a Philadelphia community, a six-week summer youth organizing program, Homeward Bound, engaged twenty-two Vietnamese immigrant and US-born youth aged 14–21 years (Nguyen & Quinn, 2017). The program aimed to shape the critical racial consciousness of its participants through engagement in critical analyses of both historical and contemporary Vietnamese and African American experiences and relations in the United States, conducting oral histories and interviews and designing and implementing an assessment of community issues. Participants were also provided professional training and opportunities in community-based research, advocacy, and leadership. Results indicated that youth reported having more empathy for others and a better ability to see things from others' perspectives as they linked the interwoven histories of Vietnamese and African Americans to the contemporary struggles of marginalized communities within the United States. Participating youth became more critically reflective of the root causes of interracial tensions in their community, challenged their own preconceptions of apprehension and prejudice toward African American youth, and came to see a shared history of struggles. From this new understanding, youth expressed greater solidarity with their peers and identified possible solutions to address these tensions.

The success of OST programs aimed at promoting CC also hinges on how well activities strengthen youth communication and teamwork skills with both adults and peers. Within these OST programs, CC development entails discussion, critiquing, and questioning of issues within the community, which result in joint action to address those concerns. Therefore, activities often include small group discussions and dialogues, debates, interviews with community members, and presentations to various stakeholders in the community. Photovoice is a participatory methodology used to explore social issues from the perspectives of marginalized youth and adults (Wang, 1999). Youth programs have used photovoice to empower youth to examine and enact change in their communities (Tang Yan et al., 2019). Foster-Fishman et al. (2010) facilitated group dialogue to promote critical reflection among youth by eliciting the photographer's meaning about the photo and analyzing the community context in a deeper way. Photovoice projects also typically conclude with an exhibit for youth to share their knowledge and strengthen CC among the community, requiring public speaking skills. The ability to communicate with program peers as well as the larger community was evident in several programs (Groves Price & Mencke, 2013; Harper et al., 2017). For example, Harper and colleagues (2017) engaged with eight youth in a YPAR photovoice project related to farm-to-school food initiatives in Holyoke, MA. The project was implemented in several phases that all required strong communication and collaboration among several parties, including youth leaders, program staff, university partners, community representatives, and diverse frontline staff on the farm-to-school pipeline. First, youth and adult facilitators worked together to define the problem and design the project.

Second, the team worked on the photovoice research process, including reviewing and discussing the photos that were taken and linking the photos to larger social issues and systems in the community. Third, youth leveraged the photovoice project to gain a voice in their school's food policy discussion and present their project to the local school committee. Finally, the youth engaged in data analysis and dialogic editing of a research article on the process.

Of fundamental importance in all of these skill-building activities is to ensure that youth are engaged in all elements of the activities and stages of the program. The significance of active engagement in promoting these skills is reflected by Groves Price and Mencke's (2013) position that "It was clear to us that the 'doing' – the generating of research questions, conducting interviews, listening to others deeply, and representing their work in a multimedia format – significantly impacted how students thought of themselves as active change agents" (p. 98).

OPPORTUNITIES FOR YOUTH CONTRIBUTION AND LEADERSHIP

Providing opportunities for youth to contribute to their communities and hold leadership roles is the final "Big Three" component of OST programs that fosters CC. However, for youth of color it is often a typical experience that they feel limited in their opportunities to change their contexts and communities (Christens & Dolan, 2011). These experiences are often grounded in systemic inequities, as youth of color are often constrained in their capacity to contribute due to exclusion from or lack of access to contexts where acts of contribution occur, such as schools, shelters, and youth programs (Ginwright & Cammarota, 2002; Hope & Jagers, 2014). The types of contribution that may be valued and relevant for youth of color to grow in CC may also differ from traditional notions of contribution, such as charity work, volunteering, and tutoring (Hershberg et al., 2015). Actions such as organizing, protesting, and other forms of youth activism to effect social change may better measure contribution and promote CC among youth of color (Ginwright & Cammarota, 2002; Hershberg et al., 2015; Hope & Jagers, 2014).

The influential factors leading to contribution and leadership of activities may also differ for youth of color (Hershberg et al., 2015). For example, to best promote contribution among youth, practitioners must be well prepared to navigate and coordinate family, school, and community settings (Eccles & Gootman, 2002; Finn-Stevenson, 2014; Simpkins et al., 2017). Practitioners working with marginalized young people such as youth of color must be particularly skilled at leveraging the resources provided by these settings because the lives of marginalized youth in their home, school, and community contexts often have different – and, at times, conflicting – norms and expectations (Larson & Walker, 2010; Ngo, 2017; Simpkins et al., 2017). Navigating the tensions between the lives of youth within the program setting and in settings external to the program has been identified as a key dilemma of practice for program staff (Larson & Walker, 2010).

CC develops as a response to one's experiences and individual contexts; thus, when youth engage in activities centered on contributing to their communities (e.g., community-based activities) they are more likely to gain critical awareness (i.e., critical reflection) of the sociopolitical issues impacting their communities. Further, as youth engage in civic and community-based activities that seek to disrupt social inequality, they are likely to participate in forms of critical action to help change marginalizing or oppressive forces affecting their communities (Christens & Dolan, 2011; Heberle et al., 2020; Gonzalez et al., 2020; Roy et al., 2019). It is important to note that while critical action (i.e., intentionally participating in activities that promote more socially just systems) can be classified as youth contribution, not all forms of contribution can be defined as critical action (e.g., neighborhood clean-up, volunteering at a soup kitchen). Critical action must involve youth's motivation to dismantle current oppressive systems and create a more equitable place for others. For example, six of sixty-seven studies reviewed by Heberle and colleagues found that participation in community-based activities is associated with youth's CC development and included subtle distinctions of what constituted critical action (for full review, see Heberle et al., 2020). Therefore, for programs to promote CC in youth of color, opportunities for contribution must involve youth taking the lead in organizing and activism to address local inequities and injustices (Ginwright & James, 2002).

SJYD-framed OST programs that include community engagement activities serve as important spaces for CC development among youth of color. For example, Winans-Solis (2014) investigated how service-learning within the community promoted CC among urban, African American high school boys. In this qualitative case study, two major themes emerged that indicate the support of CC development through service-learning. First, youth participants indicated that they gained an awareness of the oppressive structures faced by their communities (i.e., critical reflection; Winans-Solis, 2014). Second, the boys also became active participants in community action through service-learning activities (Winans-Solis, 2014). The youth's work in the community necessitated that they be involved in every step of the process. This allowed for participants to critically engage with the history of social problems and seek solutions to correct the issues faced by their communities.

Christens and Dolan (2011) similarly found that when youth participating in an OST program were provided space to critically reflect on violence within their community, they took action to correct these issues in the form of youth organizing. In this qualitative study, twenty youth (90% Latinx) identifying as youth leaders in their program took an active organizing role that led to positive community-level outcomes and sociopolitical development among program youth (Christens & Dolan, 2011). Additionally, when the youth organized initiatives, this leadership led to a shift in the relationships between the participating youth and their peers and local adults, both within the program and those considered "adults in power" (e.g., local officials, law enforcement officers, school administration; Christens & Dolan, 2011, p. 536). Through engaging in youth organizing, youth expressed confidence in their capacity to take on leadership roles to enact change within their communities and became critically aware of power dynamics and their impact on the community.

Youth are expected to contribute through sharing what they know, teaching others, and taking responsibility for the actions and goals of these social justice–oriented OST programs; that is, they are expected to take on clear leadership roles within the program. For example, Delia and Krasny (2018) used narrative inquiry to explore the experiences of youth of color in Brooklyn, New York, who served as interns in an urban agriculture, environmental education program. Youth were between 15 and 18 years of age, and their ethnicities and race varied, including African American and youth of Dominican, Guyanese, Jamaican, Nigerian, and Puerto Rican descent. Returning interns reported that the program was somewhere to practice leadership as they learned about responsibility and accountability and grew into leadership roles. These youth were expected to provide leadership in several ways, including leading crews of first-year interns, managing farm and farmers' market responsibilities, speaking at conferences, and teaching workshops. Youth saw themselves as the experts working within the program, and they reported they developed a new sense of self (Delia & Krasny, 2018).

Across the programs reviewed, youth were expected to grow into their own leadership roles as they were given the responsibility of guiding conversations and covering program content (Brown et al., 2018). Indeed, recognition as experts was also an important outcome in Foster-Fishman and colleagues' (2010) YPAR project, as youth participants were invited to serve on an expert panel at several community events to discuss youth engagement and local youth concerns. Promoting youth empowerment and agency through the development of leadership skills is an essential goal of SJYD programs.

Youth contribution and leadership opportunities that support CC development can extend beyond direct physical engagement in their communities. OST contexts also provide youth the space to contribute through various forms of multimedia, such as digital online content creation and community theater. Youth are not only consumers of multimedia but active in its creation and dissemination (Montgomery et al., 2004; Montgomery & Gottlieb-Robles, 2013; Wernick et al., 2014). Research on CC in youth experiencing marginalization has revealed that programs that incorporate multimedia expand the ways in which OST contexts can support CC development among youth (Gonzalez et al., 2020). Additionally, OST programs that utilize multimedia can provide greater access to civic education for youth as well as provide a greater space for youth's voices to be heard (Gonzalez et al., 2020). An example of such programming is #PassTheMicYouth, a podcast and blog led by students promoting youth activism and resources for developing CC among youth (Gonzalez et al., 2020). This program is housed in an ongoing extension program at a southeastern public university and highlights youth who contribute through activism and critical action in their schools and communities (Gonzalez et al., 2020). The podcasts are hosted by students, and each episode focuses on a social issue, includes an interview with a youth activist, and features youth-submitted contributions (e.g., a poem or original music; Gonzalez et al., 2020). These podcasts and blogs can be used to create critical dialogue and reflection for youth and serve as examples of ways in which youth can be agents of change in their communities.

Wernick and colleagues (2014) examined how participating in community theater projects promoted CC among youth experiencing marginalization. They found that participating in theater games and scripted performances promoted youth's CC development by providing space for them to contextualize and understand their own and their peers' experiences of marginalization (Wernick et al., 2014). Further, through collective storytelling in the form of performance, program youth were able to speak as experts on social issues to an audience of adults and peers with the intent of enacting change (Wernick et al., 2014). In other words, performance provided a safe and structured space for youth to express and bring awareness to their lived experiences of marginalization and see themselves as able to effect change. Whether engaging proximal or distal systems, the potential of youth to create social change is recognized within social justice–oriented OST programs as youth are supported and empowered to take on leadership roles when engaging in critical action.

IMPLICATIONS AND FUTURE DIRECTIONS

Based on our literature review, we provide several recommendations for practitioners, policy makers, and researchers who want to leverage the resources of OST programs to optimize young people's CC development.

Practice

In incorporating the "Big Three" into an OST program, we recommend that providers in OST programs ground their program in SJYD principles (e.g., Ginwright & James, 2002). Recasting the "Big Three" based on the contemporary evidence base of OST programming and SJYD principles has implications for OST program design and implementation as well as practitioner capacity building. Most of the studies reviewed in this chapter focus on youth programs with specific social justice–oriented aims to promote CC. However, the principles and practices of SJYD can be integrated into youth programs with a diversity of goals not explicitly aimed at promoting activism.

OST Program Design and Implementation A fundamental prerequisite in implementing quality OST programming is that practitioners must ensure that they provide a physically and psychologically safe space for youth to engage in activities that promote critical reflection, motivation, and action. Safety is a fundamental element of all effective OST programs (e.g., Eccles & Gootman, 2002); however, the assurance of a safe space is particularly relevant for CC development, given the difficult topics and issues that may arise in activities. Further, youth of color often report being misunderstood, marginalized, and discriminated against when participating in OST activities (e.g., Lin et al., 2016). Safe spaces are places in which youth feel comfortable, cared for, and supported; youth autonomy and voice are respected; and youth know they will not be judged for their thoughts, feelings, or actions.

Consistent with SJYD principles, these spaces must be coconstructed by adults and youth in which mutually agreed upon boundaries are clear. Under the guidance of staff, youth can take the lead in creating community agreements (e.g., "use 'I' statements"; "show respect to others and yourself"), which can be posted on a wall in the space where programming takes place. These agreements can be revisited daily to remind youth of the expectations. Another way to create a safe space for youth of color in an OST program aimed at promoting CC is for staff and youth to engage in daily relationship-building activities, such as journaling, group circles, and sticky note activities. These daily activities help to promote rapport, trust, and discussions among youth and staff. Creating a safe space will pave the way for staff and youth to engage in discussions about social justice and controversial topics. Researchers have found that when incidents of discrimination, offensive remarks, and uncomfortable intercultural contacts arise within OST programs, best practices support directly engaging with the incidents and facilitating reflective dialogue with youth (Gutiérrez et al., 2017) to ensure a safe and inclusive environment. Reflective dialogue includes asking open-ended questions, asking guiding questions about youth's emotions, engaging in two-way conversations with youth (rather than a lecture by an adult), listening to youth's viewpoints and emotions, and guiding exploration activities to help youth learn more about the social justice issue or topic at hand in the program.

Once youth feel safe and have developed trust and a rapport with adult leaders, program leaders can implement problem-posing methodologies to promote critical reflection and motivation among youth (Brion-Meisels et al., 2020; Freire, 2000; Groves Price & Mencke, 2013). In implementing a problem-posing framework, practitioners must resist the temptation to provide their answers to a problem raised by youth or to expect that there are specific "right answers" that youth should produce. This "adultism" (Brion-Meisels et al., 2020) arises when adults view themselves as having more expertise, wisdom, and power to make decisions than youth; in short, adults know better than youth. Practitioners should work to cocreate spaces with youth where youth can make mistakes and share prior mistakes without fear of judgment or critique as they work through difficult topics. Practitioners must give up the belief that they must be the experts and authorities within these spaces. They must be willing to give up control and be prepared for the missteps that may arise if youth agency and autonomy is honored when implementing social change activities. We suggest practitioners build in explicit structured times in which youth and adults provide feedback on the process (Brion-Meisels et al., 2020).

Several other promising practices linked to promoting critical reflection and motivation can be readily integrated into OST programs. Texts, films, and artifacts of marginalized peoples were frequently included in programs to engage youth in critically reflective practices (Brown et al., 2018; Nguyen & Quinn, 2018). These resources promoted discussion and reflection on the roots of injustices experienced by youth living in marginalizing systems. They also supported youth coming to a deeper understanding of their own selves in connection with the greater world. Another practice helpful in guiding discussions on the complex systemic causes of inequities was the "big circle–small circle" activity (Nguyen & Quinn, 2018). In this activity, adult facilitators draw out two concentric circles. Within the inner circle, youth provide possible reasons for why an issue existed, such as gun violence. Within the outer circle, youth are guided in considering the root causes for that issue. The reasons youth identify for the systemic ways of interpreting these complex social issues can then be leveraged for generating solutions to these issues.

In applying SJYD principles within their programs, we recommend practitioners find creative ways that youth can express their experiences and further reflect on systems of oppression. For example, the creation of media such as podcasts, digital stories, and photograph exhibitions was central to the CC development of youth in several studies (e.g., Gonzalez et al., 2020; Groves Price & Mencke, 2013). Photovoice was a method used by several programs (e.g., Foster-Fishman et al., 2010; Harper et al., 2017) that allowed youth to engage in critical reflection and build awareness of inequities and insight into how power operates. Identifying the unique spaces and modalities that youth may find more accessible embraces youth culture and encourages authentic and deeper youth engagement (Ginwright & James, 2002) in the skill-building activities essential to CC development.

We also recommend that OST programs incorporate YPAR projects into their programs. Several studies included YPAR projects to promote life skills linked to CC. YPAR projects can provide a structure to implement the "Big Three" as youth learn by doing under the guidance of engaged and supportive adults. The output of YPAR projects also allows for opportunities for contribution and leadership as youth engage with their communities and grow as change agents. Practitioners interested in YPAR are encouraged to connect with local researchers who may help design, implement, and evaluate a YPAR project successfully.

Practitioner Capacity Building Practitioners who aim to incorporate SJYD principles and practices into their programs must be well equipped; just connecting youth to caring adults is not enough (Kraus et al., 2014). Therefore, we recommend comprehensive training be established in these programs (Sánchez et al., 2020). Practitioners must be prepared to foster open dialogue about difficult issues, such as systemic injustice, race, gender, and class (among other topics), while also nurturing positive relationships with youth and between youth. Mentors and program staff must also be trained in how to build youth–adult partnerships with program participants so that they can jointly contribute to the decision-making processes of the program and collaborate on enacting change in the community. Youth coconstructing activities with adults is essential to both promoting CC and providing activities with cultural humility. Mentors and program staff not only need to be trained explicitly on social justice issues and how to facilitate discussion and partnerships with youth but must also learn the self-reflective skills to consider their own role in reinforcing marginalizing systems. Therefore, we recommend that cultural humility be a central component of practitioner training (Anderson & Sánchez, 2021). These types of trainings can promote program staff's own CC, which is necessary in OST programs aimed at facilitating the CC of youth.

Program administration and staff should also work to cocreate safe and supportive spaces in which staff members are able to discuss how issues of race, culture, and socioeconomic status have shaped their own identities and interactions with others. These spaces could become a regular part of staff meetings and trainings to ensure that staff relationships are strong and that staff are prepared to address these issues with youth. Lack of thoughtful preparation and anticipation for engaging in these discussions with youth can lead to exacerbating existing inequities and intergroup differences (Ettekal et al., 2020). Programs might conduct an "ideological interview"

(Brown et al., 2018) in which potential staff members are given scenarios based on events such as a youth revealing a pregnancy, school disengagement, or wanting to go to college.

Philanthropy and Policy

Foundations and funding agencies focused on OST programs tend to use frames such as the "Big Three" in evaluating logic models of programs seeking funding and identifying the targeted outcomes of these programs. Through a re-envisioned "Big Three," priorities and expectations of these philanthropic organizations are shifted as CC and the practices that support its development are prioritized. In prioritizing CC, funders and philanthropic organizations must also reimagine their approach to funding programs (Fabiano, 2019). Often, the funders' focus on youth is from a deficit model rather than a PYD approach (Baldridge, 2019; Fabiano, 2019). Grant cycles are also often poorly aligned with the complexity and time that is required to conduct meaningful work with youth of color. Funders can recast the language within funding requests to reflect a PYD perspective of youth and identify outcomes aligned with that perspective. Funders could also become creative with leveraging their own resources to support the efforts of OST programs. As indicated, many OST activities that promote CC involve the creation of media, which requires investments in new technology software, hardware, and human capital. Calls for funding can cover the costs of obtaining this capital, but funders might also work with grantees to provide professional development opportunities in this area, develop learning communities among their grant-ees, or allow their own IT staff members to support these efforts within grantee OST programs (Fabiano, 2020).

Policy makers should take a systems approach when looking to promote CC and well-being in youth, recognizing the role that race, class, and culture have on youth development (Baldridge, 2019). OST programs serve as a key setting in which systemic influences come together, but they are also a setting that provides youth of color opportunities to consider their multiple iden-tities – racial, cultural, academic, and political – in ways that settings such as schools are not well structured to do (Baldridge, 2019). Promoting CC and thriving in youth of color in any meaningful way requires a great deal of time and effort through the development of deep relationships among youth and adults. This approach would counter growing calls for programs to achieve efficiency at scale through as few touchpoints as possible. Therefore, consist-ent support from municipalities to protect these safe spaces for youth of color are needed in the face of political, economic, and social forces. Funders should also provide for enough time, space, and flexibility so programs are able to build the deep relationships required for this type of work. In addition, long-term funding should be provided to support cross-contextual collaborations between the multiple settings in which youth are embedded. Youth frequently aim to enact change in other institutions within their communities. Through organized systemwide approaches to youth development such as comprehensive community initiatives (Kubisch et al., 2010), youth efforts are more likely to be successful.

To ensure full youth engagement in these settings, policy makers must ensure that the young have opportunities to fully participate in the institutions in their communities. Factors that promote engagement in the institutions of civic society (e.g., schools and local government) may differ for youth living within marginalizing systems (Godfrey & Burson, 2018; Hershberg et al., 2015). Youth of color are subject to marginalizing forces that result in their exclusion, lack of access, or incomplete participation in contexts where they can contribute, such as schools, youth programs, and governmental bodies (Ginwright & Cammarota, 2002). Therefore, youth rights to fully engage in these contexts should be protected through appropriate legislative measures.

Research

The research reviewed in this chapter provides a great deal of evidence for the benefits of social justice–oriented youth programs for CC development in youth of color; however, there are several limitations to this body of work. Much of the work on OST programming and CC development in youth of color has involved small-scale, short-term studies that are qualitative in nature. Although it is mostly qualitative in nature, these studies provide a thick description of what happens inside OST programs aimed at promoting CC. The preponderance of evidence coming from qualitative studies, however, limits the ability to identify direct or causal links between program characteristics and CC dimensions.

Incorporating additional methodological designs will allow for a deeper understanding of the processes linking OST participation to CC development. Although the qualitative studies included in this review pointed to promising practices linked to CC, they typically focused on skills or proxies related to critical consciousness, sometimes inferring that the dimensions of CC developed; however, there were no clear constructs of critical reflection, motivation, or action included in the studies. Future research could examine what aspects of the "Big Three" are related to the three dimensions of CC. Certain program features may be more likely to influence a certain dimension of CC. For example, exploration of historical and contemporary experiences of marginalized peoples may spur critical reflection, youth–adult partnerships might empower youth to be motivated to enact change, and skill-building opportunities may be needed for youth to take action. Research is needed to identify the role of specific activities, projects, and types of support provided by adults to nurture CC. Therefore, we recommend that scholars interested in exploring how the resources provided by OST programs promote CC in youth of color conduct longitudinal mixed-method studies that unpack these processes and explicitly address CC dimensions.

The existing small-scale studies also limit consideration of intersectionality and the ability to explore the experiences of CC development within subgroups of youth based on gender, race, ethnicity, or social class, obscuring the diversity of experiences of these youth. Future research must consider the multiple overlapping systems of injustice and oppression that lead to differentiated experiences of individuals (Crenshaw, 1990; Godfrey & Burson, 2018). Studies involving larger samples of youth and programs will also allow for the consideration of the other settings with which youth engage when building CC. The OST setting might be a place where CC development begins, but it may further develop through engaging in settings beyond the program.

CONCLUSION

As this chapter has detailed, OST programs can serve as key sociocultural contexts to promote CC in youth of color. Exploring the links between OST participation and CC also points to promising possibilities for PYD research, practice, and policy. Youth of color in the United States often live within marginalizing systems that present numerous barriers to their success. Culturally relevant strengths such as CC are essential capacities for healthy and positive development within these systems. Most work aimed at promoting CC within OST programs has been derived from practice and scholarship networks that have yet to permeate the broad fields of mentoring, OST programs, and youth development. Therefore, leveraging a well-known frame for youth programs such as the "Big Three" to help identify how these three components are also linked to CC development may ease the process of adoption and integration of these practices into diverse OST programs. Drawing on both SJYD (Ginwright & James, 2002) principles and current literature on OST programming with youth of color, we aimed to recast the "Big Three" in order to inform OST practitioners, scholars, and policy makers who aim to nurture CC for youth of color. OST programs can best support CC in young people by ensuring these reimagined "Big Three" of effective youth programs are present. OST programs that connect youth with caring and consistent adult partners who support young people as they build life skills that empower them to lead change efforts within the community not only benefit youth, these "efforts of young people often lead to better public policy, stronger organizations, more relevant services, and healthier communities" (Ginwright & James, 2002, p. 33).

REFERENCES

Agans, J. P., Champine, R. B., Johnson, S. K., Erickson, K., & Yalin, C. (2015). Promoting healthy lifestyles through youth activity participation: Lessons from research. In E. P. Bowers, G. Geldhof, S. Johnson, et al. (Eds.), *Promoting positive youth development: Lessons from the 4-H Study* (pp. 137–158). Springer International Publishing.

Albright, J. N., Hurd, N. M., & Hussain, S. B. (2017). Applying a social justice lens to youth mentoring: A review of the literature and recommendations for practice. *American Journal of Community Psychology*, 59(3–4), 363–381.

Anderson, A. J., & Sánchez, B. (2021). A pilot evaluation of a social justice and race equity training for volunteer mentors. *American Journal of Community Psychology*, 69(1–2), 3–17. https://doi.org/10.1002/ajcp.12541.

Baldridge, B. J. (2019). *Reclaiming community: Race and the uncertain future of youth work*. Stanford University Press.

Barbarin, O. A., Tolan, P. H., Gaylord-Harden, N., & Murry, V. (2020). Promoting social justice for African-American boys and young men through research and intervention: A challenge for developmental science. *Applied Developmental Science*, 24, 196–207.

Bean, C., Harlow, M., & Forneris, T. (2017). Examining the importance of supporting youth's basic needs in one youth leadership programme: A case study exploring programme quality. *International Journal of Adolescence and Youth*, 22(2), 195–209.

Bowers, E. P., Bolding, C. J., Rapa, L. J., & Sandoval, A. M. (2021). Predicting contribution in high achieving Black and Latinx youth: The role of critical reflection, hope, and mentoring. *Frontiers in Psychology*, 12, 681574. https://doi:10.3389/fpsyg.2021.681574.

Bowers, E. P., Johnson, S. K., Warren, D. J., Tirrell, J. M., & Lerner, J. V. (2015). Youth–adult relationships and positive youth development. In E. P. Bowers, G. Geldhof, S. Johnson, et al. (Eds.), *Promoting positive youth development: Lessons from the 4-H Study* (pp. 97–120). Springer International Publishing.

Bowers, E. P., Winburn, E. N., Sandoval, A. M., & Clanton, T. (2020). Culturally relevant strengths and positive development in high achieving youth of color. *Journal of Applied Developmental Psychology*, 70, 101182. https://doi.org/10.1016/j.appdev.2020.101182.

Brion-Meisels, G., Fei, J. T., & Vasudevan, D. S. (Eds.). (2020). *At our best: Building youth–adult partnerships in out-of-school time settings*. Information Age Publishing.

Brown, A. A., Outley, C. W., & Pinckney, H. P. (2018). Examining the use of leisure for the sociopolitical development of Black youth in out-of-school time programs. *Leisure Sciences*, 40, 686–696. http://dx.doi.org/10.1080/01490400.2018.1534625.

Burson, E., & Godfrey, E. B. (2020). Intraminority solidarity: The role of critical consciousness. *European Journal of Social Psychology*, 50(6), 1362–1377.

Cabrera, N. J. (2013). Positive development of minority children and commentaries. *Social Policy Report*, 27(2), 1–30.

Cabrera, N. L., Milem, J. F., Jaquette, O., & Marx, R. W. (2014). Missing the (student achievement) forest for all the (political) trees: Empiricism and the Mexican

American studies controversy in Tucson. *American Educational Research Journal, 51*(6), 1084–1118.

Case, A. D. (2017). A critical-positive youth development model for intervening with minority youth at risk for delinquency. *American Journal of Orthopsychiatry, 87* (5), 510–519. https://doi.org/10.1037/ort0000273.

Causadias, J. M., & Umaña-Taylor, A. J. (2018). Reframing marginalization and youth development: Introduction to the special issue. *American Psychologist, 73*(6), 707–712. https://doi.org/10.1037/amp0000336.

Christens, B. D., & Dolan, T. (2011). Interweaving youth development, community development, and social change through youth organizing. *Youth & Society, 43*, 528–548. http://dx.doi.org/10.1177/0044118X10383647.

Clonan-Roy, K., Jacobs, C. E., & Nakkula, M. J. (2016). Towards a model of positive youth development specific to girls of color: Perspectives on development, resilience, and empowerment. *Gender Issues, 33*(2), 96–121.

Crenshaw, K. (1990). Mapping the margins: Intersectionality, identity politics, and violence against women of color. *Stanford Law Review, 43*(6), 1241–1299. https://doi.org/10.2307/1229039.

Delia, J., & Krasny, M. E. (2018). Cultivating positive youth development, critical consciousness, and authentic care in urban environmental education. *Frontiers in Psychology, 8*, 2340. http://dx.doi.org/10.3389/fpsyg.2017.02340.

Deutsch, N. L. (2008). *Pride in the projects: Teens building identities in urban contexts.* New York University Press.

Diemer, M. A. (2009). Pathways to occupational attainment among poor youth of color: The role of sociopolitical development. *The Counseling Psychologist, 37*(1), 6–35.

Diemer, M. A., & Blustein, D. L. (2006). Critical consciousness and career development among urban youth. *Journal of Vocational Behavior, 68*(2), 220–232.

Diemer, M. A., Kauffman, A., Koenig, N., Trahan, E., & Hsieh, C. A. (2006). Challenging racism, sexism, and social injustice: Support for urban adolescents' critical consciousness development. *Cultural Diversity and Ethnic Minority Psychology, 12*(3), 444–460.

Diemer, M. A., & Li, C. H. (2011). Critical consciousness development and political participation among marginalized youth. *Child Development, 82*(6), 1815–1833.

Diemer, M. A., McWhirter, E., Ozer, E., & Rapa, L. J. (2015). Advances in the conceptualization and measurement of critical consciousness. *The Urban Review, 47*, 809–823. https://doi.org/10.1007/s11256-015-0336-7.

Diemer, M. A., & Rapa, L. J. (2016). Unraveling the complexity of critical consciousness, political efficacy, and political action among marginalized adolescents. *Child Development, 87*(1), 221–238.

Diemer, M. A., Rapa, L. J., Voight, A. M., & McWhirter, E. H. (2016). Critical consciousness: A developmental approach to addressing marginalization and oppression. *Child Development Perspectives, 10*(4), 216–221. https://doi.org/10.1111/cdep.12193.

DuBois, D. L., Portillo, N., Rhodes, J. E., Silverthorn, N., & Valentine, J. C. (2011). How effective are mentoring programs for youth? A systematic assessment of the evidence. *Psychological Science in the Public Interest, 12*, 57–91.

Duerden, M. D., Witt, P. A., Fernandez, M., Bryant, M. J., & Theriault, D. (2012). Measuring life skills: Standardizing the assessment of youth development indicators. *Journal of Youth Development, 7*(1), 99–117.

Duncan, G. J., & Murnane, R. J. (2011). *Whither opportunity? Rising inequality, schools, and children's life chances*. Russell Sage Foundation.

Durlak, J. A., Weissberg, R. P., & Pachan, M. (2010). A meta-analysis of after-school programs that seek to promote personal and social skills in children and adolescents. *American Journal of Community Psychology, 45*(3), 294–309.

Eccles, J., & Gootman, J. A. (2002). Chapter 4: Features of positive developmental settings. In J. Eccles & J. A. Gootman (Eds.), *Community programs to promote youth development* (pp. 86–115). National Academy Press.

Erikson, E. H. (1968). *Youth in crisis*. W. W. Norton.

Ettekal, A. V., Simpkins, S. D., Menjívar, C., & Delgado, M. Y. (2020). The complexities of culturally responsive organized activities: Latino parents' and adolescents' perspectives. *Journal of Adolescent Research, 35*(3), 395–426.

Fabiano, R. (2019). Rooted in scarcity and deficit. In S. Hill & F. Vance (Eds.), *Changemakers!: Practitioners advance equity and access in out-of-school time programs* (pp. 59–72). Information Age Publishing.

Fabiano, R. (2020, December 18). OST funders, here's how to step up: Invest in organizations' capacity. *Youth Today*. https://youthtoday.org/2020/12/ost-funders-heres-how-to-step-up-invest-in-organizations-capacity/.

Fegley, C. S., Angelique, H., & Cunningham, K. (2006). Fostering critical consciousness in young people: Encouraging the "doves" to find their voices. *Journal of Applied Sociology/Sociological Practice, 23*(8), 7–27. http://dx.doi.org/10.1177/19367244062300102.

Finn-Stevenson, M. (2014). Family, school, and community partnerships: Practical strategies for afterschool programs. *New Directions for Youth Development, 2014* (144), 89–103.

Foster-Fishman, P. G., Law, K. M., Lichty, L. F., & Aoun, C. (2010). Youth ReACT for Social Change: A method for youth participatory action research. *American Journal of Community Psychology, 46*(1–2), 67–83. http://dx.doi.org/10.1007/s10464-010-9316-y.

Freire, P. (1970). *Pedagogy of the oppressed*. Continuum.

Freire, P. (1973). *Education for critical consciousness*. Continuum.

Freire, P. (2000). *Pedagogy of the freedom: Ethics, democracy, and civic courage*. Rowman & Littlefield.

García Coll, C., Crnic, K., Lamberty, G. et al. (1996). An integrative model for the study of developmental competencies in minority children. *Child Development, 67*(5), 1891–1914.

Ginwright, S. (2005). On urban ground: Understanding African-American intergenerational partnerships in urban communities. *American Journal of Community Psychology, 33*, 101–110.

Ginwright, S. A. (2010). Peace out to revolution! Activism among African American youth: An argument for radical healing. *Young, 18*(1), 77–96.

Ginwright, S. & Cammarota, J. (2002). New terrain in youth development: The promise of a social justice approach. *Social Justice, 29*(4), 82–95.

Ginwright, S., & Cammarota, J. (2007). Youth activism in the urban community: Learning critical civic praxis within community organizations. *International Journal of Qualitative Studies in Education, 20*(6), 693–710.

Ginwright, S., & James, T. (2002). From assets to agents of change: Social justice, organizing, and youth development. *New Directions for Youth Development, 96*, 27–46.

Godfrey, E. B., & Burson, E. (2018). Interrogating the intersections: How intersectional perspectives can inform developmental scholarship on critical consciousness. *New Directions for Child and Adolescent Development, 161*, 17–38.

Godfrey, E. B., & Grayman, J. K. (2014). Teaching citizens: The role of open classroom climate in fostering critical consciousness among youth. *Journal of Youth and Adolescence, 43*, 1801–1817. http://dx.doi.org/10.1007/s10964-013-0084-5.

Gonzalez, M., Kokozos, M., Byrd, C. M., & McKee, K. E. (2020). Critical positive youth development: A framework for centering critical consciousness. *Journal of Youth Development, 15*(6), 24–43.

Groves Price, P., & Mencke, P. D. (2013). Critical pedagogy and praxis with Native American youth: Cultivating change through participatory action research. *Educational Foundations, 27*, 85–102.

Gutiérrez, V., Larson, R. W., Raffaelli, M., Fernandez, M., & Guzman, S. (2017). How staff of youth programs respond to culture-related incidents: Nonengagement versus going "full-right-in." *Journal of Adolescent Research, 32*(1), 64–93.

Hall, H. R. (2015). Food for thought: Using critical pedagogy in mentoring African American adolescent males. *The Black Scholar, 45*(3), 39–53.

Harper, K., Sands, C., Horowitz, D. A. et al. (2017). Food justice youth development: Using photovoice to study urban school food systems. *The International Journal of Justice and Sustainability, 22*, 791–808. http://dx.doi.org/10.1080/13549839.2016.1274721.

Harro, B. (2000). The cycle of liberation. In M. Adams (Ed.), *Readings for diversity and social justice: An anthology on racism, antisemitism, sexism, heterosexism, ableism, and classism* (pp. 463–469). Routledge.

Heberle, A. E., Rapa, L. J., & Farago, F. (2020). Critical consciousness in children and adolescents: A systematic review, critical assessment, and recommendations for future research. *Psychological Bulletin, 146*(6), 525–551.

Hershberg, R. M., Johnson, S. K., DeSouza, L. M., Hunter, C. J., & Zaff, J. (2015). Promoting contribution among youth: Implications from positive youth development research for youth development programs. In E. P. Bowers, G. Geldhof, S. Johnson, et al. (Eds.), *Promoting positive youth development: Lessons from the 4-H Study* (pp. 97–120). Springer International Publishing.

Hope, E. C., & Jagers, R. J. (2014). The role of sociopolitical attitudes and civic education in the civic engagement of Black youth. *Journal of Research on Adolescence, 24*(3), 460–470. https://doi.org/10.1111/jora.12117.

Krauss, S. E., Collura, J., Zeldin, S. et al. (2014). Youth–adult partnership: Exploring contributions to empowerment, agency and community connections in Malaysian youth programs. *Journal of Youth and Adolescence, 43*(9), 1550–1562.

Kubisch, A., Auspos, P., Brown, P., & Dewar, T. (2010). *Voices from the field III: Lessons and challenges from two decades of community change efforts.* Aspen Institute.

Larson, R. W., & Walker, K. C. (2010). Dilemmas of practice: Challenges to program quality encountered by youth program leaders. *American Journal of Community Psychology*, 45(3), 338–349.

Lerner, R. M. (2004). *Liberty: Thriving and civic engagement among America's youth.* Sage.

Lerner, R. M., Lerner, J. V., Bowers, E. P., & Geldhof, G. J. (2015). Positive youth development and relational developmental systems. In W. F. Overton & P. C. Molenaar (Eds.), *Theory and method. Volume 1 of the Handbook of child psychology and developmental science* (7th ed., pp. 607–651). Editor-in-chief: R. M. Lerner. Wiley.

Lerner, R. M., Lerner, J. V., Lewin-Bizan, S. et al. (2011). Positive youth development: Processes, programs, and problematics. *Journal of Youth Development*, 6(3), 38–62. https://doi.org/10.5195/jyd.2011.174.

Liang, B., Spencer, R., West, J., & Rappaport, N. (2013). Expanding the reach of youth mentoring: Partnering with youth for personal growth and social change. *Journal of Adolescence*, 36(2), 257–267.

Lin, A. R., Menjívar, C., Ettekal, A. V. et al. (2016). "They will post a law about playing soccer" and other ethnic/racial microaggressions in organized activities experienced by Mexican-origin families. *Journal of Adolescent Research*, 31, 557–581.

Lopez, M. E., & Caspe, M. (2014). Family engagement in anywhere, anytime learning. *Family Involvement Network of Educators (FINE) Newsletter*, 6(3), 1–10.

Luginbuhl, P. J., McWhirter, E. H., & McWhirter, B. T. (2016). Sociopolitical development, autonomous motivation, and education outcomes: Implications for low-income Latina/o adolescents. *Journal of Latina/o Psychology*, 4, 43–59. http://dx.doi.org/10.1037/lat0000041.

Mahoney, J. L., Vandell, D. L., Simkins, S., & Zarrett, N. (2009). Adolescent out-of-school activities. In R. M. Lerner, & L. Steinberg (Eds.), *Handbook of adolescent psychology (3rd ed). Contextual Influences on Adolescent Development*, vol. 2 (pp. 228–269). Wiley.

Monjaras-Gaytan, L. Y., Sánchez, B., Anderson, A. J. et al. (2021). Act, talk, reflect, then act: The role of natural mentors in the critical consciousness of ethnically/racially diverse college students. *American Journal of Community Psychology*, 68(3–4), 292–309.

Montgomery, K., & Gottlieb-Robles, B. (2013). Youth as e-citizens: The internet's contribution to civic engagement. In D. Buckingham & R. Willett (Eds.) *Digital Generations* (pp. 143–160). Routledge.

Montgomery, K., Gottlieb-Robles, B., & Larson, G. O. (2004). Youth as E-Citizens. *Recuperado el*, 11(01), 2008.

Mueller, M. K., Phelps, E., Bowers, E. P. et al. (2011). Youth development program participation and intentional self-regulation skills: Contextual and individual bases of pathways to positive youth development. *Journal of Adolescence*, 34(6), 1115–1125.

Murray, I. E., & Milner, H. R. (2015). Toward a pedagogy of sociopolitical consciousness in outside of school programs. *Urban Review*, 47(5), 893–913. https://doi.org/10.1007/s11256-015-0339-4.

Ngo, B. (2017). Naming their world in a culturally responsive space: Experiences of Hmong adolescents in an after-school theatre program. *Journal of Adolescent Research*, 32, 37–63. http://dx.doi.org/10.1177/0743558416675233.

Nguyen, C., & Quinn, R. (2018). "We share similar struggles": How a Vietnamese immigrant youth organizing program shapes participants' critical consciousness of interracial tension. *Race, Ethnicity and Education, 21,* 626–642. http://dx .doi.org/10.1080/13613324.2016.1248833.

O'Donoghue, J. L., & Strobel, K. R. (2007). Directivity and freedom: Adult support of activism among urban youth. *American Behavioral Scientist, 51*(3), 465–485.

Osher, D., Cantor, P., Berg, J., Steyer, L., & Rose, T. (2020). Drivers of human development: How relationships and context shape learning and development. *Applied Developmental Science, 24*(1), 3–36.

Quinn, R. , & Nguyen, C. (2017). Immigrant youth organizing as civic preparation. *American Educational Research Journal, 54*(5), 972–1005.

Ramos-Zayas, A. Y. (2003). *National performances: The politics of class, race, and space in Puerto Rican Chicago.* University of Chicago Press.

Roy, A. L., Raver, C. C., Masucci, M. D., & DeJoseph, M. (2019). "If they focus on giving us a chance in life we can actually do something in this world": Poverty, inequality, and youths' critical consciousness. *Developmental Psychology, 55,* 550–561. http://dx.doi.org/10.1037/dev0000586.

Sánchez, B., Catlett, B. S., Monjaras-Gaytan, L. Y. et al. (2020). The role of mentoring and service learning in youth's critical consciousness and social change efforts. In O. Prieto-Flores & J. Feu (Eds.), *Mentoring children and young people for social inclusion: Global approaches to empowerment* (pp. 32–46). Taylor & Francis.

Simpkins, S. D., Riggs, N. R., Ngo, B., Vest Ettekal, A., & Okamoto, D. (2017). Designing culturally responsive organized after-school activities. *Journal of Adolescent Research, 32*(1), 11–36.

Spencer, M. B., & Spencer, T. R. (2014). Invited commentary: Exploring the promises, intricacies, and challenges to positive youth development. *Journal of Youth and Adolescence, 43*(6), 1027–1035.

Tang Yan, C., Moore de Peralta, A., Bowers, E. P., & Sprague Martinez, L. (2019). Realmente tenemos la capacidad: Engaging youth to explore health in the Dominican Republic through photovoice. *Journal of Community Engagement and Scholarship, 12*(1), 8.

Travis Jr., R., & Leech, T. G. (2014). Empowerment-based positive youth development: A new understanding of healthy development for African American youth. *Journal of Research on Adolescence, 24*(1), 93–116.

Tyler, C. P., Olsen S., & Geldhof, G. J. Bowers, E. P. (2020). Critical consciousness in late adolescence: Understanding if, how, and why youth act. *Journal of Applied Developmental Psychology, 70,* 101165. https://doi.org/10.1016/j.appdev.2020.101165.

Umaña-Taylor, A. J., Quintana, S. M., Lee, R. M. et al. (2014). Ethnic and racial identity during adolescence and into young adulthood: An integrated conceptualization. *Child Development, 85,* 21–39.

US Bureau of Labor Statistics. (2018). *American time use survey (ATUS).* Inter-university Consortium for Political and Social Research [distributor]. https://doi .org/10.3886/ICPSR36268.v6.

US Department of Commerce, Bureau of the Census. (2017). *Current Population Survey, 2017 Annual Social and Economic Supplement.*

Ushomirsky, N., & Williams, D. (2015). *Funding gaps 2015: Too many states still spend less on educating students who need the most.* Education Trust. https://edtrust.org /wp-content/uploads/2014/09/FundingGaps2015_TheEducationTrust1.pdf.

Van Dam, L., Smit, D., Wildschut, B. et al. (2018). Does natural mentoring matter? A multilevel meta-analysis on the association between natural mentoring and youth outcomes. *American Journal of Community Psychology, 62*(1–2), 203–220.

Vandell, D. L., Larson, R. W., Mahoney, J. L., & Watts, T. W. (2015). Children's organized activities. In R. M. Lerner (Ed. in Chief), M. H. Bornstein, & T. Leventhal (Vol. Eds.), *Handbook of child psychology and developmental science. Vol. 4: Ecological settings and processes* (7th ed., pp. 305–344). Wiley Inter-Science.

Wang, C. C. (1999). Photovoice: A participatory action research strategy applied to women's health. *Journal of Women's Health, 8*(2), 185–192.

Watts, R. J., Diemer, M. A., & Voight, A. M. (2011). Critical consciousness: Current status and future directions. *New Directions for Child and Adolescent Development, 134,* 43–57. https://doi.org/10.1002/cd.310.

Watts, R. J., Griffith, D. M., & Abdul-Adil, J. (1999). Sociopolitical development as an antidote for oppression – theory and action. *American Journal of Community Psychology, 27*(2), 255–271.

Watts, R. J., Williams, N. C., & Jagers, R. J. (2003). Sociopolitical development. *American Journal of Community Psychology, 31*(1–2), 185–194.

Weiston-Serdan, T. (2017). *Critical mentoring: A practical guide.* Stylus Publishing, LLC.

Wernick, L. J., Kulick, A., & Woodford, M. R. (2014). How theater within a transformative organizing framework cultivates individual and collective empowerment among LGBTQQ youth. *Journal of Community Psychology, 42,* 838–853. http://dx.doi.org/10.1002/jcop.21656.

Williams, J. L., & Deutsch, N. L. (2016). Beyond between-group differences: Considering race, ethnicity, and culture in research on positive youth development programs. *Applied Developmental Science, 20*(3), 203–213.

Winans-Solis, J. (2014). Reclaiming power and identity: Marginalized students' experiences of service-learning. *Equity & Excellence in Education, 47,* 604–621. http://dx .doi.org/10.1080/10665684.2014.959267.

Xing, K. , Chico, E. , Lambouths, D. L. , Brittian, A. S. , & Schwartz, S. J. (2015). Identity development in adolescence: Implications for youth policy and practice. In E. P. Bowers, G. Geldhof, S. Johnson, et al. (Eds.), *Promoting positive youth development: Lessons from the 4-H Study* (pp. 187–208). Springer International Publishing.

Zeldin, S., Larson, R., Camino, L., & O'Connor, C. (2005). Intergenerational relationships and partnerships in community programs: Purpose, practice, and directions for research. *Journal of Community Psychology, 33*(1), 1–10.

Zimmerman, M. A., Ramirez-Valles, J., & Maton, K. I. (1999). Resilience among urban African American male adolescents: A study of the protective effects of sociopolitical control on their mental health. *American Journal of Community Psychology, 27*(6), 733–751.

5

Breaking Down the Arts

A Novel Exploration of How Varying Kinds of Arts Participation Relate to Critical Consciousness among Youth of Color

DEANNA A. IBRAHIM, ANDREW NALANI, AND ERIN B. GODFREY

Youth of color constantly contend with manifestations of oppression such as structural racism, negative stereotyping, and microaggressions, all of which hinder their success and positive well-being (Ginwright & Cammarota, 2002). In this context, critical consciousness (CC) – the process of understanding structural inequities, feeling able and motivated to work toward social change, and engaging in social action – is a key developmental asset for youth of color (Diemer & Li, 2011; Freire, 1970; Rapa et al., 2018). Increasingly, studies involving youth of color show an association between CC and several positive youth development outcomes, such as higher occupational success, academic achievement, civic engagement, and socioemotional outcomes, among others (see Heberle et al., 2020). Watts and colleagues (1999) concluded that CC is an "antidote for oppression" and hence a protective factor against the negative impacts of structural oppression.

Several studies have contributed to our understanding of CC's contributions to positive outcomes for youth of color; however, more work is needed to unpack the enabling conditions for youth's CC. Following this line of inquiry, theoretical and empirical work suggest that processes such as parental racial socialization, peer socialization, and critical curiosity (or the desire to learn about social issues) contribute to CC growth among youth of color (Bañales et al., 2020; Clark & Seider, 2017; Diemer et al., 2006). Additionally, certain school settings can serve as "opportunity structures," or spaces in which youth are able to engage in critical reflection and action (Seider et al., 2017; Watts & Guessous, 2006). Beyond the classroom, extracurricular programs have been shown to promote youth's CC, a growing number of which leverage the arts to do so (Ngo, 2017; Tyson, 2002). How the arts relate to youth's CC is the focus of this chapter.

The link between the arts and CC may not be surprising, given that the arts have long been used as pedagogical tools to instigate critical dialogue and social change (Delgado, 2018; Goessling, 2020). Yet, only recently have scholars begun to examine this link between socially engaged arts programming and CC, primarily through qualitative methods. Additionally, only one study has leveraged quantitative methods to unpack the question of whether arts participation that is not explicitly concerned with social justice (e.g., the school choir or drama club) also facilitates CC development (Ibrahim et al., 2021). Another unexplored question is whether certain modalities of art contribute more to CC compared to others. As such, in this chapter we aim to understand (a) whether arts participation is related to CC among youth of color, and (b) what kinds of arts are related to CC among youth of color. For the first aim, we contrast two kinds of arts participation: social justice art, which intentionally engages youth in CC, and general arts (e.g., the school choir), which do not. We examine the extent to which these contrasting forms of arts participation relate to CC among youth of color. For the second aim, we further unpack general arts participation to explore whether certain forms (e.g., theater, film, music) are associated with CC. Our findings have implications for the pedagogical choices youth educators make to leverage the arts for CC development among youth of color.

How is Critical Consciousness Conceptualized?

In *Pedagogy of the Oppressed*, Paulo Freire described CC as a process wherein one becomes more aware of social inequities (critical reflection) and actively challenges oppression to bring about social change (critical action; Freire, 1970). Scholars have since expanded upon Freire's theory and applied it to the field of youth development, with specific attention to how minoritized youth may engage in CC to overcome structural barriers to positive development (Zimmerman et al., 1999). Building on these two CC components, reflection and action, Watts and colleagues (2011) suggest that critical reflection alone may not be enough to instigate youth engagement in critical action; indeed, one must be able to identify the possible ways to respond to injustice in order to take this action (Freire, 1973; Watts et al., 2011). This third component of CC represents an individual's perceived capacity to address injustice and is referred to as "political efficacy" or, at times, "critical motivation"; however, the term of critical motivation is distinct from political efficacy in that it often includes not only the perceived capacity but also the commitment to address injustice (Diemer et al., 2016; Watts et al., 2011). Thus, contemporary scholarship theorizes CC to consist of critical reflection, political efficacy, and critical action as distinct components that relate to and inform one another in complex ways. In practice, it is rare that studies of youth's CC examine all three components. The current study examines all three of these components in relation to arts programming and breaks down the component of political efficacy into two subcomponents: internal and external.

Political efficacy, as conceptualized by Watts et al. (2011), refers to an internal belief; thus, most CC studies conceptualize political efficacy as one's beliefs about their own (internal) ability to create social change. However, the field of political science suggests that it is crucial to consider not only youth's beliefs about their own perceived capacity to enact change (internal political efficacy) but also their beliefs about external forces, such as the government enacting change (external political efficacy). External political efficacy represents the perceived responsiveness of the government to one's needs and interests (Morrell, 2003). Indeed, several studies in the CC literature have assessed both internal and external forms of political efficacy as a part of youth's CC, uncovering complex and unexpected relations between critical reflection, political efficacy, and critical action (Diemer & Rapa, 2016; Godfrey & Grayman, 2014). There is a clear need for more studies in CC to consider all theorized components of this construct in order to more fully understand this developmental asset. The current study draws from prior CC conceptualizations to examine how arts programming relates to each component: critical reflection, political efficacy (both internal and external), and critical action (Diemer & Rapa, 2016; Freire, 1970; Watts et al., 2011).

CRITICAL CONSCIOUSNESS AMONG YOUTH OF COLOR

A growing body of evidence suggests that CC components serve as protective and promotive assets for marginalized youth, particularly in contexts of racial and socioeconomic oppression (El-Amin et al., 2017; Hope et al., 2020; Roy et al., 2019). For example, among youth of color, higher levels of CC may contribute to youth's capacity to navigate structural barriers to success, demonstrated through higher academic achievement (El-Amin et al., 2017), higher occupational attainment (Rapa et al., 2018), and more positive mental health (Christens & Peterson, 2012) than their peers who exhibit lower CC. We join these CC scholars in centering the experiences of youth of color in our conceptualization and operationalization of CC, viewing CC as an "antidote for oppression" or a tool that young people of color can leverage to challenge structural forces of oppression that stem from racial injustice (Watts et al., 1999).

Research on CC among marginalized youth has focused primarily on the experiences of youth from Black and Latine communities – communities that have historically faced structural oppression in the United States (Heberle et al., 2020). However, less is known about CC among youth of color from other racial/ethnic groups, including Asian and Asian American youth (with the exception of some qualitative studies that document how pedagogical experiences in community youth programs nurture CC for these youth; e.g., Ngo, 2017). In this chapter, within a sample of youth that identify primarily as Hispanic or Latine and Asian or Asian American, we delineate how participating in the arts relates to various components of CC for youth of these racial/ethnic groups.

Why Might Art Relate to Critical Consciousness Development among Youth of Color?

There are several mechanisms through which arts engagement may contribute to CC development among youth of color. To explicate these mechanisms, we first draw from an empirically grounded and practice-informed framework developed through the Boston Youth Arts Evaluation Project (BYAEP; 2012). The framework emerged from a synthesis and empirical examination of arts programs' logic models across five nonprofits with broad national consultation with research and policy experts and nonprofit leaders. The framework describes three major processes of youth development through the arts: (a) building artistic, problem-solving, critical thinking, and expressive skills; (b) strengthening identity; and (c) developing meaningful relationships through an inclusive community. We make the case that these same mechanisms can promote CC. To do so, we further interpret this framework specifically through a developmental perspective, which views adolescence as a fruitful time to engage youth in building cognitive and expressive skills, as youth gain the ability to think complexly and structurally about issues such as fairness and justice during this stage (National Academies of Sciences, Engineering, and Medicine, 2019).

Skill Building According to CC theory, critical thinking is necessary for engaging in critical reflection and critical action (Freire, 1970): individuals must be able to think critically about society and their respective social standing in order to challenge and change social structures. More recently, CC scholars suggest that related skills, such as empathy and perspective-taking skills, are necessary for youth to engage with issues of power and oppression and learn about social justice issues (Clark & Seider, 2017; Diemer & Blustein, 2006).

Expressive skills are also key to consciousness-building, as one must be able to express their views and feelings about issues of inequity in order to begin to confront these issues. Freire emphasized the importance of expressing instances of injustice, stating that "To exist, humanly, is to name the world, to change it. Once named, the world in its turn reappears [to those who name it] as a problem and requires of them a new naming" (p. 88). Arts engagement, in other words, provides youth with more developmentally attuned language forms (theater, movement, poetry, music) through which they may be able to express their views and feelings around issues of injustice than they would have in traditional talk alone (Boal, 1979).

Finally, art positions youth as creators, providing them with the tools they need to author their own stories rather than passively reproduce their socialization (Vasudevan et al., 2010). This repositioning aligns with the critique levied against deficit approaches to youth development that focus solely on behavioral modification or academic achievement at the expense of skills for navigating and countering oppressive social structures (Baldridge, 2014). Additionally, intentionally reframing youth as creators is a responsive pedagogical choice given youth's developmental readiness to contribute meaningfully to social life (Fuligni, 2019). Thus, arts engagement capitalizes on youth's new capacities for cognitive skill building to not only cultivate their ability to critically reflect on the injustices they face but also to actively name and confront these injustices.

Identity Exploration The second major way in which arts engagement supports youth's CC is through facilitating youth's identity exploration. From a developmental lens, identity exploration is often considered the main task of adolescence as youth develop the capacity to actively reflect on their personal beliefs and explore new possibilities (National Academies of Sciences, Engineering, and Medicine, 2019). Through creating and attending to art, youth can explore who they are and what they want to convey to the world. Additionally, art builds youth's capacity for creative thinking, which allows youth to imagine and explore new possibilities for themselves and to synthesize various aspects of themselves in a coherent sense of self (Barbot & Heuser, 2017; Goessling, 2020). For youth of color specifically, art can be consequential for identity exploration as it provides opportunities to confront and resist harmful stereotypes about their race, culture, and/or language in traditional educational spaces and cultivate a more affirming sense of self (Case & Hunter, 2012; Shirazi, 2019; Way et al., 2013). Arts programs shift the focus to youth's strengths as culture creators (vs. culture victims) and facilitate a climate of trust and openness which allows genuine self-expression to occur. Thus, arts programs have the potential to serve as counterspaces (Case & Hunter, 2012) in which youth of minoritized backgrounds may feel supported enough to confront and even resist negative stereotypes as they build new identities through creative expression.

The depth of self-reflection and the exploration of new possible identities that the arts afford youth of color are both crucial for CC as well. Freire (1970) emphasizes the importance of being aware of reality, the self, and new possibilities for the self. He refers to this knowledge of the self and the "creative possibilities" for the self as necessary for movement toward liberation (p. 137; see also Petrovic, 1965). More recent theorizing on CC and identity development connects racial/ethnic identity exploration to building one's critical reflection (Mathews et al., 2020). This emerging theoretical work further lends credence to our conjecture that arts engagement may relate to CC through providing opportunities for identity reflection and exploration.

Enhanced Social Connection The last major mechanism through which arts engagement facilitates CC is through enhanced social connections. Adolescence is a time for expanding social circles, as youth have the opportunity to engage with settings – including extracurricular arts organizations – outside of the classroom or home (Eccles et al., 2003). When young people join others in engaging with art, there is potential for cultivating relationships of care and support. Yet for youth of color specifically, discourses that emphasize care and support may unwittingly reproduce deficit and paternalistic views of young people "who need help" rather than advance strengths-based ones (Baldridge, 2014, 2020). In contrast, for youth of color, responsive support and care may best be expressed in the form of solidarity (Greene et al., 2013). Indeed, scholars suggest that the participatory and collaborative nature of creating art often facilitates empathy and solidarity across language, economic, intergenerational, and cultural barriers (Goessling, 2020; Hickey-Moody, 2017). We draw from CC theory to highlight the importance of solidarity in working toward social change. Freire (1970) notes that humanity and liberation can only be achieved through solidarity, including solidarity between educators and students as they cocreate new conditions for a more socially just world. By positioning youth as cocreators (artists) alongside adults, youth arts programs have the potential to facilitate youth–adult partnerships, an effective form of youth participation in which youth and adults collaborate on group decision-making (Zeldin et al., 2014). When young people work collaboratively with other youth and adults to express themselves through art, they can build social connections and efficacy (Zeldin et al., 2014), providing youth with the support and solidarity necessary to work toward positive changes for themselves and society.

Drawing from interdisciplinary theories in youth arts programming, CC, and youth development, we can see that arts programs are developmentally attuned to engage youth of color in CC through skill building, identity exploration, and social connection. However, the research literature examining relations between arts programming and CC remains nascent. In the following sections, we summarize existing evidence for this link between arts and CC in two main contexts: social justice art programs and general art programs.

Differentiating Arts Participation and its Contributions to CC Development

Social Justice Art Participation and CC *Social justice* refers to creating a more equitable society and stems from an awareness of structural inequities in society and action toward addressing inequity (Ginwright & Cammarota, 2002). It follows that social justice art – "artwork that addresses or attempts to directly affect social injustice" – has been increasingly leveraged to promote youth's CC development (Dewhurst, 2014). In fact, the CC scholarship points to a growing number of curricular and extracurricular CC interventions that involve literature and the arts or theater (Heberle et al., 2020). Most of these programs engage youth of color in arts-based activities to build CC (e.g., Osorio, 2018). For instance, one ethnographic study showcased how a group of Hmong adolescents engaged in a community-based theater program used theater to name their world, envision new ways of confronting stereotypes, and perform different ways of challenging oppression in front of an audience (Ngo, 2017).

In addition to the studies cited in the CC literature, studies across disciplines of art education, urban education, and others suggest that engaging youth in art for social justice can promote youth's CC (Greene et al., 2013; Rhoades, 2012; Vasudevan et al., 2010).

For instance, one article describes an Alternative to Incarceration Program in which youth of color leveraged storytelling and performance to critically reflect on their experiences with systemic oppression and become authors of their own narratives (Vasudevan et al., 2010). In another account, film was used as an artistic tool to spark dialogue, facilitating youth's ability to articulate and confront challenges facing the Navajo community (Squires & Inlander, 1990). Although the current chapter focuses on how arts participation relates to CC specifically among youth of color, it is important to recognize the growing number of social justice art programs that engage youth of other minoritized identities, particularly LGBTQ+ youth (see Wernick et al., 2014). Across art modalities (theater, film), and populations of youth (youth of color, LGBTQ+ youth), social justice art activates common processes for youth's self-expression, reflection, authorship, and social change, thereby facilitating CC development. However, the current body of research investigating the relationship between social justice art engagement and CC remains qualitative – and we consider this in-depth portrayal of such engagement a strength. Even so, a quantitative examination of this relationship is necessary to bolster our understanding of the arts–CC association and to test the extent to which social justice art relates to each CC component.

General Arts Participation and CC In contrast to social justice art, general arts programs (e.g., the school choir or dance classes) typically do not intentionally engage youth with social justice issues. Recent research has linked general arts participation to CC development for the first time, demonstrating that youth who participate in general arts experience growth in critical reflection and critical action over the course of a school year, adjusting for baseline CC and covariates (Ibrahim et al., 2021). Thus, it is likely that general arts participation may engage youth in processes that are conducive to CC even without the explicit focus on social justice.

Drawing from theory on youth arts development (Boston Youth Arts Evaluation Project, 2012) and CC theory (Freire, 1970), we know that mechanisms such as skill building and social connection are key facets of arts programming that relate to CC. Recent research in arts education provides evidence in support of these relations. For instance, several studies demonstrate that youth who participate in general arts experience growth in critical thinking, empathy, tolerance, and perspective-taking (Bowen et al., 2014; Bowen & Kisida, 2019; Greene et al., 2018; Lampert, 2011). This research supports the notion that arts programming may provide youth with the building blocks (e.g., critical thinking, self-expression) necessary to engage in CC. Additionally, a study among adults found that arts engagement is related to higher feelings of social connectedness, characterized by having social opportunities, sharing with others, feeling a sense of belonging, and building a collective understanding (Perkins et al., 2021). Given the importance of supporting CC for youth of color's thriving and the potential for arts programming to function as an opportunity structure for CC engagement, it is crucial to extend the scholarship on arts education and CC to bridge these two disciplines. Further, the current study also aims to expand our understanding of which modalities of art settings relate to youth's CC.

Are Certain Art Modalities More Related to CC than Others?

Scholarship on CC development suggests that different settings and activities young people participate in can promote different components of CC (Seider et al., 2017). In a study examining how various schools with distinct pedagogical models influence youth's CC development, the researchers were able to theorize which schools would promote certain CC components based on their pedagogies and related activities. Schools with problem-posing or habits-of-mind pedagogies, which engage youth in activities that emphasize inquiry and critical thinking, promoted critical reflection. In contrast, a school with an expeditionary learning model, which engages youth in more experiential activities, promoted critical action. We adopt this same logic – that different settings and activities can relate to CC in different ways – to suggest that different general arts organizations may relate to different components of CC. All kinds of arts programs, from a slam poetry club to a dance team, can engage youth in skill development, identity exploration, and building social connections as a road to CC. However, each type of program involves youth in distinct activities and social norms, which may arguably facilitate distinct CC components.

The distinction between social justice art programming and general arts programming is clear from the research cited earlier, which demonstrates that social justice art specifically leverages activities and norms to target CC, whereas general arts programming does not; however, the distinctions in the ways different general art modalities associate with CC are less clear. Within the large umbrella of general arts programming is a range of art modalities – each with the potential to tap into certain areas of CC. For instance, an arts organization specializing in theater is likely to engage youth in group-based improvisation activities, in which youth must work as a team to create a story or work of art. This collaborative work requires skills such as empathy, tolerance, and perspective-taking, which have been empirically linked to participation in theater activities (Goldstein et al., 2017; Greene et al., 2018). We know from CC theory that these skills are important for critical reflection; thus, we might expect participation in theater organizations to be linked more strongly with critical reflection than other components. Further, theory and research in music education suggest that making music in a group setting, which involves gaining mastery of an instrument with the validation of others, can enhance youth's self-esteem and self-efficacy (Clements-Cortés & Chow, 2018). Skills such as self-esteem and self-efficacy may be especially conducive to internal political efficacy, as youth first must see themselves as capable and agentic to feel able to make social change. It is crucial to understand which kinds of arts settings and activities relate to specific CC components to inform practitioners' work in developing effective arts-based tools for promoting each CC component.

Current Study

The current study seeks to understand whether and which kinds of arts activities are associated with CC among youth of color. We explore how two different types of arts participation (general arts participation and social justice art participation) uniquely relate to CC, conceptualized as the three distinct but interrelated components of critical reflection, critical action, and political efficacy (with subcomponents of internal and external political efficacy) introduced earlier. We expect both general art and social justice art participation to be positively associated with CC among youth of color. Further, we expect social justice art participation to be more robustly related to CC than general arts participation, given the intentional use of art in addressing social and political issues. Next, we aim to explore potential differences in the ways that participation in specific kinds of general arts programs (visual arts, theater, music, dance, film) relates to CC. To our knowledge, the current study is the first to examine the possibility that distinct art modalities are differentially related to each component of CC. Given the novelty of this research question, we do not make specific a priori hypotheses but aim to uncover any emerging patterns.

METHOD

Procedure

The current study is a secondary analysis of the Stanford Civic Purpose Project: Longitudinal Study of Youth Civic Engagement in California (Damon, 2011–2013). The study primarily aimed to investigate civic experiences, attitudes, and motivations among a diverse sample of adolescents. The research team recruited youth from seven high schools in California, with intentional selection based on socioeconomic, ethnic, and immigrant diversity. Youth completed surveys in their school's computer lab during a required class, and they were invited to participate in a second study approximately two years later (Malin et al., 2017).

Participants

The sample for this study consists of 1,469 high school seniors of color from California. Hispanic or Latine (50%) and Asian or Asian American (27%) subgroups made up the majority of the sample, with smaller percentages of youth identifying as Black or African American, Mixed, American Indian or Native American, or Other. Most students were 17 years old (median = 17; mean = 16.88; range = 15–20); 52% of youth identified as female, and 47% identified as male; the survey did not include nonbinary or other gender options.[1] In the tables that follow, we provide additional sample demographics (Table 5.1), and a breakdown of participation in the arts (Table 5.2).

TABLE 5.1 Sample demographics

Race	N	%
Hispanic or Latine	723	49
Asian or Asian American	401	27
Black or African American	85	6
Mixed	153	10
American Indian or Native American	5	0.3
Other	102	7
Gender	**N**	**%**
Female	763	52
Male	694	47
Born in the United States	**N**	**%**
Yes	1,221	83
No	237	16
Mother's Education Status	**N**	**%**
Up to and including high school	742	51
More than high school	474	32

[1] The survey asked participants to select their gender, but the two options offered were "female" and "male." We acknowledge that the results may reflect youth's sex given the options offered.

TABLE 5.2 Sample arts participation

General and Social Justice Art Participation		
General Arts Participation	*N*	**%**
Never	767	52
At least once	659	45
Social Justice Art Participation	*N*	**%**
Never	551	38
At least once	801	55
Combined Participation Across General and Social Justice Arts	*N*	**%**
Both general and social justice arts participation	430	29
Only general arts participation	229	16
Only social justice arts participation	371	25
No arts participation	439	30
Arts Participation by Modality		
	N	**%**
Visual	375	26
Theater	147	10
Music	257	18
Dance	211	14
Film or digital media	200	14
Other	70	5

Follow-up analyses suggested no meaningful differences in demographic characteristics (age, race, gender, SES) across arts participation categories (see Tables 5.3 and 5.4).

Measures

General Arts Participation To assess their participation in extracurricular arts, youth were asked "How often have you participated in each of the following types of organizations since the time you started high school?" followed by the option "arts organizations." Youth rated their frequency of participation by choosing one of four response options: 1 (*never*), 2 (*once or twice*), 3 (*a few times*), and 4 (*always*).

TABLE 5.3 ANOVA comparisons of average youth's age (in years) across arts participation categories

			Bonferroni Post-hoc Comparisons			
Arts Participation Category	Mean	SD	Both Social Justice Arts and General Arts	General Arts Only	Social Justice Arts Only	No Arts
Both Social Justice Arts and General Arts	16.90	0.50				
General Arts Only	16.89	0.53				
Social Justice Arts Only	16.92	0.58				
Neither General Nor Social Justice Arts	16.82	0.54			< 0.05	

Note. There was a significant difference in mean age across the four groups, $F(3) = 2.81, p < 0.05$. Post-hoc analyses showed that youth in the social justice arts only category were slightly older compared to their counterparts not participating in any arts (mean difference = 0.10 (CI: 0.00–0.20)). Only significant post-hoc comparisons are reported in this table.

TABLE 5.4 Chi-square comparisons of the proportion of youth participating in each arts category by gender

	Arts Participation Category (% proportions in parentheses)			
	Both Social Justice Arts and General Arts	General Arts Only	Social Justice Arts Only	No Arts
Female Youth	241 (31.6)	134 (17.6)	181 (23.7)	207 (27.1)
Male Youth	185 (26.7)	91 (13.1)	188 (27.1)	230 (33.1)

$\chi^2 (3) = 13.69, p < 0.01$

Note. After adjusting for multiple comparisons using Bonferroni corrections, post-hoc analyses showed that the observed proportions of males and the proportion of females in the "no arts" category were marginally statistically different ($p = 0.05$ for both comparisons) than we would expect under the null hypothesis that the proportions of males and the proportions of females across the four arts participation types are all equal, respectively. We found no differences in arts participation according to youth's race or mother's education level.

Modalities of Arts Organizations Following the main question assessing overall participation in an arts organization, students were asked six questions assessing participation in specific kinds of arts. Each question began with "What type of arts organizations have you participated in? Select all that apply"; each question listed a specific kind of art, including visual art, theater, music, dance, film, and other.

Social Justice Art Engagement To assess youth's participation in art for social justice, youth were asked to respond to one item from the Youth Inventory of Involvement (Pancer et al., 2007). The item asked "How often have you participated in each of the following types of activities since the time you started high school?" followed by [the activity] "Used art, music or digital media (art/graffiti/music/spoken word/dance/videos/rap) to express my views about political or social issues." Youth rated their frequency of social justice art engagement by choosing one of four response options: 1 (*never*), 2 (*once or twice*), 3 (*a few times*), and 4 (*always*).

Critical Reflection Critical reflection was assessed using three items from the Belief in America as a Just Society measure (Flanagan et al., 2007). Participants rated their level of agreement on a scale of 1 (*strongly disagree*) to 5 (*strongly agree*). This scale included items such as "America is a fair society where everyone has an equal chance to get ahead" and demonstrated high internal consistency ($a = 0.89$). On average, youth's responses to the US fairness items ($M = 2.84$; $SD = 1.05$) fell between "disagree" and "neither agree nor disagree." This suggests that, overall, youth did not agree that the United States is fair, indicating moderate to high critical reflection.

Internal Political Efficacy Internal political efficacy was assessed using a 5-item scale of political efficacy, adapted from an earlier measure (Craig et al., 1990). Participants reported on their perceived political efficacy by rating their level of agreement on a scale of 1 (*strongly disagree*) to 5 (*strongly agree*). This scale included items such as "I have a role to play in the political process" and demonstrated high internal consistency ($a = 0.85$). On average, youth's responses to the internal political efficacy items ($M = 2.87$; $SD = 0.78$) fell between "disagree" and "neither agree nor disagree." This suggests that, overall, youth did not agree that they have a role in effecting political change.

External Political Efficacy External political efficacy was assessed using four items adapted from the California Civic Index (Kahne et al., 2005). Participants reported on their beliefs in the government by rating their level of agreement on a scale of 1 (*strongly disagree*) to 5 (*strongly agree*). This scale included items such as "The government doesn't care about us ordinary people" and demonstrated high internal consistency ($a = 0.85$). On average, youth's responses to the external political efficacy items ($M = 2.76$; $SD = 0.83$) fell between "disagree" and "neither agree nor disagree." This suggests that, overall, youth did not agree that the government is responsive, reflecting low levels of external political efficacy.

Critical Action Critical action was assessed using a measure of civic activities adapted from the Youth Inventory of Involvement (Pancer et al., 2007). Participants were asked "How often have you participated in each of the following activities since the time you started high school?," followed by a series of twenty-two items describing civic activities. We used twenty-one of the twenty-two items to assess critical action, as one item was used to assess social justice art engagement, as described earlier. Youth rated their frequency of participation by choosing one of four response options: 1 (*never*), 2 (*once or twice*), 3 (*a few times*), and 4 (*always*). The original research team conducted a Principle Axis Factor analysis with Varimax rotation to confirm that fifteen of the original twenty-two items loaded onto the following three factors: political activities, expressive activities, and community service (Damon, 2011–2013; Malin et al., 2017). Based on the conceptualization of critical action as engagement in justice-oriented activities (Diemer et al., 2016), we excluded the community service factor from our model. We included political activities and expressive activities as two distinct factors, representing two different forms of critical action. The political activities subscale included six items, such as "Attended a protest march, meeting, or demonstration," and demonstrated high internal consistency ($\alpha = 0.73$). The expressive activities subscale consisted of three items, such as "Contacted a political representative to tell him/her how you felt about a particular issue" and demonstrated lower but adequate internal consistency ($\alpha = 0.67$). On average, youth participated close to "once or twice" in political activities ($M = 1.59$; $SD = 0.59$), and expressive activities ($M = 1.68$; $SD = 0.69$).

Covariates A set of covariates, chosen based on theory, were included in these analyses. These variables included youth's age, immigration status (whether or not youth were born in the United States), gender (youth's identification as female or male), and mother's education status (whether or not youth's mothers received education beyond a high school degree). See Table 5.1 for descriptive statistics.

Analytic Plan

In order to understand the extent to which social justice art and/or general arts relate to youth's CC, and the extent to which specific modalities of art relate to CC, we tested two structural models in Mplus (Muthén & Muthén, 1998–2017). In model 1, dependent variables (CC components) were regressed on independent variables (indicators of arts participation), adjusting for demographic characteristics that could potentially relate to both youth's arts participation and youth's CC levels based on theory: age, gender, immigrant status, and mother's education level. Importantly, to understand the extent to which different types of arts participation relate to CC, we included three independent variables as our indicators of arts participation: social justice art participation only, general arts participation only, and participation in both social justice and general (our reference group was participation in no arts). Thus, we were able to examine the specific relations between each type of arts participation, adjusting for other types and demographic covariates (see Figure 5.1 for conceptual model). In model 2, we examined the extent to which specific modalities of general arts programs relate to CC. Dependent variables (CC components) were regressed on independent variables. Each independent variable was a binary indicator of a specific art modality, including visual arts, theater, music, dance, and film.[2] For instance, the variable representing visual arts was modeled as a binary variable, with 0 indicating that the student did not participate in visual arts and 1 indicating participation in visual arts. Finally, the binary variable representing social justice art participation only and the demographic variables were included as covariates in model 2.

In both models, all CC components and subcomponents (critical reflection, internal political efficacy, external political efficacy, political action, and expressive

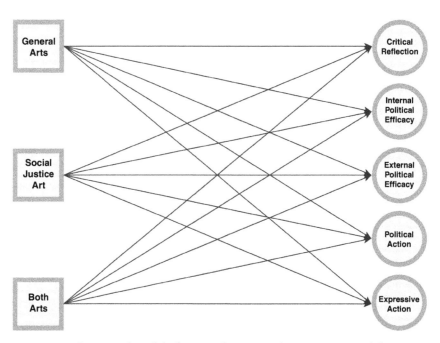

FIGURE 5.1 Conceptual model of arts predicting CC dimensions in model 1.
Note. Demographic characteristics are included in the model as covariates but not shown in the figure. The reference group is 'no arts participation' in model 1. We did not include art modalities (model 2) in this figure, as we did not have a priori hypotheses guiding those analyses.

---

[2]   For consistent interpretation across art modality categories, we excluded student responses ($N = 70$) that indicated participation in an "other" type of art.

TABLE 5.5 Model fit including all CC indicators as latent variables

Model Fit Index	CFA	Model 1	Model 2
CFI	0.93	0.92	0.91
TLI	0.92	0.90	0.89
RMSEA	0.05	0.05	0.05
SRMR	0.05	0.04	0.04
N	1,452	1,192	1,105

Note. CC components of critical reflection, internal and external political efficacy, political action, and expressive action are modeled as latent variables in the confirmatory factor analysis (CFA) and both structural models. Model 1 examines how general arts and social justice art participation relate to CC components, and model 2 examines how specific art modalities relate to CC components.

action) were modeled as latent variables. The fit statistics for each of our models demonstrated good model fit (Brown, 2015; Kline, 2011; see Table 5.5 for model fit statistics). Analyses were conducted using Maximum Likelihood (ML) estimation; under ML estimation, only cases with missingness on observed covariates ($N = 336$) are deleted, and the observed information matrix is used to compute standard errors for parameter estimates with missing data on other variables (Kenward & Molenberghs, 1998; Muthén & Muthén, 1998–2017).

Correlations among CC components within this sample of primarily Hispanic or Latine youth and Asian or Asian American youth reflect previous findings among Latine youth in some ways but contradict previous findings in others. Specifically, as in prior work, we found a negative association between critical reflection and external political efficacy, such that higher levels of perceived inequity were linked to lower levels of perceived government responsiveness. Similarly, as in prior work, we found that internal political efficacy was positively associated with political action, and we did not find a significant relationship between critical reflection and political action (Diemer & Rapa, 2016). However, although prior work suggests no relationship between critical reflection and internal political efficacy, we found a negative relationship, such that higher levels of perceived inequity were linked to lower levels of perceived capacity to effect change in this study. Additionally, although prior work suggests a negative correlation between internal and external political efficacy (Diemer & Rapa, 2016), we did not find a significant correlation between these two components (see correlations in Table 5.6).

TABLE 5.6 Correlations among CC components

	US Fair (Reflection)	Internal Political Efficacy	External Political Efficacy	Political Action
US Fair (Reflection)				
Internal Political Efficacy	0.14**			
External Political Efficacy	0.29**	0.03		
Political Action	0.014	0.50**	0.06†	
Expressive Action	0.10**	0.39**	−0.06†	0.50**

Note. †$p \leq 0.10$; *$p \leq 0.05$; **$p \leq 0.01$. Higher scores on US Fair indicate lower levels of critical reflection.

RESULTS

Does Social Justice Art Relate to Critical Consciousness among Youth of Color?

The results of model 1 (see Table 5.7) showed that, compared to youth of color who did not participate in any arts whatsoever, youth who participated in social justice art exhibited higher levels of internal political efficacy ($b = 0.31$; $SE = 0.05$, $\beta = 0.23$, $p < 0.01$), indicating a higher level of CC. In addition, youth participating in social justice art exhibited higher engagement in political activities ($b = 0.35$; $SE = 0.07$, $\beta = 0.20$, $p < 0.01$) and expressive activities ($b = 0.51$; $SE = 0.06$, $\beta = 0.36$, $p < 0.01$) compared to youth who did not participate in any arts. No associations were found between participation in social justice art and critical reflection or external political efficacy.

Does General Arts Participation Relate to Critical Consciousness among Youth of Color?

Compared to youth of color who did not participate in any arts whatsoever, youth of color who participated in general arts were more likely to view US society as fair, indicating lower levels of critical reflection ($b = 0.19$; $SE = 0.09$, $\beta = 0.08$, $p < 0.05$), adjusting for covariates. Participation in general arts was not associated with internal political efficacy, but it was associated with higher external political efficacy; that is, compared to their counterparts who did not participate in any arts, youth who participated in general arts alone were more likely to view the government as responsive to people's needs ($b = 0.24$; $SE = 0.08$, $\beta = 0.11$, $p < 0.01$) – another indicator of lower CC. However, compared to their peers in no arts, youth who participated in general arts exhibited higher levels of critical action as indicated by engagement in political activities ($b = 0.30$; $SE = 0.08$, $\beta = 0.16$, $p < 0.01$) and expressive activities ($b = 0.17$; $SE = 0.07$, $\beta = 0.10$, $p < 0.05$).

TABLE 5.7 Overview of paths for structural model 1

Path	Standardized Estimate	SE
Social Justice Arts → Critical Reflection	−0.01	0.04
Social Justice Arts → Internal Political Efficacy	**0.23**	0.04
Social Justice Arts → External Political Efficacy	−0.05	0.04
Social Justice Arts → Political Action	**0.2**	0.04
Social Justice Arts → Expressive Action	**0.36**	0.04
General Arts → Critical Reflection	0.08	0.04
General Arts → Internal Political Efficacy	0.05	0.04
General Arts → External Political Efficacy	0.11	0.08
General Arts → Political Action	**0.16**	0.04
General Arts → Expressive Action	**0.1**	0.04
Both Arts → Critical Reflection	0.04	0.04
Both Arts → Internal Political Efficacy	**0.3**	0.04
Both Arts → External Political Efficacy	−0.03	0.04
Both Arts → Political Action	**0.43**	0.04
Both Arts → Expressive Action	**0.5**	0.04

Note. Significant standardized estimates ($p < 0.05$) are shown in bold. Positive coefficients for critical reflection indicate lower levels for this attribute. Demographic characteristics were included as covariates in the model. The reference group is no arts participation.

Both Social Justice and General Arts and Critical Consciousness among Youth of Color

Participation in both social justice and general arts was related to CC components in similar ways to social justice art participation. Compared to youth of color who participated in no arts, those who participated in both social justice and general arts had higher levels of internal political efficacy ($b = 0.39$; $SE = 0.05$, $\beta = 0.30$, $p < 0.01$) and higher engagement in political activities ($b = 0.67$; $SE = 0.07$, $\beta = 0.43$, $p < .01$) and expressive activities ($b = 0.69$; $SE = 0.06$, $\beta = 0.50$, $p < 0.01$), indicating higher levels of CC.

What Can We Learn about Specific General Art Modalities and Critical Consciousness?

The results of model 2 (see Table 5.8) address our second aim of investigating whether specific modalities of general arts organizations relate to CC in differing ways. Adjusting for demographic characteristics and social justice

TABLE 5.8 Coefficients of paths for structural model 1

	Critical Reflection	Internal Political Efficacy	External Political Efficacy	Political Activity	Expressive Activity
Visual Arts	0.03(0.03)	−0.03(0.03)	0.03(0.03)	−0.01(0.04)	0.00(0.03)
Theater	0.03(0.04)	0.03(0.04)	0.06(0.04)	**0.08(0.04)**	0.03(0.04)
Music	0.01(0.04)	**0.08(0.04)**	0.04(0.04)	**0.16(0.04)**	**0.08(0.04)**
Dance	0.03(0.04)	0.05(0.04)	−0.02(0.04)	**0.13(0.04)**	<u>0.06(0.04)</u>
Film	0.03(0.03)	0.00(0.03)	−0.05(0.04)	0.05(0.04)	0.02(0.03)

Note. Significant standardized estimates ($p < 0.05$) are given in bold; marginally significant standardized estimates ($p < 0.10$) are underlined.

art participation, music participation was positively associated with youth's internal political efficacy ($b = 0.12$; $SE = 0.06$, $\beta = 0.08$, $p < 0.05$). Theater ($b = 0.20$; $SE = 0.09$, $\beta = 0.08$, $p < 0.05$), music ($b = 0.29$; $SE = 0.07$, $\beta = 0.16$, $p < 0.01$), and dance ($b = 0.27$; $SE = 0.08$, $\beta = 0.13$, $p < 0.01$) were all positively associated with youth's political activity. Lastly, music was positively associated with expressive activity ($b = 0.14$; $SE = 0.06$, $\beta = 0.08$, $p < 0.05$), and dance was marginally significantly associated with expressive activity in the positive direction ($b = 0.11$; $SE = 0.07$, $\beta = 0.06$, $p < 0.09$). Importantly, no specific modality was significantly associated with critical reflection or external political efficacy, and visual arts were not associated with any CC components.

DISCUSSION

Art has long been used as a tool for self-expression, social change, and individual and community empowerment, particularly among youth of color (Delgado, 2018; Dewhurst, 2014). Social justice art programs have engaged youth in art-making to reflect on experiences with oppression, imagine new possibilities for a more socially just world, and create art that actively challenges injustice (Greene et al., 2013; Ngo, 2017; Vasudevan et al., 2010). However, to our knowledge, no study has quantitatively examined how social justice art participation among youth of color relates to each of the CC components. Further, general arts participation has been linked to CC-related outcomes such as voting and participating in a political campaign (Catterall, 2012; Thomas & McFarland, 2010), and also to CC precursors such as critical thinking, perspective-taking, and empathy

(Bowen et al., 2014; Bowen & Kisida, 2019; Greene et al., 2018). Yet, as far as we know, only one study has examined the direct link between participation in general arts activities and CC among both youth of color and white youth (Ibrahim et al., 2021). Indeed, there is strong theoretical and developmental reasoning in support of this link between arts participation and CC, including the ability of arts participation to build developmentally appropriate skills, identity exploration, and social connections (BYAEP, 2012; National Academies of Sciences, Engineering, and Medicine, 2019). The current results expand on prior research in several ways. First, our findings suggest that both social justice art engagement and general arts programs may relate to CC levels among youth of color, but in distinct ways. Second, our findings suggest there is more nuance to be understood beyond the relationship of general arts to CC, such that specific modalities used in general arts organizations (visual arts, theater, music, dance, film) relate to CC in unique ways. Third, our findings demonstrate complex relations both among CC components themselves and between CC components and each kind of art participation, highlighting the need to understand how arts participation and other processes relate to each CC component rather than considering CC as a general, undifferentiated construct.

How Social Justice and General Art Engagement Relate to Critical Consciousness

Our findings support what we know from the extant qualitative literature – that there is a positive relationship between social justice art and CC among youth of color (Ngo, 2017; Wernick et al., 2014). More specifically, we found that, compared to youth who did not participate in any art, youth who engaged in social justice art demonstrated higher internal political efficacy, political action, and expressive action. The novel link this study establishes between social justice art engagement and internal political efficacy aligns with previous studies demonstrating that social justice art programs might contribute to youth's levels of agency (Ngo, 2017); if youth feel able to make changes in their lives, they may also feel more able to make social and political change. Thus, the current study adds to the social justice art scholarship to link social justice art participation to internal political efficacy using quantitative methods. However, the lack of association between social justice art and critical reflection is surprising given that previous qualitative work suggests youth engage in critical dialogue and analysis of social inequity through the arts (Dewhurst, 2014; Squires & Inlander, 1990). One potential reason for this inconsistency could be the measurement approach used in the current study, which operationalizes critical reflection as the perception that the United States is fair. Perhaps youth are better able to recognize inequity when applied to concrete disparities that may be specific and more immediate to their lived experiences.

Additionally, the novel finding that social justice art engagement is associated with higher political and expressive action aligns with the extant literature suggesting that social justice art programming provides a platform for youth to take action through art, which can motivate youth to join advocacy efforts outside of the context of the art program (Wernick et al., 2014). However, this study is the first of our knowledge to quantitatively assess the relationship between social justice art and these specific political activities (e.g., attending a protest march, meeting, or demonstration) and expressive activities (e.g., contacting a political representative to express their views on an issue). Thus, we provide important evidence that youth of color who participate in social justice art engage in social action not only symbolically through art itself (confronting and challenging injustice through a play, art exhibit, or song), but also in terms of direct action as well. This may suggest long-term engagement in social and political action extended beyond the practice of social justice art engagement. Still, it is important to keep in mind the cross-sectional nature of this study, and thus the possibility that youth with higher CC levels may be more likely to choose to engage in social justice art because they may feel more of a need to express their views about social or political issues than their peers with lower CC levels. This possibility should guide future research toward longitudinal, experimental studies of the relationship between engagement in social justice art and CC.

The extant literature linking general arts participation to CC is much more nascent than that of social justice art education. In addition to the one study demonstrating a longitudinal, quantitative association between general arts participation and CC components (critical reflection and action; Ibrahim et al., 2021), other studies in arts education link general arts to skills necessary for CC (e.g., critical thinking and perspective-taking; Greene et al., 2018; Lampert, 2011) and activities that overlap with critical action (e.g., participating in government and school service clubs, political campaigns, and voting; Catterall, 2012; Thomas & McFarland, 2010). The first major finding around general arts is that, compared to no arts participation whatsoever, participation in general arts only was associated with lower critical reflection and lower external political efficacy – an indication of lower CC (Godfrey & Grayman, 2014). This finding is surprising given that it contrasts the recent finding that youth who participate in higher general arts activities experience higher levels of critical reflection (Ibrahim et al., 2021). One potential reason for this inconsistency, as mentioned earlier, is that the measurement of critical reflection in this study differs from that of the previous study examining general arts and CC, which used the Critical Consciousness Scale (CCS; Diemer et al., 2017). While the CCS asks about specific injustices, including disparities in access to education and job opportunities for women, people of color, and people from low-income communities, the current study asks about youth's overall perception that the United States is fair, which may be more difficult to detect than other forms of injustice that are specific and more immediate to youth's lives.

Another potential reason for the inconsistent findings around the relationship between general arts participation and critical reflection is that general arts participation and CC look different for youth of differing levels of privilege and marginalization. Previous research found evidence for this association primarily for white youth, showing that white youth are especially likely to experience gains in critical reflection following general arts engagement (Ibrahim et al., 2021). Given that the sample for the current study consisted primarily of Latine and Asian or Asian American youth, whose experiences of oppression based on their membership in a historically marginalized racial-ethnic group differs from the experiences of white youth, it could be that general arts programs are not quite optimized to facilitate critical reflection among students of color as they are for other CC components. For instance, whereas general arts programs have been shown to enhance socioemotional skills (e.g., empathy) that play a key role in youth's abilities to reject social inequities and youth's desire to learn about social justice issues (Bowen & Kisida, 2019; Diemer & Blustein, 2006), youth of color – who are already likely to have faced various forms of racial inequity and systemic injustice – may not need to lean as heavily on these skills to understand inequity as their white counterparts. Thus, the socioemotional skills that general arts programs develop may be more conducive to white youth's critical reflection. Additionally, general arts programs may need a more explicit framing around culture, inequity, and oppression if they are to remain responsive to and supportive of critical reflection among youth of color (Simpkins et al., 2017).

Alternatively, it is also possible that our findings may be due to a selection effect, such that youth who have more optimistic views of US society are more likely to choose to enroll in general arts programming – due to the feelings of hope associated with creating art – than those who do not have hopeful, optimistic views and thus do not join arts programs. However, in prior research demonstrating that general arts participation contributes to higher critical reflection, this potential selection bias was addressed by examining the relationship between general arts participation and CC over time (adjusting for baseline CC and other potential confounders; Ibrahim et al., 2021). Thus, selection bias is not likely to be driving this association. Art may indeed support youth's efforts to express and share a hopeful vision for themselves and for the future. Yet, for youth to be able to envision a future that challenges current social structures, they must be encouraged to think critically about those structures. If not paired with a critical analysis of social structures, these positive feelings may encourage youth to believe that they currently do have a fair chance of succeeding and getting ahead in America. This interpretation aligns with the finding that general arts programs, particularly those tied to formal school curricula, seldom integrate critical pedagogies, often due to the belief that addressing inequity should be reserved for out-of-school, community-based programs (Chappell & Cahmann-Taylor, 2013).

Another major finding around general arts and CC is that, compared to no arts participation, general arts participation was associated with higher political action and expressive action. This finding aligns with the existing arts education literature, suggesting links between participating in the arts and participating in government and school service clubs, political campaigns, and voting (Catterall, 2012; Thomas & McFarland, 2010). However, it is somewhat surprising to see that youth who participate in general arts have higher critical action but lower critical reflection than youth who participate in no arts. Recognition of structural inequities is certainly considered a key step toward critical action, but, given the cyclical nature of the CC praxis (Freire, 1970; Watts et al., 2011), critical reflection may not be the only entryway into CC engagement. For instance, a young person may meet peers through an arts organization who are also involved in an activist group and join them; by engaging in critical action first, they may deepen their understanding of the social structures driving the issues they work to address, and come to feel more capable as an agent of change. Indeed, recent research found reciprocal associations between advocacy and sociopolitical efficacy, such that youth's engagement in advocacy at the beginning of the school year was related to higher levels of sociopolitical efficacy at the end of the year, adjusting for initial advocacy; the reverse relationship was also found (Poteat et al., 2020). If general arts participation is associated with higher levels of action, it is possible that action may inform youth's critical reflection and political efficacy as a result.

Overall, these findings suggest that social justice art participation is more positively linked to CC than general arts participation, which was expected due to the explicit intent of social justice art to engage young people in analyzing and challenging injustice (Dewhurst, 2014). However, general arts programs still hold potential for serving as opportunity structures, particularly for youth's critical action. Interestingly, the association between social justice art and expressive activity was stronger than that between general arts and CC, but the associations with political activity were similar in magnitude. This finding may illuminate the role of creative expression in engaging youth in CC. As Gaztambide-Fernández and colleagues (2018) indicate, the act of creating a new work of art inherently involves a greater amount of imagination and creativity than reproducing an existing work of art. While general arts programs certainly do provide the space for creative expression, youth may not always be creating original work in these settings, and when they are, they may not be expressing their own social or political views. Social justice art is more likely to engage youth in the creation of new work involving critical reflection; thus, youth may be more likely to leverage their self-expression toward critical action. While we know that both general and social justice art participation relates to youth's critical action, these nuanced differences point to the need to leverage future research to unpack the potential processes (e.g., creative expression) that may be working to engage youth in CC in different arts settings.

How Different Art Modalities Relate to Critical Consciousness

We also examined the associations between specific modalities of general arts organizations and CC components. Each art modality was uniquely associated with a different combination of CC dimensions, pointing to the complex and unique nature of participation in each kind of art. For instance, we found that music participation was associated with most CC dimensions, including internal political efficacy and both forms of critical action, whereas visual arts participation was not associated with any of the CC components. These findings highlight music as a potentially powerful tool for building youth's perceived efficacy in effecting social change and engaging in critical action. This link between music participation and perceived efficacy in effecting change aligns with scholarship in music education, which suggests that making music with others can enhance youth's self-esteem and self-efficacy (Clements-Cortés & Chow, 2018). A developmental cascade effect across domains is plausible, such that youth's self-efficacy in the context of music may influence their sense of efficacy with respect to their perceived role in society; if they feel able to create change, they may be more likely to participate in activities toward social and political change. This is not to say that other art modalities do not engage youth's self-esteem and self-efficacy; rather, we can be more confident in music's capacity to do so due to the larger body of research evidence in this area.

Additionally, theater, music, and dance were all significantly associated with increased political activity, suggesting that even across modalities there may be shared processes of art-making (such as creative expression, empathy, support from peers) that position arts-based settings well for encouraging critical action. Finally, no art modalities were associated with critical reflection or external political efficacy. Given that general arts participation was associated with both of these outcomes, it is possible that another art modality not assessed in the current study may be driving that association. It is also possible (and perhaps more likely) that we are unable to detect the associations between specific art modalities and these CC components given the imprecision of large standard error estimates due to small sample sizes of youth participating in each art modality ($N = 147-375$). Thus, additional research is needed to more fully understand how these art modalities have been and can be leveraged for CC development.

How Critical Consciousness Components Relate to Each Other

Finally, our findings underscore the complex nature of CC itself, which holds implications for the way in which CC relates to different kinds of arts engagement. Although scholarship sometimes treats CC as an undifferentiated construct, especially when seeking to understand potential factors that relate to it, CC has long been theorized as a complex set of interrelated components (Watts et al., 2011). The nature of those interrelations is as yet unknown, as are the ways in which arts participation relates to each component. In this study, the interrelations reflect prior work in some ways, but not in others. For instance, prior research among Latine youth found that lower levels of critical reflection (perceived inequity) were linked to higher levels of external political efficacy (Diemer & Rapa, 2016). We found the same pattern in this sample of primarily Hispanic or Latine youth as well. Additionally, in both prior work and the current study, internal political efficacy was positively associated with critical action, and there was no relationship between critical reflection and political action (Diemer & Rapa, 2016). As previous scholars have indicated, these relations are complex and not always intuitive – for instance, although we might expect critical reflection to be positively associated with political action based on CC theory, this is not what we or previous scholars found. Interestingly, we also found patterns in these relations that differ from prior work, including a negative association between critical reflection and internal political efficacy (contradicting a lack of association in prior work) and no association between internal and external political efficacy (contradicting a negative relationship in prior work; Diemer & Rapa, 2016). One potential reason for this difference in associations among components compared to previous work conducted with Latine youth is that the racial/ethnic demographic of the current sample differs slightly, consisting of about half Hispanic or Latine, a quarter Asian or Asian American, and the remainder primarily mixed or Black or African American youth. From previous research, we know more about the ways in which Hispanic or Latine and Black or African American youth experience CC than other historically marginalized racial/ethnic groups. Thus, the ways in which our findings contradict previous work could highlight that youth may experience CC differently based on their racial/ethnic identity and accompanying experiences (Mathews et al., 2020). Further, these nuanced interrelations between CC components highlight the complexity of CC and the need to understand its unique components both as they relate to one another and as they relate to arts engagement. This study is a step toward unpacking the relationships between arts and CC components as related but distinct processes.

Limitations and Implications for Future Research

While the current study provides novel evidence of the nuanced ways in which arts participation relates to CC among youth of color, several limitations should be noted. First, given the cross-sectional and nonexperimental nature of the current design, we cannot make causal inferences regarding the directionality of the relationships between arts participation and CC. However, the purpose of this study is to understand what CC levels look like among youth involved in social justice art and general arts. We call on future research to continue to examine these relationships using a longitudinal approach to better understand the developmental trajectories of arts participation and CC among adolescents.

Another major limitation of the current study is the lack of information on the kinds of arts organizations youth are participating in and the ways in which youth are expressing their social and political views through art. For instance, a drama club may look very different from one school to the next, depending on the ethos, mission, and goals of the school and the facilitators (Ibrahim & Godfrey, in prep). One school or facilitator may adopt a more Freirean perspective and aim to engage youth in social justice work, whereas another school or facilitator may be solely focused on academic and artistic achievement. The contextual features of each organization, which largely inform what youth gain from the organization, are not included in the data. Further, our indicator of social justice art participation asks about the frequency with which youth expressed their social or political views through art or digital media; thus, we do not know which youth were engaging in social justice art individually (e.g., at home) or in a group setting (e.g., a community-based program or school club). These two settings can bring about vastly different processes and outcomes for youth, and without this contextual information we cannot make assumptions about the specific ways in which youth are engaging in social justice art. Finally, this quantitative examination of the relations between arts participation and CC is unable to capture much of experiential qualities of arts-based programming. Although we are unable to capture the more experiential qualities of arts engagement, a rich body of social justice art literature does this through qualitative inquiry (Wernick et al., 2014). We view this study as a complimentary line of inquiry, contributing quantitative evidence of the complex relations between a range of arts programs and each of the theorized CC components. Future research could leverage mixed-methods approaches to examine the specific arts-based organizations and settings in which youth participate and the ways in which contextual features relate to youth's engagement with CC processes. Integrating both variance and interpretive methodologies could prove generative in unpacking these processes and understanding their nuance across ethnic/racial subgroups.

Implications for Practice

Given the ongoing presence of structural racism and other forms of systemic marginalization and their implications in American society, it is crucial to understand the ways in which the contexts youth engage in can center CC: motivating youth to be critically aware of the inequities, to feel able to effect social change, and to be active agents of change in their communities. Our findings contribute to the CC literature by identifying and unpacking potential opportunity structures for youth's engagement in CC, illustrating the nuanced ways in which opportunity structures are uniquely related to distinct CC components.

Our findings also provide a novel perspective and contribution to the arts education literature by positioning the arts as an opportunity structure specifically for youth of color – not simply as a tool for improving academic achievement among minoritized youth, as in much of the research with minoritized youth participants (Chappell & Cahnmann-Taylor, 2013), but as a potential tool for individual and social transformation. In her article "Educating for Social Change Through Art: A Personal Reckoning," Dipti Desai (2020) discusses social justice art education as an epistemological frame that can counter social injustice and acknowledge the racist, classist, and Eurocentric underpinnings of social activity. Art-making by individuals from minoritized, historically silenced, and invisibilized communities can be an act of social change (Desai, 2020). Thus, we argue that it is important to continue to provide opportunities and contexts through which youth of color can express themselves through general arts activities. However, in order to truly work toward social change through art-making, arts educators should explicitly draw on a critical awareness of inequities to frame their pedagogical activities and provide opportunities for youth to engage in social action. As the current findings suggest, although general arts programs may be effective in promoting critical action among youth of color, they may not currently be effective in serving youth's abilities to critically analyze social inequities. Thus, we argue that the epistemological frame of social justice art education should be leveraged across schools and communities to create and expand existing social justice art programs in which youth of color can affirm their visibility while acknowledging and working to challenge inequity. Additionally, we join other scholars in urging general arts organizations to adopt the kinds of critical, transformative practices utilized in social justice arts settings (typically community-based, out-of-school programs) to more intentionally center youth voice and self-expression, and even to engage youth in artistic material that acknowledges and challenges social inequity (Chappell & Cahnmann-Taylor, 2013; see also Case & Hunter, 2012 and Simpkins et al., 2017 for complimentary frameworks).

To begin integrating more justice-oriented practices into general arts settings, arts educators can borrow and adapt activities from existing curricula in social justice art education. For instance, educators in the field of visual arts can find concrete activities that engage youth in connecting to issues of injustice and critically analyzing the root causes of structural issues in *Social justice art* (Dewhurst, 2014). Similarly, theater educators can replicate or adapt improvisational exercises and theater games from Theatre of the Oppressed (see *Games for actors and non-actors*; Boal, 2002) or Hope is Vital (see *Theatre for community, conflict and dialogue*; Rohd, 1998) that engage youth in recognizing, naming, and confronting instances of oppression. For instance, the adult facilitator of a high school drama club (a general arts setting) might try integrating one justice-oriented activity, "Complete the Image," into a weekly session before rehearsing a play. In this activity, two people create a visual image together with their bodies using nonverbal dialogue, and the remaining participants interpret the image. This activity can serve as a bridge between general and social justice art engagement, as educators can begin by asking youth to create images about general themes (e.g., "create an image that represents family") and slowly evolve into themes that spark dialogue about experiences of injustice (e.g., "create an image that represents power"). The group reflection then allows space for youth to discuss what power means to them, how they experience power dynamics, and what it looks like. Further, we can see how seemingly simple exercises like "Complete the Image" can further youth's CC development through the theorized mechanisms of skill development. In creating images, youth think critically about the themes they are embodying. In observing images, they engage in perspective-taking to understand the story behind each image. Additionally, youth engage in identity development when, for instance, they tap into their personal experiences with a given theme to embody it in an image. They may also enhance social connections through collaborating with a partner to create an image and engage in group dialogue to reflect on complex themes. Thus, we encourage general arts educators to draw from these existing resources in justice-oriented, arts-based practice to bridge opportunities for youth's creative expression more fully to meaning-making about their lived experiences. We hope that the current findings illuminate the need to integrate a social justice ethos into more traditional arts activities and settings and motivate collaborations among researchers and arts educators to further unpack the nuances of arts practices as they relate to positive outcomes for youth of color.

REFERENCES

Baldridge, B. J. (2014). Relocating the deficit: Reimagining Black youth in neoliberal times. *American Educational Research Journal, 51*(3), 440–472.

Baldridge, B. J. (2020). The youthwork paradox: A case for studying the complexity of community-based youth work in education research. *Educational Researcher, 49* (8), 618–625.

Bañales, J., Marchand, A. D., Skinner, O. D. et al. (2020). Black adolescents' critical reflection development: Parents' racial socialization and attributions about race achievement gaps. *Journal of Research on Adolescence, 30,* 403–417.

Barbot, B., & Heuser, B. (2017). Creativity and identity formation in adolescence: A developmental perspective. In M. Karwowski & J. C. Kaufman (Eds.), *The creative self* (pp. 87–98). Academic Press.

Boal, A. (1979). *Theatre of the oppressed*. Theatre Communications Group.

Boal, A. (2002). *Games for actors and non-actors*. Routledge.

Boston Youth Arts Evaluation Project (BYAEP). (2012). *Boston Youth Arts Evaluation Project Handbook and Workbook*. Boston, MA.

Bowen, D. H., Greene, J. P., & Kisida, B. (2014). Learning to think critically: A visual art experiment. *Educational Researcher*, 43(1), 37–44.

Bowen, D. H., & Kisida, B. (2019). Investigating causal effects of arts education experiences: Experimental evidence from Houston's Arts Access Initiative. *Houston Education Research Consortium Research Report for the Houston Independent School District*, 7(4), 1–28.

Brown, T. A. (2015). *Confirmatory factor analysis for applied research*. Guilford Publications.

Case, A. D., & Hunter, C. D. (2012). Counterspaces: A unit of analysis for understanding the role of settings in marginalized individuals' adaptive responses to oppression. *American Journal of Community Psychology*, 50(1–2), 257–270.

Catterall, J. S. (2012). The Arts and Achievement in At-Risk Youth: Findings from Four Longitudinal Studies. Research Report# 55. *National Endowment for the Arts*.

Chappell, S. V., & Cahnmann-Taylor, M. (2013). No child left with crayons: The imperative of arts-based education and research with language "minority" and other minoritized communities. *Review of Research in Education*, 37(1), 243–268.

Christens, B. D., & Peterson, N. A. (2012). The role of empowerment in youth development: A study of sociopolitical control as mediator of ecological systems' influence on developmental outcomes. *Journal of Youth and Adolescence*, 41(5), 623–635.

Clark, S., & Seider, S. (2017). Developing critical curiosity in adolescents. *Equity & Excellence in Education*, 50(2), 125–141.

Clements-Cortés, A., & Chow, S. (2018). Enhancing self-esteem in the music classroom. *The Canadian Music Educator*, 59(2), 23–26.

Craig, S. C., Niemi, R. G., & Silver, G. E. (1990). Political efficacy and trust: A report on the NES pilot study items. *Political Behavior*, 12(3), 289–314.

Damon, W. *Stanford Civic Purpose Project: Longitudinal Study of Youth Civic Engagement in California*, 2011–2013. Inter-university Consortium for Political and Social Research [distributor], 2017-11-10. https://doi.org/10.3886/ICPSR36561.v1.

Delgado, M. (2018). *Music, song, dance, and theatre: Broadway meets social justice youth community practice*. Oxford University Press.

Desai, D. (2020). Educating for social change through art: A personal reckoning. *Studies in Art Education*, 61(1), 10–23.

Dewhurst, M. (2014). *Social justice art: A framework for activist art pedagogy*. Harvard Education Press.

Diemer, M. A., & Blustein, D. L. (2006). Critical consciousness and career development among urban youth. *Journal of Vocational Behavior*, 68(2), 220–232.

Diemer, M. A., Kauffman, A., Koenig, N., Trahan, E., & Hsieh, C. A. (2006). Challenging racism, sexism, and social injustice: support for urban adolescents' critical consciousness development. *Cultural Diversity and Ethnic Minority Psychology*, 12(3), 444.

Diemer, M. A., & Li, C. H. (2011). Critical consciousness development and political participation among marginalized youth. *Child Development, 82*(6), 1815–1833.

Diemer, M. A., & Rapa, L. J. (2016). Unraveling the complexity of critical consciousness, political efficacy, and political action among marginalized adolescents. *Child Development, 87*(1), 221–238.

Diemer, M. A., Rapa, L. J., Park, C. J., & Perry, J. C. (2017). Development and validation of the critical consciousness scale. *Youth & Society, 49*(4), 461–483.

Diemer, M. A., Rapa, L. J., Voight, A. M., & McWhirter, E. H. (2016). Critical consciousness: A developmental approach to addressing marginalization and oppression. *Child Development Perspectives, 10*(4), 216–221.

Eccles, J. S., Barber, B. L., Stone, M., & Hunt, J. (2003). Extracurricular activities and adolescent development. *Journal of Social Issues, 59*(4), 865–889. https://doi.org/10.1046/j.0022-4537.2003.00095.x.

El-Amin, A., Seider, S., Graves, D. et al. (2017). Critical consciousness: A key to student achievement. *Phi Delta Kappan, 98*(5), 18–23.

Flanagan, C. A., Cumsille, P., Gill, S., & Gallay, L. S. (2007). School and community climates and civic commitments: Patterns for ethnic minority and majority students. *Journal of Educational Psychology, 99*(2), 421–431. https://doi.org/10.1037/0022-0663.99.

Freire, P. (1970). *Pedagogy of the oppressed* (M. B. Ramos, Trans.). Continuum.

Freire, P. (1973). Education, liberation and the Church. *Study Encounter, IX*(1), 1–15.

Fuligni, A. J. (2019). The need to contribute during adolescence. *Perspectives on Psychological Science, 14*(3), 331–343.

Gaztambide-Fernández, R., Kraehe, A. M., & Carpenter, B. S. (2018). The arts as white property: An introduction to race, racism, and the arts in education. In *The Palgrave handbook of race and the arts in education* (pp. 1–31). Palgrave Macmillan.

Ginwright, S., & Cammarota, J. (2002). New terrain in youth development: The promise of a social justice approach. *Social Justice, 29*(4), 82–95.

Godfrey, E. B., & Grayman, J. K. (2014). Teaching citizens: The role of open classroom climate in fostering critical consciousness among youth. *Journal of Youth and Adolescence, 43*(11), 1801–1817.

Goessling, K. P. (2020). Youth participatory action research, trauma, and the arts: Designing youthspaces for equity and healing. *International Journal of Qualitative Studies in Education, 33*(1), 12–31.

Goldstein, T. R., Lerner, M. D., & Winner, E. (2017). The arts as a venue for developmental science: Realizing a latent opportunity. *Child Development, 88* (5), 1505–1512.

Greene, S., Burke, K., & McKenna, M. (2013). Forms of voice: Exploring the empowerment of youth at the intersection of art and action. *The Urban Review, 45*(3), 311–334.

Greene, J. P., Erickson, H. H., Watson, A. R., & Beck, M. I. (2018). The play's the thing: Experimentally examining the social and cognitive effects of school field trips to live theater performances. *Educational Researcher, 47*(4), 246–254.

Heberle, A. E., Rapa, L. J., & Farago, F. (2020). Critical consciousness in children and adolescents: A systematic review, critical assessment, and recommendations for future research. *Psychological Bulletin, 146*(6), 525.

Hickey-Moody, A. C. (2017). Arts practice as method, urban spaces and intra-active faiths. *International Journal of Inclusive Education*, 21(11), 1083–1096.

Hope, E. C., Smith, C. D., Cryer-Coupet, Q. R., & Briggs, A. S. (2020). Relations between racial stress and critical consciousness for Black adolescents. *Journal of Applied Developmental Psychology*, 70, 101184.

Ibrahim, D. A., & Godfrey, E. Understanding the developmental processes and contextual features of social justice arts education: An ecologically informed theory of change. *Manuscript in preparation*.

Ibrahim, D. A., Godfrey, E. B., Cappella, E., & Burson, E. (2021). The art of social justice: Examining arts programming as a context for critical consciousness development. *Journal of Youth and Adolescence*, 51(3), 409–427. https://doi.org/10.1007/s10964-021-01527-8.

Kahne, J., Middaugh, E., & Schutjer-Mance, K. (2005). *California Civic Index [Monograph]*. Carnegie Corporation and Annenberg Foundation.

Kenward, M. G., & Molenberghs, G. (1998). Likelihood based frequentist inference when data are missing at random. *Statistical Science*, 13, 236–247.

Kline, R. (2011). *Principles and practice of structural equation modeling*. The Guilford Press.

Lampert, N. (2011). A study of an after-school art programme and critical thinking. *International Journal of Education through Art*, 7(1), 55–67.

Malin, H., Han, H., & Liauw, I. (2017). Civic purpose in late adolescence: Factors that prevent decline in civic engagement after high school. *Developmental Psychology*, 53(7), 1384.

Mathews, C. J., Medina, M. A., Bañales, J. et al. (2020). Mapping the intersections of adolescents' ethnic-racial identity and critical consciousness. *Adolescent Research Review*, 5(4), 363–379.

Morrell, M. E. (2003). Survey and experimental evidence for a reliable and valid measure of internal political efficacy. *The Public Opinion Quarterly*, 67(4), 589–602.

Muthén, L. K. and Muthén, B. O. (1998–2017). *Mplus User's Guide*. 8th Ed. Muthén & Muthén.

National Academies of Sciences, Engineering, and Medicine. (2019). *The promise of adolescence: Realizing opportunity for all youth*. National Academies Press.

Ngo, B. (2017). Naming their world in a culturally responsive space: Experiences of Hmong adolescents in an after–school theatre program. *Journal of Adolescent Research*, 32(1), 37–63.

Osorio, S. L. (2018). Toward a humanizing pedagogy: Using Latinx children's literature with early childhood students. *Bilingual Research Journal*, 41, 5–22. http://dx.doi.org/10.1080/15235882.2018.1425165.

Pancer, S. M., Pratt, M., Hunsberger, B., & Alisat, S. (2007). Community and political involvement in adolescence: What distinguishes the activists from the uninvolved? *Journal of Community Psychology*, 35, 741–759. http://dx.doi.org/10.1002/jcop.20176.

Perkins, R., Mason-Bertrand, A., Tymoszuk, U. et al. (2021). Arts engagement supports social connectedness in adulthood: Findings from the HEartS Survey. *BMC Public Health*, 21(1), 1–15.

Petrovic, Gajo. (1965). "Man and Freedom," in *Socialist Humanism* (pp. 274–276), ed. E. Fromm. Doubleday.

Poteat, V. P., Godfrey, E. B., Brion-Meisels, G., & Calzo, J. P. (2020). Development of youth advocacy and sociopolitical efficacy as dimensions of critical consciousness within gender-sexuality alliances. *Developmental Psychology*, 56(6), 1207.

Rapa, L. J., Diemer, M. A., & Bañales, J. (2018). Critical action as a pathway to social mobility among marginalized youth. *Developmental Psychology*, 54(1), 127.

Rhoades, M. (2012). LGBTQ youth+ video artivism: Arts-based critical civic praxis. *Studies in Art Education*, 53(4), 317–329.

Rohd, M. (1998). *Theatre for community, conflict and dialogue: The hope is vital training manual.* Heinemann.

Roy, A. L., Raver, C. C., Masucci, M. D., & DeJoseph, M. (2019). "If they focus on giving us a chance in life we can actually do something in this world": Poverty, inequality, and youths' critical consciousness. *Developmental Psychology*, 55(3), 550.

Seider, S., Tamerat, J., Clark, S., & Soutter, M. (2017). Investigating adolescents' critical consciousness development through a character framework. *Journal of Youth and Adolescence*, 46(6), 1162–1178.

Shirazi, R. (2019). "Somewhere we can breathe": Diasporic counterspaces of education as sites of epistemological possibility. *Comparative Education Review*, 63(4), 480–501.

Simpkins, S. D., Riggs, N. R., Ngo, B., Vest Ettekal, A., & Okamoto, D. (2017). Designing culturally responsive organized after-school activities. *Journal of Adolescent Research*, 32(1), 11–36.

Squires, N., & Inlander, R. (1990). A Freirian-inspired video curriculum for at-risk high-school students. *English Journal*, 79(2), 49.

Thomas, R. J., & McFarland, D. A. (2010). Joining young, voting young: The effects of youth voluntary associations on early adult voting. CIRCLE Working Paper# 73. *Center for Information and Research on Civic Learning and Engagement (CIRCLE)*.

Tyson, C. A. (2002). "Get up off that thing": African American middle school students respond to literature to develop a framework for understanding social action. *Theory and Research in Social Education*, 30, 42–65. http://dx.doi.org/10.1080/00933104.2002.10473178.

Vasudevan, L., Stageman, D., Rodriguez, K., Fernandez, E., & Dattatreyan, E. G. (2010). Authoring new narratives with youth at the intersection of the arts and justice. Penn GSE. *Perspectives on Urban Education*, 7(1), 54–65.

Wernick, L. J., Kulick, A., & Woodford, M. R. (2014). How theater within a transformative organizing framework cultivates individual and collective empowerment among LGBTQQ youth. *Journal of Community Psychology*, 42(7), 838–853.

Watts, R. J., Diemer, M. A., & Voight, A. M. (2011). Critical consciousness: Current status and future directions. *New Directions for Child and Adolescent Development*, 2011(134), 43–57. https://doi.org/10.1002/cd.310.

Watts, R. J., Griffith, D. M., & Abdul-Adil, J. (1999). Sociopolitical development as an antidote for oppression – theory and action. *American Journal of Community Psychology*, 27(2), 255–271.

Watts, R., & Guessous, O. (2006). Sociopolitical development: The missing link in research and policy on adolescents. In S. Ginwright, P. Noguera, & J. Cammarota (Eds.), *Beyond resistance! Youth activism and community change: new democratic possibilities for practice and policy for America's youth* (pp. 59–80). Routledge.

Way, N., Hernández, M. G., Rogers, L. O., & Hughes, D. L. (2013). "I'm not going to become no rapper": Stereotypes as a context of ethnic and racial identity development. *Journal of Adolescent Research, 28*(4), 407–430.

Zeldin, S., Krauss, S. E., Collura, J., Lucchesi, M., & Sulaiman, A. H. (2014). Conceptualizing and measuring youth–adult partnership in community programs: A cross national study. *American Journal of Community Psychology, 54* (3–4), 337–347.

Zimmerman, M. A., Ramirez-Valles, J., & Maton, K. I. (1999). Resilience among urban African American male adolescents: A study of the protective effects of sociopolitical control on their mental health. *American Journal of Community Psychology, 27*(6), 733–751.

6

"Listening is Where Love Begins"
Advocacy for System-Impacted Youth as a Setting of Critical Consciousness Development

SHABNAM JAVDANI, ERIN B. GODFREY, CHRISTINA DUCAT,
AND SELIMA JUMARALI

The structural violence against Black, Latine, Asian, and Indigenous people, the visible rise of white supremacy, and the ongoing toll of gender-based violence have laid bare the extent to which structural racism, patriarchy, and systemic inequity shape US society (Barroso & Minkin, 2020; Bonilla-Silva, 1997). They have also contributed to a growing awareness of social injustice and structural oppression, particularly among more privileged youth. Amidst this wide-scale recognition, growing scholarly attention has leveraged critical consciousness (CC) development as a framework to understand how individuals reckon with and resist structural injustice and marginalization. Focusing on beliefs, motivations, and actions in response to social inequity, CC is typically conceptualized as three interrelated and mutually reinforcing components (Watts et al., 2011). *Critical reflection* refers to youths' critical analysis of current social realities and recognition of how social, economic, and political conditions limit access to opportunity and perpetuate systemic injustices. *Critical motivation* (also referred to as *sociopolitical efficacy*) encompasses the perceived importance of, and perceived ability to, act to change these conditions. *Critical action* is the extent to which individuals take individual and collective action to redress inequity.

CC is most often conceptualized as a process of moving from oppression to liberation. Indeed, it has been termed an "antidote to oppression" (Watts et al., 1999) due to its potential to empower marginalized people to navigate and challenge systemic inequity (Freire, 1970, 1973; Watts et al., 2011). Because of this, and the pervasiveness of racism in shaping structural inequity in the United States, much research to date focuses on the CC development of Black and Latine youth (Heberle et al., 2020). However, scholars and practitioners highlight the need to better understand and promote CC among people facing various forms of oppression, as well as those experiencing relatively more structural privilege and interlocking experiences of privilege and marginalization (Godfrey & Burson, 2018). Systems of oppression cannot be fully dismantled until people from all backgrounds recognize structural inequity, feel motivated and efficacious to change it, and take action to challenge and transform it.

Given their demographic composition and their status as purveyors of educational and social privilege, larger public and private universities and colleges are potentially powerful sites for promoting CC among more privileged youth through pedagogical programs and approaches such as service learning. They typically house large sustained student bodies who are often (though not always) attending during a developmental window when responsibilities are relatively light and openness to experience and innovation peaks (e.g., Roberts & DelVecchio, 2000). Universities and colleges also employ faculty and educational workforces who have the privilege of engaging with social issues through critical lenses and who are charged with creating intellectual communities. Moreover, many institutions espouse a mission to serve the public interest and engage in public-facing, community-relevant work. That these institutions remain a relatively untapped setting for the implementation and interrogation of CC-relevant work *with respect to their own constituents* is surprising yet opportune. Undergraduate students in particular represent an untapped collective that can more readily be drawn upon to "learn by doing" through consciousness-raising, community-engaged experiences like those provided through service learning. This would support the public interest aspirations of many university and college settings while cultivating students' skills in critically analyzing and resisting the status quo power dynamics that shape their social and political worlds.

One concrete way in which universities have incorporated this vision of public service and learning into their curricula is through formal and informal service learning. Indeed, the concept of service learning has deep roots in many disciplines, and a robust body of scholarship points to its many benefits for high school and university students' academic, vocational, moral, and leadership development (e.g., Astin et al., 2000). Traditional service learning is typically defined as experientially grounded educational approaches that provide a service to the community while simultaneously cultivating skills through reflection and action for students (e.g., Center for Community Engaged Learning, 2021). We argue that there is a clear and important difference between this type of service learning and *critical service learning* (Butin, 2015; Latta et al., 2018; Mitchell, 2008). We distinguish critical service learning as a specific type of experiential approach that attends to structural inequity and issues of power, privilege, and marginalization. In contrast to traditional service learning, it explicitly and deliberately seeks to redistribute power and resources in ways that redress and challenge inequity and raise CC among its participants. This distinction between critical service learning and traditional service learning becomes all the more important when the service learning experience involves working with historically marginalized communities experiencing racism, sexism, and economic and educational precarity (e.g., Davis et al., 2022). Without a critical approach, service-learning approaches on behalf of these communities could inadvertently reify harmful power inequities and victim-blaming narratives.

This chapter presents a critical service learning approach, the Resilience, Opportunity, Safety, Education, and Strength (ROSES) program. ROSES is an advocacy-based intervention in which undergraduate students in a university setting work in partnership with a minoritized girl[1] who is impacted by the juvenile legal and/or child welfare system. As such, the population served by ROSES faces myriad intersecting structural oppressions stemming from racial, ethnic, gender, and economic inequities produced by social subjugation that are reified by the ineffective response of systems of surveillance (Chesney-Lind & Shelden, 2013; Granski, Javdani, Anderson, & Caires, 2020; Javdani et al., 2011a). We examine how participating as an advocate in ROSES influences undergraduate students' skill and CC development across a myriad of indicators of critical reflection, critical motivation, and critical action.

A central goal of service learning is to promote reflection and action, thus service learning in general, and critical service learning in particular, are natural bedfellows for the promotion of CC (Barrera et al., 2017; Flanagan & Faison, 2001; Rondini, 2015). Although service-learning approaches have been applied to juvenile legal and child welfare system-impacted communities (Holsinger, 2008, 2012; Holsinger & Ayers, 2004; Tilton, 2013), this work has not been intentionally designed, described, or interrogated through a CC lens. This lens is imperative given the structural and power disparities between universities and system-impacted communities and the historic and ongoing burdens and harms placed on marginalized communities in the name of education and scholarship (e.g., Javorka, 2020). Moreover, scholarship on CC has been relatively silent on juvenile legal or child welfare system-impacted communities and young people (see Singh et al., 2021 for a notable exception), despite a conceptual and epistemic stance that seeks to interrogate and disrupt oppressive social forces and power dynamics. Thus, the time is ripe to understand how critical service learning approaches, such as the advocacy-based ROSES program, can promote CC among relatively more privileged undergraduate students and serve as an important stepping stone to foster allyship to address social injustice – and, ultimately, an important facilitator of critical action to promote equity and social justice.

---

[1] We use the term "girl" to refer to youth placed on the girls' side of the juvenile legal and child welfare systems, which include youth who are cisgender, gender nonconforming, nonbinary and transgender, and we recognize the diversity of experiences across the gender continuum.

ROSES: Advocacy as Critical Consciousness-Promoting Critical Service Learning

Community-based advocacy programs such as ROSES were developed out of community partnerships between universities and marginalized populations, including survivors of violence, with the primary goal of promoting access to self-determined resources (Davidson & Rapp, 1976; Sullivan & Bybee, 1999; Sullivan, Bybee & Allen, 2022), those subject to racial and gender inequity, and those contending with entrapment in carceral systems (Javdani, 2021; Javdani & Allen, 2016). These programs target the social context of marginalized populations by identifying the self-determined needs of community members and advocating with them, and on their behalf, to obtain needed and desired resources. ROSES employs a relationship-based approach to change that pairs system-involved girls with intensively trained paraprofessional student advocates who build nonjudgmental, emotionally supportive relationships, identify and promote girls' strengths, and mobilize resources to enhance these strengths. ROSES advocates work one-to-one with, or on behalf of, girls for 10 hours per week for 12 intensive intervention weeks (for a total of 120 hours) and tailors the intervention process to meet the unique needs of each girl. ROSES explicitly targets girls' contexts, including informal (e.g., peer, family) and formal (e.g., school, juvenile justice system) environments. ROSES advocates receive extensive training on gender and race equity, structural marginalization, and intersectionality, and employ trauma-informed principles of care.

The ROSES program constitutes a critical service learning opportunity for participants. Paraprofessional student advocates are advanced university students receiving internship or course credit. Prospective advocates complete an application and interview process and are selected based on their experience and capacity to work with high-risk youth, navigate the local area, and devote ten hours per week to the intervention for a full academic year. Advocates complete forty hours of training over the course of one month prior to providing the advocacy intervention. Training comprises about four all-day in-person sessions, as well as asynchronous didactic content. Advocates receive extensive training on the unique needs of girls involved in the legal system, correlates of girls' disruptive behavior and risk for legal system involvement, the historical and sociocultural context of girls' pathways from home, and the multilayered motivations for girls' behavior (e.g., understanding girls' running away from home as potentially motivated by experience of abuse in the home; Javdani et al., 2011b). They also receive training on adolescent development, crisis response skills, safety and mandatory reporting, and empathy and active listening skills (Javdani & Allen, 2016; Sullivan, 2003). Training is administered via didactics, small group discussions, and role plays, all of which are led by supervisors, including a PhD-level faculty director and supervisors who were former advocates. Following best practice in skill acquisition (Sullivan et al., 1992), advocates are required to demonstrate mastery of the principles of advocacy as assessed by supervisors' observation of skills (e.g., active listening, nonjudgmental stance), oral presentations evaluated by peers and supervisors, quizzes on each content area, and live assessments of advocacy skills during training. During each intervention cycle, advocates receive at least two hours of weekly direct supervision on their interaction with clients using a manualized supervision protocol. Advocates present the prior week's intervention goals, achievements, and barriers, and work with supervisors and fellow advocates to determine a plan to navigate challenges and outline goals for the next intervention week.

When it is viewed superficially – or implemented without fidelity to its underlying values orientation – the advocacy approach might be confused with traditional casework or referral-based clinical approaches. However, there are several key aspects of ROSES that differentiate it from these more traditional approaches and position it as a potential site for CC development. Key among these is that its primary goal is to promote a radical shift away from changing the client to changing their context. This necessitates embracing a paradigm shift that, we hypothesize, fosters advocates' own attunement to social power (aligned with critical reflection), motivates them to act in equity-promoting ways (aligned with critical motivation), and creates concrete opportunities for critical action. We detail the specific strategies used throughout advocate training, intervention, and supervision to create this fundamental paradigm shift and, we propose, transform advocates' orientation to social inequity. We first describe the overarching framework of care incorporated across the ROSES program. We then organize this description by each CC component, but we acknowledge that each strategy may influence other components of CC as well. We also hypothesize that, as the components themselves mutually reinforce each other, the experience of training, advocacy intervention, and supervision will result in a mutually reinforcing, virtuous cycle of CC development.

ROSES' Framework of Care Much of the training, advocacy implementation, and supervision work that advocates undertake is likely to influence the views they hold about social inequity, their understanding of the historical, social, and economic root forces that create and sustain inequity, and their motivation and behaviors to challenge and dismantle it. Although advocates self-select into the program from a university pool, and therefore arguably hold a more critically conscious stance to start, we hypothesize that the training and advocacy experience serve to concretize, deepen, and personalize their CC. Undergirding the ROSES approach is the cognitive shift advocates must make from "helping" to "advocacy." This involves building a transformed foundation rooted in a rights-based approach and troubling the foundations of traditional direct service work, which can rest on white savior and medical model frameworks that reinforce individual blame attributions of structural disparities and disease and deficit-based paradigms of helping (Dunst & Trivette, 1996; Langhout, 2015). During training, advocates are welcomed for their desire to help, while simultaneously invited to question that desire and to problematize the status quo assumptions dictating "helping." Through dialogue, discussion, and modeling, advocates are invited to question assumptions associated with the western medical models of care, which communicates that the person receiving the help is not the expert (i.e., the doctor is), is expected to adapt to the provider's schedule (i.e., not their own), to comply or have services terminated, and to locate the problem (and its causes) within the individual in need of help and not the context or structure they inhabit. When applied to social services and supports, advocates can begin to see how typical programs easily become hierarchical and compliance focused, and social causes and contextual solutions overlooked and underaddressed. Inverting typical models of helping in this way enables advocates to see white supremacy in action, understand the deep-seated and insidious ways our society places blame on marginalized individuals for structural and systemic inequity, and define social problems – and the solutions for them – through a structural lens (e.g., Caplan & Nelson, 1973). It also opens up new pathways and opportunities for students to challenge this status quo and provides them with a concrete vision for what a liberatory counterspace looks like, building their critical motivation and action more broadly.

Critical Reflection With this in view, a central goal of advocate training and supervision is to promote a more critical and nuanced understanding of power and privilege at societal and interpersonal levels – understanding that is clearly linked to critical reflection, when viewed through the CC framework. In training, advocates spend time reading about and discussing structural power and positionality, including how racism, sexism, and other intersecting forces of marginalization structure lived experience in the United States broadly and with regard to the juvenile legal system. Learning from the voices of impacted girls and women are prioritized throughout this endeavor. In addition, during training, advocacy supervisors mirror and model how to attend to and acknowledge multiple dimensions of power within interpersonal and collective spaces through specific exercises and skill training.[2]

---

[2] One training exercise involves a supervisor intentionally arriving at a training session several minutes late. Once there, they engage the group of advocates in a dialogue around who gets to be late, at what cost, and who stands to gain and lose from this action. Experiencing this difference in relative social power in vivo, advocates readily identify the ways in which it is more consequential for any individual advocate trainee to be just as late as their supervisor was, due to relative differences in the power they hold within the advocacy program alone. This helps advocates understand their relative positions of power with respect to their future girl clients, and to simultaneously validate the relative and contextual nature of social power itself.

Advocacy also conceptualizes the construct of "needs" with an intentional lens of equity and an awareness that models of helping often impose needs on oppressed communities. Young people "receiving" advocacy are centered as the experts on their own needs, how they define those needs, and whether and how they prioritize them. The right of young people to change their minds and shift their goals is also prioritized. Alongside this self-determination, community-level needs and resources are gathered to shift the gaze away from "fixing" the girl and toward changing her context. This conceptualization of needs represents a critical shift that, we argue, helps enhance advocates' critical reflection by concretizing their understanding of structural power and marginalization and learning how to "practice what they preach."

These new perspectives are reinforced during supervision of intervention cycles, when advocates inevitably run into values conflicts, emphasize individual over structural attributions for girls' feelings and actions, more readily identify individual-level (over contextual or systems-level) targets of change, and have trouble fully unpacking the needs and desires of girls (over that of system actors or adults in girls' lives). To overcome these challenges and support a liberatory vision among advocates, supervisors collectively unpack inherent assumptions around dominant social problem definitions (e.g., double standards around girls' sexuality) and identify creative ways that advocates can engage girls to unpack their own imaginations about their goals (e.g., creating vision boards). They also provide permission and encouragement for advocates to follow girls' leads regarding their needs while simultaneously planning to mitigate any negative consequences of doing so (e.g., creating plans for girls to avoid school when they do not feel safe while simultaneously communicating this plan to school stakeholders and making arrangements for girls to complete and submit schoolwork).

Similarly, as advocates work with young people during the intervention and supervision experience, advocacy supervisors continue to recast accountability, compliance, and program success as the responsibility of the program and not the responsibility of the young person enrolled in it. In this way, supervisors take ownership of the challenges of each advocacy case, identify structural solutions to meeting these challenges, and intentionally name strengths about each advocate's approach to consistently orient them toward success. These supervision strategies create a parallel process whereby advocates personally experience what it feels like and looks like to have social power shifted: their supervisors are accountable to them, their own strengths are highlighted, and their experiences as advocates are validated. This, in turn, facilitates advocates' capacity and motivation to mirror this process with their own clients. We believe this experience also likely enhances advocates' critical reflection in that it models attention to structural power, privilege, and accountability in every facet of the advocacy experience and creates a counterspace through which the typical oppressive forces structuring our experiences can be more readily seen and interrogated.

Critical Motivation The training and advocacy process also, we suspect, leads to changes in advocate's motivation to address social inequity and their feelings of efficacy to do so. That is, we expect critical motivation to be enhanced within advocates as a result of their participation in the ROSES program. Throughout training and supervision, humanization and compassion are viewed as underlying precursors to learn skills and unlearn habits to support an intentional and unfamiliar way of being with others. Advocates learn skills that enable them to sit with (instead of dismiss) pain, tolerate (instead of change) distress, and surface the emotional roots of experiences. This is engaged through a number of strategies, including concrete skills building (e.g., reflecting, listening, and identifying emotions), as well as through supervisors' modeling of radical acceptance skills in order to invite and expect emotions and reduce the urge to gloss over pain (Linehan, 2014; Robins et al., 2004). Thus, advocates are provided with concrete ways to embrace, rather than push away, the pain associated with acknowledging social inequity and to empathize with others in different positions of social power. We argue that this combination of collective distress tolerance and skill-building enhances critical motivation and supports advocates' perceived efficacy to act against inequity. These skills are practiced and modeled throughout the training and supervision process. The goal is again to create a parallel process so that advocates feel motivated and able to engage in humanizing conversations with their own clients and can expect this exact type of humanizing space cultivated for them in supervision and training. In this way, supervision and training model counterspaces for advocates, which are settings that are built to "hold" and name adaptive responses to oppression (Case & Hunter, 2012). Thus, ROSES supervision and training is likely to deepen advocates' critical motivation and provide them with concrete interpersonal skills to take action against inequity.

Advocates' critical motivation and efficacy is further supported through specific training on how to identify and leverage community resources in support of girls' self-determined goals and advocate on their behalf. Training provides advocates with concrete and effective strategies to advocate for girls' rights and needs within the juvenile legal system (e.g., providing character references, showing up to girls' court hearings, positioning ROSES – rather than law enforcement – as the first call made in a crisis involving the girl). In supervision, supervisors and fellow advocates rally around each advocate to provide concrete strategies for dealing with other issues that arise during advocacy, such as securing needed resources for a client (e.g., emergency housing) and disrupting oppressive pathways (e.g., fighting exclusionary school disciplinary practices). These concrete strategies to navigate, and advocate for, girls within oppressive systems allow advocates to learn how to exercise social power to redress inequity and builds their motivation and efficacy to do so through modeling, strengths validation, role play, and skill-building through the mastery model. Advocates not only *want* to make change, they are armed with specific tools and concrete strategies to do so, which builds their feelings of efficacy and capability to make change as well. Structurally, it is worth mentioning that critical service learning models such as ROSES might further support students' extrinsic motivation by providing university capital (e.g., giving course credits, fulfilling internship requirements).

Critical Action Not only are advocates trained in identifying and enacting concrete strategies to advocate for girls, but the advocacy intervention experience itself embeds opportunities to engage in these kinds of specific actions within a structural values framework (i.e., to change the context, not the girl) and to interrogate these actions with attention to both the intended and unintended social consequences. Indeed, the advocacy intervention itself is a form of critical action that disrupts oppressive structures. Advocates have the opportunity to act in concrete ways that fight back against the oppressive dynamics they learn about and discuss in training, and they know they will be asked to use this knowledge in service of specific action. We believe this guided experience of engaging in action, and seeing firsthand the impact it has on a real person, will foster more critical action from advocates in other spheres of their life as well. For example, the advocacy skills developed through the ROSES program may provide advocates with the capacity to identify gatekeepers that can influence whether settings and systems deploy resources when requested, brainstorm multiple solutions to challenging social problems and select a concrete course of action based on the youth-determined pros and cons of each, monitor deployed actions actively and deploy alternative strategies if the original ones were ineffective, and leverage and build social capital in support of youth needs (e.g., collecting many positive letters of reference to present to a family court judge). These skills may very well generalize in ways that advocates learn how to pursue and engage in critical action after advocacy ends. We also suspect that engaging in a concrete opportunity for critical action – the advocacy intervention itself – creates a positive feedback loop that begets more action, especially because the training, supports, and supervision provided through ROSES mean that most advocacy cycles are successful in creating meaningful change for girls. Experiencing a successful critical action opportunity such as this likely promotes more engagement in action over the long term.

Current Study

Using ROSES as an example, our primary aim in this chapter is to interrogate whether and to what degree undergraduate students enrolled in a large private university demonstrate shifts in their CC over the course of their engagement in a critical service learning opportunity. We aim to understand how critical service learning programs can serve to promote CC in a largely untapped setting (i.e., universities), for an untapped workforce (i.e., university students), and an undertreated, marginalized population (i.e., system-impacted girls). We expect advocates to enter ROSES advocacy with relatively high levels of critical reflection and critical motivation given their self-selection into this experience. However, we also expect ROSES training, intervention, and supervision experiences to increase this critical reflection and motivation, and to promote critical action due to the strategies and processes described herein. Using survey data from advocates, we examine changes in multiple measures of CC in two phases: from pretraining to posttraining, and from pretraining to postadvocacy. Exploring changes across these two phases allows us to further unpack how aspects of the ROSES training, intervention, and supervision process are associated with different components of CC.

METHOD

Data for our study come from exploratory survey data collection on advocate experiences embedded within a randomized control trial (RCT) of the efficacy of the ROSES intervention. The trial was conducted through a large private university in a large northeastern city from 2016 to 2020. Six full training cycles were provided to six cohorts of advocates; 106 students were trained as advocates, and of those, 99 demonstrated sufficient mastery of the advocacy model in training to participate in advocacy delivery and supervision. Upon completion of training, advocates were assigned to work on behalf of a single adolescent girl. Over the course of this time, 253 girls were enrolled in the larger ROSES RCT, 130 of whom were randomly assigned to work with a ROSES advocate. ROSES youth were referred directly from a large urban jurisdiction's juvenile legal and child welfare system (approximately 70%), with a smaller percentage referred directly from court (10%) or from girls' and families themselves (10%). Girls ranged in age from 11 to 18 years ($M = 14.5$; $SD = 1.6$) The majority of girls self-identified as Black, Hispanic, or Latina/x ($n = 195$; 88.6%), and 21% ($n = 47$) of girls reported lesbian, gay, bisexual, transgender, and/or gender-expansive identities. Almost half of girls' families reported an annual family income of $15,000 or less ($n = 107$; 47%).

   In the exploratory data collection, advocates were asked to complete a survey containing information about advocate demographics, characteristics, and attitudes prior to starting ROSES training (pretraining survey).

Advocates completed this survey again roughly two weeks later upon completion of ROSES training (posttraining survey) and again three to four months later, after completing their first full cycle of advocacy and supervision with a system-impacted girl (postadvocacy survey). In total, 88 (88.9%) advocates completed pretraining surveys, 50 (50.1%) completed posttraining surveys, and 45 (45.5%) completed postadvocacy surveys. Forty-two (47.7%) advocates completed both pretraining and postadvocacy surveys, among whom 36 (85.7%) also completed posttraining surveys. These represent the analytic sample for each phase examined. Although the sample sizes are different across the two windows (pretraining to posttraining and pretraining to postadvocacy), the samples are entirely overlapping and there are no observed demographic differences between samples. Due to the small sample size and exploratory nature of this data, we consider all findings preliminary and suggestive. Figure 6.1 details a typical timeline of training, advocacy, and data collection.

All advocates were advanced undergraduate students enrolled in courses at a private university and recruited through multiple departments and schools within the university, particularly psychology, children and adolescent health studies, public health, and social work. Applicants were required to submit a cover letter and résumé, and complete an in-depth applicant screening and interview process, before being offered acceptance. They committed to volunteering with the program for a minimum of one academic year. They received no monetary compensation for their time, but received course credit or fulfilled applied research requirements. At baseline, advocates were between the ages of 18 and 25 ($M = 20.5$; $SD = 1.2$) and all but one reported a female gender identity. Advocates were predominantly Black, Middle Eastern/North African, Asian, Multiracial, Latinx, or Indigenous ($n = 55$; 60.4%) and 32.2% ($n = 28$) self-reported lesbian, gay, bisexual, transgender, and/or gender-expansive identities. Most advocates were born in the United States ($n = 74$; 82.2%) and the majority self-reported their socioeconomic status as "Middle Class" or "Upper Class" ($n = 48$; 80.0%). On average, advocates provided 153 hours ($SD = 95$) of advocacy addressing roughly 68 youth-determined goals (range 3–137) during each ROSES intervention.

FIGURE 6.1 Timeline of training, advocacy, and advocate data collection.

Measures

At each survey point (pretraining, posttraining, and postadvocacy), we collected information on advocates' interpersonal skills that we consider fundamental to engaging in advocacy work and that have been hypothesized to underlie the development of CC (see also Ibrahim et al., 2022; Ibrahim & Godfrey, in prep; Ibrahim et al., Chapter 5 [this volume]; Rapa et al., in press). We then administered a broad array of indicators of critical reflection, critical motivation, and critical action, including some indicators from validated measures of CC and others that have been used as proxy measures of CC in scholarship (see Rapa et al., in press). This approach was appropriate for our exploratory aims in that it allowed us to examine potential change across a variety of subdimensions and varying conceptualizations of critical reflection, motivation, and action. All measures are presented in Table 6.1 for ease of reference.

Interpersonal Skills Three scales were used to capture critical interpersonal skills instrumental to the effective delivery of advocacy and core to CC development. Two subscales from the Interpersonal Reactivity Index (Davis, 1983) assessed advocates' emotional capacity (7 items; e.g., "When I see someone being taken advantage of, I feel kind of protective toward them"; α = 0.69) and perspective taking (7 items; e.g., "When I am upset at someone, I usually try to put myself in their shoes for a while"; α = 0.80; both measured on a 5-point scale from "doesn't describe me well" to "describes me very well"). We also measured advocates' tendency to prioritize youth-centered versus provider (i.e., advocate-focused) interventions (adapted from Javdani, 2013; 9 items, 5-point scale from "strongly disagree" to "strongly agree"; e.g., "When working with a client, the professional helper or service provider should be responsible for setting goals for the client to achieve"; α = 0.71).

Critical Reflection We assessed advocates' critical reflection on social inequity through nine measures tapping into three aspects of critical reflection: awareness of inequity, attributions for social problems, and system-justifying worldviews.

    Awareness of Inequity. Awareness of inequity was assessed using four scales. First, we administered slightly reworded versions of the two critical reflection subscales from the Critical Consciousness Scale (CCS; Diemer et al., 2017): perceived inequality, assessing general awareness of inequality for racial/ethnic, gender, and class groups (8 items; α = 0.92; e.g., "People of color have fewer chances to get good jobs") and egalitarianism, assessing beliefs that groups should be equal in our society (5 items; α = 0.81; e.g., "Group equality should be our ideal"; both measured on a 6-point scale from "strongly disagree" to "strongly agree"). We then also measured advocates' perceptions of the prevalence of racism in today's society using the Modern

TABLE 6.1 List of measures and key properties, organized by domain

# of Items	Scale Name and (Source)	Sample Item	Cronbach's Alpha (α)
Interpersonal Skills			
Emotional capacity	7 Interpersonal Reactivity Index (Davis, 1983)	"When I see someone being taken advantage of, I feel kind of protective toward them"	α = 0.69
Perspective taking	7 Interpersonal Reactivity Index (Davis, 1983)	"When I am upset at someone, I usually try to put myself in their shoes for a while"	α = 0.80
Advocate (vs. youth) centered	9 Youth-Centered Orientation to Service (Javdani, 2013)	"When working with a client, the professional helper or service provider should be responsible for setting goals for the client to achieve" (reverse)	α = 0.80
Critical Reflection			
Perceived inequality	8 Critical Consciousness Scale (slightly reworded, Diemer et al., 2017)	"People of color have fewer chances to get good jobs"	α = 0.92
Egalitarianism	5 Critical Consciousness Scale (slightly reworded, Diemer et al., 2017)	"Group equality should be our ideal"	α = 0.81
Modern racism	7 Modern Racism Scale (McConahay, 1986)	"Blacks are getting too demanding in their push for equal rights"	α = 0.70
Critical understanding of poverty	6 Perceptions of Poverty Scale (adapted from Delavega et al., 2017)	"Poverty is created by people in power"	α = 0.71
Victim-blaming attributions	15 Victim Blaming Scale (slightly modified from Johnson et al., 2002)	"People who are negatively affected by social problems lack ability" (reverse)	α = 0.77
Society-blaming attributions	22 Society Blaming Scale (Johnson et al., 2002)	"Agencies are quick to shift priorities in order to help people"	α = 0.75

TABLE 6.1 *(Cont.)*

# of Items	Scale Name and (Source)	Sample Item	Cronbach's Alpha (α)
Girl-blaming attributions 17	Girls and the System Scale (adapted for this study, based on Javdani, 2013)	"Better individual choices would help girls stay out of trouble with the system"	α = 0.80
System justification 6	System Justification Scale (forward coded items, slightly adapted from Kay & Jost, 2003)	"In general, you find society or 'the world' to be fair"	α = 0.86
Meritocratic ideology 8	The Meritocracy Ideology Scale (McCoy et al., 2013)	"If people work hard, they almost always get what they want"	α = 0.84

Racism Scale (McConahay, 1986; 7 items; α = 0.70; e.g., "Blacks are getting too demanding in their push for equal rights"; measured on a 7-point scale from "strongly agree" to "strongly disagree") and the extent to which poverty is created by social systems and related to racism and sexism using the Perceptions of Poverty Scale (created for this study, based on Delavega et al., 2017; 6 items, α = 0.71; e.g., "Poverty is created by people in power"; measured on a 5-point scale from "strongly disagree" to "strongly agree").

Attributions for Social Problems. We used three scales to assess advocate's structural (vs. individual) attributions for social problems, assuming more structural attributions represent higher critical reflection (e.g., Godfrey & Wolf, 2016). First, we administered a slightly modified version of the Victim Blaming Scale (Johnson et al., 2002) measuring individual vs. structural attributions about the causes of social problems (15 items; α = 0.77; 5-point scale from "strongly disagree" to "strongly agree"; e.g., "People who are negatively affected by social problems lack ability" (reverse-coded)). Second, we administered a modified version of the Society Blaming Scale (Johnson et al., 2002), which assesses perceptions of the role social institutions and services play in redressing or perpetuating social problems (22 items; α = 0.75; e.g., "Agencies are quick to shift priorities in order to help people"; measured on a 5-point scale from "strongly disagree" to "strongly agree"). Third, we included the Girls and the System Scale (adapted for this study, based on Javdani, 2013), which assessed individual (vs. structural) attributions for the causes of system involvement for girls in particular (17 items; α = 0.80; e.g., "Better individual choices would help girls stay out of trouble with the system"; measured on a 4-point scale from "strongly disagree" to "strongly agree").

System-Justifying Worldviews. Two scales were used to assess system-justifying worldviews. The first was a lightly adapted version (Sichel et al., 2022) of the System Justification Scale (Kay & Jost, 2003) tapping into perceptions of US society as fair and just (6 items; α = 0.86; e.g., "In general, you find society or "the world" to be fair"; measured on a 7-point scale from "strongly disagree" to "strongly agree"). Second, we administered the Meritocracy Ideology Scale (McCoy et al., 2013), which assesses beliefs that hard work inevitably leads to success (8 items; α = 0.84; e.g., "If people work hard, they almost always get what they want"; measured on a 6-point scale from "strongly disagree" to "strongly agree"). Rejecting these ideologies places blame on systems rather than individuals for inequality, representing greater critical reflection (e.g., Godfrey et al., 2019).

Critical Motivation Critical motivation and efficacy were assessed via five measures tapping into the importance advocates placed on taking action to address inequity, and their perceived ability to take such action. First, a modified version of the Social Attitudes Scale (Leung et al., 2006) was used to measure the importance advocates placed on working to address inequities (17 items; α = 0.84; e.g., "I am responsible for doing something about improving the community"; measured on a 9-point scale from "no confidence at all" to "complete confidence"). Second, items from the Social Issues Questionnaire (Miller et al., 2009) tapped into advocate's perceived confidence to address inequity (e.g., 20 items; α = 0.95; e.g., "how much confidence do you have in your ability to actively support needs of marginalized social groups?"; measured on a 9-point scale from "no confidence at all" to "complete confidence"). Third, the Commitment to Activism scale (Astin et al., 2000) assessed how much advocates prioritized doing social justice work (4 items; α = 0.75; e.g., "It is important to me to participate in advocacy or political action groups"; measured on a 5-point scale from "strongly disagree" to "strongly agree"). Finally, we administered two subscales of the Social Justice Scale (Torres-Harding et al., 2012): the attitudes subscale measured the importance of working with others to address inequity (11 items; α = 0.92; e.g., "I believe that it is important to talk to others about societal systems of power, privilege, and oppression.") and the perceived behavioral control subscale measured feelings of efficacy to promote equity (5 items; α = 0.77; e.g., "If I choose to do so, I am capable of influencing others to promote fairness and equality"; both measured on a 7-point scale from "strongly disagree" to "strongly agree").

Critical Action Critical action was assessed using three measures. First, we used the behavioral intentions subscale of the Social Justice Scale (Torres-Harding et al., 2012) to tap into advocates' willingness to engage in action in the future (4 items; α = 0.90; e.g., "In the future, I intend to engage in activities that will promote social justice"; measured on a 7-point scale from "strongly disagree" to "strongly agree"). Second, we administered an adaptation of the Pursuit of Social Action Scale (Krings et al., 2020) asking advocates to share how often they have done specific actions in pursuit of social change (8 items; $\alpha = 0.86$; e.g., "Have you attended demonstrations, protests, or rallies in pursuit of social action?"; measured on a 9-point scale from "not at all" to "quite extremely"). Finally, we used a subset of items from the Youth Inventory of Involvement (Pancer et al., 2007) to assess how often advocates engaged in critical actions in their communities, such as protesting, contacting public officials, and helping community members in need (11 items; $\alpha = 0.79$; e.g., "Contacted a public official by phone or mail to tell him/her how you felt about a particular issue"; measured on a 5-point scale from "you never did this" to "you did this a lot").

Implementation Characteristics We also utilized implementation data about each advocacy cycle taken from weekly reports made by advocates to their supervisor. From these reports, we calculated two important characteristics about the advocacy intervention: the total number of hours each advocate spent engaging in advocacy directly with and on behalf of their clients, and the average number of the client's self-determined goals the pair worked on each week. These implementation characteristics were used to examine whether and how advocacy intervention characteristics influenced changes in advocate's skills and CC following the implementation of advocacy.

RESULTS AND DISCUSSION

What Were Advocates' Interpersonal and Critical Consciousness Skills Prior to ROSES?

As a first step toward understanding how ROSES might be associated with CC outcomes among advocates, we examined advocates' reports of their interpersonal skills and CC prior to completing ROSES training or engaging in advocacy and supervision.

As shown in Table 6.2, even prior to training, advocates endorsed high interpersonal skills and high CC. They reported a high awareness of inequity across a range of measures, endorsed structural attributions for social problems, and had relatively low system-justifying ideologies. Advocates also reported high motivation and efficacy to address social inequity, high intentions to take critical action, and higher levels of actual action taken. Indicators in each domain were generally moderately to strongly correlated with each other (significant $|rs|$ ranged from 0.25 to 0.69), indicating that they are tapping into related but distinct aspects of each domain. Thus, as might be expected, undergraduate students who applied for and were selected to join ROSES advocacy already reported CC levels at levels higher than scale midpoints across a wide range of indicators and domains. However, an important

TABLE 6.2 Descriptive statistics and bivariate correlations for key study variables among advocates, pretraining (N = 88)

	Scale Range	Mean	SD	Bivariate Correlations																		
				1	2	3	4	5	6	7	8	9	10	11	12	13	14	15	16	17	18	19
Interpersonal Skills																						
1. Emotional capacity	1–5	4.55	0.43	–																		
2. Perspective taking	1–5	4.23	0.59	0.46**	–																		
3. Advocate- (vs. youth-) centered approach	1–5	2.79	0.52	–0.06	0.09	–																	
Critical Reflection				1	2	3	4	5	6	7	8	9	10	11	12	13	14	15	16	17	18	19
4. Perceived inequality	1–6	5.27	0.63	0.25*	0.19	–0.09	–															
5. Egalitarianism	1–6	5.66	0.59	0.09	0.07	–0.03	0.19	–														
6. Modern racism	1–7	1.30	0.42	–0.29*	–0.18	0.23	–0.58**	–0.28*	–													
7. Critical understanding of poverty	1–5	4.18	0.46	0.26*	0.26*	–0.33**	0.45**	0.15	–0.29*	–												
8. Victim-blaming attributions	1–5	2.17	0.46	–0.30**	–0.25*	0.22*	–0.48**	–0.24*	0.48**	–0.55**	–											
9. Society-blaming attributions	1–5	3.76	0.35	0.26*	0.35**	–0.42**	0.42**	0.14	–0.39**	0.43**	–0.45**	–										
10. Girl-blaming attributions	1–4	1.89	0.33	–0.29**	–0.28**	0.40**	–0.50**	–0.25*	0.46**	–0.45**	0.64**	–0.57**	–									
11. System justification	1–7	2.47	1.04	–0.19	–0.17	0.20	–0.43**	–0.28*	0.39**	–0.37**	0.53**	–0.52**	0.53**	–								
12. Meritocratic ideology	1–6	5.24	0.66	–0.35**	–0.41**	0.37**	–0.65**	–0.22	0.59**	–0.54**	0.67**	–0.65**	0.67**	0.70**	–							

TABLE 6.2 (*Cont.*)

	Scale Range	Mean	SD	Bivariate Correlations																		
				1	2	3	4	5	6	7	8	9	10	11	12	13	14	15	16	17	18	19
Critical Motivation																						
13. Importance of addressing inequity	1–5	4.23	0.37	0.48**	0.32**	−0.14	0.34**	0.24*	−0.38**	0.38**	−0.35**	0.43**	−0.40**	−0.29**	−0.49**	–						
14. Confidence in addressing inequity	1–9	7.85	1.30	0.37**	0.33**	−0.13	0.11	0.07	−0.07	0.01	−0.24*	0.05	−0.20	−0.27**	−0.10	0.31**	–					
15. Commitment to activism	1–5	4.28	0.55	0.12	0.13	0.02	0.15	−0.03	−0.06	0.07	−0.18	0.30**	−0.22*	−0.20	−0.15	0.51**	0.15	–				
16. Importance of working with others to address inequity	1–7	6.87	0.28	0.35**	0.15	−0.12	0.39**	0.18	−0.56**	0.24	−0.40**	0.29**	−0.32**	−0.39**	−0.54**	0.32**	0.22*	0.14	–			
17. Perceived control in addressing inequity	1–7	6.26	0.62	0.31**	0.27**	−0.15	0.24*	0.30**	−0.18	0.09	−0.30**	0.29**	−0.39**	−0.42**	−0.37**	0.45**	0.32**	0.31**	0.43**	–		
Critical Action																						
18. Behavioral intentions	1–7	6.71	0.45	0.32**	0.13	−0.19	0.40**	0.32**	−0.35**	0.03	−0.35**	0.33**	−0.28**	−0.43**	−0.43**	0.41**	0.15	0.34**	0.48**	0.55**	–	
19. Pursuit of social action	1–5	3.38	1.00	−0.01	−0.02	−0.08	0.22*	−0.01	−0.02	0.22	−0.15	0.24*	−0.27**	−0.34**	−0.29*	0.21*	0.02	0.34**	0.09	0.32**	0.24*	–
20. Engagement in critical action	1–6	2.99	0.64	0.38**	0.28*	−0.20	0.14	0.01	−0.07	0.23	−0.19	0.35**	−0.28*	−0.20	−0.21	0.21	0.32**	0.26*	0.08	0.23	0.07	0.67**

Note. SD = Standard deviation.
*$p < 0.05$; ** $p < 0.01$

question is whether these already higher levels can be meaningfully enhanced through a critical service learning approach such as ROSES.

What Happens after Training?

A key question in scholarship and practice on service learning involves the extent to which the curricular aspects of the service learning experience are central to any gains students' make in their reckoning with social injustice. Service learning courses typically include a classroom component in which students are invited to reflect and learn more about their experiences in the community. To make service learning courses truly critical, some scholars argue that this curricular space must provide critical perspectives and discussions that allow students to dig deeper into the inequities they see and the frustrations they experience during community service, otherwise they run the risk of reifying dominant victim-blaming and helping narratives (Holsinger, 2008, 2012; Javdani, 2013). In line with this thinking, ROSES advocates often expressed how important the ROSES training period was to them in serving as a counterspace in which they were able to critically engage in understanding inequity and transform their own perspectives and understanding (Javdani et al., under review). Similarly, many (but not all) CC-related interventions incorporate curricular features (e.g., Hatcher et al., 2011; Singh et al., 2018) or values-affirmations (e.g., Rapa et al., 2020) that parallel aspects of ROSES's training. To explore the role of training itself, we conducted a set of initial analyses to examine shifts in advocates' interpersonal skills and CC after training and prior to implementing an advocacy intervention. We used a series of one-way repeated measures multivariate analysis of variance (RM MANOVA) models to assess change from baseline to posttraining. RM MANOVA models examine whether there were significant changes in each of our indicators across two time points. RM MANOVAs account for the fact that measures in each domain are conceptually related and correlated to each other. They provide a summary F-statistic that indicates an overall significant change in that domain across timepoints, correcting for the fact that we are running multiple tests on related measures. We ran separate RM MANOVAs for each domain (interpersonal skills, critical reflection, critical motivation, and critical action) and followed those with univariate tests of specific outcomes within each domain. This is followed by univariate tests of specific measures, to examine change over time between advocate's reports prior to training and after training, including effect sizes measured using Cohen's d (with effect sizes of around 0.2 considered a small effect; d around 0.5 is considered a medium effect, and d around 0.8 is considered a large effect; Cohen, 1988). F statistics (presented in Table 6.3) from the RM MANOVAs suggest wholesale increases in interpersonal skills ($F(2,31) = 9.65, p < 0.001$), critical reflection ($F(8,43) = 9.54$,

TABLE 6.3 Comparison of pre- and posttraining outcomes (training ~40 hours in 1 month; $N = 45$)

	Pretraining M (SD)	Posttraining M (SD)	Univariate Test	Cohen's d
Interpersonal Skills	One-Way RM MANOVA $F(2,31) = 9.65$, $p <0.001$			
Emotional capacity	4.34 (0.49)	4.42 (0.45)	$t(1, 34) = -1.31$, $p =0.19$	0.23
Perspective taking	4.21 (0.55)	4.31 (0.59)	$t(1, 34) = -1.20$, $p =0.24$	0.40
Advocate- (vs. youth-) centered	2.75 (0.50)	2.18 (0.53)	$t(1, 34) = 5.37$, $p <0.001$	0.85
Critical Reflection	One-Way RM MANOVA $F(8,43) = 9.54$, $p =0.002$			
Perceived inequality	5.16 (0.73)	5.39 (0.72)	$t(1, 35) = -2.56$, $p <0.05$	0.43
Egalitarianism	5.82 (0.40)	5.72 (0.44)	$t(1, 34) = 1.49$, $p =0.15$	0.19
Modern racism	1.30 (0.42)	1.21 (0.35)	$t(1, 34) = 1.57$, $p =0.14$	0.39
Critical understanding of poverty	4.18 (0.46)	4.41 (0.44)	$t(1, 34) = -4.07$, $p <0.001$	0.91
Victim-blaming attributions	2.17 (0.46)	2.14 (0.43)	$t(1,34) = 3.41$, $p <0.01$	0.59
Society-blaming attributions	3.76 (0.35)	4.03 (0.38)	$t(1, 34) = -4.40$, $p <0.001$	0.77
Girl-blaming attributions	1.92 (0.34)	1.73 (0.31)	$t(1, 34) = 3.97$, $p <0.001$	0.61
System justification	2.58 (0.88)	2.35 (0.97)	$t(1, 34) = 2.47$, $p <0.05$	0.43
Meritocratic ideology	5.42 (0.58)	5.11 (0.79)	$t(1, 34) = 2.45$, $p <0.05$	0.51
Critical Motivation	One-Way RM MANOVA $F(4,31) = 2.73$, $p =0.04$			
Importance of addressing inequity	4.23 (0.37)	4.28 (0.35)	$t(1, 32) = 2.26$, $p <0.05$	0.39
Confidence in addressing inequity	7.85 (1.30)	8.29 (1.11)	$t(1, 32) = -2.67$, $p <0.01$	0.46
Commitment to activism	4.28 (0.55)	4.46 (0.57)	$t(1, 32) = -1.99$, $p =0.05$	0.35
Importance of working with others to address inequity	6.87 (0.28)	6.92 (0.21)	$t(1, 32) = -2.15$, $p <0.05$	0.37

TABLE 6.3 *(Cont.)*

	Pretraining M (SD)	Posttraining M (SD)	Univariate Test	Cohen's *d*
Perceived control in addressing inequity	6.26 (0.62)	6.33 (0.71)	$t(1, 32) = -1.79$, $p =0.08$	0.31
Critical Action	One-Way RM MANOVA $F(2,30) = 4.25, p =0.04$			
Behavioral intentions	6.66 (0.52)	6.83 (0.34)	$t(1, 35) = -2.08$, $p <0.05$	0.36
Pursuit of social action	3.30 (1.00)	3.59 (0.98)	$t(1, 32) = -3.02$, $p <0.01$	0.50
Engagement in critical action	3.18 (0.76)	3.11 (0.67)	$t(1, 32) = 0.92$, $p =0.37$	0.29

Note. M = Mean; SD = Standard deviation; RM = Repeated measures.

$p = 0.002$), critical motivation ($F(4,31) = 2.73$, $p = 0.04$), and critical action ($F(2,30) = 4.25$, $p = 0.04$) from pre- to posttraining.

Looking at average reports on individual measures prior to training and after training shows changes in the expected directions (indicating increases in interpersonal skills and CC) for every measure of each domain. In the interpersonal domain, follow-up univariate tests revealed a significant and large increase in advocates' prioritization of youth goals in advocacy. After training alone, we do not see significant changes in emotional capacity or perspective taking. In the critical reflection domain, univariate tests showed significant changes in seven of the nine measures representing medium to large effect sizes. Specifically, we see advocates perceiving greater social inequality, making fewer individual attributions for social problems in general, holding society more accountable for social problems, reporting fewer blame attributions about system-impacted girls, expressing a more critical understanding of poverty, reporting lower meritocratic ideologies, and endorsing fewer system-justifying beliefs. We see no change in endorsement of modern racism or egalitarian worldviews. In the critical motivation domain, we see changes reported across three of the five measures with small to medium effect sizes. After engaging in training, advocates reported a significant increase in their perceived confidence to address inequity, placed higher priority on doing social justice work, and felt it was even more important to work with others to address inequity. Finally, within the critical action domain, we see significantly higher intentions to take action against social injustice posttraining, and also greater reports of engaging in actions in the pursuit of social change. These changes represented small to medium effect sizes. Finally, after training alone, we do not see significant changes in engagement in specific critical actions.

Taken together, these patterns suggest that training is an important foundation to supporting interpersonal and CC skill development in advocates, particularly around the domains of critical reflection and motivation. This is not surprising given the didactic, experiential, and dialogue-promoting exercises that advocates engage in during training, but is important to underscore because training can be such a time- and resource-intensive experience. That said, advocates did not have the option of a "training only" experience and therefore experienced training through the lens of a person who would imminently be engaged in community-based advocacy. Thus, training successfully engaged advocates in structural and critical thinking, but was likely not experienced as abstract. Further, the attitudinal and motivational patterns of changes evidenced after training require examination after intervention implementation to understand consistency and maintenance of observed effects, alongside additional skill development – the focus of our next section.

How Did Advocate's Interpersonal and Critical Consciousness Skills Change after Training and Advocacy?

To answer this question, we undertook a set of exploratory analyses to examine whether advocates' reports of their interpersonal skills and CC changed after completing ROSES training and advocacy. As we mentioned earlier, only roughly half of the nearly 100 advocates were able to complete surveys, so we consider our analyses to be exploratory. However, they provide important initial evidence that ROSES in particular, and critical service learning in general, may be an effective context for CC development. We employed the same approach as described earier, using a series of one-way RM models to assess change from baseline to postadvocacy. This window was inclusive of the training period, but also encompassed implementation of an advocacy intervention following training. As above, we ran separate RM MANOVAs for each domain (interpersonal skills, critical reflection, critical motivation, and critical action) and followed those with univariate tests of specific outcomes within each domain.

Table 6.4 presents results of the RM MANOVAs and follow-up univariate tests examining change in advocates' reports of interpersonal skills and CC from pretraining to postadvocacy, after advocates engaged in both 40 hours of training and ~120 hours of advocacy hours paired with supervision. F statistics from RM MANOVAs suggest significant increases in interpersonal skills ($F(2,41) = 19.56$, $p < 0.001$), critical reflection ($F(8,31) = 4.60$, $p = 0.002$), critical motivation ($F(4,41) = 3.08$, $p = 0.02$), and critical action ($F(2,31) = 4.44$, $p = 0.04$).

A look at means on individual measures prior to training and after advocacy shows changes in the expected directions (increases in interpersonal skills and CC) for almost every domain indicator. These shifts were significant for most, but not all individual indicators. In the interpersonal

TABLE 6.4 Comparison of pretraining and postadvocacy outcomes (training + advocacy; *N*= 50)

	Pretraining M (SD)	Postadvocacy M (SD)	Univariate Test	Cohen's *d*
Interpersonal Skills	One-Way RM MANOVA $F_{(2,41)}$ = 19.56, *p* <0.001			
Emotional capacity	4.43(0.48)	4.41 (0.49)	$t_{(1, 46)}$ =0.23, *p* =0.88	0.02
Perspective taking	4.18 (0.59)	4.30 (0.53)	$t_{(1, 46)}$ = −2.01, *p* <0.05	0.29
Advocate- (vs. youth-) centered	2.80 (0.57)	2.28 (0.63)	$t_{(1, 48)}$ = 6.71, *p* <0.001	0.90
Critical Reflection	One-Way RM MANOVA $F_{(8,31)}$ = 4.60, *p* =0.002			
Perceived inequality	5.27 (0.63)	5.34 (0.84)	$t_{(1, 42)}$ = −0.76, *p* =0.45	0.12
Egalitarianism	5.66 (0.59)	5.66 (0.49)	$t_{(1, 42)}$ = −0.16, *p* =0.88	0.02
Modern racism	1.30 (0.42)	1.16 (0.25)	$t_{(1, 26)}$ = 2.02, *p* <0.05	0.39
Critical understand- ing of poverty	4.18 (0.46)	4.31 (0.41)	$t_{(1, 25)}$ = −1.70, *p* =0.10	0.15
Victim-blaming attributions	2.17 (0.46)	1.97 (0.45)	$t_{(1, 41)}$ = 3.59, *p* <0.001	0.55
Society-blaming attributions	3.76 (0.35)	3.99 (0.36)	$t_{(1, 41)}$ = −5.05, *p* <0.001	0.78
Girl-blaming attributions	1.89 (0.33)	1.63 (0.36)	$t_{(1, 39)}$ = 5.96, *p* <0.001	0.94
System justification	2.37 (0.89)	2.13 (0.98)	$t_{(1, 41)}$ = 3.62, *p* <0.01	0.52
Meritocratic ideology	5.52 (0.57)	5.24 (0.66)	$t_{(1, 25)}$ = 2.93, *p* <0.01	0.57
Critical Motivation	One-Way RM MANOVA $F_{(4,41)}$ = 3.08, *p* =0.02			
Importance of addressing inequity	4.15 (0.3)	4.27 (0.35)	$t_{(1, 41)}$ = −2.02, *p* <0.05	0.36
Confidence in addressing inequity	7.85 (1.30)	8.28 (0.96)	$t_{(1, 40)}$ = −3.85, *p* <0.001	0.60
Commitment to activism	4.28 (0.55)	4.24 (0.52)	$t_{(1, 41)}$ = −1.98, *p* <0.05	0.31

TABLE 6.4 *(Cont.)*

	Pretraining M (SD)	Postadvocacy M (SD)	Univariate Test	Cohen's *d*
Importance of working with others to address inequity	6.87 (0.28)	6.95 (0.14)	$t(1, 41) = -2.97$, p <0.01	0.46
Perceived control in addressing inequity	6.19 (0.61)	6.26 (0.64)	$t(1, 41) = -0.88$, p =0.38	0.14
Critical Action	One-Way RM MANOVA $F(2,31) = 4.44$, p =0.04			
Behavioral intentions	6.71 (0.45)	6.84 (0.34)	$t(1, 41) = -2.33$, p <0.05	0.36
Pursuit of social action	3.24 (0.88)	3.32 (0.63)	$t(1, 40) = -1.36$, p =0.18	0.21
Engagement in critical action	2.97 (0.59)	3.26 (0.68)	$t(1,31) = -2.26$, p <0.05	0.74

Note. M = Mean; SD = Standard deviation; RM = Repeated measures.

domain, follow-up univariate tests revealed significant changes in two of three measures: an increase in perspective taking and advocates' prioritization of youth goals in advocacy. The Cohen's *d* effect size for these changes were 0.29 and 0.90, indicating a shift from pretraining to postadvocacy of 0.25 to almost 1 full standard deviation in the variability of this measure postadvocacy compared to baseline. In the critical reflection domain, univariate tests showed significant changes in six of the nine measures, representing medium to large effect sizes. After engaging in training and advocacy, advocates had lower endorsement of modern racism, made fewer individual attributions for social problems and for girls' system involvement, held society more accountable for social problems, held fewer system-justifying beliefs, and endorsed lower meritocratic beliefs. In the critical motivation domain, three of five measures showed significant changes with small to medium effect sizes. After engaging in ROSES advocacy, advocates reported a significant increase in their perceived confidence to address inequity. They also placed higher priority on doing social justice work and felt it was even more important to work with others to address inequity. In addition, we saw a marginal effect suggesting that advocates place greater importance on addressing social inequity. In the critical action domain, advocates also reported significantly higher intentions to take action against social injustice and significantly greater engagement in social justice-related actions. These represented medium effect sizes.

Overall, these results suggest that critical service-learning programs such as ROSES can be quite effective in further enhancing advocates' interpersonal skills and CC. Importantly, they also show that these shifts can occur even for those who self-select into this experience and report higher than midpoint levels of CC. It is interesting that advocates' prioritization of youth goals in advocacy and increased perspective taking were primary drivers of change in the interpersonal domain, but that there were no significant changes in emotional capacity. This makes sense, given that an emphasis throughout training and advocacy is to rethink the role of helping and shift away from deficit-oriented medical models to strengths- and rights-driven perspectives. Advocates entered ROSES with high emotional capacity, which they maintained, but this kind of critical service learning experience was able to enhance their perspective-taking and ability to shift away from predominant models of helping that prioritize white savior modes and toward youth-centered visions and goals. These shifts demonstrate advocates' increased ability to recognize that "youth are the experts" in their own lives and support them to express their needs, which is a particularly important correlate of system-impacted girls' mental health outcomes (Granski, Javdani, Sichel, & Rentko, 2020).

Notably, we see significant increases in all indicators of critical reflection except critical reflection: perceived inequality, egalitarianism, or critical understanding of poverty. This could be due to high endorsement on these scales already; however, other indicators also have high endorsement to start. Both perceived inequality and critical understanding of poverty increased, but these changes were not significant. It might be that for students who self-select into experiences such as ROSES, it is the more insidious and deeper attributional processes and ideology endorsements that shift as a result of this kind of critical service learning experience, instead of basic awareness of inequity. That is, the perspectives provided in training, alongside the lived experience advocating with and on behalf of someone affected by multiple oppressions, could lay bare the plethora of structural and interlocking barriers perpetuated by inequity. This could function as a "magic elixir" to upset deep-seated attributional tendencies, ideologies, and motivations that are difficult to change and often operate outside of conscious awareness (Jost et al., 2004).

For critical motivation, we see increases in advocates' confidence to address inequity, the importance of addressing inequity, the importance of working with others to do so, and their commitment to activism. The one indicator that did not change significantly was perceived control in addressing inequity, but the means on this indicator did increase from pretraining to postadvocacy intervention. Thus, across multiple indicators of motivation and efficacy, the experience of training for and engaging in advocacy seems to bolster advocates desire to enact change and their perceived ability to do so. We attribute shifts in these indicators to the training and experiences advocates receive in ROSES to create humanizing counterspaces to hold and resist experiences of oppression and concrete strategies advocates develop and employ to change the context, not the girl.

Finally, it is notable that we saw evidence for changes in critical action as well, especially given that the act of advocacy itself is already a critical action of its own accord. Many scholars have noted the need for CC intervention and scholarship to move beyond critical reflection and focus more on the promotion of action for social change (e.g., Diemer et al., 2021; Watts & Hipolito-Delgado, 2015). Indeed, both intentions to engage in critical action following advocacy and involvement in such actions at the end of advocacy significantly increased from pretraining levels, with the latter having a particularly strong effect size. Although advocates' pursuit of social actions did not change significantly following advocacy, this more general indicator moved in the expected and positive direction.

Importantly, these critical action indicators were general and assessed across multiple contexts in advocates' lives (e.g., school, community, social organizations), suggesting that advocates report realizing a more robust set of intentions to engage in a variety of critical actions. We believe these increases in action stem both from the scaffolding of action strategies provided throughout ROSES training and intervention and the virtuous action–reflection cycle that ensues when youth are provided with scaffolded opportunities to act.

How Do Features of Advocacy Influence Change in Advocates' Skills and Critical Consciousness?

We then explored whether two features of the advocacy intervention itself moderated any of the patterns of change we saw in advocates' interpersonal skills and CC: (1) whether advocates engaged in 120 hours or more of advocacy or not; and (2) whether they worked on more than six goals per week on average. ROSES is designed so that advocates spend roughly 10 hours per week for 12 weeks working directly with a client or on behalf of her goals. Interventions in which advocates engage in 120 hours of advocacy or more are therefore considered to be fully implemented, while those with less than 120 hours are not. Similarly, advocates work with girls to establish multiple youth-determined goals, with many accompanying subgoals that vary week to week. The top need areas addressed by advocacy included goals around education, emotional support, healthcare, creative pursuits, housing, and safety. An average of six goals per week or more over the course of advocacy represents an intervention in which many goals were identified and addressed, indicating successful implementation of advocacy and providing an opportunity for advocates to work on multiple goals with girls.

To explore whether these features of advocacy changed ROSES' influence on advocates' interpersonal skills and CC from pretraining to postadvocacy, we introduced interaction terms into our RM ANOVAs. In the critical reflection domain, we found that advocates reported significantly greater perceived inequality only in cases where they engaged in 120 hours or more of advocacy ($n = 38$) compared to those who engaged in fewer hours ($n = 14$) (F $(1,47) = 4.11$; $p < 0.05$; $\eta p^2 = 0.08$). In addition, advocates who identified and worked on a greater number of client-centered goals (i.e., > 6 goals per week; $n = 29$) had a more critical understanding of poverty after advocacy, while those who worked on fewer goals did not ($n = 23$) ($F(1,30) = 4.22$; $p < 0.05$; $\eta p^2 = 0.12$). For critical action, we found that the significant increase in intentions to engage in action to redress inequity was particularly pronounced for advocates who engaged in 120 or more hours of advocacy in their intervention ($F(1,11) = 7.80$; $p = 0.02$; $\eta p^2 = 0.42$) relative to those who engaged in fewer hours. There were no differences in any changes in indicator of critical motivation or efficacy by either of these features.

Upon consideration, it makes sense that two of the three indicators of critical reflection that did not significantly shift from pretraining to posttraining overall did shift for advocates who implemented a "full" intervention of 120 or more hours of advocacy. Implementing this much advocacy may have been what was needed to move this already high perception even further. Similarly, advocates' critical understanding of poverty also increased when their advocacy intervention involved more than six goals per week on average. This is likely because working on this many goals reinforced the structural set of barriers that low-income girls of color face, making the structural nature of poverty plain. Witnessing firsthand the lived experience of an individual girl facing these challenges may have been needed to move advocates' already high level of critical thinking around poverty even further. Finally, implementing more than 120 hours of advocacy also strengthened advocate's intentions to take critical action. We understand this finding in a similar way to the findings for critical reflection. Advocates who implemented a full intervention are able to witness firsthand the ways in which contextual and structural barriers can constrain the freedom and opportunities of low-income girls of color. They also were able to experience working directly on behalf of girls to create counterspaces of liberation, navigate barriers, and secure resources. This enhanced reflection, paired with direct opportunities to make a demonstrable difference in a real person's life, reflects the virtuous cycle of reflection and action hypothesized in the CC literature and likely increased advocates' intention to take further action in the future.

What Patterns are Present from Baseline to Posttraining and Postadvocacy?

Overall, we see a relatively consistent pattern of results emerge supporting interpersonal skill and CC development across the posttraining and postadvocacy comparison windows (see Table 6.5 for comparison of patterns).

TABLE 6.5 Pattern of results from (A) pretraining to posttraining and (B) pretraining to postadvocacy, organized by domain

	(A) Pretraining to Posttraining (N = 45)	Significant Effect Size Range	(B) Pretraining to Postadvocacy (N = 50)	Significant Effect Size Range
Interpersonal Skills	One-Way RM MANOVA F (2,31) = 9.65, $p <$ 0.001	*Cohen's* $d = 0.9$	One-Way RM MANOVA $F_{(2,41)} =$ 19.56, $p < 0.001$	*Cohen's* $ds = 0.4$ to 0.9
Emotional capacity	–		–	
Perspective taking	–		* significant	
Advocate (vs. youth) centered	* significant		* significant	
Critical Reflection	One-Way RM MANOVA F (8,43) = 9.54, $p = 0.002$	*Cohen's ds=* 0.4 to 0.9	One-Way RM MANOVA $F(8,31) =$ 4.60, $p = 0.002$	*Cohen's ds =* 0.4 to 0.9
Perceived inequality	* significant		–	
Egalitarianism	–		–	
Modern racism	–		* significant	
Critical understanding of poverty	* significant		*marginal*	
Victim-blaming attributions	* significant		* significant	
Society-blaming attributions	* significant		* significant	
Girl-blaming attributions	* significant		* significant	
System justification	* significant		* significant	
Meritocratic ideology	* significant		* significant	
Critical Motivation	One-Way RM MANOVA F (4,31) = 2.73, $p = 0.04$	*Cohen's ds=0.4*	One-Way RM MANOVA $F(4,41) =$ 3.08, $p = 0.02$	*Cohen's ds =0.5* to 0.6
Importance of addressing inequity	* significant		* significant	

TABLE 6.5 (*Cont.*)

	(A) Pretraining to Posttraining (N = 45)	Significant Effect Size Range	(B) Pretraining to Postadvocacy (N = 50)	Significant Effect Size Range
Confidence in addressing inequity	* significant		* significant	
Commitment to activism	*marginal*		* significant	
Importance of working with others	* significant		* significant	
Perceived control in addressing inequity	*marginal*		–	
Critical Action	One-Way RM MANOVA *F* (2,30) = 4.25, *p* = 0.04	*Cohen's ds* = 0.4 to 0.5	One-Way RM MANOVA F(2,31) = 4.44, p = 0.04	*Cohen's ds* = 0.4 to 0.7
Behavioral intentions	* significant		* significant	
Pursuit of social action	* significant		–	
Engagement in critical action	–		* significant	

Note. "–" indicates nonsignificant difference; "*significant" = results with *p*-values < 0.05; "marginal" = *p*-values < 0.10.

In particular, training supports gains in interpersonal kill and CC development, which are by and large maintained and strengthened following intervention implementation. This points to the importance of the curricular content and activities in critical service-learning approaches. The training advocates engaged in was intensive, and it offered multiple opportunities for advocates to question core assumptions, discuss power and privilege, learn specifics about structural realities facing girls of color, and practice engaging with these ideas through role plays and modeling activities. Advocates practiced until they gained mastery with these skills and ideas. Moreover, advocates had the opportunity to engage with this knowledge and skill-building while knowing they would be directly responsible for implementing an intervention with a young person, making the experience less abstract and more concrete, current, and pressing. Indeed, we also see advocates reporting higher perceptions of inequality posttraining, a change that was not significant post-advocacy except for advocates who engaged in 120 hours or more of advocacy in their intervention; and greater engagement in actions in the pursuit of social change, which was not demonstrated postadvocacy. We believe these training features create a foundation that supports advocates in developing their inter-personal skills and CC, fostering their embrace of youth-centered practice and further cultivating their critical reflection, motivation, and action.

It is interesting to note how certain critical reflection skills were fostered somewhat differently through the experience of training alone vs. training plus advocacy. After training alone we see no difference in advocates' perspective taking, or their endorsement of modern racism, but these latter two indicators of critical reflection did shift postadvocacy. Our best guess is that while training can enhance historical and structural knowledge regarding its origins and manifest-ations, the experience of getting close to and working firsthand with a girl facing oppression is needed to truly understand the pernicious nature of racism and the complicated and nuanced perspective taking required to unpack the ways in which racism and patriarchy play out in juvenile legal and child welfare systems.

Another notable difference we see is in the domain of critical action. Posttraining, we see increases in intentions to act in addition to actual pursuit of action. However, pursuit of action is no longer significantly different after advocacy, whereas engagement in more specific critical actions is only significant postadvocacy. Our interpretation of this has to do with the nature of advocacy itself. As mentioned earlier, the implementation of an advocacy intervention is itself a version of critical action. Although it is conducted on behalf of one individual, the actions that are taken are designed to "change the context, not the girl" and so are directed at intervening in structural barriers and making structural changes to girls' contexts to enable them to meet their own self-determined goals. Thus, they often represent concrete and daily versions of critical action. In addition, the advocacy relationship itself, which transforms power relations and radically places control and expertise in the hands of youth themselves, is also an action in the form of a creation of a counterspace for liberation vs. oppression. Given this, advocates may not report pursuing more action during the course of advocacy when advocacy is the main focus of their action. However, postadvocacy their intentions remain enhanced, and they report engagement in specific critical actions assessed across a variety of contexts.

IMPLICATIONS, LIMITATIONS, AND CONCLUSION

Advocacy is presented here as an exemplary setting of critical service learning because of its unique structural and relational features. These features func-tion to raise awareness and tune into social power, invoke emotion, and invite discomfort, while simultaneously providing an opportunity for concrete skill development, the creation of contextual change strategies, and scaffolded action as advocates work with system-impacted young people. The context of critical service learning described here engages the vision of abolition feminism and represents a setting in which advocates are invited to imagine and hold a radical vision of social justice while simultaneously engaging in daily action that is messy, challenging, and labor intensive (Davis et al., 2022). This combination of radical imagination and engagement in critical action through advocacy may be both generative and transformative for advocates' CC, especially when scaffolded by accessible supervision that models the equity-enhancing processes advocates are asked to uphold with their clients.

Indeed, the transformative liberatory space that advocacy strives to create through training and supervision begins with radical and critical listening, which begets and builds love (Battle, 2022; Rogers, 1979). Although "love" is not a word typically used to describe service learning or intervention, its roots in abolition are ever-present because it allows for a collective to first acknowledge historical and contemporary manifestations of oppression, and then to reject this reality by critically acting to change it (Davis et al., 2022). In the ROSES model, the self-reflection generated and modeled throughout advocacy is inextricably tied to advocates' critical reflection about the world. Validation of advocates' emotions and challenges serves to promote and model acceptance and acknowledgment of the pain people navigate in their lives; additionally, the unwavering support advocates experience may generate respect for and commitment to honoring the lived experiences of others. At the same time, ROSES strives to move beyond reflection toward action through specific skill-building and a scaffolded set of change strategies and structural supports through supervision and relationship-building within the advocate community. These realities are based in the concept of love, and advocacy's foundational skills are rooted in active listening and radical acceptance (e.g., Linehan; 2014; Rogers, 1979), first through seeking to understand one another during training, then through critical dialogue about social inequities (e.g., Watts et al., 2011), and finally through the presence of acceptance that advocates bring to their interactions with system-impacted girls, all of which are reinforced and modeled during supervision. This is compassion paired with accountability, and empathic validation coupled with the pursuit of human rights and self-determination.

We contend that these are the seeds that may give rise to ROSES, and other critical service learning experiences, as a setting that promotes CC. Unsurprisingly, advocates demonstrated significant gains in interpersonal skills over the course of training, which are further strengthened after engagement in advocacy. But we also found that ROSES was related to promising changes in each dimension of CC as well. Even among students already motivated to engage in this work, we saw further increases in their critical reflection, motivation, and action after engaging in ROSES intensive training, and even more so after engaging in community-based social justice advocacy with system-impacted girls. This is notable given that the sample, although diverse in terms of racial/ethnic background and lesbian, gay, bisexual, transgender, and gender-expansive identity, is still a very privileged one socioeconomically and by virtue of their status as students in a resource-rich private university. Through their experiences in training and advocacy, advocates deepened their critical reflection of social injustice. Through training, advocates became even more aware of inequities that exist, made more structural attributions for these inequities, and also held fewer meritocratic and system-justifying beliefs. These changes remained through advocacy delivery, and we also saw them deepen to include even lower reports of modern racism. This shows the power of ROSES as a critical service learning experience: the invitation to reconsider power and privilege paired with the actual work of advocacy worked together to create effective circumstances for a nuanced and deep understanding of inequity.

It is important that the didactic, skill-building, and framework shifts prioritized in training are paired with actual opportunities to enact change strategies and take action. Scholars point to the importance of pairing critical reflection with opportunities to take action, seeing this as central to fostering real CC rather than "armchair activism" (Watts & Hipolito-Delgado, 2015). Pairing reflection-building with concrete change strategies and opportunities for action is also critical in transforming the discomfort and pain that comes from greater reflection into motivation for change. Accordingly, we see gains in advocates' critical motivation and efficacy across training and advocacy intervention. This is likely due in no small part to the fact that advocates know they will be charged to act with and on behalf of a system-impacted girl following training and are armed with specific tools and techniques to shift girls' contexts to better meet their self-determined goals. These tools and techniques are reinforced during advocacy supervision with group problem-solving on structural issues and resource navigation, providing advocates an avenue to create change. As a result, we see advocates' actual intentions and engagements in critical action increase after advocacy intervention. Thus, the experience of ROSES training, advocacy intervention and supervision mirrors and scaffolds the reflection–motivation–action cycle assumed to underlie CC development.

In keeping with this premise, service learning is theorized to counter the oppressive nature of schooling and reframe what it means to engage in active learning (Winans-Solis, 2014). Though important case studies exemplify this process, ours is one of the first to interrogate the degree to which the structure of one critical service learning experience can foster CC over multiple student cohorts and multiple CC indicators (Winans-Solis, 2014). Opportunities for critical reflection, paired with skill-building and linked with immediate opportunities for advocacy, may create a new process of learning for advocates in ways that promote personal and collective growth through CC. As such, ROSES may function as an empowered and critically conscious context with particular group- and setting-level features that warrant future study and consideration (Heberle et al., 2020; Zimmerman, 1990).

We acknowledge several limitations and invite readers to interpret these results with informed caution given the relatively small sample size and correlational design of our analyses. However, we note that significant patterns in our findings represent large effect sizes due to low statistical power, and that observed patterns were all in expected directions, evident across multiple indicators, and were observed across two comparison windows (baseline to both posttraining and postadvocacy). Although some of the observed differences from baseline to posttraining versus postadvocacy could be driven by differences in samples across these two comparison windows, the samples are entirely overlapping and there are no observed demographic differences between samples. That said, we emphasize the overall pattern of findings across comparison windows. We also note a likely inflated Type I error rate given multiple comparisons, though this was offset in part by conducting MANOVAs and interpreting omnibus tests prior to univariate follow-ups. We also report each univariate test's p-value and effect size to guide readers in their ability to draw even more conservative conclusions (e.g., by setting a different alpha level).

Despite this, the results are promising. They represent a path for making a real difference in changing oppressive contexts while simultaneously leveraging university resources and fostering deeper and sustained CC with students who hold considerable privilege. We encourage critical service learning approaches to proliferate, and, as they do, to take these tenets into account when developing their goals and structure so that these settings can emerge as tools for consciousness-raising and fighting injustice.

REFERENCES

Astin, A., Vogelgesang, L., Ikeda, E., & Yee, J. (2000). How service learning affects students. Los Angeles, Higher Education Research Institute, UCLA. https://www.heri.ucla.edu/PDFs/HSLAS/HSLAS.PDF.

Barrera, D., Willner, L., & Kukahiko, K. (2017). Assessing the development of an emerging CC through service learning. *Journal of Critical Thought and Practice, 6* (3), 17–35. https://doi.org/10.31274/jctp-180810-82.

Barroso, A., & Minkin, R. (2020). Recent protest attendees are more racially and ethnically diverse, younger than Americans overall. Pew Research Center. www.pewresearch.org/fact-tank/2020/06/24/recent-protest-attendees-are-more-racially-and-ethnically-diverse-younger-than-americans-overall/.

Battle, B. P. (2022). "Everything I believe in is rooted in love": Women and non-binary activists of color fighting for the practice and promise of abolition. *Qualitative Criminology*, 11(3).

Bonilla-Silva, E. (1997). Rethinking racism: Toward a structural interpretation. *American Sociological Review*, 62, 465–480. http://doi.org/10.2307/2657316.

Butin, D. (2015). Dreaming of justice: Critical service-learning and the need to wake up. *Theory Into Practice*, 54(1), 5–10.

Caplan, N., & Nelson, S. D. (1973). On being useful: The nature and consequences of psychological research on social problems. *American Psychologist*, 28(3), 199–211. https://doi.org/10.1037/h0034433.

Case, A. D., & Hunter, C. D. (2012). Counterspaces: A unit of analysis for understanding the role of settings in marginalized individuals' adaptive responses to oppression. *American Journal of Community Psychology*, 50(1), 257–270.

Center for Community Engaged Learning (2021, November 5). What is community engaged learning? https://communityengagedlearning.msu.edu.

Chesney-Lind, M., & Shelden, R. G. (2013). *Girls, delinquency, and juvenile justice*. John Wiley & Sons.

Cohen, J. (1988). *Statistical power analysis for the behavioral sciences* (2nd ed.). Erlbaum.

Davidson, W. S., & Rapp, C. A. (1976). Child advocacy in the justice system. *Social Work*, 21(3), 225–232.

Davis, A. Y., Dent, G., Meiners, E. R., & Richie, B. E. (2022). *Abolition. Feminism. Now.* Haymarket Books.

Davis, M. (1983). Measuring individual differences in empathy: Evidence for a multidimensional approach. *Journal of Personality and Social Psychology*, 44(1), 113–126.

Delavega, E., Kindle, P. A., Peterson, S., & Schwartz, C. (2017). The blame index: Exploring the change in social work students' perceptions of poverty. *Journal of Social Work Education*, 53(4), 664–675.

Diemer, M. A., Rapa, L. J., Park, C. J., & Perry, J. C. (2017). Development and validation of the CC scale. *Youth & Society*, 49(4), 461–483. https://doi.org/10.1177/0044118X14538289.

Diemer, M. A., Pinedo, A., Bañales, J. et al. (2021). Recentering action in critical consciousness. *Child Development Perspectives*, 15(1), 12–17.

Dunst, C. J., & Trivette, C. M. (1996). Empowerment, effective helpgiving practices and family-centered care. *Pediatric Nursing*, 22(4), 334–338.

Flanagan, C., & Faison, N. (2001). Youth civic development: Implications of research for social policy and programs. *Social Policy Report*, 15(1), 1–16. https://doi.org/10.1002/j.2379-3988.2001.tb00040.x.

Freire, P. (1970). *Pedagogy of the oppressed*. Herder and Herder.

Freire, P. (1973). *Education for critical consciousness*. Seabury Press.

Godfrey, E. B., & Burson, E. (2018). Interrogating the intersections: How intersectional perspectives can inform developmental scholarship on critical consciousness. *New Directions for Child and Adolescent Development*, 161, 17–38.

Godfrey, E. B., Burson, E. L., Yanisch, T. M., Hughes, D., & Way, N. (2019). A bitter pill to swallow? Patterns of CC and socioemotional and academic well-being in early adolescence. *Developmental Psychology, 55*(3), 525–537. https://doi.org/10.1037/devo000558.

Godfrey, E. B., & Wolf, S. (2016). Developing CC or justifying the system? A qualitative analysis of attributions for poverty and wealth among low-income racial/ethnic minority and immigrant women. *Cultural Diversity and Ethnic Minority Psychology, 22*(1), 93–103. https://doi.org/10.1037/cdp0000048.

Granski, M., Javdani, S., Anderson, V. R., & Caires, R. (2020). A meta-analysis of program characteristics for youth with disruptive behavior problems: The moderating role of program format and youth gender. *American Journal of Community Psychology, 65*(1–2), 201–222.

Granski, M., Javdani, S., Sichel, C. E., & Rentko, M. (2020). Gender differences in the relationship between self-silencing, trauma, and mental health among juvenile legal system-involved youth. *Feminist Criminology, 15*(5), 545–566.

Hatcher, A., de Wet, J., Bonell, C. P. et al. (2011). Promoting critical consciousness and social mobilization in HIV/AIDS programmes: Lessons and curricular tools from a South African intervention. *Health Education Research, 26*(3), 542–555.

Heberle, A. E., Rapa, L. J., & Farago, F. (2020). Critical consciousness in children and adolescents: A systematic review, critical assessment, and recommendations for future research. *Psychological Bulletin, 146*(6), 525–551. https://doi.org/10.1037/bul0000230.

Holsinger, K. (2008). Teaching to make a difference. *Feminist Criminology, 3*, 319–335.

Holsinger, K. (2012). *Teaching justice: Solving social justice problems through university education.* Ashgate Publishing Ltd.

Holsinger, K., & Ayers, P. (2004). Mentoring girls in juvenile facilities: Connecting college students with incarcerated girls. *Journal of Criminal Justice Education, 15*, 351–372.

Ibrahim, D. A., & Godfrey, E. B. (in prep). Understanding the processes and contextual features of arts programming conducive to critical consciousness for youth: An ecologically iInformed theory of change. *Manuscript in Preparation.*

Ibrahim, D. A., Godfrey, E. B., Burson, E., & Cappella, E. (2022). The art of social justice: Arts programming as a context for CC development among youth. *Journal of Youth and Adolescence, 51*(3), 409–427.

Javdani, S. (2013). Gender matters: Using an ecological lens to understand female crime and disruptive behavior. In B. L. Russell (Ed.), *Perceptions of female offenders* (pp. 9–24). Springer.

Javdani, S. (2021). Reducing crime for girls in the juvenile justice system through research-practitioner partnerships. *Office of Justice Programs, National Criminal Justice Reference Services.*

Javdani, S., & Allen, N. E. (2016). An ecological model for intervention for juvenile justice-involved girls: Development and preliminary prospective evaluation. *Feminist Criminology, 11*(2), 135–162.

Javdani, S., Sadeh, N., & Verona, E. (2011a). Gendered social forces: A review of the impact of institutionalized factors on women and girls' criminal justice trajectories. *Psychology, Public Policy, and Law, 17*(2), 161.

Javdani, S., Sadeh, N., & Verona, E. (2011b). Expanding our lens: Female pathways to antisocial behavior in adolescence and adulthood. *Clinical Psychology Review, 31* (8), 1324–1348.

Javdani, S., Walden, A. L., Jumarali, S. N., & Allen N. E. (under review). Community-based advocacy as trauma-informed care: Targeting the social contexts of girls with juvenile legal system involvement.

Javorka, M. (2020). Partnering with oppressive institutions for social change: Roles, ethics, and a framework for practicing accountability. *American Journal of Community Psychology, 68*(1–2), 3–17. https://doi.org/10.1002/ajcp.12489.

Johnson, L. M., Mullick, R., & Mulford, C. L. (2002). General versus specific victim blaming. *The Journal of Social Psychology, 142*(2), 249–263.

Jost, J. T., Banaji, M. R., & Nosek, B. A. (2004). A decade of system justification theory: Accumulated evidence of conscious and unconscious bolstering of the status quo. *Political Psychology, 25*(6), 881–919.

Kay, A. C., & Jost, J. T. (2003). Complementary justice: Effects of "Poor but happy" and "Poor but honest" stereotype exemplars on system justification and implicit activation of the justice motive. *Journal of Personality and Social Psychology, 85* (5), 823–837. https://doi.org/10.1037/0022-3514.85.5.823.

Krings, A., Trubey-Hockman, C., Dentato, M., & Grossman, S. (2020). Recalibrating micro and macro social work: Student perceptions of social action. *Social Work Education, 39*(2), 160–174. https://doi.org/10.1080/02615479.2019.1616686.

Langhout, R. D. (2015). Considering community psychology competencies: A love letter to budding scholar-activists who wonder if they have what it takes. *American Journal of Community Psychology, 55*(3), 266–278.

Latta, M., Kruger, T. M., Payne, L., Weaver, L., & VanSickle, J. L. (2018). Approaching critical service-learning: A model for reflection on positionality and possibility. *Journal of Higher Education Outreach and Engagement, 22*(2), 31–55.

Leung, K., Liu, W., & Wang, W. (2006). Factors affecting students' evaluation in a community service-learning program. *Advances in Health and Science Education, 12*, 475–490.

Linehan, M. (2014). *DBT Skills training manual.* Guilford Publications.

McCoy, S. K., Wellman, J. D., Cosley, B., Saslow, L., & Epel, E. (2013). Is the belief in meritocracy palliative for members of low status groups? Evidence for a benefit for self-esteem and physical health via perceived control. *European Journal of Social Psychology, 43*(4), 307–318.

Miller, M. J., Sendrowitz, K., Connacher, C. et al. (2009). College students' social justice interest and commitment: A social-cognitive perspective. *Journal of Counseling Psychology, 56*, 495–507. https://doi.org/10.1037/a0017220.

Mitchell, T. D. (2008). Traditional vs. critical service-learning: Engaging the literature to differentiate two models. *Michigan Journal of Community Service Learning, 14*(2), 50–65.

Pancer, S., Pratt, M., Hunsberger, B., & Alisat, S. (2007). Community and political involvement in adolescence: What distinguishes the activists from the uninvolved? *Journal of Community Psychology, 35*(6), 741–759. https://doi.org/10.1002/jcop.20176.

Rapa, L. J., Bolding, C. W., & Allyn Books, C. (in press). Integrating critical conscious-ness and social empathy: A new framework to enhance conscientization. In L. J. Rapa & E. B. Godfrey (Eds). *Critical consciousness: Expanding theory and measurement.* Cambridge University Press.

Rapa, L. J., Diemer, M. A., & Roseth, C. J. (2020). Can a values-affirmation interven-tion bolster academic achievement and raise CC? Results from a small-scale field experiment. *Social Psychology of Education, 23*(2), 537–557.

Rapa, L. J., McKellar, S. E., & Godfrey, E. B. (in press). Critical consciousness measurement: A brief history, current status, and new directions. In L. J. Rapa & E. B. Godfrey (Eds). *Critical consciousness: Expanding theory and measure-ment.* Cambridge University Press.

Roberts, B. W., & DelVecchio, W. F. (2000). The rank-order consistency of personality traits from childhood to old age: A quantitative review of longitudinal studies. *Psychological Bulletin, 126*(1), 3–25. https://doi.org/10.1037/0033-2909.126.1.3.

Robins, C. J., Schmidt III, H., & Linehan, M. M. (2004). Dialectical behavior therapy: Synthesizing radical acceptance with skillful means. In S. C. Hayes, V. M. Follette, & M. M. Linehan (Eds.), *Mindfulness and acceptance: Expanding the cognitive-behavioral tradition* (pp. 30–44). The Guilford Press.

Rogers, C. R. (1979). The foundations of the person-centered approach. *Education, 100* (2), 98–107.

Rondini, A. C. (2015). Observations of CC development in the context of service learning. *Teaching Sociology, 43*(2), 137–145.

Sichel, C. E., Javdani, S., & Yi, J. (2022). Perceiving fairness in an unfair world: System justification and the mental health of girls in detention facilities. *American Journal of Community Psychology, 69*(3–4), 451–462.

Singh, S., Berezin, M. N., Wallach, L. N., Godfrey, E. B., & Javdani, S. (2021). Traumatic incidents and experiences of racism and sexism: Examining associ-ations with components of CC for system-involved girls of color. *American Journal of Community Psychology, 67*(1–2), 64–75.

Singh, S., Granski, M., Victoria, M. D. P., & Javdani, S. (2018). The praxis of decoloni-ality in researcher training and community-based data collection. *American Journal of Community Psychology, 62*(3–4), 385–395.

Sullivan, C. M. (2003). Using the ESID model to reduce intimate male violence against women. *American Journal of Community Psychology, 32*(3), 295–303.

Sullivan, C. M., & Bybee D. I. (1999). Reducing violence using community-based advocacy for women with abusive partners. *Journal of Consulting and Clinical Psychology, 67*(1), 43–53. https://doi.org/10.1037/0022-006X.67.1.43.

Sullivan, C. M., Bybee, D. I., & Allen, N. E. (2002). Findings from a community-based program for battered women and their children. *Journal of Interpersonal Violence, 17*(9), 915–936.

Sullivan, C. M., Tan, C., Basta, J., Rumptz, M., & Davidson, W. S. (1992). An advocacy intervention program for women with abusive partners: Initial evaluation. *American Journal of Community Psychology, 20*(3), 309–332.

Tilton, J. (2013). Rethinking youth voice and institutional power: Reflections from inside a service learning partnership in a California juvenile hall. *Children and Youth Services Review, 35*(8), 1189–1196.

Torres-Harding, S. R., Siers, B., & Olson, B. D. (2012). Development and psychometric evaluation of the Social Justice Scale (SJS). *American Journal of Community Psychology*, *50*, 77–88. https://doi.org/10.1007/s10464-011-9478-2.

Watts, R., Diemer, M., & Voight, A. (2011). Critical Consciousness: Current status and future directions. *New Directions for Child and Adolescent Development*, *134*, 43–57. https://doi.org/10.1002/cd.310.

Watts, R., Griffith, D., & Abdul-Adil, J. (1999). Sociopolitical development as an antidote for oppression: Theory and action. *American Journal of Community Psychology*, *27*(2), 255–271. https://doi.org/10.1023/A:1022839818873.

Watts, R. J., & Hipolito-Delgado, C. P. (2015). Thinking ourselves to liberation? Advancing sociopolitical action in critical consciousness. *The Urban Review*, *47* (5), 847–867.

Winans-Solis, J. (2014). Reclaiming power and identity: Marginalized students' experiences of service-learning. *Equity & Excellence in Education*, *47*(4), 604–621.

PART III

SOCIETAL CONTEXTS

7

Critical Race Consciousness

Conceptualizing a Model of Race-Specific Critical Consciousness among Youth

JOSEFINA BAÑALES, ADRIANA ALDANA, AND ELAN C. HOPE

In the past three decades, theory and research on youth's critical conscious-ness, or how youth come to analyze social inequality and act against these inequalities, has expanded. Critical consciousness scholars recognize that racism and other systems of oppression are contexts in which all youth develop (see Heberle et al., 2020; Wray-Lake et al., in press). As youth develop within these racialized and oppressive contexts, they also develop understand-ings, feelings, and actions in response to these oppressive social systems (Anyiwo et al., 2018; Diemer et al., 2016; Seaton et al., 2018). Still, critical consciousness scholarship has yet to articulate potentially unique psycho-logical and behavioral processes that allow youth to critically analyze and challenge racism in particular (Bañales et al., 2019). In other words, limited theoretical and empirical work examines how youth develop beliefs and actions that challenge racism, or develop critical race consciousness (CRC). A focus on how youth develop CRC in the context of racism is necessary, as racism is a system of oppression that is embedded in the fabric of the United States, is intertwined with other systems of oppression (e.g., sexism, classism, ableism), and continues to shape the life outcomes of all people in this country (Bonilla-Silva, 2017; Delgado & Stefancic, 2017).

The goal of this chapter is to fill this theoretical gap in critical conscious-ness theory and research by developing an integrative model that articulates the nature and dynamics of youth CRC. To do so, we integrate several bodies of research across diverse fields of study (e.g., liberation psychology, develop-mental psychology, counseling psychology, sociology, social work) to describe a conceptual framework of CRC that applies to youth of color and white youth. A detailed and nuanced understanding of how youth develop CRC will better inform research and practice that aims to stimulate this developmental process. To build the conceptual framework, we first describe the nature of racism in the United States and explain how this system of oppression serves as a developmental context for youth CRC. Then, we discuss relevant theory that grounds our integrative conceptual model, followed by a more in-depth discussion of each component of the model. Next, we discuss the psychological processes and social contexts that may facilitate or hinder CRC praxis and development. We conclude with recommendations for future CRC research and practice.

Racism: The Developmental Context of Racial Oppression in the United States

The United States has a longstanding history of white supremacy upon which the country was established. The legacy of racism in the United States includes, but is certainly not limited to, the colonization of Indigenous people's land, the enslavement of African people, and the internment of Japanese people (Aldana & Vazquez, 2020; Zinn, 2015). Racism is a multidimensional system of racial advantage and oppression that is embedded in all facets of society, resulting in the disenfranchisement of racialized racial/ethnic groups and the advancement of white people. The system of racism manifests on structural, institutional, cultural, interpersonal, and intrapersonal levels – manifestations that map onto the levels of society (Jones, 1997; Miller & Garran, 2017; Neblett, 2019). The levels of racism are dynamic in that their structure and manifestations reinforce one another and change with shifts in the sociopolitical landscape; changes in one dimension inform shifts in another (Bonilla-Silva, 2017; Miller & Garran, 2017; Rozas & Miller, 2009). Critical race scholars underscore the "ordinariness" of racism within all institutions and day-to-day interactions, calling attention to the social construction of race and its intersections with other forms of oppression, such as sexism, cis-heterosexism, religious oppression, and classism (Delgado & Stefancic, 2017). Accordingly, we conceptualize racism as a matrix of oppression with multiple levels that socially construct the developmental ecology of youth.

Consistent with theoretical models of youth development, we contend that racial oppression operates on all levels of society (García Coll et al., 1996; Spencer et al., 1997), thereby shaping the nature of CRC for youth. Framing racism as part of youth's developmental ecology is necessary to fully comprehend the pervasiveness of white supremacy in shaping the lives of young people. Racism negatively affects the livelihood of youth of color (Benner et al., 2018; García Coll et al., 1996; Paradies et al., 2015) and systematically benefits white youth (Bonilla-Silva, 2017; Richards-Schuster & Aldana, 2013). At the societal and cultural levels, racism is maintained through cultural dominance over racialized racial/ethnic groups by the dominant group (Jones, 1997; Utsey & Ponterotto, 1996). For example, the criminalization of Black and Latinx people in media representations, political discourse, the school-to-prison pipeline, and the criminal legal system are ubiquitous expressions of societal racism (Rios, 2011; Thomas & Blackmon, 2015; Wray-Lake et al., 2018). Institutional racism manifests in policies, laws, and practices of institutions and organizations that disproportionately exclude, punish, or negatively impact marginalized racial/ethnic groups, irrespective of intent. Color-evasive ideology, or racist beliefs that code racial dynamics and issues as nonracial, become ingrained in the practices of established institutions, resulting in inequitable outcomes between racial/ethnic groups (Bonilla-Silva, 2017). For instance, zero-tolerance discipline policies in schools purport to promote school safety, but disproportionately punish Black and brown students for misconduct with school-based arrests and expulsions (Husband & Bertrand, 2021; Losen et al., 2015).

Interpersonal racism includes individuals' or groups' involvement in intentional or unintentional discriminatory behaviors toward others (Jones, 1997). This may include using a racial slur to insult someone or acts of racial bias that cause agony or harm to the target of the interaction, whether intentional or not. A teacher may applaud a Black student for being "articulate" or demonstrate delight that a Latinx student "wants to go to college" without considering the underlying racialized assumption that Black and Latinx students do not have the capacity or the desire to excel academically. At the intrapersonal level, racism manifests as prejudice attitudes, beliefs, and assumptions rooted in stereotypes *within* an individual.

Interpersonal and intrapersonal racism are often considered quintessential forms of racism in the United States (Bonilla-Silva, 2017; Tatum, 2017). This understanding of racism corresponds with the dominant discourse, which posits that racism is the result of mean-spirited "racist people" who endorse negative attitudes or beliefs toward other racial/ethnic groups and engage in intentional forms of racial discrimination (Bonilla-Silva, 2017; Raval et al., 2021). In other words, people often analyze racism at the level of individuals and not societal practices, culture, and institutions. Regardless of people's good intention to not be racist, the structural racialized nature of United States culture and institutions embeds racism throughout everyday life. Without active and intentional antiracist action that disrupts whiteness and the oppression of people of color, individuals contribute to and sustain a system of white advantage (Tatum, 2017; Kendi, 2019).

Given that adolescence is considered an important period for psychosocial and behavioral development in racist social systems (García Coll et al., 1996; Spencer et al., 1997), how youth come to understand racism and engage in antiracism efforts should also be of concern (Aldana et al., 2019; Toraif et al., 2021). As youth negotiate their values, beliefs, and actions alongside biological, sociocognitive, and contextual changes, youth may reflect on the nature of racial affairs in the United States, which may prompt them to seek out new information or experiences to learn about their racial/ethnic group or the racial experiences of others (Rivas-Drake & Umaña-Taylor, 2019). Thus, adolescence is a time when youth commitments to racial justice and other forms of justice are especially malleable (Bañales et al., 2020; Flanagan et al., 2009).

Researchers have investigated how youth reflect on and challenge racism through qualitative and youth participatory action research studies (Aldana et al., 2019; Cabrera et al., 2013; Hope et al., 2015; Richards-Schuster & Aldana, 2013; Roberts et al., 2008), providing valuable insights into the nature of youth's capacities to critically analyze and challenge racism. Psychologists have also validated quantitative measures that capture youth antiracism actions and orientations (Aldana et al., 2019; Hope et al., 2019; McWhirter & McWhirter, 2016) and explore causes and correlates of anti-racist beliefs and behavior. In light of this growing body of research, we put forth a conceptual model of CRC to situate how youth come to understand racism and act to dismantle it.

CRITICAL RACE CONSCIOUSNESS

Our conceptualization of CRC includes three dimensions: *racism analysis, racial reflexivity*, and *antiracism action* (see Figure 7.1). To summarize, *racism analysis* is a multidimensional sociocognitive skill that includes the recognition and critique of white supremacy operating on different societal levels, the ability to link historical and modern racism, and an understanding of how racialization intersects with other forms of oppression (Aldana et al., 2012; Bañales, Aldana et al., 2021; Bañales & Rivas-Drake, 2022). *Racial reflexivity* is

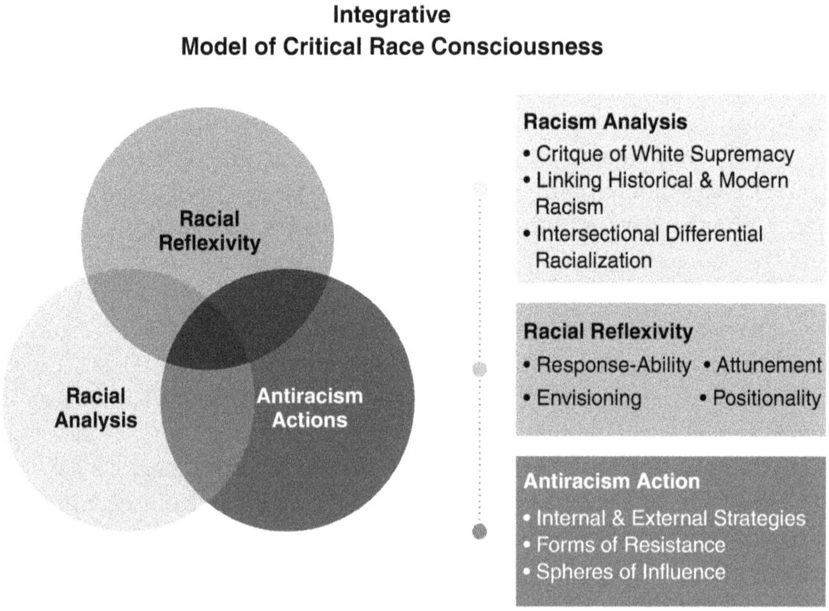

Integrative Model of Critical Race Consciousness

Racism Analysis
• Critque of White Supremacy
• Linking Historical & Modern Racism
• Intersectional Differential Racialization

Racial Reflexivity
• Response-Ability   • Attunement
• Envisioning   • Positionality

Antiracism Action
• Internal & External Strategies
• Forms of Resistance
• Spheres of Influence

FIGURE 7.1 Integrative model of critical race consciousness.

the ongoing and moment-to-moment practice of situating oneself within an analysis of racism that allows one to engage in reflective and contextually informed antiracism action. *Antiracism action* is involvement in actions that challenge racism on interpersonal, communal, and political levels. In the following sections, we further articulate the nature of each component and how the development of each component of CRC might differ for youth of color and white youth. We also conceptualize youth CRC as praxis and development. CRC *praxis* refers to the three dimensions of CRC, and CRC *development* refers to the formation of these phenomena in social context and relation to one another.

In this model of CRC, we explicitly acknowledge the role of white supremacy in youth's personal lived experiences and structure of society and challenge the notion that reflecting on, critiquing, and challenging racism are processes that "only people of color have to deal with" (Helms, 2014). White people, including youth, are also affected by racism in that they receive interpersonal, cultural, and structural advantages in society, whereas people of color are disadvantaged by this system of oppression (Miller & Garran, 2017; Tatum, 2017). Thus, the development of CRC is a relevant process for youth of all racial/ethnic backgrounds. However, the extent to which youth engage in this process, resist learning about race and white supremacy, and are exposed to experiences that initiate this process will depend on their social position in the United States' racialized power hierarchy and other power structures. For instance, for white youth, CRC might involve becoming aware of their active and unintentional involvement in white supremacy and determining if and how they will relinquish their white racial advantage in pursuit of racial justice (Heberle et al., 2020; Neville et al., 2014).

Theoretical Foundations of Youth Critical Race Consciousness

Our model of CRC is informed by several theories and frameworks from multiple social science disciplines that focus on critical consciousness and sociopolitical development among youth, ethnic/racial identity, and ideologies/beliefs that perpetuate the system of racism, ecological systems theories, and developmental perspectives on the origins of beliefs about race and racism (see Table 7.1). In particular, the current model is grounded in foundational critical consciousness theory that articulates that a critique of and action against inequality is vital for social change among adults who are marginalized by classism (Freire, 2018). Freire articulated *conscientização* as the process by which oppressed people come to critically reflect and act upon unjust societal issues affecting their lives. He proposed that transformation cannot occur unless there is social action that builds on reflection. Freire (2018) also underscored that political and educational efforts seeking anti-oppressive change need to attend to the interdependent nature of action-reflection through

TABLE 7.1 Theoretical models and frameworks that inform the integrative model of critical race consciousness among youth

		Ethnic/Racial Identity		
Frameworks	Discipline	Tenets/Concepts	Communities of Focus (i.e., Racial/Ethnic Groups, Age)	Sources
Ethnic-Racial Identity (ERI)	Developmental psychology Social psychology	• ERI development is a normative developmental task • ERI is multidimensional in content and process • ERI is informed by social context • There are intersections between ERI and CC/SPD processes	• Different racial/ethnic groups, primarily including Latinx and African American youth • Youth, approximately 14–18 years old	Anyiwo et al. (2018) Mathews et al. (2020) Sellers et al. (1998) Umaña-Taylor et al. (2014) Williams et al. (2020)
People of Color Racial Identity Ego Statuses and Information-Processing Strategies White Racial Identity Ego Statuses and Information-Processing Strategies	Counseling psychology	• The content of racial identity and the processes by which this content develops looks differently between white adults and adults of color • Among white people, integrative awareness includes the ability to emphasize and collaborate with people from oppressed groups	• White adults • Adults of color	Helms (2005) Helms (2014)

Ideologies/Beliefs That Perpetuate the System of Racism

Colorblind Ideology	Sociology	• Race/color-evasive belief system that minimizes the role of racism in structuring society is the dominant racial ideology in the United States • White people endorse colorblind ideology (e.g., abstract liberalism, minimization of race) which perpetuates the white racial status quo	• Primarily white adults • Emerging work with adults of color	Bonilla-Silva (2017) Rendón et al. (2020)
Colorblind Attitudes	Counseling psychology	• Colorblind attitudes deny, distort, and minimize the reality of racial differences in societal outcomes and the existence of structural power that advantages white people • Envisions solutions and alternatives to colorblind attitudes (e.g., a multicultural perspective)	• White college students • Smaller body of research with college students of color	Neville et al. (2013) Bar & Neville (2008)
System-Justification Beliefs	Social psychology	• People endorse system-justification to address psychological needs of certainty, to assuage insecurity, and to coordinate social relationships • Dominant and marginalized groups may adopt system-justification beliefs	• Adults with dominant statuses (e.g., white, Christians) in the United States and across the world	Jost & Hunyady (2005) Jost (2019)

TABLE 7.1 (*Cont.*)

		Ethnic/Racial Identity		
Frameworks	Discipline	Tenets/Concepts	Communities of Focus (i.e., Racial/Ethnic Groups, Age)	Sources
Internalized Racism	Social psychology Clinical psychology	• People of color may internalize dominant and deficient narratives about their racial groups if they have not critically examined socialization of dominant beliefs.	• Adults of color	David et al. (2019)
Ecological Models				
Ecological System Models	Developmental psychology Human development	• Youths' psychological and behavioral development is informed by multiple overlapping contexts • Youth of color's psychological competencies are shaped by racism at various levels	• Diverse racial/ethnic groups • Children, youth, and adults across the lifespan	Bronfenbrenner & Morris (2006) García Coll et al. (1996) Spencer et al. (1997)

Developmental Perspectives on the Origins of Beliefs about Race and Racism

Ethnic Perspective Taking and Critical Analysis of Racism	Developmental psychology	• Children develop more abstract and complex beliefs about race and stereotypes over time • Youth may endorse contradictory beliefs about racism • Youths' structural analysis of racism may increase throughout adolescence	• Diverse racial/ethnic groups • Children and youth of different racial/ethnic backgrounds	Bañales, Aldana et al. (2021) McKown (2004) Quintana (1998) Quintana (2008) Seider et al. (2020)

Note. Table does not include critical consciousness and sociopolitical development theories, as they are reviewed in depth in the manuscript.

dialogic pedagogy that attends to the "various levels of perceptions of themselves and of the world in which and with which they exist" (p. 95).

Expanding on Freire's concept of *conscientização*, a conceptualization of critical consciousness informed by developmental psychology (Diemer et al., 2016) includes critical reflection (i.e., the ability to identify social issues and attribute their causes to structural factors), political efficacy (i.e., a personal sense of confidence that one can contribute to social change), and critical action (i.e., involvement in individual and collective behaviors that challenge the status quo). Other work conceptualizes external political efficacy, or perceptions that the government and government officials can enact social change, as another dimension of critical consciousness (Diemer & Rapa, 2016). Emerging work recognizes that perceptions that social change can happen alongside community members, or collective efficacy, is another key component of critical consciousness (Bañales, Sarissa Pech et al., 2021; Sánchez Carmen et al., 2015). Critical consciousness research has focused primarily on marginalized youth, primarily African American, Latinx, and low-income youth, informing questions about critical consciousness processes for more privileged youth (e.g., white youth; Diemer et al., 2021). This conceptualization of critical consciousness has been broad in that it applies to how youth develop an analysis of oppression in general. Only a few studies have centered racism and examined the development of awareness of interpersonal and structural racism over time among youth of color (Bañales et al., 2019; Seider et al., 2019) and associations between racism and antiracism action for youth of color (see Hope et al., Chapter 8 [this volume] for a review).

The proposed CRC model departs from prevailing developmental models of critical consciousness in that it does not include political efficacy (sometimes called agency or critical motivation) as a primary component of CRC. Instead, we suggest that racial reflexivity is an essential component of CRC that links racism analysis and antiracism action. While we expect that political efficacy may be related to various aspects of racial reflexivity and antiracism action, we do not purport that this component of generalized critical consciousness is a primary component of CRC. Our theoretical divergence is not intended to replace political efficacy in existing conceptualizations of critical consciousness. Rather, we anchor our conceptualization of the three CRC dimensions in Freire's (2018) notion that a critical analysis is foundational to action and that analysis and action are multidimensional, interrelated phenomena that constitute conscientization (Freire, 2018). Thus, our conceptualization of CRC focuses on the complex psychological and behavioral processes that undergird analysis of a racialized world and critical analysis of the self (i.e., reflexivity) necessary for taking action to address racism. Racial reflexivity, as we describe in more detail later in this chapter, integrates *conscientização* with other concepts from liberation psychology, including deideologizing (reconstructing ideas about one's reality through analysis of dominant white supremacist culture and problematizing), questioning, and critiquing circumstances created through conditions of oppression (Rivera, 2020). Grounded in liberation psychology and critical theories on race (e.g., Collins, 2002; Rivera, 2020), our integrative CRC framework considers the role of one's social location within society (positionality) and its relation to how one makes meaning of racism in relation to personal lived experiences, vision for social change, and one's ability to respond to racial oppression, which shapes how one takes antiracism action.

Along with critical consciousness, Watts' model of sociopolitical development (Watts et al., 1999; Watts & Guessous, 2006) has informed our CRC framework. Sociopolitical development and critical consciousness are related but different phenomena (Hope et al., in press). Both sociopolitical development and critical consciousness frameworks focus on how youth come to understand, negotiate, and challenge systems of oppression, such as racism, classism, and sexism (Watts et al., 2011; Watts & Guessous, 2006). The sociopolitical development model, however, is a race-focused framework that considers how youth develop critical consciousness and other related sociopolitical skills within a racialized context, grounded in Black liberation theory, research, and practice (for a review, see Hope et al., in press; Watts et al., 1999). Models of sociopolitical development contend that the extent to which youth critically analyze the structure of society and act upon these issues is dependent on the developmental characteristics (e.g., age, social, and cognitive abilities) and opportunity structures (e.g., schooling, racial socialization, community engagement) provided to youth to gain awareness of the reality of historical and contemporary oppression in the United States (Watts & Flanagan, 2007; Watts & Guessous, 2006).

Both sociopolitical development and critical consciousness theories and research aim to understand how youth understand, critique, negotiate, and challenge unjust social conditions. Both traditions are rooted in Paulo Freire's (2018) conceptualization of critical consciousness, although sociopolitical development theory is also explicitly grounded in Black liberation thought and practice (Hope et al., in press; Watts et al., 1999). Both bodies of work have focused primarily on youth of color, yet there has been limited explicit theory and measurement of the multidimensional nature of conscientization in the context of race and racism. We draw from the race-specific focus of youth sociopolitical development research to inform our conceptualization of CRC. Sociopolitical development research helps us differentiate how youth understand and critique racism specifically and engage in various behaviors that challenge this multilayered system of oppression in ways that center racism (see Aldana et al., 2019; Anyiwo et al., 2018; Bañales et al., 2020; Hope et al., 2019, for foundational articles that ground critical consciousness and sociopolitical development processes in the system of racism in the United States).

In addition to critical consciousness and sociopolitical development, other related frameworks and theories contribute to our understanding of the role of race and racism in youth's CRC development. The formation of beliefs, feelings, and actions toward the nature of one's racialized self, others, and the structure and dynamics of society – as explicated in various social science theories – coincide or overlap with sociopolitical and critical consciousness development (Anyiwo et al., 2018; Bañales et al., 2020; Mathews et al., 2020). In Table 7.1, we highlight these related frameworks, their corresponding disciplines, and the key tenets or theoretical concepts that informed our conceptualization of CRC. In general, ecological models that articulate how psychological and behavioral development is informed by proximal and distal social contexts (including structural racism) inform the current model of youth CRC (Bronfenbrenner & Morris, 2006; García Coll et al., 1996; Spencer et al., 1997). Our conceptual framework was also informed by theories of ethnic/racial identity (Sellers et al., 1998; Umaña-Taylor et al., 2014; Williams et al., 2020), ideologies that perpetuate systemic racism (Bar & Neville, 2008; Bonilla-Silva, 2017; David et al., 2019; Helms, 2005, 2014; Jost, 2019; Jost et al., 2004; Neville et al., 2013; Rendón et al., 2020), and developmental perspectives on the origins of beliefs about race and racism (Bañales, Aldana et al., 2021; McKown, 2004; Quintana, 1998, 2008; Seider et al., 2020). Throughout the chapter, we weave these perspectives together to develop and describe the CRC conceptual framework.

In summary, we integrate these diverse bodies of theory and research on how adults and youth develop notions of themselves as racialized beings and navigate the racialized United States to inform the dimensions of CRC, as presented in the sections that follow. Our CRC model focuses on youth's awareness and critical analysis of racism and the nature of behaviors used to challenge these conditions and achieve liberation, and of the conditions and environments that promote wellness and thriving. A focus on youth's critical analysis of racism does not imply that youth can, as Watts and Hipolito-Delgado (2015) describe it, "think themselves into liberation." Instead, in alignment with core tenets of liberation psychology (see Rivera, 2020), we see youth's ability to act upon unjust racial conditions as predicated on their awareness and critique of the existence of racism. This is a complex skill that also incorporates the ability to reflect on their positionality within racialized social systems and contexts, which then informs their involvement in antiracism actions. Our model elucidates the underlying developmental processes and components that comprise CRC among youth of color and white youth: *racism analysis*, *racial reflexivity*, and *antiracism action*.

Racism Analysis An analysis of racism is foundational to CRC and includes the synthesis of three forms of racial literacy. First, youth must recognize and critique white supremacy. To do so, there must be knowledge that race is a social construct that is created by historical and contemporary policy and results in inequitable social, economic, and political dynamics in society (Bonilla-Silva, 2017; Tatum, 2017). Youth of color and white youth have the potential to see race as a social construct, although many youth see race as immutable, inherited, or biological (Bañales, 2020; Byrd & Hope, 2011). Youth's conceptions of race as a fixed biological trait are informed by mainstream assumptions and resulting socialization about the nature of race across the United States (Bonilla-Silva, 2017; Raval et al., 2021). Central to understanding race as a social construct is recognizing that race was created to justify the subjugation of people of color and used to propagate the myth of intellectual, physical, and behavioral superiority of white people, particularly white men (Crenshaw, 2017; Delgado & Stefancic, 2017; Omi & Winant, 2018). This racial subjugation occurs on interpersonal, cultural, and structural levels (Miller & Garran, 2017). Thus, youth's critique of white supremacy includes the ability to recognize that white people's quest for white dominance, and the oppression of people of color, operated and continues to function on different levels of society.

Youth of color have the potential for a multidimensional analysis of racism, as they recognize the interpersonal (Montoro et al., 2021; Seaton & Iida, 2019), cultural (Hope et al., 2019; Cammarota, 2004), institutional, and structural racism (Bañales et al., 2019; Hope & Bañales, 2019; McWhirter et al., 2019; Richards-Schuster & Aldana, 2013) that they personally experience and witness in society. It is not guaranteed that youth of color will automatically recognize or be able to name forms of racism that are more distal to their immediate social contexts (e.g., institutional and structural racism). Youth of color, like all youth, are reared in the same color-evasive[1] United States society that frames racism as individuals' involvement in intentional and visible discriminatory behaviors (Bonilla-Silva, 2017; Neville et al., 2013). Research suggests that the internalization of color-evasive principles related to meritocracy and individualism, along with racial segregation, minimizes the ability to apply a critical race analysis to their experiences of racism (Bonilla-Silva & Embrick, 2001; Rendón et al., 2020; Young, 2006). Given that youth of color experience interpersonal forms of racial discrimination (Benner et al., 2018), they might be more likely to recognize interpersonal forms of racism than institutional or structural manifestations of racism (Bañales et al., 2020). However, how and why certain youth of color might be more likely than other youth of color to recognize and critique cultural, institutional, and structural racism is a standing empirical question that should be investigated.

---

[1] Color-evasive is a nonableist term that recognizes the propensity to avoid and ignore race in societal dynamics without implicating blindness or visual impairment (see Annamma et al., 2016).

In their potential critique of white supremacy, white youth may be especially likely to misinterpret all acts of intergroup exclusion as interpersonal racism, as they voice knowledge that people of color face this form of interpersonal racism, but they also indicate that they personally experience interpersonal racial discrimination (Bañales et al., 2020; Flanagan et al., 2009). White youths' perceptions of personal experiences with racial discrimination (or experiences with "reverse racism") must be questioned as racism is a system of oppression that advantages white people (Tatum, 2017). The extent to which white youth perceive cultural, institutional, and structural racism is unclear, partly because the majority of research on white people's racism awareness has been with college students (Neville et al., 2013). Researchers find that white youth have the ability to recognize the structural nature of oppression, including racism, and that this skill may be informed by their exposure to socializing opportunities that are offered as a result of their socioeconomic status (Bañales et al., 2020; Flanagan et al., 2014).

Along with critiquing white supremacy across the levels of racism, linking historical racism with modern racial dynamics, disparities, and experiences is another key dimension of racism analysis (Richards-Schuster & Aldana, 2013; see also Burson & Godfrey, 2020). Youth who connect the historical roots of racism, such as redlining – or the systematic denial of people of color from obtaining loans to buy homes in white communities – with contemporary racial issues (e.g., racial segregation in neighborhoods and school) can recognize that these everyday racial issues have not developed by accident. Contemporary racism is the product of anti-Black, anti-Indigenous, and white supremacist ideologies and practices (e.g., capitalism) that form the policies and practices that negatively affected the lives of people of color and advanced the lives of white people. These policies and practices continue to reverberate in contemporary society and strengthen as new policies and practices that advantage white people's lives are created. Thus, the ability to link contemporary racism with an understanding of the historical structural factors that created or perpetuate these issues is key in youth's racism analysis, which may, in turn, facilitate psychological and behavioral outcomes that promote racial justice, such as solidarity against social injustice among minoritized communities (Bañales & Rivas-Drake, 2022; Burson & Godfrey, 2020).

Third, an *intersectional understanding of differential racialization* is foundational to racism analysis. Racialization refers to the ongoing sociohistorical process through which bodies, groups, interactions, and social structures come to be assigned racial meaning and significance (Hochman, 2019). In essence, racialization is the cumulation of the social construction of race – not simply as a categorical label but as a tool of white supremacy – to (re)create a caste system that targets people deemed nonwhite. The racialization of individuals is not limited to associating physical markers of racial/ethnic background (e.g., phenotype, hair texture), but also styles of dress, hairstyles, body sizes, speaking styles, and languages spoken (Rosa, 2018). Youth recognize that people are racialized in the United States (Bañales et al., 2020), particularly youth who are racialized themselves (Rios, 2011; Sirin et al., 2008).

To offer one example of racialization, we turn to the experience of Muslim people in the United States. Muslim people are not considered a racial group, but rather a religious group. However, preceding and following 9/11, Muslim people encountered discrimination based on their skin tone, women's wearing of hijabs, style of dress, language use, and surnames. Muslim people's experiences with racialization in the United States post-9/11 occurred when they experienced "de-Americanization," which stripped them of privileges associated with citizenship because they were perceived and treated as "national threats," "terrorists," and "Anti-American" (Selod, 2015). As the experiences of Muslim Americans suggests, the racialization process is imposed on groups by some agent in particular time periods and social contexts.

Accordingly, differential racialization, a tenet of critical race theory, further suggests that social groups are racialized in differing ways at different times to serve the interests and needs of whiteness (Delgado & Stefancic, 2017). In revisiting the experience of Muslim Americans, a critical race analysis of the "War on Terror" would suggest that the racialization of Muslims in the United States was employed to justify the creation of Immigration and Customs Enforcement (ICE), an agency founded in 2003 within the Department of Homeland Security. While ICE was part of the federal government's response to the September 11, 2001 attack, its enforcement has largely and acutely targeted undocumented immigrants (of any race) from Latin America, which has accompanied the xenophobic and anti-immigrant public policies of the Trump administration (Allen & Goetz, 2021). As another example of differential racialization, we can look at the resurgence of anti-Asian discrimination that arose during the COVID-19 pandemic. Although influenced by former President Trump's scapegoating tactics, the recent rise in anti-Asian racism is reflective of the racialization of Asian Americans as disease-prone foreigners (e.g., "yellow peril") used to restrict immigration of Asian countries to the United States throughout history (Li & Nicholson, 2021). In the examples provided here, the racialization process involves othering these groups as non-American citizens (i.e., forever foreign) to maintain the association between national citizenship and whiteness.

Taken together, youth's racism analysis includes a critique of white supremacy; the ability to link historical racism with contemporary racial disparities, issues, and patterns; and an intersectional knowledge of differential racialization. These dimensions of a racism analysis are developmental competencies that evolve over time, are interdependent, and inform one another (Bañales et al., 2020; Neville et al., 2014), suggesting that youths' CRC is an active and malleable process in and of itself (Hope & Bañales, 2019).

Racial Reflexivity Critical consciousness scholars have long understood the interdependent nature of reflection and action. Indeed, Freire (2018) asserts that reflection and action co-occur in the conscientization process. The skill of reflection is beneficial when there is a need to recognize or become aware of inequality, but reflecting upon the world on its own is not sufficient for involvement in actions that challenge the status quo (Aldana et al., 2019; Norton & Sliep, 2018). In explaining praxis, Freire (2018) argued that it is essential for the oppressed to situate themselves in their analysis of social conditions and to be critically aware of their role as subjects of change rather than objects. We argue that critical self-reflection is also crucial for white people who act in solidarity with racially marginalized groups from a place of privilege. Nevertheless, the role of critical reflection of oneself as a subject of an oppressive system to transform society has been given less attention within the critical consciousness literature. As such, in our conceptualization of CRC we include racial reflexivity as a conduit that connects racism analysis to antiracism action.

Reflexivity is distinct from racism analysis as it involves locating oneself in the structure of society, one's relations with others in society, and reconciling potential incongruence between one's beliefs and actions that aim to influence societal norms, practices, and systems. Among social work, health, and educational practitioners, reflexivity involves the process by which individuals recognize how their roles as researchers, educators, and practitioners shape interactions and experiences in research and practice settings (Norton & Sliep, 2018; Sakamoto & Pitner, 2005). Norton and Sliep's (2018) critical reflexive model indicates that the process involves "an ongoing critical appraisal of the self and others in action" (p. 46). This model incorporates an understanding of how one's social contexts, awareness of personal values, and position in society lead to the simultaneous critical examination of one's agency, which informs performance and actions. Thus, critical reflexivity builds upon reflection to embody thoughtful action in response to one's context, power relations, and those with whom one interacts.

In social science research, feminist and race scholars have long argued for the use of reflexivity as a critical research method to interrogate presumptions of dominant epistemologies and advance critical knowledge production. For instance, in explicating Black women's epistemic agency and standpoint, Patricia Hill Collins (2002) underscores the need for scholars to critically examine how our social location within intersecting systems of oppression structure relationships with the people and issues under investigation. Similarly, Emirbayer and Desmond (2012) have called for the integration of racial reflexivity, or the recognition of how a scholar's social location in the racial order affects their assumptions, analysis of the social world, and political imagination in the sociological study of race. The study and analysis of race and oppression is not exclusive to members of the academy or social leaders (Collins, 2002; Freire, 2018). Therefore, we argue that given the centrality of race and racism to the social order in the United States, building capacity to examine racism, and how it affects our day-to-day lives, is necessary for every individual.

Drawing on multidisciplinary conceptualizations of reflexivity, we put forth a multifaceted notion of *racial reflexivity* as an aspect of youth CRC. Racial reflexivity is the ongoing and moment-to-moment practice of situating oneself within an analysis of racism that allows one to engage in reflective and contextually informed antiracism action. Specifically, racial reflexivity is the dynamic embodiment of one's *response-ability, envisioning, attunement,* and *positionality* (REAP). We elaborate on each as follows:

> **Response-ability:** The critical appraisal of one's ability to enact change (individual and collective agency) *and* sense of obligation to effectively respond to racism while taking into account one's positionality, contextual risks and rewards, and opportunity for action.
>
> **Envisioning:** The ability to radically imagine, dream, visualize, or propose new possibilities for being in, relating to, and enacting a more racially just future. This includes the individual or collective practice of critical hopefulness and an ethic of communal love.
>
> **Attunement:** Cognitive-emotional alignment between one's racial values, beliefs, goals, affective reactions to (e.g., anger, guilt, apathy) and behaviors toward racism. Attunement involves awareness of, but is not equivalent to, motivations for disrupting racial hegemony.
>
> **Positionality:** Intentional engagement in the world informed by an understanding of how one's sociopolitical positioning (e.g., access to resources, school and home residence, how people treat individuals and those around them) is affected by racial hierarchies and structural power (social location), with particular attention to the ways race and racism inform one's standpoint, interactions with others, and roles within a given context. One might engage in antiracism actions, or respond to racism, as a member of a target/marginalized group (i.e., people of color, racialized groups), a member of the agent/dominant group (i.e., white allies), or someone holding a liminal social location between two or more target and agent groups (e.g., a biracial person).

Youth's embodiment of racial reflexivity supports the interdependent relationship between a racism analysis and antiracism action. Racial reflexivity differs from racism analysis in that the latter involves acquiring and utilizing a foundational understanding of the system of racism, such as the different levels of racism and statistics on the racial disparities. Racial reflexivity involves coming to understand and reflect on one's own racial narrative and other people's racial stories, one's relations with other racial groups, racial contexts and systems, the roles one has in how these contexts and systems function, reflection on one's emotions in response to these interactions, and a consideration of whether one's values and beliefs match actions and adjustments made to settle any incongruence. In this way, youth's embodied racial reflexivity facilitates a racism analysis so that new knowledge learned about racism is more personal and less abstract (this may be particularly relevant for white youth) and that racialized experiences of people of color are seen as interconnected and interdependent. Racial reflexivity also informs and is interdependent with antiracism action. The synergy between the various aspects of racial reflexivity is an ongoing process that occurs as youth engage in antiracism behaviors with others.

Racial reflexivity is also related to ethnic/racial identity processes that enable young people to engage in a racialized world in a conscientious manner. For example, the Integrative Awareness status within the white racial identity ego status model includes the ability to empathize and collaborate with people from oppressed groups (Helms, 1994). The ability to empathize with others' unique sociopolitical experiences is akin to the "emotional faculties" theorized to underlie sociopolitical development (Watts et al., 2003), and the ability to collaborate with others includes engagement in collective action behaviors (e.g., activism, critical action) that aim to advance racial justice alongside other people of color (Aldana et al., 2019; Anyiwo et al., 2020; Mathews et al., in press).

Understanding racism and acting to dismantle racism may operate differently for youth of color and white youth. Thus, taking into account the role of racial reflexivity in whether and how a person chooses to act, speak out, or intervene to address racism is necessary to fully understand antiracism praxis. Freire (2018) states that "a critical analysis of reality may, however, reveal that a particular form of action is impossible or inappropriate at the present time. Those who through reflection perceive the infeasibility of inappropriateness of one or another form of action . . . cannot thereby be accused of inaction" (p. 128). To illustrate, a youth of color who chooses to remain silent after experiencing a racial microaggression in class may do so as an act of resistance against serving as a token spokesperson for their race or the emotional labor associated with teaching white peers about race. In this example, the student has considered their positionality, response-ability, and attunement within this specific racialized classroom situation. While the student may envision a radical education environment wherein they do not experience racism, they are also reflexive on their options within the moment. This behavior is in fact a form of antiracism action when interpreted through a lens of racial reflexivity. As another example, a white youth ally who engages in racial reflexivity may decide to listen or remain silent in a collective action planning meeting rather than offer strategies to maintain a collaborative space that centers the expertise of youth of color. In this way, the white youth ally is considerate of their positionality and the collective envisioning and response-ability that prioritizes the experiences and voices of their racially minoritized peers.

In psychology's conceptualization of critical consciousness, the under-lying assumption is that youth who have a greater recognition and critique of societal inequality will feel more agentic to challenge these social inequities and, in turn, will engage in behaviors that challenge these inequities via range of civic and political behaviors (Watts et al., 2011). In our CRC framework, we contend that youth who reflect on and question their positions in systems of privilege and oppression will be better equipped to develop a sense of collective agency and social responsibility and enact antiracism actions that challenge oppression, as youth better understand how their lives are connected to others (Aldana et al., 2021; Norton & Sliep, 2018; Richards-Schuster & Aldana, 2013). Our inclusion of racial reflexivity in the CRC model departs from existing conceptualizations of critical consciousness that name political efficacy (or agency or critical motivation) as a core component (Diemer et al., 2016; Watts et al., 2011). Indeed, empirical research suggests that political efficacy is related to critical action among youth, such that a greater sense of efficacy is related to more engagement in critical action (Barnes & Hope, 2017; Diemer & Rapa, 2016; Hope et al., 2020). Empirical research, however, is mixed on whether and how political efficacy connects critical reflection to action in the general critical consciousness literature (Diemer & Rapa, 2016; Heberle et al., 2020).

In our conceptual framework, we contend that CRC is a reciprocal process wherein racial reflexivity connects racism analysis and antiracism action. Political efficacy is integrated as a peripheral aspect of racial reflexivity, mainly via response-ability and attunement. For instance, within racial reflexivity, youth make regular and ongoing evaluations of their individual and collective agency (determined by the current state of their racism analysis, the opportunities for antiracism action, and other factors), along with evaluations of their obligation and commitment to pursue racial justice (i.e., response-ability). Political efficacy is likely one of several factors that shapes both a sense of obligation to challenge racism, which implies a role of accountability, as well as the act of attunement necessary to act accordingly. In this way, political efficacy or agency is related to CRC praxis, but it is not a primary component of CRC.

To encourage racial reflexivity, youth may be asked the following questions to expose and interrogate their assumptions about race and racism and positionality in the United States' racial hierarchy:

- What values do I have about understanding the nature of race, racial difference, racial diversity, and challenging racial inequality?
- Am I engaging in behaviors that are consistent with these values?
- Are the nature and functioning of my social contexts (e.g., friends, schools, neighborhoods) congruent with my values and beliefs?
- Are my race-related behaviors informed by my own values or the values of others?

These questions, and the larger racial reflexivity practice, help youth avoid intellectualizing an understanding of racism, which is common among white people as they learn about and reflect on racism (Saul & Burkholder, 2020).

Youth of color who engage in raising these questions may be encouraged to reflect on internalized racism (Atkin et al., 2018; Smith & Hope, 2020) or the extent to which they have unconsciously or consciously adopted white supremacist, anti-Black, or anti-Indigenous ideologies in their lives. Youth of color who engage in racial reflexivity may also ask:

- Are there ways of knowing the world that your family, relatives, or ancestors have taught you that are incongruent with what your school or media is teaching you?
- Do you feel that you can show up as a true, whole self in predominantly white spaces?
- Do you feel a longing to learn more about your race, ethnicity, and culture because you feel something might be missing in your lives?

Youth of color may reflect on the answers to these questions through collective storytelling with other peers, families, and ancestors to invoke knowledge that may have been lost through racial trauma (e.g., capitalism, immigration), love for and belonging among same and other racially marginalized communities, and resistance against racial oppression (Bañales & Rivas-Drake, 2022; Chavez-Dueñas et al., 2019; Sánchez Carmen et al., 2015). Youth who engage in racial reflexivity will be better equipped to engage in antiracism actions that are congruent with their values, positionality in the United States' racial hierarchy, relationships with others in social contexts, their psychological needs, and contextual constraints.

Antiracism Action The third component of CRC is antiracism action. Antiracism actions are enacted to resist white supremacy, reduce racial inequality that is a function of societal structures, and create antiracist cultures and climates (Aldana et al., 2019; Kendi, 2019). The ultimate goal of antiracism within the CRC framework is liberation – a healthy environment that is conducive to thriving and well-being. There are various ways youth may engage in antiracism action to challenge racism and other linked systems of oppression and achieve liberation (Aldana et al., 2019; Hope et al., 2019; McWhirter & McWhirter, 2016; McWhirter et al., 2019). Antiracism actions can target racism as it manifests in individuals, institutions, and culture. Actions that challenge systems of oppression may be more impactful in dismantling the structural roots of racism (Watts & Hipolito-Delgado, 2015), whereas antiracism actions that resist individual behavior and interpersonal interactions may help mitigate bias and discrimination (Rozas & Miller, 2009).

The fundamental distinction between antiracism action in this CRC framework and critical action in the critical consciousness framework is that antiracism action specifically centers the destruction of racism and fostering of liberation that grows from equalizing and uplifting racially minoritized individuals and communities. Critical action, as articulated in the critical consciousness literature, is generally framed more broadly and is most often associated with externally facing social justice actions to transform unjust social and political systems and contribute equality and liberation (Diemer et al., 2021), through individual and collective mobilization (Watts & Hipolito-Delgado, 2015). Hope and colleagues (Chapter 8 [this volume]), provide a conceptual model for understanding critical action along four dimensions: domain, actor, risk, and target. The domain is the ecological sphere that the action is centered in (e.g., interpersonal, political) and the actor is the individual or collective that is pursuing the action. This framework also considers the risk (relative consequences and rewards of engagement for the target) and the target, the ideal result or social change the action will generate. Antiracism action is thus encompassed by critical action but is specific to any and all actions that work toward racial justice in particular. This may include antiracism actions that target racism broadly (see Aldana et al., 2019) or antiracism actions specific to the unique ways that racism manifests for one particular racial/ethnic group (see Hope et al., 2019).

Given that white supremacy manifests on multiple levels (Jones, 1997; Miller & Garran, 2007), youth may challenge racism at multiple levels using internal strategies and external strategies (Aldana et al., 2019; Rozas & Miller, 2009). Internal strategies for antiracism action include involvement in activities that increase self-awareness and critical analysis of racism. For example, an internal antiracism action involves seeking out resources that increase one's knowledge about within-group diversity among other racial groups to reduce one's stereotypes and prejudices toward those groups. Internal strategies for antiracism action provide the tools and opportunity for youth to generate and sustain their racism analysis and racial reflexivity. While racism analysis and racial reflexivity are processes, they can be initiated and sustained passively through education settings, peer and family socialization, and culture/media exposure.

External antiracism actions involve ongoing behaviors in alliance or coalition with others, including friends, family members, coworkers, or strangers of similar or different racial/ethnic backgrounds. Internal and external strategies may occur in youth's homes, schools, work, and community settings (Aldana et al., 2019; Hope et al., 2019). Internal antiracism actions also provide foundational skills for external antiracism actions (Rozas & Miller, 2009). We contend that many forms of external antiracism action are valuable and accessible, particularly for youth. For children and adolescents, antiracism action depends on access to opportunities to engage in these behaviors, safety associated with actions, and the development of skills to support racism analysis and racial reflexivity that facilitate action. Here, we highlight two models for considering antiracism action, with a focus on forms of resistance and spheres of influence. Forms of resistance are similar to domains in Hope and colleagues' model of critical action and include the types of actions that one can engage in (e.g., dialogue, protests). Spheres of influence are similar to the target in Hope and colleagues' model and include the target audience of the antiracism action (e.g., peers, policy makers).

Informed by youth's voices through youth participatory action research, Aldana and colleagues (2019) consider antiracism action broadly across and within racial/ethnic groups. They contend that external antiracism action occurs through interpersonal interactions, communal contexts, and political channels. Interpersonal antiracism action includes directly challenging individual-level forms of racism (e.g., racial slurs, stereotypes) enacted by individuals (e.g., adults, strangers) in youth's immediate social contexts. Communal antiracism action challenges racism with others in school or community groups. Political antiracism action involves resisting racism through participation in protests, contacting local political officials, and leadership efforts. In this model of antiracism action, forms of resistance, or domains, include interpersonal and communal conversations and leadership as well as more conventional forms of activism and political involvement specific to antiracist causes. The spheres of influence, or targets, for antiracism action include individuals (e.g., peers, family, strangers), systems (e.g., media, schools), and systems-change actors (e.g., policy makers, politicians). Each of these types of antiracism action can contribute to the overall goal of redressing racism and supporting people and communities who have been most nega- tively impacted by racial oppression.

Another approach to antiracism action is to consider resistance to racism that advances the well-being of specific racially minoritized communities. For example, Hope and colleagues (2019) conceptualized external antiracism actions specific to Black communities to focus on anti-Black racism in the United States. In this conceptualization, the forms of resistance, or domains, are considered alongside risk. Antiracism action in support of Black commu- nities in this framework can be low-risk, relatively safe forms of resistance, such as confronting family or friends who make racist jokes or comments or wearing clothing that express positive messages about Blackness. These actions are not without risk and often focus on the interpersonal domain with spheres of influence, or targets, that are other close individuals. The costs of these interactions may be relational and emotional.

The potential rewards may also include improved interpersonal inter- actions and broadening racism analysis and racial reflexivity within one's immediate sphere of influence. Antiracism actions that support a specific racially minoritized community can also be high-risk, including protests and demonstrations that are likely to result in physical harm or arrest. These high-risk actions are most like traditional conceptualizations of activ- ism and organized resistance that influences broader policy and structural change (Corning & Myers, 2002). The personal risks of these actions may include burnout (Gorski, 2019), risk to physical well-being, and reputational harm. The benefits, however, include the possibility of large-scale sociopolitical change by way of policy and laws. Finally, there are political forms of resistance that are specific to a minoritized racial/ethnic group, such as keeping track of views of a member of Congress that are specific to that racial/ethnic group or campaigning for a politician who supports addressing structural issues relevant to that racial/ethnic group. For these types of politically based antiracism actions, the sphere of influence is policy makers and policy from within existing political structures.

These frameworks are two examples of conceptualizing antiracism action that focuses on how youth challenge the manifestations of racism, anti-Black racism, and, in some cases, the risks associated with varying forms of resistance. However, questions remain regarding how youth determine the forms of resistance and spheres of influence they will engage through antiracism action and what the results of these actions might be. These questions may be answered in part by considering how racial reflexivity informs antiracism action. Through racial reflexivity, youth consider which racial communities are impacted by various actions, the risk and rewards associated with involvement in these behaviors as informed by youth's response-ability, their unique racial positionality, the consequences of different antiracism actions on youth's well-being and development, and the potential impact of participation. For example, it could be that interpersonal antiracism action with other youth or adults is a relatively low-risk behavior for white youth since their racial privilege protects them from physical and socioemotional harm from racism, whereas youth of color who engage in interpersonal antiracism action may face relational and emotional consequences due to hostility toward their racial/ethnic groups. However, any youth who engages in antiracism faces some level of risk, such as exclusion from certain family members and friends, which may have negative consequences on other important developmental processes (e.g., sense of belonging).

To be clear, we believe that antiracism action might look different for youth who are Black, Indigenous, Latinx, Asian, white, and/or biracial, and that within-group differences in antiracism action are likely, given youth's positionality in other systems of oppression that are interlocked with racism. For example, later-generation Latinx youth who actively work to learn or retain the Spanish language or Indigenous languages in their lives are engaging in antiracism action, as they are actively working against white supremacy – a system that attempts to strip non-English speakers from their native languages through the assimilation process (Bañales & Rivas-Drake, 2022). For these youth, learning and practicing Spanish or Indigenous languages allows them to connect to their cultural roots and other non-European ways of knowing, which promotes their healing from white supremacy (Cammarota & Aguilera, 2012; French et al., 2020). Other youth who do not have family members who speak Spanish and do not identify as Latinx might learn Spanish due to their appreciation of the Spanish language or desire to communicate with Spanish speakers, which is commendable. However, for these youth, learning Spanish does not have the same intent, meaning, or emotional toll in their lives as they do not have a familial history with attempted forced Spanish language loss. Their learning of Spanish may contribute to antiracism actions, such as translating legal documents written in Spanish into English as a social worker with Spanish speaking clients, but their learning of Spanish, in and of itself, is not a form of antiracism action.

PSYCHOLOGICAL, BEHAVIORAL, AND CONTEXTUAL FACILITATORS AND BARRIERS OF CRITICAL RACE CONSCIOUSNESS

Youth CRC is likely associated with other psychological, behavioral, and contextual factors. Such psychological processes may include various forms of efficacy, such as internal political efficacy and collective efficacy (Diemer & Rapa, 2016; Sánchez Carmen et al., 2015). Similar to the broader critical consciousness literature, these constructs have been conceptualized and measured generally and not in the context of race and racism, raising questions about whether these phenomena facilitate dimensions of youth CRC in domain-specific or general ways. For example, it could be that a general collective efficacy does not relate to antiracism but that a collective efficacy that is grounded in individuals' sense that they and their racial communities can create racial change is associated with antiracism action (Bañales, Sarissa Pech et al., 2021).

Race-related psychological processes and experiences are especially likely to facilitate or hinder youth's CRC development. Ethnic/racial identity has been theoretically and empirically linked with CRC, particularly among Black youth (Anyiwo et al., 2018). Ideological dimensions of ethnic/racial identity are likely to inform youth's beliefs about and the actions they take to disrupt social injustice (Bañales, Lozada et al., 2021). For example, Hope and colleagues (2019) found that Black youth's nationalist ideologies, or a philosophical stance that emphasizes the unique racial experiences of Black people in the United States, were associated with high- and low-risk Black community activist orientation. Youth's ethnic/racial centrality, or the importance placed on race in one's self concept, might be especially important in youth's CRC development because a central ethnic/racial identity increases the likelihood that one will be attuned to information about race and racism (Sellers et al., 1998). Further, ethnic/racial identity awareness (Williams et al., 2020), which includes people's perceptions that ethnic/racial groups are categorized with social meaningfulness, maps onto how youth perceive inequality in society (Diemer et al., 2016).

Ethnic/racial identity scholars contend that people's development of a critical consciousness around race and racism may coincide with more complex forms of ethnic/racial identity development, suggesting that ethnic/racial identity and critical consciousness development are distinct yet overlapping processes (Tatum, 2017). *Color-evasive racial attitudes*, or the unawareness of racial privilege, racial issues, and institutional discrimination, should also be considered as barriers to CRC development (Aldana et al., 2012). Research has found color-evasive attitudes to be associated with less intergroup empathy and lower positive emotions toward other group members (Yi et al., 2020). These, in turn, are associated with lower confidence in taking internal and external strategies that challenge oppression among college students of different racial/ethnic backgrounds.

Similarly, *racial/ethnic socialization*, or the implicit and explicit messages individuals provide to youth about race, racism, and race relations, in the context of parents, schools, peers, and the media likely inform CRC (Aldana & Byrd, 2015; Anyiwo et al., 2018; Bañales et al., 2019). In their foundational conceptual article, Anyiwo and colleagues (2018) outlined how parental cultural pride socialization and preparation for bias socialization – two common racial socialization messages among African American families – may support African American youth's sociopolitical development. Cultural pride socialization refers to messages that increase youth's pride in and knowledge of their racial/ethnic group, and preparation for bias socialization refers to messages that increase youth's awareness of racism and that provide youth with skills to cope with racism (Hughes et al., 2006). By learning about one's racial group's history through cultural pride socialization, youth may become more sensitized to race, and their awareness of social movements or their critical analysis may increase (Anyiwo et al., 2018). At the same time, preparation for bias messages are expected to increase African American youth's awareness of systemic and individual racism, as these messages inherently intend to increase youth's awareness of racism (Anyiwo et al., 2018). Preparation for bias messages may also be communicated through involvement in activism, which has been described as a community-level support youth may engage to cope with racial oppression (Anyiwo et al., 2018; O'Leary & Romero, 2011).

Given that the messages youth receive about race and the opportunities they have to disrupt racism are especially likely to stimulate youths' CRC development (Anyiwo et al., 2018; Bañales et al., 2019), future research should investigate the extent to which certain racial/ethnic socialization messages in different social contexts from unique socializing agents interact to inform youth's CRC. One study with racially/ethnically diverse youth examined associations between parental and school racial socialization and other racial and social contextual variables via cluster analysis, finding that youth who reported the highest levels of parental and school racial/ethnic socialization were more likely to report a higher critical consciousness on all dimensions, compared to youth in clusters who reported fewer of these messages (Byrd & Ahn, 2020). Building on this work, future research should examine the unique, structural associations different parental and school racial socialization messages have on CRC. It could be that youth who receive preparation for bias messages from their parents but also receive color-evasive socialization at school might trust the lessons they learn at home, given the amount of time they have spent with their parents. However, the extent to which youth deem certain racial/ethnic socialization messages as more credible than others will depend on other social and contextual factors, such as the quality of the parent–child relationship or the extent to which youth question adult authority at home or in school (Deutsch & Jones, 2008; Frabutt et al., 2002).

Racial/ethnic-racial socialization could also be a barrier to CRC. Given the deep-seated nature of anti-Black racism in the United States and across the world, youth of color and white youth are likely to receive racial/ethnic socialization from the media, home, and schools that spreads anti-Black ideologies. Youth who receive anti-Black socialization could internalize these messages and, as a result, may not engage in activism that promotes the well-being of Black communities because youth may think Black people "deserve" the conditions in which they live. Black youth and other youth of color who receive and internalize anti-Black racial socialization and other manifestations of white supremacy, such as colorism, display internalized oppression, which may result in lower CRC on all dimensions due to feelings of self-blame, anger, sadness, or disappointment. Any youth can internalize and act upon anti-Black socialization. Thus, there is a need for antiracist, programs, dialogues, and youth participatory action research in schools and communities that offer opportunities for youth to critique, navigate, and disrupt white supremacy.

Antiracism programs, dialogues, and youth participatory action research in schools and communities also serve as forms of racial-ethnic socialization that aim to facilitate CRC. These experiences are particularly powerful as they promote the critique and dismantling of white supremacy (racism analysis), the development of authentic and productive cross-racial coalitions (antiracism action), and a critical self-reflection and negotiation of one's positionality and how this positionality shapes types of antiracism action (racial reflexivity). Thus, youth who participate in these experiences are likely to engage in CRC praxis, such as gaining knowledge about racial inequality and working toward racial justice in community with other racial group members (Aldana et al., 2021; Griffin et al., 2012; Richards-Schuster & Aldana, 2013). Given that CRC is an active and communal process that needs to be intentionally cultivated and constructed, youth's racial reflexivity, for example, may be stimulated through communal storytelling as they reflect on their life narratives and how their experiences with white supremacy are different from those in the shared communal space (Norton & Sliep, 2018). Within this practice, youth may be encouraged to focus on their everyday beliefs, thoughts, feelings, and actions in order to gain insight into whether their racial values are congruent with their behaviors. Intervention and educational programs that foster critical consciousness, broadly speaking, may help support CRC. However, in order to avoid inadvertently upholding dominant color-evasive ideology that minimizes the role of racism in discourse, research, and pedagogy, explicit and consistent attention to race, racism, and racial justice are necessary to adequately support CRC. In this way, youth organizing spaces meet the need for young people to understand who they are, how they view the world, and how they are shaped by the world as racialized beings.

CONCLUSION AND FUTURE DIRECTIONS

In the current chapter, we propose an integrative conceptual model of youth CRC. CRC is an active, reciprocal, and multidimensional process that involves the development of beliefs, feelings, metacognitions, and actions that challenge racism. Indeed, scholarship on systemic racism demonstrates that oppression is multileveled and requires multilevel analysis and response (Jones, 1997; Watts & Hipolito-Delgado, 2015). Therefore, a central contribution of the CRC model to the literature is that our model accounts for, and intentionally centers, the multilevel manifestation of racism. Moreover, it may be that the color-evasive approach that is dominant in academic research (Quiñones-Rosado, 2020) has limited our ability to think critically about the role of racism in critical consciousness scholarship. While the critical consciousness literature considers oppression broadly, we contribute a race-specific model to intentionally foreground racism and antiracism.

We encourage future researchers to test the theoretical postulates of the CRC conceptual model with youth of different racial/ethnic backgrounds across varying genders, social classes, abilities, sexualities, and other experiences of oppression. It is also important to understand how manifestations and associations between CRC constructs are dependent on youths' social contexts, sociohistorical time periods, relationships with same and other racial/ethnic group members in their social contexts, and the needs and demands of youth themselves and those in their communities. The conceptual model must be tested separately with youth who identify with the same racial group, such as Black youth, non-Black Latinx youth, white youth, and Asian youth, to examine within-group differences in the nature of and associations between CRC dimensions.

Given that the components of youths' CRC are dynamic, relational, and coconstructed in the community, testing the current conceptual model lends itself to a range of research methodologies and approaches, including youth participatory action research, mixed-methods research, and ecological momentary assessment. Mixed-methods research should also be leveraged to create new quantitative measures that assess dimensions of youth's CRC, as there are limited measures that assess youth's beliefs, feelings, and actions that challenge racism (see Aldana et al., 2019; Hope et al., 2019). Youth should be included as partners in empirical research so their voices are used to inform the formation of measures (Aldana et al., 2019).

Critical research on white youth's CRC is needed, given that there is minimal research on white youth's development of beliefs, feelings, and actions toward racism in general. Perhaps there is less research on white youth's perceptions of and actions toward racism because researchers do not consider research on race and racism relevant to the lives of white people, which is informed by myopic beliefs that only people of color experience racial, ethnic, and cultural processes (Causadias et al., 2018; Helms, 2014). It could also be the case that quantitative studies, for example, do include white youth in research on youth's racism awareness but that this work is not published because little variation is expressed among youth's responses on measures that assess perceptions of cultural, institutional, and structural racism. Youth who report fewer perceptions of these forms of racism may have an underdeveloped or inaccurate understanding of cultural, institutional, and structural racism. The inability to recognize the presence of these more distal forms of racism among white youth is informed by youth's experiences with white racial privilege, or a set of calculated and implicit structural, ideologies, and cultural practices that render structural white dominance and the subjugation of people of color invisible through racial socialization (Hagerman, 2018). Mixed-methods research on the nature and extent of white youths' CRC is needed.

Although the current conceptual model is grounded in the experiences of adolescents, future research should examine adults' (e.g., parents', school officials') CRC. Adult CRC likely shapes the opportunities they provide youth to explore and challenge racism. For example, in considering Black youth's and parents' reports of parental racial/ethnic socialization, research found that neither Black youth's nor parents' reports of racial/ethnic pride socialization were associated with youths' critical analysis, but that youth's reports of racial/ethnic pride socialization were associated with critical agency (Bañales, Hope et al., 2021). Both youth and parent reports of preparation for bias socialization were associated with youth's critical analysis (Bañales, Hope et al., 2021). Additional research should explore whether parents' own CRC might explain the types and frequency of racial/ethnic socialization messages they provide their youth, and whether parents' CRC shapes associations between parental racial socialization and youth CRC. Further, we acknowledge that while adolescence is an optimal time to concretize CRC praxis, adults who did not develop CRC as children and adolescents may still engage in dynamic racism analysis, racial reflexivity, and antiracism action as adults.

Taken together, youth involvement in critiquing and challenging racism is nothing new, despite the recent uptick in attention on the topic in response to antiracism action specific to police brutality. The current chapter integrated an interdisciplinary body of research, primarily rooted in liberation psychology and research on youth critical consciousness and sociopolitical development, to create a multidimensional model of CRC. The future testing and application of this model may be used to inform research and practice that aims to understand and facilitate youth's CRC. Without youth who understand the structural roots and current repercussions of racism (racism analysis), recognize who they are in relation to a racialized world (racial reflexivity), and seek opportunities to dismantle racism in their immediate communities and larger institutional policies (antiracism action), racism will proliferate. Through CRC, our next generation of leaders will continue to transform our racialized society toward racial justice.

REFERENCES

Aldana, A., Bañales, J., & Richards-Schuster, K. (2019). Youth anti-racist engagement: Conceptualization, development, and validation of an anti-racism action scale. *Adolescent Research Review*, 4(4), 369–381. https://doi.org/gb82.

Aldana, A., & Byrd, C. M. (2015). School ethnic-racial socialization: Learning about race and ethnicity among African American students. *The Urban Review*, 47(3), 563–576. https://doi.org/10.1007/s11256-014-0319-0.

Aldana, A., Richards-Schuster, K., & Checkoway, B. (2021). "Down woodward": A case study of empowering youth to see and disrupt segregation using photovoice methods. *Journal of Adolescent Research*, 36(1), 34–67. https://doi.org/10.1177/0743558420933220.

Aldana, A., Rowley, S. J., Checkoway, B., & Richards-Schuster, K. (2012). Raising ethnic-racial consciousness: The relationship between intergroup dialogues and adolescents' ethnic-racial identity and racism awareness. *Equity and Excellence in Education*, 45(1), 120–137. https://doi.org/10.1080/10665684.2012.641863.

Aldana, A. & Vazquez, N. (2020). From colorblind racism to critical race theory: The road toward anti-racist social work in the United States. In G. Singh and S. Masocha (Eds.) *Anti-racist social work: International perspectives* (pp. 129–148). Red Globe Press.

Allen, R., & Goetz, E. G. (2021). A home for xenophobia: US public housing policy under Trump. *International Journal of Housing Policy*, 21(1), 127–137.

Annamma, S. A., Jackson, D. D., & Morrison, D. (2016). Conceptualizing color-evasiveness: Using dis/ability critical race theory to expand a color-blind racial ideology in education and society. *Race Ethnicity and Education*, 20(2), 1–16. https://doi.org/10.1080/13613324.2016.1248837.

Anyiwo, N., Bañales, J., Rowley, S. J., Watkins, D. C., & Richards-Schuster, K. (2018). Sociocultural influences on the sociopolitical development of African American youth. *Child Development Perspectives*, 12(3), 165–170. https://doi.org/10.1111/cdep.12276.

Anyiwo, N., Palmer, G. J., Garrett, J. M., Starck, J. G., & Hope, E. C. (2020). Racial and political resistance: An examination of the sociopolitical action of racially marginalized youth. *Current Opinion in Psychology*, *35*, 86–91. https://doi.org/10.1016/j.copsyc.2020.03.005.

Atkin, A. L., Yoo, H. C., Jager, J., & Yeh, C. J. (2018). Internalization of the model minority myth, school racial composition, and psychological distress among Asian American adolescents. *Asian American Journal of Psychology*, *9*(2), 108–116. https://doi.org/10.1037/aap0000096.

Bañales, J. (2020). Adolescent critical racial consciousness (unpublished doctoral dissertation). University of Michigan.

Bañales, J., Aldana, A., Richards-Schuster-K., & Merritt, A. (2021). Something you can see, hear, and feel: A descriptive, exploratory mixed-methods analysis of youths' articulations about racism. *Journal of Adolescent Research.* https://doi.org/10.1177/07435584211062117.

Bañales, J., Hoffman, A. J., Rivas-Drake, D., & Jagers, R. J. (2020). The development of ethnic-racial identity process and its relation to civic beliefs among Latinx and Black American adolescents. *Journal of Youth and Adolescence*, *49*(12), 2495–2508. https://doi.org/10.1007/s10964-020-01254-6.

Bañales, J., Hope, E. C., & Rowley, S. J., & Cryer-Coupet, Q. (2021). Raising justice-minded youth: Parental political and ethnic-racial socialization on Black youths' critical consciousness. *Journal of Social Issues*, *77*(4), 964–986.

Bañales, J., Lozada, F. T., Channey, J., & Jagers, R. J. (2021). Relating through oppression: Longitudinal relations between parental racial socialization, school racial climate, oppressed minority ideology, and empathy in Black male adolescents' prosocial development. *American Journal of Community Psychology*, *68*(1–2), 88–99. https://doi.org/10.1002/ajcp.12496.

Bañales, J., Marchand, A. D., Skinner, O. D. et al. (2019). Black adolescents' critical reflection development: Parents' racial socialization and attributions about race achievement gaps. *Journal of Research on Adolescence*, *30*(S2), 403–417. https://doi.org/10.1111/jora.12485.

Bañales, J., & Rivas-Drake, D. (2022). Showing up: A theoretical model of anti-racist identity and action for Latinx youth. *Journal of Research on Adolescence.* https://doi.org/10.1111/jora.12747.

Bañales, J., Sarissa Pech, A., Pinetta, B. J. et al. (2021). Critiquing inequality on campus and in society: Peers and faculty in civic and academic outcomes of college students. *Research in Higher Education*, *63*, 589–609. https://doi.org/10.1007/s11162-09663-7.

Barnes, C. Y., & Hope, E. C. (2017). Means-tested public assistance programs and adolescent political socialization. *Journal of Youth and Adolescence*, *46*(7), 1611–1621. https://doi.org/10.1007/s10964-016-0624-x.

Barr, S. C., & Neville, H. (2008). Examination of the link between parent racial socialization messages and racial ideology among Black college students. *Journal of Black Psychology*, *34*(2), 131–155. https://doi.org/10.1177/0095798408314138.

Benner, A. D., Wang, Y., Shen, Y. et al. (2018). Racial/ethnic discrimination and well-being during adolescence: A meta-analytic review. *American Psychologist*, *73*(7), 855–883. https://doi.org/10.1037/amp0000204.supp.

Bonilla-Silva, E. (2017). *Racism without racists: Colorblind racism and the persistence of racial inequality in America.* (5th ed.) Rowman & Littlefield Publishers.

Bonilla-Silva, E., & Embrick, D. G. (2001). Are Blacks color blind too? An interview-based analysis of Black Detroiters' racial views. *Race and Society, 4*(1), 47–67. https://doi.org/10.1016/s1090-9524(02)00034-7.

Bronfenbrenner, U., & Morris, P. A. (2006). The bioecological model of human development. In R. M. Lerner & W. Damon (Eds.), *Handbook of child psychology: Theoretical models of human development* (pp. 793–828). John Wiley & Sons Inc.

Burson, E., & Godfrey, E. B. (2020). Intraminority solidarity: The role of critical consciousness. *European Journal of Social Psychology, 50*(6), 1362–1377. https://doi.org/10.1002/ejsp.2679.

Byrd, C. M., & Ahn, L. H. R. (2020). Profiles of ethnic-racial socialization from family, school, neighborhood, and the Internet: Relations to adolescent outcomes. *Journal of Community Psychology, 48*(6), 1942–1963. https://doi.org/10.1002/jcop.22393.

Byrd, C., & Hope, E. C. (2011, April). *Understanding adolescents' conceptions of race and ethnicity using the Q-sort: Implications for racial/ethnic identity research.* Society for Research in Child Development.

Cabrera, N. L., Meza, E. L., Romero, A. J., & Cintli Rodríguez, R. (2013). "If there is no struggle, there is no progress": Transformative youth activism and the school of ethnic studies. *Urban Review, 45*(1), 7–22. https://doi.org/10.1007/s11256-012-0220-7.

Cammarota, J. (2004). The gendered and racialized pathways of Latina and Latino youth: Different struggles, different resistances in the urban context. *Anthropology and Education Quarterly, 35*(1), 53–74. https://doi.org/10.1525/aeq.2004.35.1.53.

Cammarota, J., & Aguilera, M. (2012). "By the time I get to Arizona": Race, language, and education in America's racist state. *Race Ethnicity and Education, 15*(4), 485–500.

Causadias, J. M., Vitriol, J. A., & Atkin, A. L. (2018). Do we overemphasize the role of culture in the behavior of racial/ethnic minorities? Evidence of a cultural (mis)attribution bias in American psychology. *American Psychologist, 73*(3), 243–255. https://doi.org/10.1037/amp0000099.

Chavez-Dueñas, N. Y., Adames, H. Y., Perez-Chavez, J. G., & Salas, S. P. (2019). Healing ethno-racial trauma in Latinx immigrant communities: Cultivating hope, resistance, and action. *American Psychologist, 74*(1), 49–62. https://doi.org/10.1037/amp0000289.

Collins, P. H. (2002). *Black feminist thought: Knowledge, consciousness, and the politics of empowerment.* Routledge.

Corning, A. F., & Myers, D. J. (2002). Individual orientation toward engagement in social action. *Political Psychology, 23*(4), 703–729. https://doi.org/10.1111/0162-895x.00304.

Crenshaw, K. W. (2017). *On intersectionality: Essential writings.* The New Press.

David, E. J. R., Schroeder, T. M., & Fernandez, J. (2019). Internalized racism: A systematic review of the psychological literature on racism's most insidious consequence. *Journal of Social Issues, 75*, 1057–1086. https://doi.org/10.1111/josi.12350.

Delgado, R., & Stefancic, J. (2017). *Critical race theory: An introduction* (3rd ed.). NYU Press.

Deutsch, N. L., & Jones, J. N. (2008). "Show me an ounce of respect": Respect and authority in adult-youth relationships in after-school programs. *Journal of Adolescent Research, 23*(6), 667–688. https://doi.org/10.1177/0743558408322250.

Diemer, M. A., Pinedo, A., Bañales, J. et al. (2021). Recentering action in critical consciousness. *Child Development Perspectives, 15*(1), 12–17. https://doi.org/10 .1111/cdep.12393.

Diemer, M. A., & Rapa, L. J. (2016). Unraveling the complexity of critical consciousness, political efficacy, and political action among marginalized adolescents. *Child Development, 87*(1), 221–238. https://doi.org/10.1111/cdev.12446.

Diemer, M. A., Rapa, L. J., Voight, A. M., & McWhirter, E. H. (2016). Critical consciousness: A developmental approach to addressing marginalization and oppression. *Child Development Perspectives, 10*(4), 216–221. https://doi.org/10.1111 /cdep.12193.

Emirbayer, M., & Desmond, M. (2012). Race and reflexivity. *Ethnic and Racial Studies, 35*(4), 574–599. https://doi.org/10.1080/01419870.2011.606910.

Flanagan, C. A., Kim, T., Pykett, A. et al. (2014). Adolescents' theories about economic inequality: Why are some people poor while others are rich? *Developmental Psychology, 50*(11), 2512–2525. https://doi.org/f6pjfq.

Flanagan, C. A., Syvertsen, A. K., Gill, S., Gallay, L. S., & Cumsille, P. (2009). Ethnic awareness, prejudice, and civic commitments in four ethnic groups of American adolescents. *Journal of Youth and Adolescence, 38*(4), 500–518. https://doi.org /bjvd2k.

Frabutt, J. M., MacKinnon-Lewis, C., Walker, A. M., & MacKinnon-Lewis, C. (2002). Racial socialization messages and the quality of mother/childhood interactions in African American families. *Journal of Early Adolescence, 22*(2), 200–217. https:// doi.org/dvrt76.

Freire, P. (2018). *Pedagogy of the oppressed* (MB Ramos, Trans.; 50th Anniversary ed.). Bloomsbury Publishing. (Original work published 1970).

French, B. H., Lewis, J. A., Mosley, D. V. et al. (2020). Toward a psychological framework of radical healing in communities of color. *The Counseling Psychologist, 48*(1), 14–46. https://doi.org/d7h6.

García Coll, C., Lamberty, G., Jenkins, R. et al. (1996) An integrative model for the study of developmental competencies in minority children. *Child Development, 67*(5), 1891–1914. https://doi.org/cbjhg7.

Griffin, S. R., Brown, M., & Warren, N. M. (2012). Critical education in high schools: The promise and challenges of intergroup dialogue. *Equity and Excellence in Education, 45*(1), 159–180. https://doi.org/10.1080/10665684.2012.641868.

Gorski, P. C. (2019) Fighting racism, battling burnout: causes of activist burnout in US racial justice activists. *Ethnic and Racial Studies, 42*(5), 667–687. https://doi.org /10.1080/01419870.2018.1439981.

Hagerman, M. A. (2018). *White kids: Growing up with racial privilege in a racially divided America.* NYU Press.

Heberle, A. E., Rapa, L. J., & Farago, F. (2020). Critical consciousness in children and adolescents: A systematic review, critical assessment, and recommendations for future research. *Psychological Bulletin, 146*(6), 525–551. https://doi.org/10.1037/bulooo0230.

Helms, J. E. (1994). The conceptualization of racial identity and other "racial" constructs. In E. J. Trickett, R. J. Watts, & D. Birman (Eds.), *Human diversity: Perspectives on people in context* (pp. 285–311). Jossey-Bass/Wiley.

Helms, J. E. (2005). An update on Helms's White and People of Color racial identity models. In J. G. Ponterotto, J. M. Casas, L. A. Suzuki, and C. M. Alexander (Eds.), *Handbook of Multicultural Counseling* (pp. 181–191). Sage.

Helms, J. E. (2014). A review of White racial identity theory: The sociopolitical implications of studying White racial identity in psychology. In S. Cooper & R. Kopano (Eds.), *Proceedings of the 30th International Congress of Psychology.* (Vol. 2, pp. 12–27). Taylor & Francis Group.

Hochman, A. (2019). Racialization: A defense of the concept. *Ethnic and Racial Studies, 42*(8), 1245–1262.

Hope, E. C., Anyiwo, N., Palmer, G. J. M., Bañales, J., & Smith, C. (in press). Sociopolitical development theory: A history and overview of a Black liberatory approach to youth development. *American Psychologist.*

Hope, E. C., & Bañales, J. (2019). Black early adolescent critical reflection of inequitable sociopolitical conditions: A qualitative investigation. *Journal of Adolescent Research, 34*(2), 167–200. https://doi.org/10.1177/0743558418756360.

Hope, E. C., Gugwor, R., Riddick, K. N., & Pender, K. N. (2019). Engaged against the machine: Institutional and cultural racial discrimination and racial identity as predictors of activism orientation among Black youth. *American Journal of Community Psychology, 63*(1–2), 61–72. https://doi.org/10.1002/ajcp.12303.

Hope, E. C., Pender, K. N., & Riddick, K. N. (2019). Development and validation of the Black Community Activism Orientation Scale. *Journal of Black Psychology, 45*(3), 185–214. https://doi.org/10.1177/0095798419865416.

Hope, E. C., Skoog, A. B., & Jagers, R. J. (2015). "It'll never be the white kids, it'll always be us": Black high school students' evolving critical analysis of racial discrimination and inequity in schools. *Journal of Adolescent Research, 30*(1), 83–112. https://doi.org/10.1177/0743558414550688.

Hope, E. C., Smith, C. D., Cryer-Coupet, Q. R., & Briggs, A. S. (2020). Relations between racial stress and critical consciousness for Black adolescents. *Journal of Applied Developmental Psychology, 70*, 101184. https://doi.org/10.1016/j.appdev.2020.101184.

Hughes, D., Rodriguez, J., Smith, E. P. et al. (2006). Parents' ethnic-racial socialization practices: A review of research and directions for future study. *Developmental Psychology, 42*(5), 747–770. https://doi.org/bdqxq6.

Husband, T., & Bertrand, S. (2021). The inequitable consequences of school disciplinary policies on Black girls in Ohio. *Journal of Global Education and Research, 5*(2), 175–184. https://doi.org/10.5038/2577-509x.5.2.1075.

Jones, J. M. (1997). *Prejudice and racism* (2nd ed.). McGraw Hill Companies.

Jost, J. T. (2019). A quarter century of system justification theory: Questions, answers, criticisms, and societal applications. *British Journal of Social Psychology, 58*(2), 263–314. https://doi.org/10.1111/bjso.12297.

Jost J. T, Banaji, M. R, & Nosek, B. A. (2004). A decade of system justification theory: Accumulated evidence of conscious and unconscious bolstering of the status quo. *Political Psychology, 25*(6), 881–920. https://doi.org/10.31234/osf.io/6ue35.

Jost, J. T. & Hunyady, O. (2005). Antecedents and consequences of system-justifying ideologies. *Current Directions in Psychological Science, 14*(5), 260–265.

Kendi, I. X. (2019). *How to be an antiracist.* One World.

Li, Y., & Nicholson Jr., H. L. (2021). When "model minorities" become "yellow peril": Othering and the racialization of Asian Americans in the COVID-19 pandemic. *Sociology Compass, 15*(2), 1–13. https://doi.org/10.1111/soc4.12849.

Losen, D., Hodson, C., Keith II, M. A., Morrison, J., & Belway, S. (2015). Are we closing the school discipline gap? The Center for Civil Rights remedies. https://escholar ship.org/content/qt2t36g571/qt2t36g571.pdf.

Mathews, C. J., Bañales, J., Christophe, N. K., Briggs, A. S., & Hope, E. C. (in press). Action, but make it critical. The content and developmental processes of critical action among youth of color. In G. L. & D. Witherspoon (Eds.), *Diversity and developmental science – bridging the gaps between research, practice, and policy.* Springer.

Mathews, C. J., Medina, M., Bañales, J. et al. (2020). Mapping the intersections of adolescents' ethnic-racial identity and critical consciousness. *Adolescent Research Review, 5*(4), 363–379. https://doi.org/10.1007/s40894-019-00122-0.

McKown, C. (2004). Age and ethnic variation in children's thinking about the nature of racism. *Journal of Applied Developmental Psychology, 25*, 597–617. https:doi .org/10.1016/j.appdev.2004.08.001.

McWhirter, E. H., Gomez, D., & Rau, E. D. (2019). "Never give up. Fight for what you believe in": Perceptions of how Latina/o adolescents can make a difference. *Cultural Diversity and Ethnic Minority Psychology, 25*(3), 403–412. https://do .org/10.1037/cdp0000254.

McWhirter, E. H., & McWhirter, B. T. (2016). Critical consciousness and vocational development among Latina/o high school youth: Initial development and testing of a measure. *Journal of Career Assessment, 24*(3), 543–558. https://doi.org/f8xvkd.

Miller, J., & Garran, A. M. (2007). The web of institutional racism. *Smith College Studies in Social Work, 77*(1), 33–67. https://doi.org/10.1300/J497v77n01_03.

Miller, J., & Garran, A. M. (2017). *Racism in the United States: Implications for the helping professions.* Springer Publishing Company.

Montoro, J. P., Kilday, J. E., Rivas-Drake, D., Ryan, A. M., & Umaña-Taylor, A. J. (2021). Coping with discrimination from peers and adults: Implications for adolescents' school belonging. *Journal of Youth and Adolescence, 50*(1), 126–143. https://doi.org/10.1007/s10964-020-01360-5.

Neblett, E. W., Jr. (2019). Racism and health: Challenges and future directions in behavioral and psychological research. *Cultural Diversity and Ethnic Minority Psychology, 25*(1), 12–20. https://doi.org/10.1037/cdp0000253.

Neville, H. A., Awad, G. H., Brooks, J. E., Flores, M. P., & Bluemel, J. (2013). Color-blind racial ideology theory, training, and measurement implications in psychology. *American Psychologist, 68*(6), 455–466. https://doi.org/10.1037/a0033282.

Neville, H. A., Poteat, V. P., Lewis, J. A., & Spanierman, L. B. (2014). Changes in white college students' color-blind racial ideology over 4 years: Do diversity experiences make a difference? *Journal of Counseling Psychology, 61*(2), 179–190. https://doi.org10.1037/a0035168.

Norton, L., & Sliep, Y. (2018). A critical reflexive model: Working with life stories in health promotion education. *South African Journal of Higher Education, 32*(3), 45–63. https://doi.org/10.20853/32-3-2523.

O'Leary, A. O., & Romero, A. J. (2011). Chicana/o students respond to Arizona's anti-ethnic studies bill, SB 1108: Civic engagement, ethnic identity, and well-being. *Aztlan: A Journal of Chicano Studies, 36*(1), 9–36.

Omi, M., & Winant, H. (2018). *Racial Formation in the United States: From the 1960s to the 1990s* (pp. 222–227). Routledge.

Paradies, Y., Ben, J., Denson, N. et al. (2015). Racism as a determinant of health: A systematic review and meta-analysis. *PLoS One, 10*(9), e0138511. https://doi.org/10.1371/journal.pone.0138511.

Quiñones-Rosado, R. (2020). Liberation psychology and racism. In L. Comas-Daz & E. T. Rivera (Eds.), *Liberation psychology: Theory, method, practice, and social justice.* (pp. 53–68). American Psychological Association. https://doi.org/10.1037/0000198-004.

Quintana, S. M. (1998). Children's developmental understanding of ethnicity and race. *Applied and Preventive Psychology, 7*, 27–45. https://doi.org/10.1016/S0962-1849(98)80020-6.

Quintana, S. M. (2008). Racial perspective taking: Developmental, theoretical and empirical trends. In S. M. Quintana & C. McKown (Eds.), *Handbook of race, racism, and the developing child* (pp. 16–36). John Wiley & Sons.

Raval, V. V., Ovia, T., Freeman, M., Raj, S. P., & Daga, S. S. (2021). Discourses about race in the United States: A thematic analysis of short essays. *International Journal of Intercultural Relations, 83*(4), 98–113. https://doi.org/10.1016/j.ijintrel.2021.05.004.

Rendón, M. G., Aldana, A., & Hom, L. D. (2020). Children of Latino immigrants framing race: Making sense of criminalisation in a colour-blind era. *Journal of Ethnic and Migration Studies, 46*(11), 2407–2425.

Richards-Schuster, K., & Aldana, A. (2013). Learning to speak out about racism: Youths' insights on participation in an intergroup dialogues program. *Social Work with Groups, 36*(4), 332–348. https://doi.org/10.1080/01609513.2013.763327.

Rios, V. (2011). *Punished: Policing the lives of Black and Latino boys.* NYU Press.

Rivera, E. T. (2020). Concepts of liberation psychology. In L. Comas-Daz & E. T. Rivera (Eds.), *Liberation psychology: Theory, method, practice, and social justice* (pp. 41–51). American Psychology Association. https://doi.org/10.1037/0000198-003.

Rivas-Drake, D., & Umaña-Taylor, A. (2019). *Below the surface: Talking with teens about race, ethnicity, and identity.* Princeton University Press.

Roberts, R. A., Bell, L. A., & Murphy, B. (2008). Flipping the script: Analyzing youth talk about race and racism. *Anthropology and Education Quarterly, 39*(3), 334–354. https://doi.org/10.1111/j.1548-1492.2008.00025.x.

Rosa, J. (2018). *Looking like a language, sounding like a race: Raciolinguistic ideologies and the learning of Latinidad.* Oxford University Press.

Rozas, L. W., & Miller, J. (2009). Discourses for social justice education: The web of racism and the web of resistance. *Journal of Ethnic and Cultural Diversity in Social Work, 18*(1–2), 24–39. https://doi.org/10.1080/15313200902874953.

Sakamoto, I., & Pitner, R. O. (2005). Use of critical consciousness in anti-oppressive social work practice: Disentangling power dynamics at personal and structural levels. *British Journal of Social Work*, 35(4), 435–452. https://doi.org/10.1093/bjsw/bch190.

Sánchez Carmen, S. A., Domínguez, M., Greene, A. C. et al. (2015). Revisiting the collective in critical consciousness: Diverse sociopolitical wisdoms and onto-logical healing in sociopolitical development. *Urban Review*, 47(5), 824–846. https://doi.org/10.1007/s11256-015-0338-5.

Saul, R., & Burkholder, C. (2020). Intellectualizing whiteness as a response to campus racism: Some concerns. *Ethnic and Racial Studies*, 43(9), 1636–1653. https://doi .org/gng3.

Seaton, E. K., Gee, G. C., Neblett, E., & Spanierman, L. (2018). New directions for racial discrimination research as inspired by the integrative model. *American Psychologist*, 73(6), 768–780. https://doi.org/10.1037/amp0000315.

Seaton, E. K., & Iida, M. (2019). Racial discrimination and racial identity: Daily moderation among Black youth. *American Psychologist*, 74(1), 117–127. https://doi.org /gf9gqc.

Seider, S., Clark, S., Graves, D. et al. (2019). Black and Latinx adolescents' developing beliefs about poverty and associations with their awareness of racism. *Developmental Psychology*, 55(3), 509.

Seider, S., Clark, S., & Graves, D. (2020). The development of critical consciousness and its relation to academic achievement in adolescents of color. *Child Development*, 91(2), e451–e457. https://doi.org/10.1111/cdev.13262.

Sellers, R. M., Smith, M. A., Shelton, J. N., Rowley, S. A., & Chavous, T. M. (1998). Multidimensional model of racial identity: A reconceptualization of African American racial identity. *Personality and Social Psychology Review*, 2(1), 18–39. https://doi.org/10.1207/s15327957pspr0201_2.

Selod, S. (2015). Citizenship denied: The racialization of Muslim American men and women post-9/11. *Critical Sociology*, 41(1), 77–95.

Sirin, S. R., Bikmen, N., Mir, M. et al. (2008). Exploring dual identification among Muslim-American emerging adults: A mixed methods study. *Journal of Adolescence*, 31(2), 259–279. https://doi.org/10.1016/j.adolescence.2007.10.009.

Smith, C. D., & Hope, E. C. (2020). "We just want to break the stereotype": Tensions in Black boys' critical social analysis of their suburban school experiences. *Journal of Educational Psychology*, 112(3), 551–566. https://doi.org/10.1037/edu0000435.

Spencer, M. B., Dupree, D., & Hartmann, T. (1997). A Phenomenological Variant of Ecological Systems Theory (PVEST): A self-organization perspective in context. *Development and Psychopathology*, 9(4), 817–833. https://doi.org/10.1017 /s0954579497001454.

Tatum, B. D. (2017). *Why are all the Black kids sitting together in the cafeteria? And other conversations about race*. Basic Books.

Thomas, A. J., & Blackmon, S. M. (2015). The influence of the Trayvon Martin shooting on racial socialization practices of African American parents. *Journal of Black Psychology*, 41(1), 75–89. https://doi.org/10.1177/0095798414563610.

Toraif, N., Augsberger, A., Young, A. et al. (2021). How to be an anti-racist: Youth of color's critical perspectives on antiracism in a youth participatory action research context. *Journal of Adolescent Research*, *35*, 86–91. https://doi.org/10.1177/07435584211028224.

Umaña-Taylor, A. J., Quintana, S. M., Lee, R. M. et al. (2014). Ethnic and racial identity during adolescence and into young adulthood: An integrated conceptualization. *Child Development*, *85*(1), 21–39. https://doi.org/10.1111/cdev.12196.

Utsey, S. O., & Ponterotto, J. G. (1996). Development and validation of the Index of Race-Related Stress (IRRS). *Journal of Counseling Psychology*, *43*(4), 490–501. https://doi.org/10.1037/0022-0167.43.4.490.

Watts, R. J., Diemer, M. A., & Voight, A. M. (2011). Critical consciousness: Current status and future directions. *New Directions for Child and Adolescent Development*, *2011*(134), 43–57. https://doi.org/10.1002/cd.310.

Watts, R. J., Griffith, D. M., & Abdul-Adil, J. (1999). Sociopolitical development as an antidote for oppression: Theory and action. *American Journal of Community Psychology*, *27*, 255–271. https://doi.org/10.1023/A:1022839818873.

Watts, R. J., & Flanagan, C. (2007). Pushing the envelope on youth civic engagement: A developmental and liberation psychology perspective. *Journal of Community Psychology*, *35*(6), 779–792.

Watts, R. J., & Guessous, O. (2006). Sociopolitical development: The Missing link in research and policy on adolescents. In S. Ginwright, P. Noguera, & J. Cammarota (Eds.), *Beyond resistance! Youth resistance and community change: New democratic possibilities for practice and policy for America's youth* (pp. 59–80). Routledge.

Watts, R. J., & Hipolito-Delgado, C. P. (2015). Thinking ourselves to liberation? Advancing sociopolitical action in critical consciousness. *Urban Review*, *47*(5), 847–867. https://doi.org/10.1007/s11256-015-0341-x.

Watts, R. J., Williams, N. C., & Jagers, R. J. (2003). Sociopolitical development. *American Journal of Community Psychology*, *31*, 185–194. http://dx.doi.org/10.1023/A:1023091024140.

Williams, C. D., Byrd, C. M., Quintana, S. M. et al. (2020). A lifespan model of ethnic-racial identity. *Research in Human Development*, *17*(2–3), 99–129. https://doi.org/10.1080/15427609.2020.1831882.

Wray-Lake, L., Plummer, J. A., & Alvis, L. (2023). Adolescents' developmental pathways to critical consciousness in the contexts of racial oppression and privilege. In L. J. Rapa and E. B. Godfrey (Eds.), *Critical consciousness: Expanding theory and measurement*. Cambridge University Press.

Wray-Lake, L., Wells, R., Alvis, L. et al. (2018). Being a Latinx adolescent under a Trump presidency: Analysis of Latinx youth's reactions to immigration politics. *Children and Youth Services Review*, *87*, 192–204. https://doi.org/10.1016/j.childyouth.2018.02.032.

Yi, J., Todd, N. R., & Mekawi, Y. (2020). Racial colorblindness and confidence in and likelihood of action to address prejudice. *American Journal of Community Psychology*, *65*(3–4), 407–422. https://doi.org/10.1002/ajcp.12409.

Young, A. A. (2006). *The minds of marginalized Black men*. Princeton University Press.

Zinn, H. (2015). *A people's history of the United States: 1492-present*. Routledge.

8

The Quest for Racial Justice

An Overview of Research on Racism and Critical Action for Youth of Color

ELAN C. HOPE, CHANNING J. MATHEWS, ALEXIS S. BRIGGS,
AND ANITRA R. ALEXANDER

Social movements to seek racial justice are a regular part of the social and political milieu in the United States. The legacy of youth seeking justice from racial oppression is well established in the United States, from the Student Nonviolent Coordinating Committee of the 1960s to Black Lives Matter in more recent years (Webster, 2021). There has also been advocacy for Deferred Action for Childhood Arrivals, movements to abolish US Immigration and Customs Enforcement (ICE) detention centers, fights for water and land rights at Standing Rock, activism to remove the travel ban from Muslim-majority countries, and advocacy to protect Asian American and Pacific Islander (AAPI) communities against increased racial violence (Carasik, 2016; Collingwood et al., 2018; Huber et al., 2014; Tessler et al., 2020). Following the murders of George Floyd and Breonna Taylor in the summer of 2020, there were thousands of protests and demonstrations seeking criminal legal system reform and racial justice in the United States (Kishi & Jones, 2020). These social movements have centered the needs of racially marginalized communities to seek justice and liberation from racially oppressive laws, practices, and culture. By liberation, we mean the disruption and dismantling of systemic racism and the ability for racially marginalized communities to pursue wholeness and wellness as well as "live and function in environments in which they are not constantly at battle to survive and prove their worth" (Thompson & Alfred, 2009, p. 485).

Critical action is social, political, or civic engagement with the specific goal of liberation of oppressed people and transformation of inequitable systems (Diemer et al., 2020). Activism and organizing, inclusive of protests, demonstrations, and boycotts, are commonly associated with critical action (Conner, 2015; Corning & Myers, 2002). Critical action, however, is not limited to activism and social movements. It also includes behaviors to combat oppression and seek social justice (Aldana et al., 2019; Diemer et al., 2020; Watts & Hipolito-Delgado, 2015). There has been growing interest in understanding how experiences of racism are related to critical action.

Although racial injustice is persistent, youth who are forced to develop in this oppressive racial hierarchy are equally tenacious in resisting and acting against it (Diemer et al., 2020; Mathews et al., in press). In this chapter, we will review the current research on how racism is related to critical action for racial justice and social change among youth of color.

WHAT DO WE MEAN BY RACISM?

Racism is a system that affords sociopolitical privileges and power to white individuals over nonwhite individuals (Bonilla-Silva, 1997). In the United States, racism is a normative societal context of youth development (English et al., 2020; García-Coll et al., 1996). Racism is systemic and endemic and operates across several ecological levels – through culture (e.g., media, policies), institutions (e.g., education, criminal justice system), and individuals (e.g., discrimination, racial microaggressions; Jones, 1997).

At the cultural level, racism is fostered by the historical and cultural dominance of the majority group over minoritized groups (Jones, 1997; Utsey & Ponterotto, 1996). In this way, racism is pervasive and maintained through cultural norms, media, laws, and the overarching rules of society. For example, cultural racism is perpetuated through negative media portrayals of Black people in television and films (Martin, 2008) and on social media (Stewart et al., 2019) that influence how youth reify racial hierarchies that uphold whiteness as standard and superior. The predominant messages that youth of color learn about their race, rooted in cultural racism, have been linked to negative mental health outcomes such as depression and stress (Gibson et al., 2021; Hope et al., 2021).

At the institutional level, racism is rooted in inequitable societal systems, such as education, the criminal legal system, and the labor market (Fulbright-Anderson et al., 2005; Jones, 1997). Racist beliefs become ingrained in the practices and policies of established institutions, resulting in inequitable outcomes between racial groups (Bonilla-Silva, 1997). For example, Black, Latinx, and Pacific Islander students are overrepresented in school suspensions and expulsions (Gopalan & Nelson, 2019; Nguyen et al., 2019) but underrepresented in referrals and admittance into academic giftedness programs (Goings & Ford, 2018). Disparities such as these impact the opportunity structure for youth of color (Cuellar & Markowitz, 2015). The pervasive nature of institutional racism enacted in systems and policies can also invoke chronic stress for youth of color (Harrell, 2000), which negatively affects their psychological health, including depression, anxiety, and emotion regulation (Driscoll et al., 2015; Henderson et al., 2019).

At the individual level, racism manifests as actions and ideologies held by members of the dominant racial group that have differential and negative effects on people from racially marginalized groups (Williams et al., 2003).

This is commonly understood as bigotry, racial prejudice, racial microaggressions, and racial discrimination. For youth, individual racism includes experiences such as being singled out by a teacher, being bullied and teased, and being assumed incompetent because of one's race (Benner et al., 2018; Hope et al., 2015). Individual racism experiences are typical for racially marginalized adolescents (Benner et al., 2018) and emerging adults (Lewis et al., 2021). English and colleagues (2020) found that Black adolescents experience an average of five experiences of racial discrimination (i.e., individual, vicarious, online, offline, and teasing) per day. Further, youth from racially marginalized backgrounds are vulnerable to the negative effects of being targets of racism at the individual level, including academic (Butler-Barnes & Inniss-Thompson, 2020; Montoro et al., 2020), psychological (Cheeks et al., 2020; Keels et al., 2017), and physical health consequences (Brody et al., 2014; Volpe et al., 2019). Racism is ubiquitous in the United States in interpersonal interactions, in institutional policies, and through larger cultural customs. Yet, as often as youth experience racism, young people act and demand racial justice.

WHAT DO WE MEAN BY CRITICAL ACTION?

Critical consciousness is one of several liberation frameworks (see also Fanon, 1968; Woodson, 1933) that posits that people who face oppression must pursue freedom and justice to thrive and live in optimal conditions for physical and psychological well-being (Thompson & Alfred, 2009). From the critical consciousness perspective, cultivating liberatory knowledge through literacy and education serves as the impetus for this resistance and critical action (Freire, 1970). While critical reflection (analysis of structural roots of oppression) and agency (motivation or efficacy to seek justice) are central components of critical consciousness, it is impossible to "think ourselves into liberation" (Watts & Hipolito-Delgado, 2015, p. 847). Actions engender enduring social change and may, in turn, inspire deeper critical reflection (Diemer et al., 2016). A focus on experiences of and stress from racism as it relates to critical action is particularly relevant to the study of critical consciousness because youth of the global majority who experience racism do not begin their journey at critical reflection. Often, racially marginalized youth experience racial awakenings or encounters with racism that spark reflection and action (Neville & Cross, 2017). Thus, understanding critical action from a critical consciousness perspective is insufficient and incomplete without specific consideration of how racism relates to action for youth of color.

Here, we focus on the critical action of racially marginalized youth, in alignment with liberation psychology that focuses on understanding how people from racially marginalized communities gain power and understand, reject, and change the conditions of their racial oppression (Anyiwo et al., 2020; Bryant-Davis & Moore-Lobban, 2020). To define and provide an

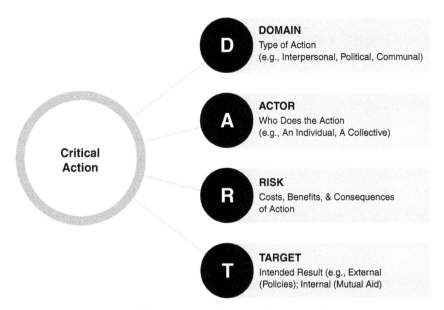

FIGURE 8.1 DART classification system for describing critical action.

overview of critical action from the literature, we have devised a novel organizational structure to classify critical action based on the existing literature on
youth civic engagement, activism, and antiracism (see Aldana et al., 2019;
Hope, Pender et al., 2019; Watts & Hipolito-Delgado, 2015). In our classification system (see Figure 8.1), we describe critical action according to domain
(the type of action), actors (those doing the action), risk (potential threat of
doing the action), and target (the change objective of the action).

Domains of Critical Action for Racial Justice

Watts and Hipolito-Delgado (2015) describe critical action as justice-oriented
behaviors that people engage with to reform individual beliefs, interpersonal
interactions, and institutional policies and practices. Aldana and colleagues
(2019) propose three domains of critical action specific to addressing racism:
interpersonal, communal, and political change. Interpersonal critical action
occurs between individuals (e.g., defending a person who was the target of
a racial slur or joke). Communal critical action accounts for collective action
(e.g., leading an activist organization), and political change critical action
includes engagement within existing political structures (e.g., engaging public
officials). Time, context, and developmental stage may affect the ways that
young people push back against racism and participate in critical action across
these dimensions. For example, youth may not have access to opportunities

for collective or political change action but may be committed to interpersonal action within their friend group or family.

Actors of Critical Action

In addition to the domain of critical action, Watts and Hipolito-Delgado (2015) posit critical action can be performed by individuals or a collective. For example, critical action can be a conversation with another person to challenge their belief system rooted in racism. Critical action can also be a collective or group of individuals that mobilize a community to protest policies that result in undue and disparate harm (e.g., protests, community organizing). Both individual and collective actors can challenge individual and institutional inequities and may work in tandem to promote social change.

Risks of Critical Action

We also consider critical action along a risk spectrum (see Corning & Myer, 2002; Hope, Pender et al., 2019). Low-risk critical action is typically performed individually or within interpersonal interactions and small, familiar group settings. Low-risk actions are not completely devoid of risk, but the risks have fewer long-term implications and are generally constrained to temporary changes in affect (e.g., heightened negative emotions) or changes in relationships (e.g., losing a friend). High-risk critical action has likely and identifiable consequences,including damage to one's person, possessions, or reputation. The risks associated with these types of actions may involve more resources to resolve and the implications may be longer-term (e.g., posting bail after an arrest). These categorizations of risk are an important starting point for considering the potential impact of critical action on youth of color. Some actions confer more risk of physical harm and future self (e.g., protesting when police confrontation is likely). This does not render other types of critical action risk free. For instance, interpersonal critical action (e.g., confronting a racist joke within a friend group) may be risky in terms of reputation or relationships.

Scholars have also investigated why youth may perceive some forms of critical action as more or less risky than others. Oosterhoff and colleagues (2021) propose that there are costs and benefits to political participation and that racially marginalized youth and white youth experience these costs and benefits differently. This is in part because racism permeates political systems, and, for youth of color, participation may be a tool for liberation that challenges the status quo and upsets members of the racial majority who benefit from unjust systems. Youth report that participation in politics could have negative ramifications on their mental health, family relationships, friendships, and financial/legal circumstances, and may become an obsession and distraction from daily life. Along with costs, youth also recognize benefits to political participation, including pride, empowerment, and better relationships with family and friends (Oosterhoff et al., 2021). In addition to personal benefits, critical action may lead to liberation, which is the ultimate benefit. Applying this cost–benefit framework alongside risk, we can consider how racially marginalized youth weigh factors to determine the risks they may take when pursuing racial justice.

Targets of Critical Action

Watts and Hipolito-Delgado (2015) also distinguish between the focus of critical action in terms of external and internal targets. Critical action can have external goals, such as changes to structural manifestations of oppression, like policies and laws. This might be the target of youth organizing and activism as reflected in the communal domain (Aldana et al., 2019). Participation in traditional political systems might also have external targets. For instance, at the time of the 2020 US presidential election, 68% of youth reported that voting is a way to disrupt racism and violence against people of color (Lundberg et al., 2021). Critical action with internal targets focuses on interpersonal interactions between members of marginalized communities and their allies and accomplices to offer community support and increase capacity for engagement (Watts & Hipolito-Delgado, 2015). For example, youth might engage in mutual aid campaigns to provide food and supplies to families facing underemployment. Each of these perspectives of critical action (domain, actor, risk, target) are important to assess the dynamic and adaptive nature of critical action and the creative and varied ways that young people decide to demand that society acknowledges the fullness of their humanity and works to change racist systems.

RACISM AND CRITICAL ACTION IN THEORY

Scholars have proposed two ways that critical action functions in relation to racism. First, critical action is an adaptive coping mechanism (Hope & Spencer, 2017). For people of color, witnessing and experiencing racism causes racism-related stress: the inability to access and activate resources to cope with race-related threats (Harrell, 2000). Experiences of racism can also catalyze racially marginalized youth toward action to effect change and reduce future instances and conditions of racism. Critical action is one way that racially marginalized youth respond to racism to resist the negative effects of racism on individual and community health and well-being (Ginwright, 2010; Hope & Spencer, 2017). Critical action can buffer stress associated with experiencing racism and, over time, it can become an acquired response to the vulnerabilities that result from racism-related stress. Second, the goal of critical action, by definition, is to eradicate systems that create and sustain racism and to seek liberation (Freire, 1970; Watts & Hipolito-Delgado, 2015). Through critical action, racially marginalized youth take an active role in changing the sociopolitical conditions that contribute to their vulnerability. In this way, racially marginalized youth engage in critical action to navigate racial oppression and alter these conditions to reduce future risk for themselves and their communities.

Mosley and colleagues (2021) document how Black activists who experience and witness anti-Black racism process those experiences. In their resulting model of critical consciousness against anti-Black racism, they found that the processing of racism builds agency, which leads to critical action against anti-Black racism and toward racial justice. This conceptual framework aligns with sociopolitical development theory, which suggests that awareness of and experiences with racism influence how youth understand racial oppression (critical reflection) and determine if and how they will act to change those systems (Anyiwo et al., 2018; Watts & Guessous, 2006). Scholars have also linked other sociocultural processes to critical action, suggesting that racial identity, racial socialization, and coping with race-related stress may mediate or moderate the associations between experiences of racism and critical action (e.g., Bañales et al., 2021; Hope, Cryer-Coupet et al., 2020; Mathews et al., 2019). As young people develop, they concurrently and reciprocally experience racism and explore who they are as racialized beings (Spencer et al., 2003), and these processes may, directly and indirectly, influence decisions to participate in critical action or not (Hope & Spencer, 2017). Given these theoretical assertions, scholars have sought to understand associations between experiences of racism and critical action for racially marginalized youth.

RACISM AND CRITICAL ACTION IN THE EMPIRICAL RESEARCH

Researchers have begun to explore associations between racism and critical action, and to describe how different experiences with racism might be differentially associated with types of critical action. Questions remain regarding the nature and nuance of how experiences of and stress from racism at multiple levels and dimensions of critical action may relate to each other. In this chapter, we provide a review of the quantitative empirical studies with racially marginalized youth that examine racism and critical action to help synthesize this growing area of research. Empirical qualitative studies were excluded, given our focus on the patterns of associations between racism and critical action to marginalized youth of color. While qualitative work provides important nuance as to how these associations may manifest in the lives of marginalized youth, we specifically document the frequency and patterns in which these associations occur.

Study Inclusion Process and Criteria

We conducted a comprehensive search of the PsycINFO, ERIC, and AcademicComplete databases to extract relevant studies published through January 24, 2022. We used the following keywords: youth or adolesc* or teen* or child*; racism or discrimination or prejudice or racial bias; activism or social movements or social justice or protest or civic engagement. Additional studies were located by examining prior reviews of and references to included articles. This initial search produced 1,990 unique articles. Studies were included if they met the following criteria: (a) they included a US-based sample; (b) they sampled youth from racially and ethnically marginalized communities; (c) they included at least one measure of critical action (inclusive of behavior and engagement across civic and political domains); (d) they included at least one measure of racism; (e) they were published in English; and (f) they were peer-reviewed. We did not include studies that only measured awareness of racism or critical reflection of oppression (e.g., Clark & Seider, 2019). When a study had a sample with multiple age groups, inclusive of youth, the study was included. These selection criteria resulted in a final sample of twenty-six articles.

Study Characteristics

In Table 8.1 we provide the study characteristics for the twenty-six studies included in this review. Throughout our discussion of these studies, we will use the language of the original authors when we refer to the race and ethnicity of the participants. The participants in these studies were Black and African American youth ($n = 13$), racially and ethnically diverse youth samples ($n = 5$), Asian and Pacific Islander youth ($n = 3$), both Black/African American and Latinx/Hispanic youth ($n = 3$), and both Latinx/Hispanic and Asian youth ($n = 1$). Most of the studies had average participant ages of between 18 and 20 years ($n = 14$), and nine studies focused on adolescents with average ages of between 12 and 17 years old. Among included studies, eight were published before 2017, and eighteen studies were published between 2017 and 2022. Similarly, eight studies were longitudinal, and eighteen studies were cross-sectional.

Overview of the Findings

Across the studies examined in this review, racism and critical action were associated, with few exceptions. Associations were evident across various measures of racism and diverse conceptualizations of critical action,

TABLE 8.1 Characteristics of quantitative studies examining racism and critical action

Study	N	M Age (SD)	Race/Ethnicity	% Girls / Women	Location	Design	Racism Measure	Critical Action Measure
Ballard (2015)	400	17.34 (0.41)	53.25% Asian 46.75% Latino	61%	California	Longitudinal	Individual experiences	Protest, petition, political art, political expression, internet political discussion
Bañales et al. (2021)	453	13.73 (1.33)	Black	0%	Midwest	Longitudinal	Institutional experiences	Prosocial behaviors
Christophe et al. (2021)	186	18.7 (1.4)	Black	86%	Southeast	Cross-sectional	Individual experiences	Interpersonal, communal, political
Cooc & Kim (2021)	2,430	–	24% Chinese 22% Asian Indian 20% Vietnamese 10% Filipino 9% Korean	–	Austin, TX	Cross-sectional	Individual experiences	Civic engagement
Diemer et al. (2008)	2,078	12th grade	49.8% Hispanic, 33.6% Black/ African American 13.4% Asian/ Pacific Islander 3.2% Native American/ Alaska Native	51.9%	National	Cross-sectional	Individual & institutional experiences	Motivation to transform inequity (social action; helping; importance of equity work; community service)

Study	N	Age M (SD)	Race/Ethnicity	%	Region	Design	Type of experience	Outcome measure
Hope, Cryer-Coupet, et al. (2020)	286	18.7 (4.76)	64.7% African American 11.2% African 10.5% Multiethnic 5.9% Afro-Latino 5.2% Afro-Caribbean/West Indian 2.5% Other	0%	National	Cross-sectional	Individual racial stress	Black community activism orientation scale
Hope & Jagers (2014)	634	19.2 (3.12)	Black	54.8%	National	Cross-sectional	Institutional experiences	Civic and political engagement
Hope et al. (2018)	504	18.2 (0.47)	56% Latinx 44% Black	-	Midwest	Longitudinal	Individual experiences	Political activism
Hope, Gugwor et al. (2019)	893	19.7 (4.78)	66.1% Black/African American 10.4% Multiethnic 9.7% African 5.9% Afro-Caribbean or West Indian 5.3% Afro-Latinx 2.6% Other	67.4	National	Cross-sectional	Institutional & cultural experiences	Low- and high-risk Black community activism orientation

TABLE 8.1 (*Cont.*)

Study	N	M Age (SD)	Race/Ethnicity	% Girls / Women	Location	Design	Racism Measure	Critical Action Measure
Hope, Smith, et al. (2020)	549	15.44 (1.24)	91.8% Black/ African American 8.25% Biracial	47.5	National	Cross-sectional	Individual, institutional, & cultural racism stress	Critical action
Jun et al. (2021)	240	37 (14.25)	East & Southeast Asian	57.1%	National	Cross-sectional	Individual experiences	Social media activism Political activism advocacy
Leath & Chavous (2017)	322	18–22	African American	70.19%	Midwest	Longitudinal	Individual & institutional experiences	Community and political involvement
Lozada et al. (2017)	265	13.74 (1.77)	Black	0%	Midwest	Cross-sectional	Individual experiences	Prosocial behaviors
Pinedo et al. (2021)	504	18.2% (0.47)	56.2% Latinx 43.8% Black	75% Black 57% Latinx	Midwest	Longitudinal	Individual experiences	Political activism
Riley et al. (2020)	419	18.42 (0.34)	African American	76%	Southeast	Cross-sectional	Individual experiences	Civic engagement

Study	N	Mean age (SD)	Racial/ethnic composition	%	Location	Design	Type of experiences	Critical action
Singh et al. (2020)	220	14.5 (1.3)	49.1% Hispanic/Latinx 39.5% African American/Black	100%	New York	Cross-sectional	Individual experiences	Critical action
Szymanski (2012)	269	31.16 (15.91)	African American	72%	National	Cross-sectional	Individual experiences	Involvement in African American activism
Szymanski & Lewis (2015)	185	18.77 (1.75)	93% African American/Black 7% Biracial/Multiracial	63	South	Cross-sectional	Individual, institutional & cultural stress	Involvement in African American activism
Tao & Fischer (2022)	407	16.47 (0.93)	28.3% Black 27.5% East or Southeast Asian 24.8% Latinx 19.4% Indigenous	82.3	National	Cross-sectional	Online individual & vicarious experiences	Online civic publication; online activity coordination
Tyler et al. (2020)	1,578	16.87 (0.53)	46% Latinx 26% Asian 10% Multiracial 6% white 5% Black/African American 7% Other	51%	California	Cross-sectional	Individual experiences	Political action community service expressive action

TABLE 8.1 (Cont.)

Study	N	M Age (SD)	Race/Ethnicity	% Girls / Women	Location	Design	Racism Measure	Critical Action Measure
Tyler et al. (2021)	380	12.38 (0.55)	64% Black 36% Latinx	52%	–	Longitudinal	Individual experiences	Prosocial behavior
Watson-Singleton et al. (2020)	232	19.7 (2.87)	75.2% Black American 17.8% African 2.1% Caribbean 3.7% Other	72.4%	Midwest	Longitudinal	Individual experiences	Black lives matter activism and support
White-Johnson (2012)	303	20 (3.03)	African American	81.2%	Midwest, Mid-Atlantic, South	Cross-sectional	Individual experiences	Prosocial behavior in African American community
White-Johnson (2015)	295	20 (0.17)	Black	81%	Midwest, Mid-Atlantic, South	Cross-sectional	Individual experiences	Prosocial behavior in African American community
Yellow Horse et al. (2021)	3,006	18 and older	Asian	–	National	Cross-sectional	Individual experiences	Support for Black lives matter activism

from prosocial behavior to racial justice activism. Racism was measured using several approaches. In most of the studies (n = 19), researchers measured individual racism (e.g., discrimination, microaggressions). The most common approach was to measure racism as a count of lifetime experiences of discrimination (e.g., Christophe et al., 2021) or recent interpersonal interactions (e.g., Hope et al., 2016; Singh et al., 2020). Participants in four studies reported their experiences of institutional and cultural racism along with individual racism, and three studies reported experiences with just institutional and/or cultural racism (e.g., Hope & Jagers, 2014). Several studies explored individual and institutional racism in schools via measures of school racial climate and race relations in schools (e.g., Bañales et al., 2021; Diemer et al., 2008). Along with experiences of racism, researchers also assessed stress responses to, and in anticipation of, racism (e.g., Hope, Cryer-Coupet et al., 2020; Szymanski & Lewis, 2015). As such, we can speak most confidently to the association between individual racism and critical action. We are limited in understanding how experiences of institutional and cultural racism are related to young people's decisions to seek justice for oppression, particularly systems of racial oppression.

Similarly, measures of critical action were broad and varied and the domains of critical action included general critical action (n = 14) and racism-specific critical action (n = 12). Most authors provided sample items that indicated the domain or type of critical action, but less information was provided about targets, risk, and actors. Among the general critical action studies, authors commonly used the critical action subscale of the Critical Consciousness Scale (see Diemer et al., 2017) and adaptations of the Youth Involvement Inventory (see Pancer et al., 2007). Among measures of general critical action, political and civic engagement was most common (n = 8), followed by prosocial behavior (n = 3) and critical action from common critical consciousness scales (n = 3). For the racism-specific critical action, six studies measured activism and prosociality supporting the African American or Black communities, and one study measured activism supporting the Asian community. Three studies measured critical action specific to the Black Lives Matter movement, and one of those studies also examined advocacy for Deferred Action for Childhood Arrivals. Finally, one study examined antiracism action broadly, and another measured online racial justice activism broadly. Most studies included measures of frequency of past action, but two studies measured orientation toward future activism and two studies examined support for racial justice activism. Given the many different domains of critical action, it is difficult to make specific claims regarding which types of racism are associated with which domains of critical action.

Positive Associations between Racism and Critical Action In most of the cross-sectional and longitudinal research on racism and youth critical action, scholars found a positive association between the two: more experiences of and stress from racism were associated with more critical action. These findings are consistent across various types of racism, a variety of domains of critical action (e.g., interpersonal, communal), and different developmental periods (e.g., early adolescence, late adolescence, emerging adulthood).

Direct Cross-Sectional Associations between Racism and Critical Action. It is important to note that we can describe associations between racism and critical action but cannot infer directionality from cross-sectional studies. For example, we can describe whether racism and critical action were concurrently associated among a sample of youth. We cannot, however, determine whether racism at one timepoint was associated with critical action at a later timepoint using cross-sectional data.

In most cross-sectional studies, researchers examined the association of individual racism (e.g., microaggressions, racial discrimination, racist events) with critical action. White-Johnson (2012) found that for 303 Black college students at both predominantly white institutions and historically Black colleges and universities, more frequent experiences of racial discrimination within the past year were associated with more low-risk interpersonal and communal prosocial behavior specific to Black communities (e.g., community service, tutoring) and prosocial attitudes (e.g., fighting against racism; contributing to the Black community). Similarly, the positive associations between racism and critical action were evidenced in studies of youth of color from various racial and ethnic backgrounds. Singh et al. (2020) investigated associations between racism and sexism and critical consciousness for 220 adolescent girls of color (Hispanic/Latinx, Black/African American, Asian, American Indian/Native Alaskan, other) aged 11–18. They found that for adolescent girls of color, more frequent experiences of both interpersonal racism and sexism within the previous three months were related to more individual and communal critical action (e.g., protesting, campaigning).

Yellow Horse et al. (2021) examined individual racism experienced by Asians and Asian Americans in relation to support for or indifference to the Black Lives Matter movement. They found that for foreign-born and US-born Asian Americans, odds of being indifferent to the Black Lives Matter movement was lower for those who acknowledged anti-Black racism in the United States (critical reflection) and who experienced racial discrimination themselves. They also found that among US-born Asian Americans, Generation Z (18–19 years old) was the least likely to be indifferent toward the Black Lives Matter movement, compared to millennials (20–35 years old), Generation X (36–51 years old), Baby Boomers (52–72 years old), and The Greatest

Generation (73 years and older). This study is one of the few to examine how in-group experiences of racism are related to race-related critical action in support of another racially marginalized group.

There were also positive associations between critical action and institutional racism. For example, Hope & Jagers (2014) examined associations between experiences of institutional racism (e.g., "It is hard for young Black people to get ahead because they face so much discrimination.") and civic engagement among Black adolescents and young adults (ages 15–25). They found that Black adolescents and young adults who experienced more institutional racism participated in more types of civic engagement (e.g., campaigning, boycotting, protesting). Several other studies that examined institutional racism and critical action also examined moderation and mediation effects and are discussed later in the chapter.

The association between racism and critical action was mixed in studies that examined racism-related stress. In a study of 199 Black, African American, and Black biracial young adults, Szymanski & Lewis (2015) found that more stress from cultural racism was associated with more critical action in the form of activism to address issues faced by African American communities. They did not, however, find evidence that stress from individual and institutional racism was related to activism in and for African American communities.

Meditators of Racism and Critical Action. In addition to direct effects, researchers have been interested in how racism is related to critical action. One proposed process that connects experiences of and stress from racism to critical action is the components of critical consciousness: critical reflection and critical agency. The findings from these studies are mixed. For instance, in a study of 1,578 high school students (Latinx, Asian, Multiracial, white, Black/African American, other), Tyler et al. (2020) found that the adolescents who were discriminated against more frequently also participated in more political action (e.g., protesting), community service (e.g., volunteering), and expressive action (e.g., wearing political/social issue clothing). The authors tested whether discrimination was related to this action through critical reflection but found no evidence of indirect effects. In another study, Lozada et al. (2017) examined prosocial behavior (e.g., helping a classmate; donating items) among Black adolescent boys (ages 12–17) and found that more frequent experiences of racial discrimination at school were related to more prosocial critical action. They also tested whether this relationship was mediated by racial identity (operationalized as critical reflection of race and racism) and found no evidence of indirect effects.

Other scholars have found evidence to support that the experiences of racism and stress from racism are related to critical action directly and indirectly through aspects of critical consciousness. In a study of 594 Black adolescents, researchers found that stress from individual, institutional, and cultural racism was related to critical action directly, and individual and cultural racial stress were associated indirectly through both critical reflection and critical agency (Hope, Smith, et al., 2020). Further, in a national study of 858 Asian adults in the United States, researchers found that experiences of racial discrimination are related to social media activism (e.g., posting online about a social or political issue), political activism (e.g., voting for Asian American political candidates), and advocacy (e.g., donating to groups working for Asian American rights; Jun et al., 2021). This association between experiences of racial discrimination and critical action was mediated by knowledge of racial injustice (e.g., hate crimes, bullying) against Asian Americans in the United States. In both studies, there is evidence that the association between racism and critical action is facilitated through recognizing or understanding racial injustice as a broader structural issue. This aligns with the tenets of critical consciousness, which suggest that education and critical analysis of oppression facilitate action to change unjust systems, though critical analysis alone is not always a sufficient precursor to action (Diemer et al., 2020).

Two additional studies have examined mediational pathways from racism to critical action. In a study with 407 Asian, Black, Indigenous, and Latinx adolescents, researchers examined how social media activism is related to racism experienced online and how online racism mediates the relation between social media activism and health outcomes (Tao & Fisher, 2022). They found that individual and vicarious experiences of racism online were positively associated with two types of social media racial justice activism: posting and sharing racial justice content, and planning and coordinating racial justice events. They also found evidence that depressive symptoms partially mediated the associations between individual and vicarious online racism and racial justice activism on social media (Tao & Fisher, 2022). In this study, the data suggest that racism is related to more feelings of depression, which is then related to low-risk interpersonal and communal racial justice activism online.

Riley et al. (2020) examined racial discrimination, civic engagement, and emotion regulation among 419 African American college students and found that more experiences of racial discrimination were associated with more communal civic engagement. For African American young women in this sample, the association between racial discrimination and civic engagement was facilitated through cognitive reappraisal of the racist events – thinking differently about the meaning or relevance of one's emotions (Riley et al., 2020). In this study, there is evidence that how racially marginalized young people process their experiences with racism is an important component of the racism-to-action connection. The associations between racism and critical action may be facilitated by psychological and emotional responses to racism.

Moderators of Racism and Critical Action. Along with mediators, researchers have investigated factors that might strengthen or weaken the associations between racism and critical action. Proposed moderators include sociocultural factors such as racial identity, coping with racism, and racial socialization (Anyiwo et al., 2018). Hope and colleagues investigated the moderating effect of racial identity in two studies. In a study of 893 Black adolescents and young adults, Hope, Gugwor et al. (2019) found that more experiences of cultural racism were related to more low-risk activism. More experiences of institutional racism were associated with less low-risk activism and more high-risk activism. The association between institutional racism experiences and high-risk activism varied by public regard, or how positively or negatively the youth felt others view Black people. For Black youth with low public regard, more institutional racism was related to a greater orientation toward high-risk activism; for Black youth with high public regard, there was no association between institutional racism and high-risk activism orientation.

Similarly, Hope, Cryer-Coupet et al. (2020) found associations between racism-related stress and activism for 286 Black adolescent boys and young adult men. The physiological and psychological anticipation of racism was related to more low-risk activism orientation and the physiological anticipation of racism was related to more high-risk activism orientation. The association between physiological anticipation of racism and an orientation toward more high-risk critical action was strongest for young Black males for whom race was a central component of their identity and ideological beliefs (high racial centrality and nationalism ideology). Hope and colleagues also found that these associations can vary by age, suggesting some potential developmental implications to the ways racism and critical action relate across the lifespan.

Along with racial identity, scholars have considered racial coping and socialization. Szymanski (2012) examined experiences of racist events, coping styles, and critical action specific to African American communities among African American adults (64% college students) and found that more frequent experiences of individual racism were associated with more activism supporting African American communities. This relationship was stronger for those with a less planful coping style targeted toward changing the stressor or one's affective state. White-Johnson (2015) explored the interactive effect of racial discrimination and racial socialization among 295 Black college students and found that more experiences of racial discrimination were related to more prosocial behavior in the Black community but found no evidence of any moderation by racial pride, egalitarianism, or preparation for bias socialization.

A study by Christophe et al. (2021) was built on the work of White-Johnson to examine how both racial identity and racial socialization moderate the relation between racism and critical action for 186 Black undergraduate college students in the Southeast. In this study, more experiences of individual racism were associated with more communal and political antiracism critical action. For interpersonal antiracism action, past experiences of discrimination were associated with critical action, and that relationship varied by both racial identity and racial socialization. The association between discrimination and action was present for Black undergraduate students, with exceptions. There was no association between discrimination and critical action for two types of Black undergraduates: (a) those whose race was an important part of their identity and who had minimal racial socialization to prepare for racial bias, and (b) those for whom race was not a central part of their identity and had received substantial racial socialization to prepare for future experiences of racism and discrimination (Christophe et al., 2021). It may be that interpersonal types of critical action are not appealing for Black youth who do not consider race as a core component of their identity, even if they were socialized to expect and deal with racism. Similarly, interpersonal antiracist critical action may be less accessible for youth that consider race as a core component of their identity when they were not socialized to understand and expect racism as a part of their interactions and life experiences.

Longitudinal and Reciprocal Associations. Eight studies examined the associations between racism and critical action over time. The findings of these longitudinal studies are mixed, with overall evidence pointing to the reciprocal and amplifying associations between racism and critical action. There is some evidence for longitudinal associations between past experiences of racism and future activism. Watson-Singleton et al. (2020) explored racial discrimination, depressive symptoms, and Black Lives Matter activism among 232 Black college students (Black American, Caribbean, African) in the Midwest. They found a positive bivariate association between Black Lives Matter activism and both lifetime racial discrimination and racial discrimination over the previous six months. Leath & Chavous (2017) examined individual (racial stigma consciousness) and institutional racism (hostile racial climate) and found that for Black college-going women, negative experiences of institutional racism (a racially hostile campus climate with racial mistrust and racial tension) was related to more civic engagement a year later. This association between racial climate and civic engagement was strongest for Black women with high political efficacy.

Several scholars examined the relationships between racial discrimination and critical action for Black and Latinx college students in the Midwest over the first two years of college. First, Hope et al. (2016) found that more experiences of racial microaggressions in high school were related to more involvement in Black Lives Matter and Deferred Action for Childhood Arrivals advocacy during the first year of college for Latinx students, but not for Black students. Next, Hope et al. (2018) found that for both Black and Latinx students, racial microaggressions experienced over the first year of college were related to political activism at the end of the first year. Further, for Black students who were more involved in political activism, the racial microaggressions experienced were related to increased stress. Pinedo et al. (2021) expanded this investigation and found that these Black and Latinx college students experienced increasing racial microaggressions over the first two years of college and participated in more critical action over time as they experienced more racial discrimination on campus. This relationship was strongest over time for Black and Latinx students who also participated in ethnic/racial clubs on campus. It is possible that in the transition to college, Black and Latinx students establish a community of similar peers, and those peers and social connections help facilitate critical action in response to experiences of racism on campus.

In another longitudinal study, Bañales and colleagues (2021) examined prosocial community behavior (e.g., donating items to charity or someone in need) and institutional racism experiences in schools among Black adolescent boys. In this study, a racially equitable school climate in year one was not directly related to prosocial behaviors two years later. They did find some weak empirical support that a more racially equitable school climate in year one was related to adolescents feeling more empathy and beliefs in supporting marginalized groups in year two, which was related to more prosocial behaviors in year three. Altogether, this study suggests that for Black adolescent boys, racially equitable schools can support adaptive social and emotional beliefs, which in turn promote prosocial behaviors in support of their community.

In another recent study of 380 Black and Latinx early adolescents, Tyler and colleagues (2021) examined previous experiences with discrimination and prosocial behavior. Overall, they found that experiences of racial discrimination in seventh grade were related to prosocial behavior six months later (seventh grade), but not one year later (eighth grade). These findings were nuanced when considering race and ethnicity: Black early adolescents were more prosocial than their Latinx peers six months later, and there were no differences in prosociality one year later. These findings were also qualified by the influence of perceptions of self. Youth who felt more in control of their own self-esteem also reported more long-term prosocial behaviors.

There is also some evidence of a reverse association, where earlier critical action is related to experiences of racism later. In a study of 400 Latino and Asian high school seniors from California, Ballard (2015) looked at the bidirectional and longitudinal associations between civic activism (frequency of involvement over the previous nine months; attending a protest/march/demonstration; signing a petition; artistic expression of political views; political expression through clothing, buttons, bumper stickers; discussed political issues online) and discrimination (frequency of being discriminated against for any reason; the most common reason – 66% – was race/ethnicity). In this study, Latinx participants reported more frequent discrimination than Asian participants. Ballard found that frequency of discrimination during the senior year of high school was not related to civic activism one year after high school. However, civic activism during the senior year of high school was related to more reported discrimination one year after high school. The author suggests that this may be due in part to the stable nature of civic activism during the study period; Asian and Latinx late adolescents, in general, did not report much change in their civic activism over one year. These findings might also be due, in part, to the general measure of discrimination, rather than a domain-specific measure that focused on racism or sexism.

Null Association between Racism and Critical Action Among the studies that we examined, two cross-sectional studies found null results regarding the association between racism and critical action. Cooc & Kim (2021) examined critical action and racial discrimination among a sample of Asian Indian, Chinese, Filipino, Korean, and Vietnamese adults (20% emerging adults between 18 and 25 years old). To measure racial discrimination, they asked participants if they had been treated unfairly based on race or ethnicity. To measure critical action, they created a composite score of five types of civic engagement over the past year: (a) having attended a city council meeting, (b) having attended a city-hosted public meeting, (c) having contacted a city office or staff, (d) having voted in a city election, and (e) having participated in a survey from the city. They found that racial discrimination was not related to critical action for any of the Asian American Pacific Islander subgroups in their study.

Diemer and colleagues (2008) similarly found no association between racism and critical action. In their study, they examined how schools and parents influence sociopolitical development for Hispanic, Black/African American, Asian/Pacific Islander, and Native American/Alaska Native adolescents from lower socioeconomic backgrounds. In this study, racism is reflected in measures of racial relations in school, which included cross-race friendships, cross-race conflict, and teacher and principal views of cross-race conflict among students. They conceptualized critical action as participation in social action groups and community service, along with the importance of helping in the community and correcting social injustice. Racial relations in the school were not related to critical action in this sample (Diemer et al., 2008). Given the longitudinal evidence, along with evidence of mediators and moderators that facilitate the association between racism and critical action, these associations may be more nuanced in ways not captured by the models tested in these two studies.

Summary of Findings

Youth of color experience and witness racism in their schools and communities, and these experiences of racism are generally positively related to critical action. Cross-sectionally, the association between racism and critical action is clear. In all but two studies, there was a positive association between racism and critical action. In these studies, several important mediators and moderators have emerged that help distinguish which types of racism are associated with which types of critical action. Researchers found that the association between racism and critical action varies by racial identity, racial socialization, coping style, and political efficacy. For high-risk racial justice activism, the association with racism and racism-related stress was strongest for youth with more positive connections to the Black community and beliefs that others view Black people less positively (Hope, Gugwor et al., 2019; Hope, Cryer-Coupet et al., 2020). For racial socialization, there were mixed results. Racial socialization did not strengthen or weaken the association between individual racism and prosocial forms of interpersonal and communal critical action (White-Johnson, 2015). However, when combined with racial identity beliefs, preparation for bias socialization can strengthen the association between individual racism and interpersonal critical action (Christophe et al., 2021). Further, scholars identified emotion reappraisal (Riley et al., 2020) and other components of critical consciousness (Hope, Smith et al., 2020) that may be mechanisms that connect experiences of racism to critical action. Other studies, however, did not find support for critical reflection as a mediating factor (Tyler et al., 2020). For youth from racially marginalized backgrounds, cognitive reappraisal of emotions after experiencing racism and reflection on racism as a system are potential conduits to future critical action.

The longitudinal research on racism and critical action helps to elucidate and complicate our understanding of how these two experiences co-occur and relate over time. Out of eight studies that examine the associations between racism and critical action over time, seven of them find that racism is related to subsequent action (Bañales et al., 2021; Pinedo et al., 2021). This finding was robust in samples that included Black adolescents and emerging adults. In one study, racism was not related to critical action, but critical action in high school was related to subsequent experiences of discrimination (Ballard, 2015). Further, the studies with early adolescents provided fewer clear links between early individual racism and critical action years later. Given that racially marginalized youth experience racism across the lifespan, investigating the role of racism in critical action behaviors over time may help map patterns of factors that help initiate and sustain critical action. These approaches can also help us understand how critical action can help young people learn to recognize and name racism when they see and experience it.

We highlight three areas of opportunity and offer recommendations for future research to expand our understanding of if, when, and how young people who are subjected to racism challenge that racism and pursue racial justice. We ground these recommendations in the DART framework, emphasizing the importance of considering domain, actor, risk, and target of critical action.

Research with Youth of Color from Many Backgrounds

The overwhelming majority of studies that were prominent in the literature have focused on Black adolescents and young adults. While anti-Black racism is prominent and pervasive in the United States (and internationally), it is important to understand how racism and critical action function for other youth of color. Two important questions stem from examinations of youth of color beyond monoracial youth of African descent. First, how do experiences of racism inform critical action for monoracial youth not of African descent and for biracial youth? For instance, qualitative research with Chicano youth impacted by a Mexican–American studies ban in Arizona (Cabrera et al., 2013) and research on the criminalization of undocumented Latinx youth during the Development, Relief, and Education for Alien Minors Act (DREAMERS) movement (Terriquez, 2017; Terriquez et al., 2018) highlight the connection between institutional racism and critical action that are unique to the experiences of youth from Latinx backgrounds. Using the DART framework, these examples demonstrate how institutional racism is an impetus for critical action within the political domain with external targets, including state and federal policy. Further, there may be unique risks for Latinx youth who are undocumented or have undocumented family and friends as they use critical action to target racism embedded in law and policy. Therefore, it is important to understand how racism unique to the experiences of Latinx youth inform and catalyze critical action among this group with specificity.

As another example, particularly in the context of the COVID-19 pandemic, Asian youth have experienced increased racial discrimination and racial violence (Gover et al., 2020; Tessler et al., 2020), with heterogeneity among the experiences within this group. As such, it is imperative to understand how these differential experiences of racism inform critical action for youth who experience racial marginalization beyond the Black–White racial binary. A third example is the unique experiences of biracial and multiracial youth. Biracial and multiracial youth may contend with racism unique to their biracial/multiracial identity, for which their often-monoracial parents may not be able to prepare them (Atkin et al., 2021; Stokes et al., 2021). Biracial and multiracial youth may also navigate experiences of racism associated with a part of their ancestry or identity that is oppressed while also identifying with the dominant racial group (Stokes et al., 2021). These unique experiences of racism must be explored more deeply in relation to critical action across domain, action, risk, and target, particularly as youth navigate their identity and community in relation to both racism and critical action.

Second, it is important to understand how other youth of color understand racism experienced by other groups and other types of oppression that overlap with racism (e.g., heterosexism, classism). This informs how youth from racially marginalized communities make decisions to act as allies to combat oppression that might not directly impact them or their most proximal communities. Some theory and research has explored how young people from one racial/ethnic group support the social justice causes of members of another racially marginalized community (Burson & Godfrey, 2020; Hope et al., 2016; Yellow Horse et al., 2021). Scholars suggest that building coalitions and participating in intergroup dialogues could strengthen connections between one's own experiences of racism, vicarious experiences of the oppression of other marginalized groups, and critical action to support the justice causes of those groups (e.g., Christens & Dolan, 2011; Cole, 2008; Richards-Schuster & Aldana, 2013). This speaks directly to the actor and target dimensions of critical action, where we consider individual action and collective action, and internal targets. Evidence from qualitative research finds that youth are best supported in critical action to support other marginalized groups when they have opportunities to discuss race and racism, to learn to communicate with people who have had different experiences than they have had, to engage in learning how oppression is connected and interwoven, and to be leaders (Richards-Schuster & Aldana, 2013). Further, barriers to this type of coalition-building include competition and threats to identity, while facilitators to intergroup coalition-building include commonality and critical reflection that considers how the racial oppression of one group co-occurs with, is similar to, and is different from another (Burson & Godfrey, 2020). Future studies can leverage quantitative methods to uncover what other beliefs and attitudes can best support youth in pursuing critical action with internal targets and both individual and collective actors, beyond the types of oppression that they encounter most readily.

Measure Racism and Critical Action over Time

The cross-sectional association of racism and critical action is well established. Thus, it is important to better understand how racism is related to critical action over time. This should include tests of reciprocal associations to understand how racism is a catalyst for critical action and how experiences of critical action, in turn, relate to naming and understanding experiences of racism. For existing research, we have evidence to support a reciprocal process where experiences with racism can catalyze critical action (Pinedo et al., 2021), and where critical action might precede more experiences with racism (Ballard, 2015). This potentially bidirectional process can be explored further to understand how these relationships change together over time and how those change processes may look different for younger and older youth, and across the lifespan. The DART model also provides a framework to consider how various domains and targets of critical action relate to each other over time. We can answer questions about whether communal actions with internal targets predict future actions with external targets. We can also understand how experiences of racism and critical action risk co-occur over time.

In addition to the exploration of reciprocal associations between racism and critical action over time, few studies have examined mediation processes over time. In critical consciousness (Freire, 1970) and related youth development frameworks (e.g., Anyiwo et al., 2018; Bañales et al., Chapter 7 [this volume]; Watts & Guessous, 2006), scholars propose many sociocultural and sociopolitical factors that may help move youth from experiencing racism to acting to uproot racial injustice. These potential mediators could include critical reflection, agency, coping strategies, and racial identity, among others. As we have established that more experiences of racism are associated with more critical action, a next step is understanding the pathways through which young people take experiences of racism and transform them into calls and demands for liberation.

Measure Racism and Critical Action with Precision

In our review of the quantitative evidence, most studies focused on individual racism. A growing movement in psychology and related fields is to decenter the interpersonal component of racism and focus on systemic racism, upheld through institutions and culture (Jones, 1997; Seaton et al., 2018). This systematic perspective is central to the tenets of critical consciousness, which call us to understand oppression as a system that is purposefully maintained and can be intentionally deconstructed (Freire, 1970; Watts & Guessous, 2006). As such, we call for the field to attend to how youth experience racism in the institutions they frequent (e.g., schools, healthcare) and through cultural norms. Prior research also focuses on experiences of racism as conceptualized as frequency of experiences within a given time period (e.g., lifetime, past six months). Researchers have theorized that it is not only the experience of racism but the stress responses associated with those experiences that are related to various developmental and health outcomes for racially marginalized people (Harrell, 2000; Utsey & Ponterotto, 1996). By extension, researchers and practitioners interested in critical consciousness should consider how the stress of racism might facilitate or obstruct critical action and related critical consciousness and sociocultural attitudes and beliefs.

Along with measuring racism with more precision, we recommend that researchers and practitioners consider the broad spectrum of critical action more carefully. Across the literature, critical action is typically measured as frequency of participation in action. Here it is important to be specific on how frequently actions are expected within a given domain. For instance, weekly participation in protests for a sustained period may not be a reasonable expectation for young people of color. Equally, daily confrontation of family and friends who use racially harmful language and rhetoric may not be supportive of overall individual well-being.

Beyond domains of critical action and frequency of participation, it is important to consider the targets, risks, and actors of critical action. Particularly for youth, collective action may be an empowering experience that is a developmentally adaptive response to racism, rather than tackling racism individually without communal support (Watts & Hipolito-Delgado, 2015). Further, consideration of risk, or costs and benefits of critical action, takes into account the autonomy youth have to make decisions about participation in critical action. While youth may participate in actions that convey reputational, financial, physical, or social risks, they do so with consideration of the costs of not pursuing racial justice. For many youth, inaction may be just as risky, if not more so, than action. As such, we implore scholars to continue to specify the types of critical action they are studying in order to clarify the various ways youth of color do or do not act to support justice broadly – and racial justice specifically.

Expand Methods to Strengthen the Evidence Base

Finally, future research on racism and critical action would be strengthened by leveraging mixed methods and QuantCrit methodology. Mixed methods studies can holistically capture how youth are thinking about their critical action and how they understand their own experiences of racism (including vicarious racism) in relation to their critical action choices and intentions. For instance, Tyler et al. (2020) examined racially diverse adolescents' critical consciousness processes in a mixed-methods study. Through quantitative analyses, they found that more experiences of discrimination were related to more critical action (e.g., protesting, volunteering, wearing political clothing). They also found, via semistructured qualitative interviews, that oppression and inequity were a part of these adolescents' daily lived experiences and that those experiences informed the sociopolitical issues they felt connected to and wanted to act to change. Through this mixed-method investigation, we learned that these adolescents came to activism through their dissatisfaction with current sociopolitical conditions and policy as well as a desire to alter these circumstances and create lasting change. This study highlights how the combination of various methods can provide context for each other and further illuminate how experiences of racism and other oppression draw adolescents to critical action.

QuantCrit provides a useful framework to pursue antiracism through quantitative methods (Suzuki et al., 2021). QuantCrit acknowledges the historical use of statistics for the oppression of racially marginalized groups, and applies critical race theory to statistical analysis, emphasizing that research is not an objective process. Applying an actively antiracist framework can combat the perpetuation of racism in research and honor the racially marginalized adolescents and their communities that are the focus of this quantitative research. Using innovative and participatory methods to explore the intersections of experiences of racism and critical action can deepen our understanding of what brings racially marginalized adolescents to critical action and antiracism work without perpetuating racism in the process.

CONCLUSION

There is a growing body of literature that confirms that racism can be a catalyst for critical action among racially marginalized adolescents and young adults. In this chapter, we provided an overview of the quantitative evidence that echoes the evidence from qualitative and youth participatory methods. We outline the mechanisms of action – such as agency, emotion regulation, racial identity, and racial socialization – that connect racism to critical action for young people of color. As racism continues to plague the environments that young people develop in, researchers and practitioners should continue to amplify how youth take those experiences of racism and pursue liberation through critical action. Further, policy makers and institutional stakeholders should continue to support youth critical action through changes in the structures that uphold racism.

REFERENCES

Aldana, A., Bañales, J., & Richards-Schuster, K. (2019). Youth anti-racist engagement: Conceptualization, development, and validation of an anti-racism action scale. *Adolescent Research Review*, 4(4), 369–381. https://doi.org/gb82.

Anyiwo, N., Bañales, J., Rowley, S. J., Watkins, D. C., & Richards-Schuster, K. (2018). Sociocultural influences on the sociopolitical development of African American youth. *Child Development Perspectives*, 12(3), 165–170. https://doi.org/f5rm.

Anyiwo, N., Palmer, G. J., Garret, J. M., Starck, J. G., & Hope, E. C. (2020). Racial and political resistance: An examination of the sociopolitical action of racially marginalized youth. *Current Opinion in Psychology*, 35(2020), 86–91. https://doi.org/10.1016/j.copsyc.2020.03.005.

Atkin, A. L., Yoo, H. C., White, R. M. B., Tran, A. G. T. T., & Jackson, K. F. (2021). Validation of the Multiracial Youth Socialization (MY-Soc) Scale among racially diverse multiracial emerging adults. *Journal of Family Psychology, 36*(1), 13–22. https://doi.org/10.1037/fam0000879.

Ballard, P. J. (2015). Longitudinal links between discrimination and civic development among Latino and Asian adolescents. *Journal of Research on Adolescence, 26*(4), 723–737. https://doi.org/f9fcj2.

Bañales, J., Lozada, F. T., Channey, J., & Jagers, R. J. (2021). Relating through oppression: Longitudinal relations between parental racial socialization, school racial climate, oppressed minority ideology, and empathy in Black male adolescents' prosocial development. *American Journal of Community Psychology, 74*, 63–12. https://doi.org/10.1002/ajcp.12496.

Benner, A. D., Wang, Y., Shen, Y. et al. (2018). Racial/ethnic discrimination and well-being during adolescence: A meta-analytic review. *American Psychologist, 73*(7), 855–883. https://doi.org/10.1037/amp0000204.supp.

Bonilla-Silva, E. (1997). Rethinking racism: Toward a structural interpretation. *American Sociological Review, 62*, 465–480. http://doi.org/10.2307/2657316.

Brody, G. H., Lei, M., Chae, D. H. et al. (2014). Perceived discrimination among African American adolescents and allostatic load: A longitudinal analysis with buffering effects. *Child Development, 85*(3), 989–1002. https://doi.org/10.1111/cdev.12213.

Bryant-Davis, T., & Moore-Lobban, S. J. (2020). Black minds matter: Applying liberation psychology to Black Americans. In L. Comas-Díaz & E. Torres Rivera (Eds.), *Liberation psychology: Theory, method, practice, and social justice* (pp. 189–206). American Psychological Association. https://doi.org/10.1037/0000198-011.

Burson, E., & Godfrey, E. B. (2020). Intraminority solidarity: The role of critical consciousness. *European Journal of Social Psychology, 50*(6), 1362–1377. https://doi.org/10.1002/ejsp.2679.

Butler-Barnes, S. T., & Inniss-Thompson, M. N. (2020). "My teacher doesn't like me": Perceptions of teacher discrimination and school discipline among African-American and Caribbean Black adolescent girls. *Education Sciences, 10*, 44–57. https://doi.org/10.3390/educsci10020044.

Cabrera, N. L., Meza, E. L., Romero, A. J., & Rodríguez, R. C. (2013). "If there is no struggle, there is no progress": Transformative youth activism and the school of ethnic studies. *Urban Review, 45*, 7–22. https://doi.org/10.1007/s11256-012-0220-7.

Carasik, L. (2016). N Dakota Pipeline Protest Is a Harbinger of Many More. (November 21). *ALJAZEERA.* www.aljazeera.com/indepth/opinion/2016/11/dakota-pipeline-protest-harbinger-161120150300919.html.

Cheeks, B. L., Chavous, T. M., & Settles, I. H. (2020). A daily examination of African American adolescents' racial discrimination, parental racial socialization, and psychological affect. *Child Development, 29*, 57–18. https://doi.org/10.1111/cdev.13416.

Christens, B. D., & Dolan, T. (2011). Interweaving youth development, community development, and social change through youth organizing. *Youth & Society, 43*(2), 528–548. https://doi.org/10.1177/0044118x10383647.

Christophe, N. K., Martin Romero, M. Y., Hope, E. C., & Stein, G. L. (2021). Critical civic engagement in Black college students: Interplay between discrimination, centrality, and preparation for bias. *American Journal of Orthopsychiatry*, 92(2), 144–153. https://doi.org/10.1037/ort0000600.

Clark, S., & Seider, S. (2019). The role of curiosity in the sociopolitical development of Black and Latinx adolescents. *Journal of Research on Adolescence*, 30(1), 189–202. http://doi.org/10.1111/jora.12511.

Cole, E. R. (2008). Coalitions as a model for intersectionality: From practice to theory. *Sex Roles*, 59(5–6), 443–453. https://doi.org/10.1007/s11199-008-9419-1.

Collingwood, L., Lajevardi, N., & Oskooii, K. A. (2018). A change of heart? Why individual-level public opinion shifted against Trump's "Muslim Ban." *Political Behavior*, 40(4), 1035–1072. https://doi.org/10.1007/s11109-017-9439-z.

Conner, J. O. (2015). Pawns or power players: The grounds on which adults dismiss or defend youth organizers in the USA. *Journal of Youth Studies*, 19(3), 403–420. https://doi.org/10.1080/13676261.2015.1083958.

Cooc, N., & Kim, G. M. (2021). The roles of racial discrimination and English in civic outcomes for Asian Americans and Pacific Islanders. *Cultural Diversity and Ethnic Minority Psychology*, 7(3), 483–494. http://doi.org/10.1037/cdp0000443.

Corning, A. F., & Myers, D. J. (2002). Individual orientation toward engagement in social action. *Political Psychology*, 23, 703–729. https://doi.org/cqrz2s.

Cuellar, A. E., & Markowitz, S. (2015). School suspension and the school-to-prison pipeline. *International Review of Law and Economics*, 43, 98–106. https://doi.org/10.1016/j.irle.2015.06.001.

Diemer, M. A., Hsieh, C.-A., & Pan, T. (2008). School and parental influences on sociopolitical development among poor adolescents of color. *The Counseling Psychologist*, 37(2), 317–344. https://doi.org/10.1177/0011000008315971.

Diemer, M. A., Pinedo, A., Bañales, J. et al. (2020). (Re)centering action in critical consciousness. *Child Development Perspectives*, 26, 176–182. https://doi.org/gh7kq6.

Diemer, M. A., Rapa, L. J., Park, C. J., & Perry, J. C. (2017). Development and validation of the Critical Consciousness Scale. *Youth & Society*, 49(4), 461–483. https://doi.org/10.1177/0044118x14538289.

Diemer, M. A., Rapa. L., Voight, A., & McWhirter, E. (2016). Critical consciousness: A developmental approach to addressing marginalization and oppression. *Child Development Perspectives*, 10(4), 216–221. https://doi.org/10.1111/cdev.12446.

Driscoll, M. W., Reynolds, J. R., & Todman, L. C. (2015). Dimensions of race-related stress and African American life satisfaction: A test of the protective role of collective efficacy. *Journal of Black Psychology*, 41(5), 462–486.

English, D., Lambert, S. F., Tynes, B. M. et al. (2020). Daily multidimensional racial discrimination among Black US American adolescents. *Journal of Applied Developmental Psychology*, 66, 101068. https://doi.org/10.1016/j.appdev.2019.101068.

Fanon, F. (1968). *The wretched of the earth*. Grove Press.

Freire, P. (1970). *Pedagogy of the oppressed*. Continuum.

Fulbright-Anderson, K., Lawrence, K., Sutton, S., Susi, G., & Kubisch, A. (2005). *Structural Racism and Youth Development: Issues, Challenges, and Implications*. The Aspen Institute. www.aspeninstitute.org/publications/structural-racism-youth-development-issues-challenges-implications/.

García Coll, C., Lamberty, G., Jenkins, R. et al. (1996). An integrative model for the study of developmental competencies in minority children. *Child Development*, *67*, 1891–1914. https://doi.org/10.1111/j.1467-8624.1996.tb01834.x.

Gibson, S. M., Bouldin, B. M., Stokes, M. N., Lozada, F. T., & Hope, E. C. (2021). Cultural racism and depression in Black adolescents: Examining racial socialization and racial identity as moderators. *Journal of Research on Adolescence*, *32*(1), 41–48. https://doi.org/10.1111/jora.12698.

Ginwright, S. (2010). *Black youth rising: Activism and healing in urban American*. Teacher's College Press.

Goings, R. B., & Ford, D. Y. (2018). Investigating the intersection of poverty and race in gifted education journals: A 15-year analysis. *Gifted Child Quarterly*, *62*, 25–26. https://doi.org/10.1177/0016986217737618.

Gopalan, M., & Nelson, A. A. (2019). Understanding the racial discipline gap in schools. *AERA Open*, *5*(2), 1–26. https://doi.org/10.1177/2332858419844613.

Gover, A. R., Harper, S. B., & Langton, L. (2020). Anti-Asian hate crime during the COVID-19 pandemic: Exploring the reproduction of inequality. *American Journal of Criminal Justice*, *45*(4), 647–667. https://doi.org/10.1007/s12103-020-09545-1.

Harrell, S. P. (2000). A multidimensional conceptualization of racism-related stress: implications for the well-being of people of color. *American Journal of Orthopsychiatry*, *70*(1), 42–57. https://doi.org/10.1037/h0087722.

Henderson, D. X., Walker, L., Barnes, R. R. et al. (2019). A framework for race-related trauma in the public education system and implications on health for Black youth. *Journal of School Health*, *89*(11), 926–933. https://doi.org/10.1111/josh.12832.

Hope, E. C., Brinkman, M., Hoggard, L. S. et al. (2021). Black adolescents' anticipatory stress responses to multilevel racism: The role of racial identity. *American Journal of Orthopsychiatry*, *91*(4), 487–498. https://doi.org/10.1037/ort0000547.

Hope, E. C., Cryer-Coupet, Q. R., & Stokes, M. N. (2020). Race-related stress, racial identity, and activism among young Black men: A person-centered approach. *Developmental Psychology*, *56*(8), 1484–1495. https://doi.org/gb87.

Hope, E. C., Gugwor, R., Riddick, K. N., & Pender, K. N. (2019). Engaged against the machine: Institutional and cultural racial discrimination and racial identity as predictors of activism orientation among Black youth. *American Journal of Community Psychology*, *63*(1–2), 61–72. https://doi.org/gftk4q.

Hope, E. C., & Jagers, R. J. (2014). The role of sociopolitical attitudes and civic education in the civic engagement of Black youth. *Journal of Research on Adolescence*, *24*(3), 460–470. https://doi.org/10.1111/jora.12117.

Hope, E., Keels, M., & Durkee, M. (2016). Participation in Black Lives Matter and deferred action for childhood arrivals: Modern activism among Black and Latino college students. *Journal of Diversity in Higher Education*, *9*, 203–215. https://doi.org/f84zd5.

Hope, E. C., Pender, K. N., & Riddick, K. N. (2019). Development and validation of the Black Community Activism Orientation Scale. *Journal of Black Psychology*, *45*(3), 185–214. https://doi.org/10.1177/0095798419865416.

Hope, E. C., Skoog, A. B., & Jagers, R. J. (2015). "It'll never be the white kids, it'll always be us": Black high school students' evolving critical analysis of racial discrimination and inequity in schools. *Journal of Adolescent Research*, 30(1), 83–112. https://doi.org/10.1177/0743558414550688.

Hope, E. C., Smith, C. D., Cryer-Coupet, Q. R., & Briggs, A. S. (2020). Relations between racial stress and critical consciousness for Black adolescents. *Journal of Applied Developmental Psychology*, 70, 101184. https://psycnet.apa.org/doi/10.1016/j.appdev.2020.101184.

Hope, E. C., & Spencer, M. B. (2017). Civic engagement as an adaptive coping response to conditions of inequality: An application of Phenomenological Variant of Ecological Systems Theory (PVEST). In N. Cabrera, & B. Leyendecker (Eds.), *Handbook on positive development of minority children and youth* (pp. 421–435). Springer. https://doi.org/gb88ur.

Hope, E. C., Velez, G., Offidani-Bertrand, C., Keels, M., & Durkee, M. I. (2018). Political activism and mental health among Black and Latinx college students. *Cultural Diversity and Ethnic Minority Psychology*, 24(1), 26–39. https://doi.org/10.1037/cdp0000144.

Huber, L. P., Villanueva, B. P., Guarneros, N., Vélez, V. N., & Solórzano, D. G. (2014). *DACAmented in California: The impact of the Deferred Action for Childhood Arrivals program on Latina/os. CSRC Research Report. No. 18.* UCLA Chicano Studies Research Center. www.chicano.ucla.edu/publications/report-brief/daca mented-california.

Jones, J. M. (1997). *Prejudice and racism* (2nd ed.). McGraw Hill Companies.

Jun, J., Kim, J. K., & Woo, B. (2021). Fight the virus and fight the bias: Asian Americans' engagement in activism to combat anti-Asian COVID-19 racism. *Race and Justice*, Advanced Online Publication. https://doi.org/10.1177/21533687211054165.

Keels, M., Durkee, M., & Hope, E. C. (2017). The psychological and academic costs of school-based racial and ethnic microaggressions. *American Educational Research Journal*, 54(6), 1316–1344. https://doi.org/10.3102/0002831217722120.

Kishi, R., & Jones, S. (2020). *Demonstrations and political violence in America: New data for Summer 2020.* Armed Conflict Location and Event Data Project (ACLED). https://acleddata.com/2020/09/03/demonstrations-political-violence-in-america-new-data-for-summer-2020/.

Leath, S., & Chavous, T. (2017). "We really protested": The influence of sociopolitical beliefs, political self-efficacy, and campus racial climate on civic engagement among Black college students attending predominantly white institutions. *The Journal of Negro Education*, 86(3), 220–237. https://psycnet.apa.org/doi/10.7709/jnegroeducation.86.3.0220.

Lewis, J. A., Mendenhall, R., Ojiemwen, A. et al. (2021). Racial microaggressions and sense of belonging at a historically white university. *American Behavioral Scientist*, 65(8), 1049–1071. https://doi.org/10.1177/0002764219859613.

Lozada, F. T., Jagers, R. J., Smith, C. D., Bañales, J., & Hope, E. C. (2017). Prosocial behaviors of Black adolescent boys: An application of a sociopolitical development theory. *Journal of Black Psychology*, 43(5), 493–516. https://doi.org/10.1177/0095798416652021.

Lundberg, K., Kiesa, A., & Medina, A. (2021). *The 2020 election is over, but young people believe in continued engagement.* Center for Information & Research on

Civic Learning and Engagement. https://circle.tufts.edu/latest-research/2020-election-over-young-people-believe-continued-engagement.

Martin, A. C. (2008). Television media as a potential negative factor in the racial identity development of African American youth. *Academic Psychiatry*, 32(4), 338–342. https://doi.org/10.1176/appi.ap.32.4.338.

Mathews, C. J., Bañales, J., Christophe, N. K., Briggs, A. S., & Hope, E. C. (in press). Action, but make it critical: The measurement and developmental processes of critical action for Black and Latinx youth. In D. Witherspoon & G. Livas Stein (Eds.), *Diversity and developmental science: Bridging the gaps between research, practice, and policy*. Springer.

Mathews, C. J., Medina, M. A., Bañales, J. et al. (2019). Mapping the intersections of adolescents' ethnic-racial identity and critical consciousness. *Adolescent Research Review*, 43(3), 1–17. https://doi.org/10.1007/s40894-019-00122-0.

Montoro, J. P., Kilday, J. E., Rivas-Drake, D., Ryan, A. M., & Taylor, A. J. U. (2020). Coping with discrimination from peers and adults: Implications for adolescents' school belonging. *Journal of Youth and Adolescence*, 30(2), 1–18. https://doi.org/10.1007/s10964-020-01360-5.

Mosley, D. V., Hargons, C. N., Meiller, C. et al. (2021). Critical consciousness of anti-Black racism: A practical model to prevent and resist racial trauma. *Journal of Counseling Psychology*, 68(1), 1–16. https://doi.org/10.1037/cou0000430.

Neville, H. A., & Cross, W. E. (2017). Racial awakening: Epiphanies and encounters in Black racial identity. *Cultural Diversity and Ethnic Minority Psychology*, 23(1), 102–108. https://doi.org/10.1037/cdp0000105.

Nguyen, B. M. D., Noguera, P., Adkins, N., & Teranishi, R. T. (2019). Ethnic discipline gap: Unseen dimensions of racial disproportionality in school discipline. *American Educational Research Journal*, 56(5), 1973–2003. https://doi.org/10.3102/0002831219833919.

Oosterhoff, B., Poppleer, A., Hill, R. M., Fitzgerald, H., & Shook, N. J. (2021). Understanding the costs and benefits of politics among adolescents within a sociocultural context. *Infant and Child Development*, Advanced Online Publication. https://doi.org/10.1002/icd.2280.

Pancer, S. M., Pratt, M., Hunsberger, B., & Alisat, S. (2007). Community and political involvement in adolescence: What distinguishes the activists from the uninvolved? *Journal of Community Psychology*, 35(6), 741–759. https://doi.org/10.1002/jcop.20176.

Pinedo, A., Durkee, M. I., Diemer, M., & Hope, E. C. (2021). Disentangling racial discrimination and critical action among Black and Latinx college students: What role do peers play? *Cultural Diversity & Ethnic Minority Psychology*, 27(3), 546–557. https://doi.org/gb9b.

Richards-Schuster, K., & Aldana, A. (2013). Learning to speak out about racism: Youths' insights on participation in an intergroup dialogues program. *Social Work with Groups*, 36(4), 332–348. https://doi.org/10.1080/01609513.2013.763327.

Riley, T. N., DeLaney, E., Brown, D. et al. (2020). The associations between African American emerging adults' racial discrimination and civic engagement via emotion regulation. *Cultural Diversity and Ethnic Minority Psychology*, 27(2), 169–175. https://doi.org/10.1037/cdp0000335.

Seaton, E. K., Gee, G. C., Neblett, E., & Spanierman, L. (2018). New directions for racial discrimination research as inspired by the integrative model. *American Psychologist*, 73(6), 768–780. https://doi.org/10.1037/amp0000315.

Singh, S., Berezin, M. N., Wallach, L. N., Godfrey, E. B., & Javdani, S. (2020). Traumatic incidents and experiences of racism and sexism: Examining associations with components of critical consciousness for system-involved girls of color. *American Journal of Community Psychology*, 6(2), 3–12. https://doi.org/10.1002/ajcp.12479.

Spencer, M. B., Fegley, S. G., & Harpalani, V. (2003). A theoretical and empirical examination of identity as coping: Linking coping resources to the self processes of African American youth. *Applied Developmental*, 7(3), 181–188. https://doi.org/10.1207/s1532480xads0703_9.

Stewart A., Schuschke J., & Tynes B. (2019) Online racism: Adjustment and protective factors among adolescents of color. In H. Fitzgerald, D. Johnson, D. Qin, F. Villarruel, & J. Norder (Eds.), *Handbook of Children and Prejudice* (pp. 501–513). Springer. https://doi.org/10.1007/978-3-030-12228-7_28.

Stokes, M. N., Charity-Parkeer, B. M., & Hope, E. C. (2021). What does it mean to be Black and white? A meta-ethnographic review of racial socialization in multiracial families. *Journal of Family Theory and Review*, 13(2), 181–201. https://doi.org/10.1111/jftr.12413.

Suzuki, S., Morris, S. L., & Johnson, S. K. (2021). Using QuantCrit to advance an anti-racist developmental science: Applications to mixture modeling. *Journal of Adolescent Research*, 36(5), 535–560. https://doi.org/10.1177%2F07435584211028229.

Szymanski, D. M. (2012). Racist events and individual coping styles as predictors of African American activism. *Journal of Black Psychology*, 38(3), 342–367. https://doi.org/ccx55h.

Szymanski, D. M., & Lewis, J. A. (2015). Race-related stress and racial identity as predictors of African American activism. *Journal of Black Psychology*, 41(2), 170–191. https://doi.org/10.1177/0095798414520707.

Tao, X., & Fisher, C. B. (2022). Exposure to social media racial discrimination and mental health among adolescents of color. *Journal of Youth and Adolescence*, 51, 30–44. https://doi.org/10.1007/s10964-021-01514-z.

Terriquez, V. (2017). Legal status, civic organizations, and political participation among Latino young adults. *The Sociological Quarterly*, 58(2), 315–336. https://doi.org/10.1080/00380253.2017.1296756.

Terriquez, V., Brenes, T., & Lopez, A. (2018). Intersectionality as a multipurpose collective action frame: The case of the undocumented youth movement. *Ethnicities*, 18(2), 260–276. https://doi.org/10.1177/1468796817752558.

Tessler, H., Choi, M., & Kao, G. (2020). The anxiety of being Asian American: Hate crimes and negative biases during the COVID-19 pandemic. *American Journal of Criminal Justice*, 45(4), 636–646. https://doi.org/10.1007/s12103-020-09541-5.

Thompson, C. E., & Alfred, D. M. (2009). Black liberation psychology and practice. In H. A. Neville, B. M. Tynes, & S. O. Utsey (Eds.), *Handbook of African American psychology* (pp. 483–494). Sage Publications, Inc.

Tyler, C. P., Geldhof, G. J., Settersten, Jr., R. A., & Flay, B. R. (2021). How do discrimination and self-esteem control beliefs affect prosociality? An examination among Black and Latinx youth. *Journal of Early Adolescence, 41*(2), 282–308. https://doi.org/10.1177/0272431620912486.

Tyler, C. P., Olsen, S. G., Geldhof, G. J., & Bowers, E. P. (2020). Critical consciousness in late adolescence: Understanding if, how, and why youth act. *Journal of Applied Developmental Psychology, 70,* 101165. https://doi.org/10.1016/j.appdev.2020.101165.

Utsey, S. O., & Ponterotto, J. G. (1996). Development and validation of the Index of Race-Related Stress (IRRS). *Journal of Counseling Psychology, 43*(4), 490–501. https://doi.org/10.1037/0022-0167.43.4.490.

Volpe, V. V., Lee, D. B., Hoggard, L. S., & Rahal, D. (2019). Racial discrimination and acute physiological responses among Black young adults: The role of racial identity. *Journal of Adolescent Health, 64*(2), 179–185. https://doi.org/10.1016/j .jadohealth.2018.09.004.

Watson-Singleton, N. N., Mekawi, Y., Wilkins, K. V., & Jatta, I. F. (2020). Racism's effect on depressive symptoms: Examining perseverative cognition and Black Lives Matter activism as moderators. *Journal of Counseling Psychology, 68*(1), 27–37. https://doi.org/10.1037/cou0000436.

Watts, R. J., & Guessous, O. (2006). Sociopolitical development: The missing link in research and policy on adolescents. In S. Ginwright, P. Noguera, & J. Cammarota (Eds.), *Beyond resistance! Youth activism and community change: New democratic possibilities for practice and policy for America's youth* (pp. 59–80). Routledge.

Watts, R. J., & Hipolito-Delgado, C. P. (2015). Thinking ourselves to liberation? Advancing sociopolitical action in critical consciousness. *The Urban Review, 47* (5), 847–867. https://doi.org/10.1007/s11256-015-0341-x.

Webster, N. (2021). Acknowledging the historical contributions of Black youth's civic engagement in society. *Sociology Compass, 15*(5), 1–17. https://doi.org/10.1111/soc4 .12871.

White-Johnson, R. L. (2012). Prosocial involvement among African American young adults: Considering racial discrimination and racial identity. *Journal of Black Psychology, 38*(3), 313–341. https://doi.org/bzh6dt.

White-Johnson, R. L. (2015). The impact of racial socialization on the academic performance and prosocial involvement of Black emerging adults. *Journal of College Student Development, 56*(2), 140–154. https://doi.org/10.1353/csd.2015.0015.

Williams, D. R., Neighbors, H. W., & Jackson, J. S. (2003). Racial/ethnic discrimination and health: Findings from community studies. *American Journal of Public Health, 93*(2), 200–208. https://doi.org/10.2105/ajph.93.2.200.

Woodson, C. G. (1933). *The mis-education of the Negro.* Associated Publishers.

Yellow Horse, A. J., Kuo, K., Seaton, E. K., & Vargas, E. D. (2021). Asian Americans' indifference to Black Lives Matter: The role of nativity, belonging and acknowledgment of anti-Black racism. *Social Sciences, 10,* 168–183. https://doi.org/10.3390 /socsci10050168.

9

Critical Consciousness Development among Undocumented Youth

State of the Science, Historiography of Immigration Policy, and Recommendations for Research and Practice

GERMÁN A. CADENAS, RAFAEL MARTÍNEZ OROZCO, AND CARLOS AGUILAR

When Freire (1973) popularized the concept of *conscientização* (i.e., conscientization, critical consciousness) in *Pedagogy of the Oppressed*, he envisioned a pedagogical method and way of being in community that would support those who are at the receiving end of marginalization. Critical consciousness (CC) involves becoming awakened to the conditions that constrain one's options in society and recognizing social action as a necessary vehicle for progress (Watts et al., 2011). This combination of reflection and action are what Freire (1973) defined as praxis. Ideas about CC development have been advanced and clarified in academic and practical literature over the past fifty years, and most recently in the social sciences over the past twenty years (Jemal, 2017), including an expansive conceptualization of the components defining CC. Ongoing scholarship maintains the notion that CC is a pivotal developmental tool for youth belonging to groups that hold fewer privileges along intersecting social systems of racism, sexism, heterosexism, classism, ableism, ageism, and immigration status, among many others (Collins, 2000; Crenshaw, 1991). Research suggests that these youth may benefit from conscientization about the way these systems impact their overall well-being and futures (Diemer et al., 2015, 2016). Undocumented immigrants, in the United States and globally, are a group that is particularly targeted by intersecting forms of oppression, defined as a state or process of unequal and unfair use of power and resources (Watts et al., 2003). While there is an expanding understanding of illegality as juridical and sociopolitical fabrications that significantly limit the experiences of undocumented youth (De Genova, 2002), the study of CC among undocumented youth is still nascent.

Undocumented immigrants represent a community of about 11 million in the United States, a small fraction of a larger population of 272 million migrants worldwide (Edmond, 2020; Lopez et al., 2021). In the United States, youth make up a significant portion of the undocumented community, and estimates suggest that about 100,000 undocumented youth graduate from high school every year (Zong & Batalova, 2019). Due to the lack of a legal status, undocumented immigrants are subject to legal violence enforcing restrictions on most realms of their lives (Menjívar & Abrego, 2012), as well as racism, ethnoracism, economic marginalization, and exploitation, among many other systems of oppression. These vulnerabilities, caused and exacerbated by systems of oppression, may prompt undocumented immigrants to develop CC as an adaptive response. That is, placed at the intersection of varied systems of oppression (Collins, 2000), there emerges the possibility for undocumented immigrants to juxtapose their realities with ideals of justice in society. In this chapter, we provide an overview of the emerging scholarship centered on CC among undocumented youth, drawing from a literature that has flourished over the past five years. Building on this, we argue that future scholarship and practice on this topic must engage with the historical context of discriminatory immigration policies against the backdrop of which undocumented immigrants live, and how these policies provide the context for CC and resistance. Therefore, we provide an abridged summary of major policy moments and commentary on how these may inform CC. The chapter ends with recommendations for research and practice to support undocumented youth's CC through participatory research, education, social and health service delivery, and advocacy among undocumented communities and on their behalf.

AUTHORS' POSITIONALITY

The three coauthors collaborated in writing this chapter with humility and great appreciation for the undocumented immigrant community. Each of us is situated within different academic fields, including psychology, sociology, education, American studies, and borderlands studies. Yet, our focal lens when engaging in scholarship about immigration is our lived experience as currently or formerly undocumented people in the United States ourselves. The following positionality statements are intended to provide the narratives of us, the coauthors, and denote what informs our critical reading of and action related to immigration.

German A. Cadenas, PhD, identifies as a formerly undocumented immigrant who is now a US citizen, a person of Latin American ancestry, and an immigrant rights activist. He is a faculty member in counseling psychology at Lehigh University, where most of his work focuses on immigration and CC. He remains an active member of the immigrant activist community in the United States and has been involved in advocacy for institutional, state, and federal policies that are humane toward immigrants.

Rafael Martínez Orozco, PhD, self-identifies as an UndocuScholar – a scholar researching and writing about the immigrant experience from an undocumented perspective. Rafael has lived undocumented in the United States for more than thirty years while also recognizing his privilege of qualifying for the Deferred Action for Childhood Arrivals (DACA) program, which allowed him to pursue higher education and begin his career in academia. Rafael is an assistant professor at Arizona State University and is engaged in public projects that seek to connect academic work with community development.

Carlos Aguilar, AM, MS, is an undocumented immigrant and DACA beneficiary. Carlos's underlying emphasis is to explore alternative ways of thinking about theoretical frameworks surrounding undocumented immigration. Taking his positionality as a point of departure but aware of the limitations it also poses, his current work seeks to explore the experiences and opportunities that immigrants encounter in historically racialized and marginalized contexts. Carlos is a doctoral student in the Department of Sociology at the University of Pennsylvania.

THE STATE OF THE SCIENCE OF UNDOCUMENTED YOUTH CRITICAL CONSCIOUSNESS DEVELOPMENT

The development of social science regarding CC among youth experiencing social oppression has benefitted from a long period of increased inquiry over the past twenty years. A contribution that was significant in catalyzing this academic movement was the introduction of the theory of sociopolitical development (Watts et al., 1999), which envisioned a stage-by-stage developmental model that detailed how oppressed youth may move toward CC and liberation. Since then, critical consciousness research has investigated the ways in which CC may enhance the livelihood of oppressed youth in many domains of their lives, including their education and career development (Diemer & Blustein, 2007), their sociopolitical participation (Diemer & Li, 2011; Diemer & Rapa, 2016; Diemer et al., 2021), and their overall health and development (Diemer et al., 2015). Moreover, there has been expansive conceptualization of CC and its components (e.g., reflection, action, agency, and/or motivation) in extensive theoretical work (Jemal, 2017; Montero, 2009; Watts et al., 2011), paired with recent advancement in measurement and assessment of these constructs (Diemer et al., 2015). In almost parallel fashion, social science researchers have also devoted growing attention to the developmental, psychological, and sociolegal experiences of undocumented youth (Gonzales, 2015; Gonzales et al., 2013; Sullivan & Rehm, 2005), including their political activism that is exemplary of CC and liberatory action (Abrego & Negrón-Gonzales, 2020; Negrón-Gonzales, 2017). Holding great promise and new possibilities, these lines of scholarship have begun to converge in the past five years, bringing more clarity and specificity to CC development among undocumented youth. This part of the chapter focuses on reviewing this scholarship specifically; see Arce and colleagues' contribution in this volume (Chapter 10) for more on the unique processes underlying CC development for immigrant youth more generally.

Critical Consciousness and Educational Outcomes

In recent research, CC development was applied to undocumented college youth using an intersectional lens (Cadenas & Kiehne, 2021). A conceptual model was developed and tested to delineate how CC is informed by social categories where oppression is experienced (Crenshaw, 1991), specifically immigration status, social class, gender, and age. Subsequently, the model in this study positioned CC as a mediator between experiences of social oppression and academic performance, suggesting that CC helps undocumented youth transform disadvantage along these intersectional axes into higher academic performance. The model was supported when tested using robust statistical methods amongst Latinx undocumented youth who are temporarily protected by the Deferred Action for Childhood Arrivals (DACA) program. The results suggested that they held an academic advantage in contrast to Latinx US citizens, possibly due to endorsing higher CC that enabled them to read their social conditions and adjust their academic behavior accordingly.

In related research, a model that integrated action, reflection, and agency dimensions of CC among undocumented youth was developed to test whether these components, as well as social supports and barriers for CC, were predictive of undocumented youth's intent to persist in their education (Cadenas et al., 2018). This model was also tested among undocumented students protected by DACA as well as US citizens, and it yielded many findings. It was found that various forms of critical action (i.e., institutional activism and high-risk activism) were predictive of students' greater critical agency (i.e., political self-efficacy and outcome expectations). Higher agency was then predictive of higher intent to persist in college. Importantly, it was found that immigration status, race, and ethnicity moderated many of the links in the model, particularly for undocumented youth, who benefited more from social supports (e.g., encouragement from mentors) when developing CC. It was also found that undocumented Latinx youth benefited from CC just as much as their peers who were white and/or held US citizenship.

These studies clarify how undocumented youth develop CC in response to social oppression, the sequential process that connects various components of CC (i.e., between action and reflection, action and agency, reflection and agency). The evidence so far highlights that social supports are key to CC development among undocumented youth and establishes that increases in the development of this construct can be predictive of greater educational outcomes for this group of students. These findings are particularly hopeful considering the many systemic barriers experienced by undocumented youth as they navigate K–12 education. Many of these barriers include cultural mismatch of educators (Lopez & Garcia, 2019), inadequate educational content (Aguilara, 2021), and lack of support for parents of undocumented youth (Turney & Kao, 2009). These systemic barriers become far steeper at the higher education level as the law does not mandate public colleges and universities to provide accessible tuition to undocumented immigrants. A handful of states in the United States provide tuition equity and some financial support to undocumented immigrants. However, many more have enacted restrictive laws that keep undocumented immigrants from accessing higher education, and many others fall somewhere between these two ends of the continuum (Darolia & Potochnick, 2015). These inequities contribute to the low graduation rate of undocumented college students; recent estimates suggest that it is somewhere between 2.5% and 5% (Teranishi et al., 2015). In addition to facing inaccessible tuition costs and lack of financial aid, undocumented students may also contend with the challenges that come with being the first in their families to attend college and the racism and ethnoracism on college campuses (e.g., by faculty, staff, and students), not to mention the usual stressors and challenges associated with college studies (Bjorklund, 2018; Perez et al., 2009). While structural changes are needed to help undocumented youth succeed in their educational pathways, CC development can serve as a significant tool in this endeavor.

Critical Consciousness and Career Development

The workforce context is one where abundant hurdles and challenges exist for undocumented youth. However, this context is perhaps a more precarious one to navigate while developing CC, given the dearth of supports and resources available to undocumented immigrants at work, compared to those in educational settings. It is estimated that immigrants make up about 17% of workers in the United States, and this includes a large portion of undocumented workers (Budman, 2020). These workers are particularly essential in industries such as farming, construction, food service, cleaning and hospitality, and manufacturing, representing as much as 41% of the workforce in some of these industries. Although undocumented immigrants are essential to the functioning of a healthy economy (Becerra et al., 2012), contributing millions of dollars in taxes and more than $1 billion in spending power, the jobs that tend to be available to them are not considered "high-skilled," which excludes them from pathways for employment authorization through employee sponsorship (Boucher, 2020).

The lack of recognition and protection by federal and state law leaves undocumented immigrants to work in precarious conditions (Autin et al., 2018). They are vulnerable to workplace exploitation, with limited to no access to education and workforce development opportunities (e.g., English language education) or basic worker rights (e.g., paid sick leave, minimum wage). These surmounting conditions of oppression are compounded by undocumented immigrants' economic needs and responsibilities, as they often provide for families both in the United States and abroad by way of remittances (De Haas, 2005). Autin and colleagues (2018) found that both social and institutional support (i.e., in employment and educational institutions) as well as welcoming policies can counter these oppressive conditions, serving as supports for undocumented immigrants at work. This combination of social and institutional support can be critical for immigrant workers to engage in CC development. Godfrey & Wolf's (2016) research with low-income racially/ethnically minoritized immigrant women revealed that all participants in the study attributed poverty to individual factors (e.g., lack of hard work), and that less than half endorsed structural explanations for poverty. These results suggest that immigrant women may attempt to understand their own conditions by making use of two conflicting belief systems: one that is reflective of CC (e.g., structural attributions), and one that is more prevalent and reflects low CC and endorsement of meritocratic mindsets (e.g., system justification). This phenomenon may be due to low-income immigrants having fewer opportunities to engage in practices that support them in clarifying these belief systems, thereby developing CC. These results identify both a possibility and the need for heightened support for the CC development of low-income workers who are marginalized on multiple social dimensions (i.e., gender, race/ethnicity, social class, and immigration).

Given the precariousness of their career development, interventions based on CC are being developed to support undocumented youth as they prepare to enter the workforce and/or once they are in it. For instance, a recent asset-building framework for career interventions was developed specifically for Latinx immigrant youth (McWhirter et al., 2021). This framework attempts to combine college and career readiness activities and CC development activities. The framework maps out how each element of career readiness aligns with components of CC, such as reflection/awareness, action, and agency. The activities outlined in this framework can certainly be useful to those working with undocumented youth in the workforce, or in educational settings while undocumented youth are employed or prepare to seek employment.

Along the same lines, the Poder program was designed specifically for community college students, given that community colleges tend to serve undocumented youth, providing them affordable and flexible options (Cadenas et al., 2020a). Many community college students are matriculated while simultaneously maintaining employment. The Poder program is a free, cocurricular offering that supports students who hope to start their own small business or nonprofit in their communities. They learn social entrepreneurship and technology skills while engaging in a pedagogical process that is grounded in CC development. Students engage in critical dialogues about their identity and cultural strengths, work on a project that centers on connecting to community members, and receive mentorship and opportunities for seed funding. Research suggests that the Poder program is effective in promoting several career development outcomes among community college youth, including immigrant youth (Cadenas et al., 2020b), and that these outcomes were not moderated by immigration status. Several of the outcomes bolstered during the intervention include entrepreneurial skills, technology readiness, career outcome expectations, aspirations to start a business/non-profit, aspirations to finish an associate's degree and/or transfer to a university, and CC. These emerging studies and frameworks suggest that CC can be a helpful tool to embed within career development interventions for immigrant youth, as it may promote more equitable career outcomes in the face of steep structural inequities in the workforce.

Critical Consciousness and Mental Health

Extant research continues to suggest that the mental health of undocumented immigrants is marked by psychological distress that may be caused or exacerbated by experiences of marginalization, isolation, stigmatization, vulnerability, exploitability, fear, stress, and health concerns (Cobb et al., 2017; Ramos-Sánchez, 2009; Sullivan & Rehm, 2005). Given these complex psychological experiences, it is imperative to understand the role of CC in alleviating undocumented immigrants' distress. Emerging research has documented the benefits of CC development on undocumented immigrants' mental health. Cadenas and colleagues (2021) developed and tested a coping model that demonstrates the protective role that CC served among undocumented youth who experience everyday discrimination. The study focused particularly on conceptualizing critical agency as a protective factor, which may result from engagement in praxis (reflection and action), as prior research on undocumented youth has found (Cadenas et al., 2018). Results from that study found that higher everyday discrimination predicted higher anxiety among these youth. However, the link between discrimination and anxiety was diminished when critical agency was part of the model. This suggests that critical agency can be an adaptive response that is used by undocumented youth to protect their own mental health when facing discrimination.

Furthermore, community engagement can be conceptualized as form of critical action, a key component of CC (Diemer & Rapa, 2016). Research by Perez and colleagues (2010) found that undocumented students who were more engaged in their communities also tended to display more positive mental health. Moreover, a recent review of immigrant youth's community participation detailed how various forms of engagement (e.g., activism, cultural engagement, arts, and community service) may support these youth in connecting with social supports and engaging in identity development, skill development, and political empowerment, each of which may be protective to immigrant youth when they experience various forms of trauma and adverse childhood experiences (Cadenas et al., 2021). It is hopeful that research is finding the critical agency and action components of CC to be protective for undocumented youth. Recent decolonial frameworks for psychological practice have integrated CC and liberatory action as part of the healing process among immigrant communities (Chavez-Dueñas et al., 2019). Other studies have documented how activism, community participation, educational pursuits, and identity development are linked to higher resilience among undocumented students (Cadenas & Nienhusser, 2021; Gonzales et al., 2013; Hernandez, 2018; Moreno et al., 2021). Although there is growing evidence for the resilience associated with CC development, the ways in which undocumented immigrants engage with the potential drawbacks of critical consciousness development, such as activism burnout, racial battle fatigue, and tokenism in the political narrative surrounding immigration issues, are less explored (Bess et al., 2009; Gorski, 2018). Understanding the mechanisms linking CC to mental health may be fruitful for those providing services and support to undocumented youth, and for the youth themselves.

Critical Race Theory and Undocumented Youth

As the academic scholarship about undocumented youth's CC continues to evolve, this body of work benefits from more than fifty years of theorizing about concepts allied with CC. It is relevant to acknowledge these conceptual contributions as they may be informative to future scholarship and practice that more explicitly center the experiences of undocumented youth. In the United States, and specifically within educational spaces, critical race theory (CRT) has played an important role in fomenting CC among marginalized communities, offering many helpful concepts that may aid in understanding the experiences of undocumented immigrants (Ladson-Billings, 2013). This theory offers a critical analysis of the experiences of marginalized and racialized communities. Emerging in the critical legal studies movement (Crenshaw, 1991), and following a long tradition of critical theories, CRT centers the role that the concept of race(ism) has and continues to play in our society (Delgado & Stefancic, 2017). CRT was initially focused on a Black–white binary, and since its inception different off-shoots have emerged to account for the various experiences of marginalized and racialized populations. These perspectives include, but are not limited to, AsianCrit (Kolano, 2016; Museus & Iftikar, 2013), LatCrit (Solorzano & Yosso, 2001), TribalCrit (Brayboy, 2005), DisCrit (Annamma et al., 2013), and UndocuCrit (Aguilar, 2019), among others (Cabrera, 2018; Wong, 2021). As a theory preoccupied with social change, CRT offers tools to investigate white supremacy, the role of racism in society, the marginalization of different communities, and the tools to enact praxis.

A relatively recent addition to CRT, UndocuCrit centers undocumented and formerly undocumented scholars in the research process (Aguilar, 2019; Castrellón, 2021). Seeking to "validate and honor" the lived experiences and identities of undocumented immigrants (Aguilar, 2019, p. 157), UndocuCrit highlights "the fear and oppression to which we are subjected, the varied and rich-fullness of our experiences, and the ways in which we navigate and succeed despite the obstacles encountered on a daily basis" (p. 153). Attending to the sociopolitical context created by the state and the mechanisms employed to paralyze the illegalized, UndocuCrit builds on a long tradition of approaches with the objective to foster a CC. In other words, it highlights that undocumented youth are undocumented only because others impose on them the social category of "illegal," seeing them as subhuman, belonging to what Fanon (2009) described as "the zone of nonbeing." UndocuCrit specifically suggests that the lives of undocumented youth are shaped by: (a) fear that is endemic among immigrant communities, (b) states of liminality that shape experiences of reality, (c) parental *sacrificios* (e.g., sacrifices made by immigrant parents), and (d) *acompanamiento*, a form of relating that is exemplary of mentorship and community engagement. Future scholarship and practice relating to undocumented youth CC may benefit from engaging with these notions of racialized marginalization and oppression that are so prevalent in the development of undocumented youth, and which may motivate and facilitate CC development as an adaptive response.

A CRITICAL HISTORIOGRAPHY OF IMMIGRATION POLICY

The scientific inquiry about undocumented youth's CC development continues to expand and inform future research and practice. As this growth happens, we assert that scholarship and practice must also engage with the exclusionary history of anti-immigrant policy. This policy context permeates the lived experiences of undocumented youth in palpable ways, constraining their opportunities for development (Goodman, 2020). Since its inception, immigration policy in the United States has been racialized (Ngai, 1999, 2004), more harshly disadvantaging people of color (e.g., Indigenous, Latinx, Black, and Asian), thus creating oppressive structures that necessitate critical analyses and action by those impacted by it. Immigration policy serves as a reflective mirror to the ways in which citizenship is constructed in the United States. In other words, citizenship is meant to be a privileged category that is protected and afforded to a select few while creating a category for the "other" who should not be afforded the privilege of citizenship (Winant, 1986). In this section, we provide a brief critical historiography of US immigration policy through the lens of racial discourse to demonstrate the investment by the US government in discriminatory practices and policies against immigrants. We draw from scholars who have outlined the distinct ways in which immigration policy has been exclusionary based on race and we expand our analysis to focus on the legal consciousness of immigrants, which is informed by lived multigenerational experience of discrimination based on not only race, but also gender, sexuality, nationality, religion, and politics (Abrego, 2011).

We organize this historiography into three major power structure periods: exclusion from immigration and citizenship, World War II, and neoliberalism. The timeline sections we provide draw heavily on scholar A. Naomi Paik's history of immigration in the United States, which is critical and intersectional and includes race, ethnicity, gender, sexuality, and multiple other factors that create a structure of discrimination (Paik, 2020). We contrast each period of anti-immigration policies with responses character-ized by resistance and resilience, which we see as evidence of CC among immigrants. While we understand the utility of the concept of resilience specifically as it relates to the experiences of undocumented immigrants, it is also important to problematize such concepts as this individualizes the necessary responses, often absolving structural and governmental responsi-bilities. Through historic moments of immigrant resilience, we hope to highlight the historical context that may motivate immigrant youth to develop a CC. We note that this section provides a brief and comprehensive histori-ography of immigration policy aimed at providing context to immigrant CC and should not be interpreted as an extensive immigration policy history.

Exclusion from Immigration and Citizenship

The first policy regarding immigration in the United States occurred with the Naturalization Act of 1790, which confirmed citizenship as a restricted cat-egory for "white persons," and labeled all "others" as an exploitable working class (Haney-López, 2006). Race as a basis for citizenship would not be changed as a policy until 1952 (Lee, 2019). An important component of establishing citizenship based on race was the creation of a deep sense of distrust of foreigners and instilling of a sense of national pride in the new republic. As such, the Alien and Sedition Acts of 1978 were manifestations of patterns of xenophobic sentiment against foreigners and foreign languages and mistrust of cultural differences (Kanstroom, 2010).

During the nineteenth century, US immigration policy began to take shape to focus its exclusionary practices and craft ideas around what should constitute citizenship (Kettner, 1978). The 13th, 14th, and 15th Amendments confirmed slavery's abolishment, birthright citizenship, and the right to vote for individuals from historically marginalized communi-ties that had not been granted the privilege of citizenship (Zinn, 1999).

One example of one group's gains at the expense of another is the Naturalization Act of 1870, which reaffirmed citizenship of African-descent individuals as a form of apparent reparations for slavery while simultaneously denying citizenship to Asian immigrants (Wang, 2012). And while this is a difference in citizenship treatment, it is also a pattern throughout US history that one group's gain represents a loss for another. At the tail end of this section, we demonstrate how this concept of exclusion has informed a need for an intersectional consciousness and a strategic form of organizing that explores the complexities and diversity of undocumented communities in the United States. By *intersectional consciousness*, we refer to the ways in which immigrant populations and groups use critical historical knowledge about the ways in which distinct ethnic and racialized groups have been marginalized and incorporate this form of consciousness into intersectional forms of community organizing.

In studying the history of US immigration policy, we usually see scholars taking one of two approaches: focusing either on federal- or on state-level actions (Fong & Chan, 2008). This was a direct result of the Supreme Court hearing in Chy Lung v. Freeman (1875), which ruled that the federal government was to manage immigration policy at the federal level and the states would not dictate immigration policy (Gulasekaram & Ramakrishnan, 2013). The tug-of-war between the federal and state governments regarding immigration policy has impacted distinct immigrant realities and consciousness across internal geopolitical boundaries in the United States determined by state policies that differ across state lines (Chavez, 2008).

The period 1880–1920 witnessed the largest migration of ethnic southern Europeans to the United States and a period of discrimination practices based on differences in religion, particularly as experienced by Catholic and Jewish religious majorities (Dinnerstein & Reimers, 1975). This period of "new immigration" contained many European ethnic minorities that would go on to constitute a large majority of the east coast labor force, laying the foundation for forms of consciousness-raising efforts relating immigrant rights to labor movements.

The beginning of the twentieth century represented immigrant consciousness in the form of labor rights stemming from the Industrial Revolution. The United States began targeting immigrants based on political views, such as anarchism, and in later periods this was extended to communism with the Immigration Act of 1903 (Noonan, 2016). Additionally, in 1918 there was also the Anarchist Act, which linked anti-immigrant sentiments against political dissidence and added the threat of deportation (Paik, 2020). The United States continued to expand and practice the philosophy of deportation as a threat to political dissidence with the Palmer Raids, which targeted immigrant consciousness in strategic ways (Paik, 2020).

World War II

The period of World War II represents the normalization of deportation, detention, and internment (Lytle Hernández, 2010). Xenophobic sentiment was heightened during World War II, and detention practices expanded to include Japanese descent individuals living in the United States as the federal government created internment camps after the attack on Pearl Harbor. The camps radically altered the lives of Japanese descent individuals for generations, as internment occurred from 1942 to 1946 (Kaatz & Ivey, 2017). Scholars have begun to analyze early forms of Japanese internment in connection to detention, deportation, and mass movement of peoples (Harvey, 2003; Kaatz & Ivey, 2017).

The Bracero Program (1942–1964) was a temporary labor federal program with no pathway to citizenship aimed at addressing the United States agricultural production labor demand by supplementing it with foreign laborers from Mexico. The name "Bracero" comes from the Spanish word "brazo," which means "arm," to figuratively represent Mexican laborers as performing a helping hand to supply American's agricultural production shortages stemming from WWI and heightened during and after WWII (Mitchell, 2012). However, scholars have noted the long-term impacts of the racialization of labor, the medical and biological experimentation on bracero bodies, and the conditions in which laborers were forced to live during the remainder of the program (Guidotti-Hernández, 2021). As the number of Mexican laborers grew in the United States, so did xenophobic attitudes and political action that would later result in one of the largest mass deportation events, "Operation Wetback" in 1954 (Lytle Hernández, 2010). "Operation Wetback" showed how the interconnected powers of the Immigration and Naturalization Service (INS), the strengthening of one of its branches, the Border Patrol, and political power combined to result in the deportation of Mexican immigrants in large sweeps in three states: California, Texas, and Illinois (Ngai, 2004). In total, more than one million people were deported as a result of "Operation Wetback." These were mostly Mexican nationals, but it has been confirmed that US citizens were deported in the sweeps as well.

Japanese–American internment, the Bracero Program, and "Operation Wetback" are historical watershed moments that continue to live as intergenerational trauma for Japanese–American and Mexican–American descendants living in the United States. Historical events such as Japanese–American internment and deportation in Operation Wetback inform a CC that may motivate social action to protest state violence in the form of internment, detention, and deportation.

Neoliberalism

The neoliberal period is characterized by the last immigration reform in the United States: the Immigration Reform and Control Act of 1986, which created a pathway to citizenship for three million people (Bean et al., 1990).

Neoliberal logic in the 1990s was dictated by three conditions: the mobility and flow of capital and goods freely without restrictions, the restrictions of mobility of migrants and the militarization of the border, and the active detention and deportation of immigrants in the interior of the United States (Golash-Boza, 2015). No policies embodied these conditions more than the North American Free Trade Agreement (NAFTA, 1994) and the Illegal Immigration Reform and Immigrant Responsibility Act (IIRIA, 1996) (Nevins, 2010). Restriction on mobility did not mean that immigrants and their families would not begin to settle in the United States, however. In 1982, the Supreme Court case of *Plyler* v. *Doe* (1982) ensured access to a K–12 education to immigrant youth, positively impacting large numbers and helping foster consciousness that would go on to manifest in the 2000s (Abrego & Negrón-Gonzales, 2020).

Immigrant Consciousness in an Historical Perspective

We define immigrant consciousness as the process of CC development that is specifically informed by the human experiences related to the immigration process, attuned to the historic oppression of immigrants through policy and enforcement, and cognizant of social action as necessary for the liberation of immigrants. The critical historiography presented thus far suggests that from the establishment of the US nation-state in the late eighteenth century to the end of the nineteenth century, immigration policy rested on racialization of building an alien "other" who was not deemed worthy of incorporation. The classification of being unfit for incorporation or acquiring citizenship privileges grew over time to go beyond race and extended to gender, sexuality, class, respectability, political views, ethnic difference, and adaptivity to assimilation. Immigrants during this period understood that being able to assimilate to these normative categories represented not only incorporation but also survival in many instances.

Immigrant consciousness during the early period in US history took on many forms. Many times immigrants would perform these normative practices as they led to favorable outcomes in US society while continuing to practice cultural traditions within ethnic enclaves and communities. At other times, they assimilated and adopted US practices that favored representations of whiteness and capitalist outlooks. And at other times, immigrant consciousness took on the form of rejection, organizing, and performing dissidence even when such acts represented potential deportation, violence, and exclusion. During the early period of immigration policy, two notable historical forms of immigrant consciousness are worthy of mention: Emma Goldman and the Magon Brothers.

Emma Goldman was an immigrant who radicalized the labor rights movements and brought concepts of anarchism to the United States, building new CC among a generation of immigrants from the end of the nineteenth century into the beginning part of the twentieth century. Goldman's historical example of building CC among immigrant communities also represents one of the earliest examples of state violence, as she was to be deported because of her political views (Hing, 2004). Goldman would continue to organize beyond the United States in Europe and elsewhere, up until her death in Canada. Goldman's example of immigrant consciousness led to radical ideas of organizing that became the base for the labor movement in the United States and that also inspired transnational movements.

The period 1910–1920 brought a large influx of migrants from Mexico, along with radical anarchists and a particular consciousness centered on community by way of the Mexican Revolution (Gómez-Quiñones, 1981). Chicano historian Juan Gómez-Quiñones writes about the intellectual and revolutionary Magon brothers, who would go on to establish newspapers and community schools and foster an immigrant consciousness with Mexicans and Mexican Americans across the Southwest. This resulted in state violence toward one of the brothers, Ricardo Flores Magon, who would be picked up during the Palmer Raids and jailed. It is widely believed he was strategically murdered by prison guards. As a state measure, the southern border witnessed the beginning of militarization, with Congress approving the establishment of the US Border Patrol through the Labors Appropriation Act in 1924 (Lytle Hernández, 2010). The levels of organizing fueled by immigrant consciousness in examples such as that of Emma Goldman and the Magon brothers led to heavy enforcement practice responses by the immigration apparatus. This became a characteristic of the twentieth century.

More recently, scholars have begun to write about the active ways in which interned Japanese Americans resisted and formed a particular consciousness rooted in their internment experience during WWII (Harvey, 2003; Kaatz & Ivey, 2017). The Japanese example of internment represents a period in US history where immigrant consciousness takes on varied and multiple forms of practice, from complete adoption of US societal norms as a form of survival to forms of resistance practiced by interned Japanese–American citizens. From WWII to the end of the twentieth century and on to the twenty-first century, neoliberal forms of governance also sparked new forms of immigrant consciousness.

Leadership coming from immigrant youth is particularly notable in the twenty-first century. The period of the 2000s fostered some of the largest mobilization efforts in immigrant youth consciousness, efforts that moved the immigrant rights movement beyond a labor rights-based movement (Nicholls, 2013). The Dream Act was a federal bill introduced on three occasions (2001, 2007, 2010) that would have provided immigrant youth a pathway to citizenship, but it did not pass in Congress. The mobilization that fueled the legislative activism around the Dream Act led immigrant youth to push beyond organizing in civic engagement spaces to direct actions that involved civil disobedience (Vélez et al., 2008). Finally, 2006 and 2007 witnessed some of the largest immigrant rights demonstrations in the nation's history and would serve as the spark to ignite immigrant youth consciousness to develop new organizations and movements to fight for a broader inclusion and to intersect immigrant rights struggles with other social justice efforts (Escudero, 2020). Immigrant youth consciousness in the twenty-first century is unique in that it has gone beyond fighting for immigrant inclusion efforts; that is, it has expanded to fight for intersectional forms of inclusion around race, gender, sexuality, and class.[1]

This long history of immigration policy resting on difference and discriminatory practices is the foundation for contemporary forms of undocumented youth's CC. Undocumented youth who have benefited from decisions like *Plyler* v. *Doe*, and have had access to public education K–12 and state measures that made higher education accessible, may have learned about the discriminatory and racialized history of immigration policy and the treatment of diverse ethnic groups in the United States. The idea that one group's gain furthers another group's struggles has formed the historical, material, and cultural foundations for scholars and undocumented organizers to push for intersectional approaches to organizing across interlocking communal issues rather than establishing single-issue frameworks such as citizenship. A contemporary example of this is the UndocuBlack Network, which highlights the plight and struggles of Black immigrants in the United States and premises race as an interlocking issue across immigrant communities.[2] Similarly, undocumented youth also continue to organize around intersectional identities such as gender and sexuality and brought UndocuQueer[3] leadership to the broader immigrant rights movement (Chávez, 2013; Ramirez, 2020). A final example across intersectional communities that builds on the historical genealogy mentioned in this section is social movements' attention to "No One is Illegal on Stolen Land," or "No Ban on Stolen Land," in relation to immigrant communities, Indigenous communities, Middle Eastern-American, and refugee/asylum communities (Martínez & Schreiber, 2018). Therefore, we can see how these historical examples materialize in the current consciousness and organizing strategies of undocumented

---

[1] To read more about intersectionality within the undocumented youth movements, see Escudero (2020).

[2] UndocuBlack organizers argue that gaining citizenship for Black immigrants does not translate into complete equality, as they are still read as unequal due to the historical context of race in the United States and longstanding traditions in slavery and contemporary rates of incarceration. The UndocuBlack Network website can be found at https://undocublack.org.

[3] Julio Salgado is credited with coining and first using the term "UndocuQueer" in his artwork series titled *I am UndocuQueer* in 2012. The term aims to intersect the experiences and identities of being undocumented and queer. The series can be found in Salgado's website on the "timeline" section: www.juliosalgadoart.com/timeline/.

communities across multiple states in the United States. With this critical exploration into the long history of immigrant consciousness in a policy context, we now turn to recommendations for those working with undocumented immigrant communities.

RECOMMENDATIONS FOR PRACTITIONERS AND RESEARCHERS

We offer the following set of recommendations humbly, with the aim of informing practice and research to support the well-being and healthy development of undocumented youth via CC. These recommendations are based on the evolving state of the science and the historical policy context that we reviewed in this chapter. Our positionality and lived experiences as undocumented youth who underwent processes of CC also prominently inform these recommendations. The goal with these recommendations is not to be prescriptive but to offer a starting place for anyone supporting undocumented youth.

1. Conduct Participatory Research Informed by Critical Race Theories

Our first recommendation is for scholars engaging in research related to CC. We would suggest that the science on this topic is produced by using research methods that are inclusive of the voices of undocumented youth, that are responsive to their needs, and that aim to transform the very conditions that oppress them. To this end, methods such as youth participatory action research (YPAR; Anyon et al., 2018) are excellently suited. YPAR involves youth in every aspect of the research, from developing research questions to the design and implementation of a study. Most importantly, YPAR is conducted with the goal of resisting and transforming conditions that perpetuate inequalities, such as the ones that have been endured by undocumented youth for decades. An example of this is the UndocuScholars project, through which undocumented college youth conducted a study to uplift their experiences in higher education and to inform advocacy and policy change stemming from these scholarly efforts (Suárez-Orozco et al., 2015; Teranishi et al., 2015). In addition, scholars may also benefit from becoming familiar with CRTs, such as Undocumented Critical Theory (Aguilar, 2019), and infusing their research with the tenets and concepts discussed in these writings. CRTs are exemplary of many of Freire's notions, particularly as these frameworks are emerging from the perspectives of oppressed communities and are intended to encourage praxis. Research about undocumented youth is certainly enhanced when approached using CRT lenses.

2. Educate Practitioners and Youth about the Racist History of Immigration Policy

As highlighted in this chapter, we find it impossible to separate the historic and current context of anti-immigrant policy from the process of CC development among undocumented youth, given the extensive influence of these policies on their livelihood. Thus, we would recommend that practitioners who serve these youth receive ongoing education about this historical context and that this education is itself provided with a critical lens. This kind of critical education may support practitioners in challenging their neutrality when it comes to injustices experienced by immigrants. An emphasis on racist anti-immigrant policy may be embedded within professional development for allyship among educators and education staff (Cadenas et al., 2018b) and within continuing education for mental health providers (Cadenas et al., 2022). As evidenced by research, this kind of programming supports practitioners so that they are better able to listen to the experiences and ultimately identify and meet the needs of undocumented youth. Wide-scale implementation of educational programs that focus on policy, and their real-life impacts, may sensitize practitioners to create institutions that are safer for undocumented youth (Cadenas et al., 2019). Furthermore, critical education can also be provided to youth themselves. For example, courses or programs such as ethnic studies (Cammarota, 2016) have been documented to foster a CC and to translate into social action, community building, and improved outcomes in education and career. Understanding that illegality is socially constructed (De Genova, 2002) can thus open opportunities to seek out its undoing within the educational and practice community by engaging in praxis.

3. Facilitate Safe Spaces that Foster Critical Consciousness

In our current sociopolitical moment, creating safe spaces for immigrant youth can be difficult given the intersecting social positions that individuals possess. As we seek to acknowledge and further the CC of undocumented youth, it is necessary for educators, researchers, and other practitioners to facilitate opportunities, resources, and supports so that undocumented youth can create a space in which they feel seen, heard, and motivated to reflect on and act to change the injustices that impact them (Cadenas & Kiehne, 2021). Individuals who work with undocumented youth may connect them to activist organizations, such as United We Dream (2018), the largest immigrant youth-led organization in the United States. Practitioners may also attempt to connect with or create more intimate spaces, such as the Mestizo Arts & Activism Collective (MAA) in Salt Lake City, Utah, which serves to transform the thinking and understanding of overlapping oppressions to which young people of color are subjected, as well foster caring relationships within the collective (Cahill et al., 2019). These spaces may emerge in different contexts (e.g., schools, community activism, workforce development), and may also take the form of healing circles, storytelling, or other artistic outlets (Mateos-Fernández & Saavedra, 2021; Pérez, 2018; Rodriguez Vega, 2019). These spaces may allow undocumented youth to share their emotions, make sense of their experiences, map their relation to others and the world, or foster spaces of resistance and action (Cadenas et al., 2020b; Cahill et al., 2019; Vega, 2018). Exemplary of this recommendation are Undocumented Student Resource Centers (Cisneros & Valdivia, 2018), which have been pioneered in higher education to provide a range of services to undocumented youth. As evidenced by research (Cadenas et al., 2018, 2021), undocumented youth's educational and career development is bolstered when they feel supported in their CC development and have the ability to engage in critical reflection, action, and agency.

4. Practice *Acompañamiento*

The concept of *acompañamiento* was described by Aguilar (2019) in *Undocumented Critical Theory*, and it pertains to forming relationships with undocumented youth that are marked by empathy, dialogue, support, encouragement, and the fostering of a sense of belonging (Sepúlveda, 2011). *Acompañamiento* may serve to foster CC from a place of support that enables the creation of knowledge emerging from a shared experience. Given that praxis takes place within community, Cahill et al. (2019) remind us that a space in which love and care serve as a starting point can lead us to change both our ways of thinking but also of acting and moving in the world. Ultimately, as Cadenas and Kiehne (2021) find in their research, safe and brave collectives are an important aspect "of the repertoire of supports" that allow the undocumented individual to be accompanied in their awakening journeys toward CC, in academic contexts and otherwise (Aguilar, 2019). In our view, these collectives are formed through relationships that are nurtured by the elements identified in *acompañamiento*. This cultural practice is one that has the potential of leading to praxis beyond the individual level, and of supporting activism that is initiated by undocumented youth themselves (Forenza et al., 2017).

5. Identify and Deconstruct Meritocratic Narratives in Education and Career

The US educational system and workforce tend to reinforce beliefs about meritocracy, the idea that all sociocultural groups exist on a leveled playing field, and that hard work is sufficient to guarantee success in education, career, and life overall. Meritocracy ignores the systemic inequalities and barriers experienced by oppressed groups, such as undocumented youth, as they pursue "the American dream." For those individuals working with undocumented youth, regardless of the context, it is important to acknowledge and discuss the extensive barriers that a lack of a legal status will pose in immigrants' lives (Gonzales, 2011). As research has shown, even when undocumented youth have done everything that was asked of them to achieve success, such as excel academically, the lack of a legal status has kept them from reaping the benefits of their hard work (Gonzales, 2011). We believe it is also important to discuss the role that the education system itself plays in sorting out undocumented students into their "respective social position" (Aguilar 2021a; Cahill et al., 2016). CC can be strengthened, and resilience fostered, by acknowledging that the education system is not a neutral institution (Warikoo & Carter, 2009) and, thus, that "illegality" and its consequences are not inherent qualities of undocumented youth, but conditions that are imposed upon them by social systems.

CONCLUSION

In this chapter, we reviewed the emerging science about mechanisms through which CC might be developed among undocumented immigrants in the United States, including those who are undocumented and/or are beneficiaries of the Deferred Action for Childhood Arrivals (DACA). This review included the links between CC and the education, careers, and mental health of undocumented youth, as well as emerging theories aiming to uplift their experiences. The chapter also included a critical historiography of immigration policy, which described the ways in which oppressive and racialized anti-immigrant contexts may motivate CC that is specific to the experiences of immigration. Our chapter ended with an offering of recommendations for practitioners and scholars to support their efforts in promoting CC among undocumented youth in the context of education, workforce development, mental health service, community activism, and research.

REFERENCES

Abrego, L. J. (2011). Legal consciousness of undocumented Latinos: Fear and stigma as barriers to claims-making for first-and 1.5-generation immigrants. *Law and Society Review*, 45(2).

Abrego, L., & Negrón-Gonzales, G. (2020). *We are not dreamers: Undocumented scholars theorize undocumented life in the United States*. Duke University Press.

Aguilar, C. (2019). Undocumented critical theory. *Cultural Studies↔ Critical Methodologies*, 19(3), 152–160.

Aguilar, C. (2021a). Undocumented critical theory in education. In N. M. Garcia, C. Salinas Jr., & J. Cisneros (Eds.), *Studying Latinx/a/o students in higher education: A critical analysis of concepts, theory, and methodologies* (pp. 149–163). Routledge.

Aguilar, C. (2021b). Review of We are not dreamers: Undocumented scholars theorize undocumented life in the United States. *Anthropology & Education Quarterly, 52* (3), 362–363.

Annamma, S. A., Connor, D., & Ferri, B. (2013). Dis/ability critical race studies (DisCrit): Theorizing at the intersections of race and dis/ability. *Race Ethnicity and Education, 16*(1), 1–31.

Anyon, Y., Bender, K., Kennedy, H., & Dechants, J. (2018). A systematic review of youth participatory action research (YPAR) in the United States: Methodologies, youth outcomes, and future directions. *Health Education & Behavior, 45*(6), 865–878.

Autin, K. L., Duffy, R. D., Jacobson, C. J. et al. (2018). Career development among undocumented immigrant young adults: A psychology of working perspective. *Journal of Counseling Psychology, 65*(5), 605–617.

Bean, F. D., Edmonston, B., & Passel, J. S. (1990). *Undocumented migration to the United States: IRCA and the experience of the 1980s.* Rand Corp.

Becerra, D., Androff, D. K., Ayon, C., & Castillo, J. T. (2012). Fear vs. facts: Examining the economic impact of undocumented immigrants in the US. *Journal of Sociology & Social Welfare, 39*, 111–200.

Bess, K. D., Prilleltensky, I., Perkins, D. D., & Collins, L. V. (2009). Participatory organizational change in community-based health and human services: From tokenism to political engagement. *American Journal of Community Psychology, 43*(1–2), 134–148.

Bjorklund Jr., P. (2018). Undocumented students in higher education: A review of the literature, 2001 to 2016. *Review of Educational Research, 88*(5), 631–670.

Boucher, A. K. (2020). How "skill" definition affects the diversity of skilled immigration policies. *Journal of Ethnic and Migration Studies, 46*(12), 2533–2550.

Brayboy, B. M. J. (2005). Toward a tribal critical race theory in education. *The Urban Review, 37*(5), 425–446.

Budman, A. (2020). Key findings about US immigrants. Pew Research Center. www .pewresearch.org/fact-tank/2020/08/20/key-findings-about-u-s-immigrants/.

Cabrera, N. L. (2018). Where is the racial theory in critical race theory?: A constructive criticism of the crits. *The Review of Higher Education, 42*(1), 209–233.

Cadenas, G. A., Bernstein, B. L., & Tracey, T. J. (2018). Critical consciousness and intent to persist through college in DACA and US citizen students: The role of immigration status, race, and ethnicity. *Cultural Diversity and Ethnic Minority Psychology, 24*(4), 564–575. https://doi.org/10.1037/cdp0000200.

Cadenas, G. A., Cantú, E. A., Lynn, N., Spence, T., & Ruth, A. (2020a). A programmatic intervention to promote entrepreneurial self-efficacy, critical behavior, and technology readiness among underrepresented college students. *Journal of Vocational Behavior, 116*, 103350.https://doi.org/10.1016/j.jvb.2019.103350.

Cadenas, G. A., Cantú, E. A., Spence, T., & Ruth, A. (2020b). Integrating critical consciousness and technology in entrepreneurship career development with diverse community college students. *Journal of Career Development, 47*(2), 162–176. https://doi.org/10.1177/0894845318793968.

Cadenas, G. A., Cisneros, J., Todd, N. R., & Spanierman, L. B. (2018). DREAMzone: Testing two vicarious contact interventions to improve attitudes toward undocumented immigrants. *Journal of Diversity in Higher Education*, 11(3), 295–308. https://doi.org/10.1037/dhe0000055.

Cadenas, G. A., & Kiehne, E. (2021). The undocumented advantage: Intersectional predictors of critical consciousness and academic performance among US Latinxs. *Journal of Latinx Psychology*. Advance online publication. https://doi .org/10.1037/lat0000163.

Cadenas, G. A., & Nienhusser, H. K. (2021). Immigration status and college students' psychosocial well-being. *Educational Researcher*, 50(3), 197–200. https://doi.org /10.3102/0013189X20962470.

Cadenas, G. A., Neimeyer, G., Suro-Maldonado, B. et al. (2022). Developing cultural competencies for providing psychological services with immigrant populations: A cross-level training curriculum. *Training and Education in Professional Psychology*, 16(2), 121–129.

Cadenas, G. A., Peña, D., & Cisneros, J. (2019). Creating a welcoming environment of mental health equity for undocumented students. In E. Crawford & L. Dorner (Eds.), *Educational leadership of immigrants: Case studies in times of change* (pp. 71–78). Routledge.

Cadenas, G. A., Peña, D., Minero, L. P., Rojas-Araúz, B. O., & Lynn, N. (2021). Critical agency and vocational outcome expectations as coping mechanisms among undocumented immigrant students. *Journal of Latinx Psychology*, 9(2), 92–108. https://doi.org/10.1037/lat0000178.

Cadenas, G. A., Sosa, R., & Liang, C. (2021). Immigrant youth's community participation to promote immigrant rights and resist psychological and sociopolitical challenges. *Encyclopedia of Child and Adolescent Health*. https://doi.org/10.1016 /B978-0-12-818872-9.00024-8.

Cahill, C., Alberto Quijada Cerecer, D., Reyna Rivarola, A. R., Hernández Zamudio, J., & Alvarez Gutiérrez, L. (2019). "Caution, we have power": Resisting the "school-to-sweatshop pipeline" through participatory artistic praxes and critical care. *Gender and Education*, 31(5), 576–589.

Cahill, C., Alvarez Gutiérrez, L., & Quijada Cerecer, D. A. (2016). A dialectic of dreams and dispossession: The school-to-sweatshop pipeline. *Cultural Geographies*, 23(1), 121–137.

Cammarota, J. (2016). The praxis of ethnic studies: Transforming second sight into critical consciousness. *Race Ethnicity and Education*, 19(2), 233–251.

Castrellón, L. E. (2021). "Just being undocumented you gotta find loopholes": Policy enactment of an in-state resident tuition policy. *Journal of Diversity in Higher Education*, 15(4), 480–492.

Chy Lung v. Freeman. (1959). *The Yale Law Journal*, 68(8), 1596.

Chavez, K. (2013). *Queer migration politics: Activist rhetoric and coalitional possibilities*. University of Illinois Press.

Chavez, L. (2008). *The Latino threat: Constructing immigrants, citizens, and the nation*. Stanford University Press.

Chavez-Dueñas, N. Y., Adames, H. Y., Perez-Chavez, J. G., & Salas, S. P. (2019). Healing ethno-racial trauma in Latinx immigrant communities: Cultivating hope, resistance, and action. *American Psychologist*, 74(1), 49–62.

Cisneros, J., & Valdivia, D. (2018). Undocumented student resource centers: Institutional supports for undocumented students. Penn Center for Minority Serving Institutions. https://cmsi.gse.rutgers.edu/sites/default/files/USRCs.pdf.

Cobb, C. L., Meca, A., Xie, D., Schwartz, S. J., & Moise, R. K. (2017). Perceptions of legal status: Associations with psychosocial experiences among undocumented Latino/a immigrants. *Journal of Counseling Psychology, 64*(2), 167–178.

Collins, P. H. (2000). *Black feminist thought: Knowledge, consciousness, and the politics of empowerment* (2nd ed.). Routledge.

Crenshaw, K. W. (1991). Mapping the margins: Intersectionality, identity politics, and violence against women of color. *Sandford Law Review, 43*(6), 1241–1279.

Darolia, R., & Potochnick, S. (2015). Educational "when," "where," and "how" implications of in-state resident tuition policies for Latino undocumented immigrants. *The Review of Higher Education, 38*(4), 507–535.

De Genova, N. P. (2002). Migrant "illegality" and deportability in everyday life. *Annual Review of Anthropology, 31*(1), 419–447.

De Haas, H. (2005). International migration, remittances and development: Myths and facts. *Third World Quarterly, 26*(8), 1269–1284.

Delgado, R., & Stefancic, J. (2017). *Critical race theory: An introduction.* New York University Press.

Dinnerstein, L., & Reimers, D. (1975). *Ethnic Americans: A history of immigration and assimilation.* Dodd, Mead.

Diemer, M. A., & Blustein, D. L. (2007). Vocational hope and vocational identity: Urban adolescents' career development. *Journal of Career Assessment, 15*(1), 98–118.

Diemer, M. A., & Li, C. H. (2011). Critical consciousness development and political participation among marginalized youth. *Child Development, 82*(6), 1815–1833.

Diemer, M. A., McWhirter, E. H., Ozer, E. J., & Rapa, L. J. (2015). Advances in the conceptualization and measurement of critical consciousness. *The Urban Review, 47*(5), 809–823.

Diemer, M. A., Pinedo, A., Bañales, J. et al. (2021). Recentering action in critical consciousness. *Child Development Perspectives, 15*(1), 12–17.

Diemer, M. A., & Rapa. L. J. (2016). Unraveling the complexity of critical consciousness, political efficacy, and political action among marginalized adolescents. *Child Development, 87*(1), 221–238. https://doi.org/10.1111/cdev.12446.

Diemer, M. A., Rapa, L. J., Voight, A. M., & McWhirter, E. H. (2016). Critical consciousness: A developmental approach to addressing marginalization and oppression. *Child Development Perspectives, 10*(4), 216–221.

Edmond, C. (2020). Global migration, by the numbers: Who migrates, where they go and why. *World Economic Forum.* www.weforum.org/agenda/2020/01/iom-global-migration-report-international-migrants-2020/.

Escudero, K. (2020). *Organizing while undocumented: Immigrant youth's political activism under the law.* New York University Press.

Fanon, F. (2009). *Piel negra, máscaras blancas.* Ediciones Akal.

Fong, E., & Chan, E. (2008). An account of immigration studies in The United States and Canada, 1990–2004. *Sociological Quarterly, 49*(3), 483–502.

Forenza, B., Rogers, B., & Lardier, D. (2017). What facilitates and supports political activism, by and for, undocumented students? *The Urban Review*, 49, 648–667. https://doi.org/10.1007/s11256-017-0413-1.

Freire, P. (1973). *Education for critical consciousness* (Vol. 1). Bloomsbury Publishing.

Godfrey, E. B., & Wolf, S. (2016). Developing critical consciousness or justifying the system? A qualitative analysis of attributions for poverty and wealth among low-income racial/ethnic minority and immigrant women. *Cultural Diversity and Ethnic Minority Psychology*, 22(1), 93–103. http://dx.doi.org/10.1037/cdp0000048.

Golash-Boza, T. M. (2015). *Deported: Immigrant policing, disposable labor, and global capitalism*. New York University Press.

Gómez-Quiñones, J. (1981). *Porfirio Díaz, los intelectuales y la Revolución* (1st ed.). Ediciones El Caballito.

Gonzales, R. G. (2011). Learning to be illegal: Undocumented youth and shifting legal contexts in the transition to adulthood. *American Sociological Review*, 76(4), 602–619.

Gonzales, R. G. (2015). *Lives in limbo*. University of California Press.

Gonzales, R. G., Suárez-Orozco, C., & Dedios-Sanguineti, M. C. (2013). No place to belong: Contextualizing concepts of mental health among undocumented immigrant youth in the United States. *American Behavioral Scientist*, 57(8), 1174–1199.

Goodman, A. (2020). *The deportation Machine: America's long history of expelling immigrants*. Princeton University Press.

Gorski, P. C., 2018. Racial battle fatigue and activist burnout in racial justice activists of color at predominately white colleges and universities. *Race Ethnicity and Education*, 22(1), 1–20. https://doi.org/10.1080/13613324.2018.1497966.

Guidotti-Hernández, N. (2021). *Archiving Mexican masculinities in diaspora*. Duke University Press.

Gulasekaram, P., & Ramakrishnan, S. K. (2013). Immigration federalism: A reappraisal. *New York University Law Review*, 88(6), 2074–2145.

Haney-López, I. (2006). *White by law: The legal construction of race* (Rev. and updated, 10th anniversary ed.). New York University Press.

Harvey, R. (2003). *Amache: The story of Japanese internment in Colorado during World War II*. Taylor Publishing.

Hernandez, E. (2018). *Undocumented, unafraid, and unapologetic: Exploring the role of activism in DACAmented Latinas/os/xs' thwarted transition into adulthood*. Doctoral dissertation, Columbia University. Pro-Quest Dissertations and Theses Global (Order No. 10808152).

Hing, B. O. (2004). *Defining America through immigration policy*. Temple University Press.

Jemal, A. (2017). Critical consciousness: A critique and critical analysis of the literature. *The Urban Review*, 49(4), 602–626.

Kaatz, K. W., & Ivey, L. L. (2017). *Citizen internees: A second look at race and citizenship in Japanese American internment camps*. Praeger.

Kanstroom, D. (2010). *Deportation nation: Outsiders in American history*. Harvard University Press.

Kettner, J. H. (1978). *The development of American citizenship, 1608–1870*. Published for the Institute of Early American History and Culture, Williamsburg, VA, University of North Carolina Press.

Kolano, L. (2016). Smartness as cultural wealth: An AsianCrit counterstory. *Race Ethnicity and Education, 19*(6), 1149–1163.

Ladson-Billings, G. (2013). Critical race theory – What it is not! In M. Lynn, & A. D. Dixson (Eds.), *Handbook of critical race theory in education* (pp. 54–67). Routledge.

Lee, E. (2019). *America for Americans: A history of xenophobia in the United States* (1st ed.). Basic Books.

Lopez, D., & García, O. (2019). Translanguaging: Challenges and opportunities for school leaders. In E. R. Crawford, & L. M. Dorner (Eds.), *Educational leadership of immigrants* (pp. 37–47). Routledge.

Lopez, M. H., Passel, J. S., & Cohn, D. (2021). Key facts about the changing US unauthorized immigrant population. Pew Research Center. www.pewresearch.org /fact-tank/2021/04/13/key-facts-about-the-changing-u-s-unauthorized-immigrant-population/.

Lytle Hernández, K. (2010). *Migra! A history of the US Border Patrol.* University of California Press.

Martínez, R. A., & Schreiber, R. M. (2018). Sovereignty and sanctuary: a roundtable. *Chiricú Journal: Latina/o Literature, Art, and Culture, 3*(1), 141–154.

Mateos-Fernández, R., & Saavedra, J. (2021). Designing and assessing of an art-based intervention for undocumented migrants. *Arts & Health,* 1–14.

McWhirter, E. H., Cendejas, C., Fleming, M. et al. (2021) College and career ready and critically conscious: Asset-building with Latinx immigrant youth. *Journal of Career Assessment,* 1–18. https://doi.org/10.1177/1069072720987986.

Menjívar, C., & Abrego, L. (2012). Legal violence: Immigration law and the lives of Central American immigrants. *American Journal of Sociology, 117*(5), 1380–1421.

Mitchell, D. (2012). *They saved the crops: Labor, landscape, and the struggle over industrial farming in the Bracero-era California.* University of Georgia Press.

Montero, M. (2009). Methods for liberation: Critical consciousness in action. In *Psychology of liberation* (pp. 73–91). Springer.

Moreno, O., Fuentes, L., Garcia-Rodriguez, I., Corona, R., & Cadenas, G. A. (2021). Psychological impact, strengths, and handling the uncertainty among Latinx DACA recipients. *The Counseling Psychologist,* 00110000211006198.

Museus, S. D., & Iftikar, J. (2013). An Asian critical theory (AsianCrit) framework. *Asian American Students in Higher Education, 31*(10), 18–29.

Negrón-Gonzales, G. (2017). Political possibilities: Lessons from the undocumented youth movement for resistance to the Trump administration. *Anthropology & Education Quarterly, 48*(4), 420–426.

Nevins, J. (2010). *Operation gatekeeper and beyond the war on illegals and the remaking of the US-Mexico boundary* (2nd ed.). Routledge.

Ngai, M. M. (1999). The architecture of race in American immigration law: A reexamination of the Immigration Act of 1924. *The Journal of American History, 86*(1), 67–92.

Ngai, M. (2004). *Impossible subjects: Illegal aliens and the making of modern America.* Princeton University Press.

Nicholls, W. J. (2013). *The DREAMers: How the undocumented youth movement tdansformed the immigrant rights debate.* Stanford University Press.

Noonan, A. (2016). "What must be the answer of the United States to such a proposition?" anarchist exclusion and national security in the United States, 1887–1903. *Journal of American Studies, 50*(2), 347–376.

Paik, N. A. (2020). *Bans, walls, raids, sanctuary: Understanding US immigration for the twenty-first century.* University of California Press.

Perez, W., Espinoza, R., Ramos, K., Coronado, H. M., & Cortes, R. (2009). Academic resilience among undocumented Latino students. *Hispanic Journal of Behavioral Sciences, 31*(2), 149–181.

Perez, W., Espinoza, R., Ramos, K., Coronado, H., & Cortes, R. (2010). Civic engagement patterns of undocumented Mexican students. *Journal of Hispanic Higher Education, 9*(3), 245–265.

Pérez, J. B. (2018). Undocuartivism: Latino undocumented immigrant empowerment through art and activism. *Chiricù Journal: Latina/o Literature, Art, and Culture, 2* (2), 23–44.

Plyler v. Doe, 457 U.S. 202, 102 S. Ct. 2382, 72 L. Ed. 2d 786 (1982).

Ramirez, M. L. (2020). Beyond Identity: Coming Out as UndocuQueer. In L. J. Abrego, & G. Negrón-Gonzales (2020). *We are not dreamers: Undocumented scholars theorize undocumented life in the United States* (pp. 146–167). Duke University Press.

Ramos-Sánchez, L. (2009, June). The psychology of undocumented Latinos: Living an invisible existence. In J. L. Chin (Ed.), *Diversity in mind and in action, vol. 1. Multiple faces of identity* (pp. 105–115). Praeger/ABC-CLIO.

Rodriguez Vega, S. (2019). Teatro vs Trump: Children in South Central Los Angeles fight back. *Aztlán: The Journal of Chicano Studies, 44*(1), 189–198.

Sepúlveda III, E. (2011). Toward a pedagogy of acompañamiento: Mexican migrant youth writing from the underside of modernity. *Harvard Educational Review, 81* (3), 550–573.

Solorzano, D. G., & Yosso, T. J. (2001). Critical race and LatCrit theory and method: Counter-storytelling. *International Journal of Qualitative Studies in Education, 14* (4), 471–495.

Suárez-Orozco, C., Katsiaficas, D., Birchall, O. et al. (2015). Undocumented undergraduates on college campuses: Understanding their challenges and assets and what it takes to make an undocufriendly campus. *Harvard Educational Review, 85*(3), 427–463.

Sullivan, M. M., & Rehm, R. (2005). Mental health of undocumented Mexican immigrants: A review of the literature. *Advances in Nursing Science, 28*(3), 240–251.

Teranishi, R. T., Suárez-Orozco, C., & Suárez-Orozco, M. (2015). In the shadows of the ivory tower: Undocumented undergraduates and the liminal state of immigration reform. UndocuScholars Project, The Institute for Immigration, Globalization, & Education. University of California, Los Angeles.

Turney, K., Kao, G., 2009. Barriers to school involvement: Are immigrant parents disadvantaged? *The Journal of Educational Research, 102*(4), 257–271. https://doi .org/10.3200/JOER.102.4.257-271.

United We Dream. (2018). UndocuHealth. https://unitedwedream.org/undocuhealth-wellness/.

Vega, S. R. (2018). Praxis of resilience & resistance: "We can STOP Donald Trump" and other messages from immigrant children. *Association of Mexican American Educators Journal, 12*(3), 122–147.

Vélez, V., Huber, L. P., Lopez, C. B., De La Luz, A., & Solorzano, D. G. (2008). Battling for human rights and social justice: A Latina/o critical race media analysis of Latina/o student youth activism in the wake of 2006 anti-immigrant sentiment. *Social Justice, 35*(1/111), 7–27.

Wang, X. (2012). *Trial of democracy: Black suffrage and northern republicans.* University of Georgia Press.

Warikoo, N., & Carter, P. (2009). Cultural explanations for racial and ethnic stratification in academic achievement: A call for a new and improved theory. *Review of Educational Research, 79*(1), 366–394.

Watts, R. J., Diemer, M. A., & Voight, A. M. (2011). Critical consciousness: Current status and future directions. *New Directions for Child and Adolescent Development, 2011*(134), 43–57. https://doi.org/10.1002/cd.310.

Watts, R. J., Griffith, D. M., & Abdul-Adil, J. (1999). Sociopolitical development as an antidote for oppression: Theory and action. *American Journal of Community Psychology, 27*(2), 255–271.

Watts, R. J., Williams, N. C., & Jagers, R. J. (2003). Sociopolitical development. *American Journal of Community Psychology, 31*(1–2), 185–194.

Winant, H. (1986). *Racial formation in the United States: From the 1960s to the 1980s.* Routledge & Kegan Paul.

Wong, C. P. (2021). The wretched of the research: Disenchanting Man2-as-educational researcher and entering the 36th chamber of education research. *Review of Research in Education, 45*(1), 27–66.

Zinn, H. (1999). *A people's history of the United States: 1492-present* (20th anniversary ed.). HarperCollins.

Zong, J., & Batalova, J. (2019). How many unauthorized immigrants graduate from US high schools annually? Migration Policy Institute. www.migrationpolicy.org/research/unauthorized-immigrants-graduate-us-high-schools.

10

Influences of Sense of Social Responsibility, Immigrant Bargain, and Immigrant Optimism on Critical Consciousness Development among Immigrant Youth of Color

MARIA ALEJANDRA ARCE, CLAUDIA A. DELBASSO, AND GABRIEL P. KUPERMINC

Immigrant youth of color comprise one of the fastest growing segments of the US population (Migration Policy Institute, 2018), and they are subjected to oppression at multiple levels of the human ecology, ranging from racial microaggressions in everyday interactions to anti-immigrant legislation. Over the last few decades, this population has received increasing attention in social science research, particularly through research rooted in liberation psychology and critical consciousness (CC) theory (e.g., Cadenas et al., 2020; Godfrey & Wolf, 2016; Seider et al., 2017). However, much of this research has focused on group-level differences between immigrant and nonimmigrant youth. Research also has not consistently considered ways in which immigration phenomena may uniquely shape the CC development of immigrant youth of color above and beyond the core elements of CC that are frequently investigated among other marginalized groups (i.e., critical awareness, motivation, internal sociopolitical efficacy, and action). This chapter reviews the existing literature on immigration phenomena and processes relevant to CC among immigrant youth of color, with a focus on *sense of social responsibility* (e.g., Katsiaficas, 2018) as a commonly held value of young immigrants, and intersecting principles and applications of the *immigrant bargain* (e.g., Cherng & Liu, 2017) and *immigrant optimism* (Kao & Tienda, 1995) phenomena. The aim of this chapter is to outline ways in which evidence from the acculturation literature can help inform CC research and practice and facilitate our understanding of how best to support the collective empowerment of immigrant youth of color. We challenge the limits of existing theories as currently applied and encourage the reader to critically evaluate the perspectives presented in this chapter.

We begin this chapter by defining the core concepts as well as delineating the premises that guide the rest of this chapter. We then provide an introduction to theorized bidirectional influences of social identities, inequities, and responsibilities among immigrant youth of color. Next, we review the literature on immigrant family dynamics and values that may directly or indirectly shape these youth's development of a sense of social responsibility and further contribute to their participation in actions aimed at bettering their communities. Then, we synthesize the literature that supports the role of a sense of social responsibility to identity-based communities on the critical reflection and action of immigrant youth of color. Finally, we describe the immigrant optimism hypothesis and delineate potential influences on social responsibilities and action. We conclude with a discussion on limitations of existing research and make recommendations for future research and practice with young immigrants of color.

CORE CONCEPTS

This chapter conceptualizes sense of social responsibility as a sense of duty or obligation to contribute to the betterment of others (Katsiaficas, 2018; Wray-Lake & Syvertsen, 2011). We emphasize immigrant youth's perceived sense of social responsibility to both proximal (i.e., family) and distal social systems (i.e., other immigrants, society at large), and how this value is exercised through participation in a range of civic activities. Such activities include but are not limited to critical action or efforts that challenge the status quo. Thus, we distinguish the value orientation of social responsibility from its behavioral enactment and consider the two as mutually influential. Throughout the chapter, we highlight the various roles that social identities and social inequities might play in the development of this value orientation and behavioral outcomes. This chapter also considers ways in which the immigrant optimism hypothesis (Kao & Tienda, 1995) may add nuance to the already dynamic processes occurring between and among social identities, inequities, and responsibilities for immigrant youth. The immigrant optimism hypothesis posits that immigrant groups hold higher aspirations and more positive views of the host or receiving country (e.g., the United States) than their nonimmigrant peers, and this confers to them an advantage for positive development and adaptation across domains, including civic development. Thus, while it might appear that aspects of immigrant optimism could detract from the development of CC, we explore the ways that such optimism can serve to reinforce a sense of social responsibility and support different forms of action intended to uplift marginalized communities.

GUIDING THEORY AND PREMISES

Originally proposed by Freire (1968) in his liberation practice with marginalized communities in Brazil, CC theory has been applied across a range of communities in a range of oppressive contexts (e.g., Forenza, 2018; Harper et al., 2019; Singh et al., 2021). Since its origins, the theory has evolved, and there has been variation in the conceptualization and operationalization of the core elements of CC. On one hand, researchers seem to agree that critical reflection is a key and necessary aspect of CC that involves awareness of systemic inequities. However, variations in how critical reflection is conceptualized and measured make it difficult to compare across studies (see Heberle et al., 2020, for a systematic review of studies of CC in youth; see Diemer et al., 2015, for a review of CC measures). Similarly, the field recognizes that awareness of inequities alone does not constitute CC – it must be translated into action aimed at creating social change (i.e., *critical action*, e.g., Watts et al., 1999). In this chapter, we further argue that what critical action looks like in immigrant communities may differ from that in nonimmigrant groups. We emphasize the importance of intentions and define critical action in terms of the intent to create social change rather than focus on discrete categories of behaviors. For example, as we highlight in more detail in a later section, young immigrants of color – who might be the first in their families to be involved in and confront barriers in the US education system – often seek to persist and achieve academically as an act of resistance to uplift their communities (e.g., Gutiérrez, 2014). We believe it is essential to remind ourselves and the reader that, while some behaviors may be assumed by others to maintain instead of challenge the status quo, the unique experiences of immigrant youth of color in the United States might make these assumptions more nuanced and even null.

Particularly relevant to intention is the core construct of *critical motivation*, which is highlighted in more modern conceptualizations of CC theory (e.g., Rapa et al., 2020), along with *sociopolitical efficacy* (e.g., Diemer & Rapa, 2016). As Kiang et al. (2021) noted, critical motivation "has been simultaneously cast as reflecting individuals' beliefs about their commitment to create social and political change, their internal effectiveness to enact change, as well as the perception that government policies and societal structures are actually responsive" (p. 1370). Indeed, the term is often used interchangeably with sociopolitical efficacy and agency. In this chapter, we understand critical motivation and sociopolitical efficacy as related but distinct constructs. We conceptualize sociopolitical efficacy as beliefs about an individual's ability to effect sociopolitical change (e.g., Peterson et al., 2011), and we adhere to Rapa et al.'s (2020) conceptualization of critical motivation as encompassing "beliefs about the importance of correcting societal inequity and responsibility to change perceived inequalities" (p. 3). In the next section, we argue and provide support for considering ways in which a sense of social responsibility as it relates to inequities may influence the CC development of immigrant youth.

SOCIAL IDENTITIES, INEQUITIES, AND RESPONSIBILITIES

In order to understand the dynamic associations between sense of social responsibility, social inequities, and action among immigrant youth of color, we must also pay attention to these youth's various social identities.

Social identity is theorized to influence youth of color's civic engagement and CC (Anyiwo et al., 2018, 2020; Sánchez-Jankowski, 2002). Identity informs how one understands the meaning of group membership and thus is interconnected with awareness and understanding of marginalization against social identity group(s). Consequently, researchers posit that identity development and CC are likely reciprocal among minoritized youth and adults (Anyiwo et al., 2018; Mathews et al., 2020). Katsiaficas (2018) calls for more research to consider the role that intersecting identities and social inequities may play in shaping the development of social responsibility among young adults. An intersectional approach may be particularly useful in examining facilitators and barriers to civic action among immigrant youth of color because they often hold multiple social identities, including those constructed by race, ethnicity, documentation status, and religion, among others (e.g., Ghavami et al., 2016). For example, Chan's (2011) study among first- and second-generation Asian immigrant college students identified ethnic and religious identity as antecedents of action. Participants often described joining ethnic organizations as a means to explore their own identity and meet others of the same background.

Although longitudinal examinations are sparse and directionality cannot be established, there is evidence to suggest that associations between group identity and actions aimed at creating social change are bidirectional (e.g., Thomas et al., 2020). A stronger sense of belonging to a social group may both precede and follow action. This is consistent with the larger social and racial/ethnic identity literatures, which find that individuals who have a strong sense of belonging to their social group(s) feel positively about their membership(s), consider their social group(s) central to their overall self-concept, and are invested in promoting the well-being of the group (Tajfel & Turner, 1986; Turner et al., 1987; Williams et al., 2020). Particularly relevant to this chapter may be the social identity model of collective action (SIMCA), which positions both politicized social identity and perceived injustice against one's social group as key predictors of action (e.g., van Zomeren et al., 2008). Although this model has not been carefully applied to young immigrants of color in the United States (e.g., Wiley et al., 2012), its premises are supported in tests of the rejection–identification model (Branscombe et al., 1999) in immigrant-origin groups. Specifically, perceived ethnic/racial discrimination has been found to predict identifying with the targeted group and disidentifying with the dominant group (e.g., Ramos et al., 2012; Wiley et al., 2013). Similarly, research links both ethnic/racial identity and discrimination to activism in support of immigrant rights and racial equality (e.g., Tran & Curtin, 2017).

Consistent with both social identity and CC theories, Katsiaficas (2018) also suggests that experiences of inequity may motivate a sense of social responsibility among immigrant youth. Indeed, studies have found that these youth often experience a sense of social responsibility to address the inequitable social conditions of the various groups of which they are a part. Along these lines, Sánchez-Jankowski (2002) notes that youth of color share a history of systemic racialized exclusion from social and civic life that affects their identity development and their civic engagement. In their literature review of immigrant youth civic engagement, Stepick and Stepick (2002) noted that discrimination is a likely motivator for civic actions that benefit one's marginalized community – whether along dimensions of ethnicity or immigrant background. More recently, in one of few longitudinal examinations of racial discrimination and critical action, Pinedo et al. (2021) found that changes in perceived racial discrimination positively predict changes in action among Black and Latinx college students. A growing body of research has also examined ways in which immigrant youth of color (particularly those with a precarious documentation status) become aware of and challenge anti-immigrant policies and their consequences. For instance, in response to anti-immigrant rhetoric under the Trump administration, many Latinx immigrants have increased their engagement in advocacy. This was driven by a sense of responsibility to "bring visibility to these issues and take action" among those directly impacted by restrictive legislation (e.g., DACA-mented youth; Moreno et al., 2021, p. 16) and by a sense of responsibility to help vulnerable others among those with a more secured status (e.g., US citizens; Arce et al., 2020). We return to actions that challenge anti-immigrant rhetoric in a later section.

Reciprocal/Reinforcing Processes

As we have alluded to throughout this chapter, research supports a reciprocal approach to the study of social identities, inequities, and responsibilities. A strong sense of belonging to one's sociocultural group(s) may influence the development of social responsibility in both its attitudinal and behavioral manifestations. At the same time, the enactment of a sense of social responsibility via participation in civic activities can help strengthen youth's sociocultural identities. Indeed, although longitudinal quantitative research in this area is limited, evidence from evaluations of community-based programming aimed at promoting the integration and adaptation of young immigrants suggests these constructs are mutually reinforcing (see Thomas et al., 2020, for a longitudinal examination of SIMCA among ethnic groups in New Zealand).

For instance, using longitudinal ethnographic observations, Kolano and Davila (2019) found that participation in an ethnic community-based organization serving Southeast Asians facilitated critical reflection, ethnic pride, and political efficacy among Southeast Asian refugee adolescent girls. In particular, dialogue about systemic inequities and participation in advocacy efforts seemed to foster a collective identity and a sense of responsibility to support their own community and other communities of color facing injustices. Similarly, studies have found that participation in ethnic studies programming as well as service-learning curricula delivered within schools and/or ethnic community-based organizations facilitates Asian American youth's increased sense of social responsibility to stand up for their "people" which, in turn, seems to contribute to increased participation in social change efforts (Chan, 2011; Suyemoto et al., 2015). Also, among Black and Latinx college students, greater involvement in ethnic/racial clubs is associated with more frequent engagement in critical action (Pinedo et al., 2021). Along these lines, Wray-Lake and Syvertsen (2011) note that civic engagement and social responsibility are mutually reinforcing: "just as social responsibility may provoke civic action, certain kinds of civic action may enhance social responsibility" (p. 13). On the other hand, a lack of a sense of social responsibility (i.e., believing something is "not my problem" and "not my responsibility") has been identified as a barrier to action among youth (Ellis, 2004; George Mwangi et al., 2019). Existing research thus highlights the importance of considering youth's sense of belonging to their marginalized sociocultural identities and awareness of inequities that their own and other groups experience when investigating social responsibility as a value and a behavior. Next, we review relevant findings from the acculturation literature that highlight how the value orientation of social responsibilities may first develop within immigrant families in the context of other values and dynamics – such as the immigrant bargain – and inform immigrant youth's later participation in actions aimed at improving their communities.

PATHWAYS TO CRITICAL CONSCIOUSNESS FROM SENSE OF RESPONSIBILITY TO THE FAMILY

Family life provides a starting point for the development of a sense of social responsibility. Fuligni et al. (2009) note that many ethnic minority families in the United States have family traditions that emphasize the importance of children's roles in supporting and assisting family members. A strong sense of family obligation among youth in immigrant families arises not only from culturally grounded parenting practices but also from a sense of duty to repay parents for the sacrifices they made to provide better lives for their children (Borjian, 2018; Fuligni et al., 1999).

Little research has directly examined the impact of these responsibilities on CC or civic development. However, two strands of research have investigated developmental outcomes associated with immigrant youth's family responsibilities, usually focusing on academic or mental health outcomes. The first strand focuses on values and attitudes emphasizing a sense of obligation (sometimes referred to as "familism" among Latinx origin families;

Stein et al., 2014). The second focuses on behaviors, such as sibling caretaking and language or culture brokering (e.g., translating and interpreting spoken or written communications for parents; Kuperminc, Wilkins, et al., 2009). Both strands often emphasize concerns that family responsibilities can stifle healthy development. For example, specific to civic development, some studies find that youth's feelings of indebtedness to their parents for their sacrifices immigrating to the United States can potentially conflict with their participation in civic activities as their time may be consumed with other family-related responsibilities (East, 2010). Because family assistance is normative and supported in many cultures, it is likely that such assistance will only have detrimental consequences for children's development under high levels of family stress (East, 2010). Indeed, studies of normative development in immigrant families have repeatedly found that family responsibilities are unrelated to emotional distress (Kuperminc, Jurkovic, et al., 2009; Kuperminc et al., 2013) and that immigrant youth do not necessarily view daily family assistance activities as stressful, and even derive a sense of fulfillment from their contributions (Telzer & Fuligni, 2009).

There is emerging evidence that a commitment to improving their immigrant families' circumstances can motivate youth's participation in various civic activities, including critical action to address inequities related to race, ethnicity, and/or immigration status (e.g., Borjian, 2018). For example, Rubio-Hernandez and Ayón's (2016) qualitative examination of Latinx parents' perceived impact of restrictive immigration legislation on their children revealed that, in addition to fear, sadness, concern, and other unpleasant emotional experiences, parents perceived that their children felt a sense of responsibility to help improve their family's circumstances. By and large, these youth are often identified in the literature as engaging in family and community assistance behaviors, such as translating for parents and neighbors and helping them navigate unfamiliar US institutions or systems. Moreover, principles of reciprocity and, in particular, the notion of giving or paying back to immigrant parents is frequently discussed in the immigration and acculturation literature (e.g., Cherng & Liu, 2017; Dreby, 2010; Louie, 2012), although it often goes unacknowledged in studies of immigrant youth CC development.

Immigrant Bargain

The aforementioned dynamic is captured by the phenomenon of the immigrant bargain (e.g., Cherng & Liu, 2017; Dreby, 2010; Louie, 2012). As noted, immigrant parents often make great sacrifices so that their children can achieve more in the United States than they could in their countries of origin (e.g., Louie, 2012). Thus, immigrant children often grow up aware of their parents' sacrifices and this awareness seems to contribute to their sense of responsibility to improve the social conditions of their family and larger immigrant and/or ethnic community. One way immigrant youth of color seek to repay their parents for their sacrifices is through academic and career achievement, which may allow them to both financially and emotionally (via pride in their achievements) give back to their parents (e.g., Fuligni & Pedersen, 2002; Katz, 2014). For instance, in Sy and Romero's (2008) qualitative examination of Latina college women, participants described seeking to gain financial independence as a way to reduce the burden on their parents and help the family financially. Also, research has found that young immigrants' persistence in their academic and vocational goals is driven by a desire to become a source of pride and better represent their marginalized communities (Phinney, 2006). The potential role of such "humanitarian" motivations (Phinney, 2006; Uriostegui et al., 2020) in influencing the development of CC of immigrant youth of color has received little research attention and is an important focus for future research.

Using two-wave data from Black and Latinx youth, Uriostegui et al. (2020) investigated direct and indirect effects of critical reflection, sociopolitical efficacy, and critical action on academic and career plans via a range of motivations to pursue academic and career goals. Results revealed significant direct and indirect effects of sociopolitical efficacy on both indicators of motivation and on academic and career planning. However, the direction of these effects varied by type of motivation. For example, higher efficacy contributed to higher "humanitarian motivations," but such motivations were unrelated to academic and career planning activities. "Encouragement motivations," or motivations stemming from youth's perceived encouragement from a mentor or others, significantly and positively mediated the effects of efficacy on academic and career plans. In other words, higher levels of efficacy were associated with greater encouragement motivations which, in turn, contributed to greater engagement in academic and career planning activities. In contrast, negative pressure from others, particularly parents (referred to as "expectation motivations" in the study) to meet goals appeared to undermine academic and career planning. When youth endorsed higher levels of efficacy, they were more likely to report higher expectation motivations, and this contributed to less engagement in academic and career planning. Again, these findings are generally consistent with research on the immigrant bargain and family obligation (both values and behaviors) among immigrant youth of color.

The immigrant bargain thus involves a sense of duty to make the sacrifices of immigrant parents "worth it" and is considered a "moral contract between parents and children" (Katz, 2014, p. 96). Of course, to effectively fulfill their side of the bargain, immigrant youth of color need access to community and institutional resources beyond those provided by their families to facilitate successful academic/vocational achievement and upward mobility. Such resources may be out of reach for those youth. Looking beyond the immediate family, it is important to acknowledge the support that immigrant families give to each other. This support is an often overlooked resource in studies of social responsibilities and action, despite calls for greater attention to principles of reciprocity within the context of social responsibility (e.g., Katsiaficas, 2018). Indeed, the phenomenon of the immigrant bargain is in line with the larger social responsibility literature that identifies relationships and a sense of connectedness to others as a critical precursor to a sense of responsibility that extends beyond the individual (Wray-Lake & Syvertsen, 2011). In the next section, we explore potential applications of this phenomenon – which has primarily been examined within the family system – to actions aimed at bettering larger systems, including young people's immigrant, ethnic, and/or undocumented communities.

Family Responsibilities Translated to Communities

Whereas relatively little research has considered the ways that family responsibilities may contribute to the development of a broader sense of social responsibility, there are reasons to expect that it does. Katsiaficas's (2018) definition of social responsibility includes both family obligation and community engagement. Developing a strong sense of social responsibility is consistent with the interdependent world views held by many immigrant youth with origins in cultures that are described as collectivistic (Greenfield et al., 2003). Family responsibilities can lead to, rather than stifle, the development of autonomy and personal maturity, which are necessary to effectively navigate, engage with, and challenge more distal systems. Engaging in family assistance behaviors, such as language brokering, can promote the development of effective interpersonal skills (Kuperminc, Jurkovic, et al., 2009; Kuperminc et al., 2013) and offer opportunities for youth to observe social inequities, including limited access to resources and marginalization (Katsiaficas, 2018). For example, Weisskirch (2005) notes that language brokering entails more than translating and interpreting. It requires children and adolescents to negotiate power relationships between themselves, their parents, and the outside world. Whereas some research finds associations between language brokering and low well-being and increased stress (Martinez et al., 2009), others find potential benefits, such as enhanced ethnic identity (Weisskirch, 2005). Ethnic identity has long been theorized as a predictor of critical action at the individual and collective levels (e.g., Mathews et al., 2020; Sánchez-Jankowski, 2002; Tajfel, 1978). Thus, family responsibilities have the potential to expose immigrant youth to contexts in which they learn what it means to be part of a marginalized group and gain a greater sense of their ethnic and cultural identity, which in turn can lead them to develop a greater sense of solidarity with members of their own and other marginalized groups (Fuligni et al., 2009). In the following section, we expand on the potential influences of family responsibilities on the development of social responsibilities to larger communities. We further outline ways in which recognizing and resisting inequities may both be a driver and an outcome of social responsibilities among immigrant youth of color.

Awareness of Inequities and Sense of Social Responsibility to Immigrant, Ethnic, and/or Undocumented Communities

Aside from a sense of responsibility to one's parents or family members, immigrant youth of color's sense of responsibility to their identity-based communities both influences and is influenced by their critical reflection of inequities and oppression. In tandem, these processes shape young immigrants' CC development and civic engagement more broadly (e.g., Barajas-Gonzales et al., 2018; Crookes et al., 2021). Whether inequities and oppression are experienced subtly through microaggressions in interpersonal contexts or more overtly through anti-immigrant hate at the local, state, or national levels, a breadth of research identifies these experiences as fundamental drivers of social responsibilities in their attitudinal and behavioral forms among immigrant youth of color (e.g., Chan & Latzman, 2015; Gutiérrez, 2014; Suárez-Orozco et al., 2015).

For instance, Gutiérrez (2014) qualitatively examined how a sample of primarily undocumented, Spanish-speaking, recent Mexican immigrant high schoolers navigated a hostile school climate. Youth described that they and their Mexican peers were excluded from school programs and class participation, were treated as if they were dishonest and unintelligent by teachers, and were monitored and sometimes made fun of by white peers and teachers who frequently told them to "speak English" (p. 316). These overt and covert experiences of group-based marginalization contributed to their awareness of discriminatory systems and sense of responsibility to better their immigrant and Mexican communities and advocate for immigrant rights. Particularly, and consistent with past research, youth in this study were committed to pursue higher education and careers that would position them to support and defend the rights of their fellow immigrant peers.

Notably, the finding that immigrant youth of color consider education and career achievement as a means through which they can give back to their families and communities is well established in the immigration and acculturation literature. It is growing in CC research as well. In a series of studies, Cadenas and colleagues proposed and tested a model that integrated core elements of CC and social cognitive career theories (Cadenas et al., 2018, 2020, 2021), finding direct and indirect effects of CC components on academic achievement (i.e., GPA) among a racially/ethnically diverse sample of graduate students (Cadenas et al., 2021). McWhirter and others have also documented positive effects of CC components on academic and vocational outcomes among high schoolers of color (Luginbuhl et al., 2016; McWhirter & McWhirter, 2016). Their findings informed the development of a school-based intervention guided by social cognitive career and sociopolitical development theories aimed at supporting the career development of Latinx high schoolers (McWhirter, Rojas-Araúz, et al., 2019).

In a recent longitudinal study of CC components as predictors of academic achievement among youth of color, Seider and colleagues (2020) found that critical reflection and action contributed positively to academic achievement (assessed via standardized tests and school grades). However, a sense of political agency (reflecting sociopolitical control and social responsibility) was unrelated to later academic achievement. It is also important to note that critical action was operationalized as both a commitment to engage in social change efforts and a motivation to achieve personal success as a form of activism ("as a mechanism for countering hegemonic notions that achievement is a White property"; p. 458). These findings support the notion that academic and/or vocational achievement among immigrant youth of color is not just about self-actualization but an act of resistance to a range of barriers, inequities, and stereotypes.

Consistent with the immigrant bargain, immigrant youth of color identify educational and career achievement as meaningful avenues to create change in their communities – not only because of expected upward mobility for themselves and their families but also because they hope to model and encourage action in other community members (Kennedy et al., 2020). As an illustration, Suárez-Orozco and colleagues (2015) qualitatively explored profiles of civic engagement among Latinx emerging adults of varying educational level and documentation status. Analyses revealed that most youth actively participated in activities to better their community or group, and many went beyond active participation to take on leadership and organizing roles. Researchers identified a sense of social responsibility as an important driver for such actions and, in this capacity, participants often emphasized their commitment to serving as role models to other Latinx youth community members (Suárez-Orozco et al., 2015).

Furthermore, in keeping with the immigrant bargain, young immigrants' commitment to better the communities they are part of and to lead by example is also documented in studies of parental racial/ethnic socialization (e.g., Aldoney & Cabrera, 2016; Knight & Watson, 2014). For example, studies have found that West African immigrant parents often encourage their children to "do good things" for others within and across borders (Knight & Watson, 2014, p. 550). Also, Latinx parents teach their children to do right and model this by example (Aldoney & Cabrera, 2016). Latinx parents also talk to their youth about political and social justice issues in their community and teach them about their ethnic/racial history and culture, which contributes to a stronger sense of responsibility to help community members (Pinetta et al., 2020). Immigrant youth of color's sense of responsibility to give back to their communities and set a good example for similar others stems from the socialization messages they first encountered within the family system, which are later reinforced in school, community, and religious organizations, as well as other settings (Chan, 2011; Jensen, 2008; Suyemoto et al., 2015). Thus, the immigrant bargain arises between parents and children and is reinforced within their identity-based communities.

Challenging Anti-immigrant Rhetoric

Immigrant youth of color also experience a sense of responsibility to challenge anti-immigrant rhetoric, including perceptions of immigrants as "burdens on society" (p. 541), and do so through the development of sociopolitical identities and actions (Knight & Watson, 2014). Studies have found that immigrant youth of color give back to their communities not only out of concern for the conditions of their groups but also to counter negative stereotypes against their immigrant, ethnic, and/or undocumented communities (e.g., Forenza et al., 2017; Jensen, 2008; Kennedy et al., 2020). Of course, this necessitates awareness of such forms of marginalization in the first place. As such, a growing body of research investigates perceptions of and reactions to anti-immigrant legislation and other immigration-related news or events among immigrant youth of color. For example, when the custody and deportation case of the Cuban child Elián González dominated US news in the early 2000s, Stepick et al. (2008) found that Caribbean and Latinx immigrant youth in Miami were aware that the news disproportionately portrayed Cubans as angry rioters. Youth participation in demonstrations and other civic actions seemed to be driven by both a sense of injustice toward Latinxs at large and a sense of responsibility to stand in solidarity against injustice.

In recent years, with anti-immigrant sentiment rising under the Trump administration, studies have documented a range of responses to increasingly restrictive immigration legislation and general climate. Such responses include a sense of social responsibility to protect and fight for other immigrants, especially those with precarious or no documentation status. For example, in response to restrictive immigration policies implemented by the Trump administration, Arce et al. (2020) found that Latinx immigrant parents of varying residency statuses (i.e., undocumented, permanent residents, and US citizens) and their adolescent children developed a sense of responsibility to partake in actions that promote immigrant justice. Children in these families were acutely aware of the impacts that restrictive immigration policies have on their immigrant families and the immigrant community at large and were committed to pursue relevant service careers (e.g., immigration law) to defend the rights of immigrants, particularly those without a secured legal status.

Similarly, Wray-Lake et al. (2018) examined reactions to the Trump presidency shortly after the inauguration and found that Latinx adolescents were increasingly aware of racism, anti-immigrant legislation, and discrimination toward themselves, their families, and their larger immigrant and Latinx communities. For some of these youth, this heightened awareness of injustice motivated their commitment to stand up against and fight racism and discrimination on behalf of themselves and others. Consistent with CC theory, the authors highlighted that "greater motivation to stand up for one's community or become more engaged tended to coincide with awareness of the injustices of racism and negative stereotypes directed toward them and their community" (p. 199).

Similar findings have been documented in evaluations of youth programming aimed at deepening reflection on social issues. For example, Kennedy et al. (2020) examined the development of CC among Asian, Latinx, Black, and African adolescents from immigrant backgrounds involved in a multisite after-school program in the months right before, during, and after Trump's election. During this time, youth engaged in critical discussions with adult facilitators wherein they frequently articulated concern about actual and anticipated negative consequences of discriminatory rhetoric and policies (e.g., Muslim travel ban and increased funding for immigration enforcement) against their various identities. Youth further expressed a shared sense of responsibility with their community and peers toward the collective goal of resisting restrictive immigration policies under Trump (Kennedy et al., 2020). Some youth reported a commitment to their academic achievement as a necessary strategy to create social change by disproving negative stereotypes against them and using their knowledge to educate and inspire others. It is important to note, however, that youth who have negative feelings about their marginalized social group or a limited understanding of their group's history, culture, and traditions may be more negatively impacted by discrimination and thus more disengaged from civic life (Suyemoto et al., 2015).

Documented versus Undocumented Status

Although we focus on the shared experiences of immigrant youth of color, it goes without saying that this population is not homogenous. In particular, some immigrant youth experience unique barriers to certain kinds of action as a function of documentation status. Specifically, studies have established that precarious documentation status can be both a barrier to conventional political participation, on one hand, and a driver of critical action, on the other. This is especially true if the critical action relates to immigration reform or occurs in the form of mentoring or other types of community service (e.g.,

Ballard et al., 2015; Borjian, 2018; Forenza et al., 2017). With this in mind, and in line with an intersectionality framework, we briefly review relevant findings on undocu- and DACA-mented immigrants' sense of social responsibility. For a more comprehensive examination of CC development among these youth, see the contribution in this volume by Cadenas and colleagues (Chapter 9).

Undocu- and DACA-mented youth experience social responsibilities in similar and unique ways relative to their documented peers. Borjian (2018) conducted a qualitative study of "academically successful" (i.e., cumulative grade point average at or above 3.0) undocumented college students. Student narratives pointed to a strong sense of responsibility for similar others' well-being as fuel for civic activities, such as mentorship, outreach, advocacy, and volunteer involvement. Consistent with previous studies, Borjian (2018) found that undocumented youth have high regard for education as a way to improve their communities despite their restricted access to it. Students were committed to helping other immigrants succeed in higher education and highlighted the support from peers, mentors, and organizations that had made their own success possible. This provides further evidence for the phenomenon of the immigrant bargain extended to the community: Because youth recognize and appreciate what others in their community have done for them, they feel indebted and experience a sense of responsibility to do what they can to support similar others.

In fact, in their examination of the enactment of familial and community responsibilities among a national sample of Latinx undocumented college students, Katsiaficas et al. (2018) found reciprocal influences between familial and community support, cultural values (e.g., familism), and students' sense of responsibility. Students described receiving support from and recognizing the sacrifices of community and family members. This motivated participants' desire and sense of responsibility to give back to their family and community via various activities, including educational attainment, advocacy, and mentoring and translating for others in their community. Thus, both documented and undocumented immigrant youth of color are committed to give back to their immigrant, ethnic, and/or undocumented communities and seek to do so by modeling achievement and encouraging and inspiring others like them to persevere (e.g., Borjian, 2018; McWhirter, Gomez, et al., 2019). However, for undocu- and DACA-mented youth, the road to successfully and safely enacting their sense of social responsibility and fulfilling their piece of the immigrant bargain is paved with considerably more institutional barriers and risks to action than their peers. At the same time, the consequences of not traveling the road may be even more threatening to their liberation than doing so.

Influences of Immigrant Optimism on Social Responsibility and Critical
Consciousness

We now briefly evaluate the association between sense of social responsibility
and CC in light of evidence for another immigration phenomenon: the
immigrant optimism hypothesis. This hypothesis suggests that immigrant
youth often evaluate the host country more positively and have higher aspirations for their future relative to their nonimmigrant peers (Kao & Tienda,
1995). This optimism is further assumed to contribute to more positive
psychosocial outcomes, including academic achievement, in these youth
when compared to their counterparts, despite experiencing immigration
and acculturation-related challenges that their peers are unlikely to experience (e.g., De Feyter et al., 2020). In this sense, immigrant optimism appears
to function as a source of resilience that helps youth persevere in uneven
playing fields. For example, studies have found that undocumented Latinx
college students are motivated by their optimism to achieve and persevere
amidst numerous obstacles in the way of their educational achievement
(Borjian, 2018). As we have noted, immigrant youth of color often view
educational and vocational achievement as a means to enact their sense of
social responsibility and bring about change in and for their communities.
This suggests that immigrant optimism may work in tandem with a sense of
social responsibility to directly and indirectly facilitate social change efforts.

   Although direct examinations of the role of immigrant optimism on social
responsibility and CC are limited, there is theoretical and some empirical evidence to suggest it may enhance a sense of responsibility to engage in actions that
benefit young immigrants' families and communities. However, little is known
about the extent to which immigrant optimism might facilitate or hinder participation in actions specifically intended to create social change. For example, first-
generation immigrants endorse higher optimism about and trust in the fairness of
US society and the responsiveness of the government (Ballard, 2013), which has in
turn been linked to formal participation in democratic processes (Flanagan et al.,
2009). For youth in immigrant families, optimism may further emerge from their
parents' socialization practices, including conversations comparing conditions
and opportunities in the native versus host country, which may promote engagement in civic activities. Among a sample of Salvadoran and Indian immigrant
parents and their adolescent children, participants often described appreciation
for American values and its democracy as a motivator for becoming civically
active (Jensen, 2008). On the other hand, acculturation gaps between immigrant
youth and their parents' generation often represent barriers to action. For
example, Asian American college students report that their immigrant parents
sometimes discouraged or did not support their engagement in high school civic
activities because they perceived this to be a "foreign, American concept" (Chan,
2011; p. 200). This suggests that pathways from immigrant optimism to different

forms of action are nuanced and highly influenced by family practices, values, and dynamics. Importantly, appreciation for and trust in US society as it relates to immigrant optimism may be more likely to facilitate forms of engagement that support democracy in conventional ways (Flanagan et al., 2009). Here, we underscore our focus on understanding the motivations and the intended outcomes of youth's action. While participation in formal democratic or electoral behaviors, such as voting, is not typically considered *critical* action, it may very well be so for immigrant youth who might be the only or first in their family to have a political "voice" and therefore experience a unique sense of responsibility to use their voting rights to advocate for others (e.g., Arce et al., 2020). Indeed, in our research, we have found that Latinx parents who are US citizens feel they have to be the voice ("tenemos que ser la voz"; p. 113) for immigrants who do not have the documentation status to participate in US elections.

Also, the association between optimism and conventional action is likely to vary as a function of exposure to marginalization. That is, optimism about US society and related democratic processes and activities may decline with increased exposure to and awareness of inequities (e.g., Sánchez-Jankowski, 2002). For example, perceived discrimination in the last year of high school predicted a decrease in fair society beliefs one-year postgraduation among Latinx and Asian adolescents (Ballard, 2016). Also, after initially being grateful for the better access to educational materials in the United States compared to that in their native country, over time undocumented Mexican immigrant high schoolers became aware of inequitable resources for and discrimination against Mexicans specifically and immigrants more broadly (Gutiérrez, 2014). Similarly, George Mwangi et al. (2019) found that Black immigrant college students described a transition from positive views about available educational opportunities to awareness of racial inequities. Education, advocacy, and service- or civic-related careers were seen as strategies to transform the structural barriers of which they had become increasingly aware (George Mwangi et al., 2019; Gutiérrez, 2014; McWhirter, Gomez, et al., 2019). An important avenue for future research in this area is to consider the reasons and circumstances undergirding immigration to the United States. It is likely that immigrant optimism varies among those who migrate by choice versus those who are forced to migrate. For example, in an exploratory study, Arce (2021) found that young immigrants in families that experienced persecution in their country of origin had higher levels of immigrant optimism than their immigrant peers who did not have a history of persecution.

Another possibility is that immigrant optimism is related to but distinct from awareness of inequities. Immigrant youth of color may hold high regard for the host society and appreciate the opportunities it has granted them and their families yet still recognize existing inequities that negatively impact their own and others' social conditions in the host country. However, limited

research in this area and inconsistent conceptualizations and operationaliza-
tions of these constructs, particularly immigrant optimism, do not yet allow
us to draw meaningful conclusions. We return to this and other limitations of
existing research in the next section.

DISCUSSION

CC theory suggests that being aware of societal inequities and engaging
in critical action to challenge them is particularly important for the positive
development and empowerment of youth of color. To date, however, there
have been limited attempts to consider variations in CC development among
youth of color who also have an immigrant background and for whom
developmental processes may differ. This chapter thus aimed to fill gaps in
the conceptualization of CC among immigrant youth of color by describing
how key immigration phenomena may uniquely shape processes of CC in
these youth. A main focus of this chapter involved young immigrants' perceived sense of responsibility to the systems within which they are embedded.
Starting with families, we discussed ways in which socialization practices
along with mutually beneficial dynamics between immigrant parents and
children might promote the development of a sense of responsibility that
can spill over to other, more distal systems and motivate engagement in
critical action, broadly defined. We introduced the concept of the immigrant
bargain to help elucidate this matter. To a lesser extent, we also presented
potential influences of immigrant optimism on CC development.

Throughout the chapter, we have highlighted a few observations and
criticisms that we present here again as main takeaways. First, actions themselves cannot be defined as critical or not without first understanding the
motivations and intentions for such actions. This is a particularly important
consideration for immigrant youth of color who, as a function of their own or
their family's actual or presumed documentation status, and their potentially
more limited familiarity with some US systems relative to nonimmigrant
youth, may face considerable barriers to and risks in participating in narrowly
defined social change efforts. We discourage researchers and practitioners
from predetermining what constitutes critical action without explicitly assessing this given youth's unique position within society and without giving
participants an opportunity to help make that determination. After all, CC
is, in its essence, an empowering process that provides marginalized individuals and groups opportunities for self-determination, and our methods
should reflect their voice.

Second, although we conceptualize the phenomenon of the immigrant
bargain as a driver of social responsibilities, we consider it important to
recognize that the immigrant bargain may present more costs than rewards
for some youth (e.g., Louie, 2012). Indeed, as we have noted, the sense of

responsibility to make their immigrant parents' sacrifices "worth it" may be motivating to some and burdensome to others (e.g., Katz, 2014; Louie, 2012; Uriostegui et al., 2020). We suggest that in order to understand the nuances of how immigrant youth of color make sense of, respond to, affect, and are affected by these dynamics we must carefully consider interactions between and among factors at multiple levels of the human ecology. Like others have noted, the experiences of immigrants navigating and adapting to a new society are as much about their own characteristics and values as they are about the institutional supports that are or are not available to them (Louie, 2012). Indeed, we have argued that young immigrants hold high aspirations for their future and are driven to achieve academically and vocationally to fulfill their part of the immigrant bargain and give back to both their families and identity-based communities. However, we have also emphasized the need for resources that extend beyond the family.

Third, we would like to underscore the importance of attending to reciprocal and reinforcing influences between immigrant youth's attitudinal and behavioral responsibilities and their multiple systems of support. These, again, include not only those systems that are proximal and interpersonal (e.g., family, peers), but also those that are more distal and institutional (e.g., school, community organizations), and/or systemic in nature (e.g., social policy).

Limitations and Recommendations

This chapter reviews the existing literature on processes relevant to CC among immigrant youth of color, shedding light on unique immigration phenomena that may shape their pathways to critical action, but which have previously been neglected. This review and the arguments we have presented must thus be considered within the context of several gaps and limitations in existing research. First, whereas research has documented the relevance of family obligations and family support to the development of immigrant youth of color, research on community and institutional support is limited yet promising. Also, in this chapter, we have distinguished sense of social responsibility from its behavioral enactment. Future research should examine whether differences are present between pathways to attitude versus behavior and what accounts for those differences, if any, among immigrant youth of color (e.g., availability/eligibility to participate in action, risk of participating in action).

Research seeking to integrate CC and acculturation literatures could also benefit from investigations that consider the diverse ways that immigrant youth of color seek to effect social change. For example, as we have reported, immigrant youth of color often aspire to serve as role models for others in their communities and perceive their own achievement as an avenue to do this and bring about social change. However, this is not captured in existing measures of critical action. We encourage researchers to utilize mixed methods to explicitly assess intended outcomed of youth action and utilize that information to determine which behaviors constitute *critical* action among immigrant youth of color, instead of predetermining categories of action without accounting for the unique experiences reviewed in this chapter.

Intervention efforts would also benefit from greater attention to the role of intersecting identities, including nativity and citizenship. Scholars have recommended attention to activities that are accessible to the group of interest as this can help better clarify motivations and account for barriers to action (e.g., Dixon et al., 2018; Ekman & Amnå, 2012). Young immigrants' sense of responsibility and involvement in particular activities to benefit their identity-based communities is influenced by factors such as the protection offered to them and close family members via documentation status (e.g., Arce, 2021). Practitioners should carefully attend to these intersecting identities with a focus on interlocking systems of oppression and culturally relevant assets that may promote empowering settings (e.g., Buckingham et al., 2021). It is also worth noting that the findings we have reviewed on key immigration phenomena come primarily from qualitative observations, and when quantitative data have been available, these constructs have not been consistently operationalized. Future research should consider employing a mixed methods design to both quantify the influence of these processes and contextualize findings with qualitative details that may not be captured in quantitative measures.

Conclusion

Immigrants and children of immigrants make up approximately 26% of the US population, according to the 2020 Current Population Survey, with the vast majority of them being natives of Asia and Latin America (Batalova et al., 2021). Consistent with that, most research on the development of immigrant youth of color has focused on Asian and Latinx youth and finds that these youth continue to be impacted by systems of oppression. As CC is considered "an antidote for oppression" (Watts et al., 1999, p. 255), greater understanding of what promotes or hinders the CC development of these youth and clears a pathway toward liberation is crucial. We suggest that this understanding can only come from careful consideration of dynamics and processes that may be unique to the immigrant experience, including but not limited to the ones presented in this chapter.

REFERENCES

Aldoney, D., & Cabrera, N. J. (2016). Raising American citizens: Socialization goals of low-income immigrant Latino mothers and fathers of young children. *Journal of Child and Family Studies*, 25(12), 3607–3618. https://doi.org/10.1007/s10826-016-0510-x.

Anyiwo, N., Bañales, J., Rowley, S. J., Watkins, D. C., & Richards, S. K. (2018). Sociocultural influences on the sociopolitical development of African American youth. *Child Development Perspectives, 12*(3), 165–170. https://doi.org /10.1111/cdep.12276.

Anyiwo, N., Palmer, G. J., Garrett, J. M., Starck, J. G., & Hope, E. C. (2020). Racial and political resistance: An examination of the sociopolitical action of racially marginalized youth. *Current Opinion in Psychology, 35*, 86–91. https://doi.org/10.1016 /j.copsyc.2020.03.005.

Arce, M. A. (2021). Civic action among immigrant youth of color in the US: Contributions of critical reflection, sociopolitical efficacy, and immigrant optimism. Unpublished doctoral dissertation. Georgia State University.

Arce, M. A., Kumar, J. L., Kuperminc, G. P., & Roche, K. M. (2020). "Tenemos que ser la voz": Exploring resilience among Latina/o immigrant families in the context of restrictive immigration policies and practices. *International Journal of Intercultural Relations, 79*, 106–120. https://doi.org/10.1016/j.ijintrel.2020.08.006.

Ballard, P. J. (2013). The civic lives of immigrant-origin youth. Unpublished doctoral dissertation. Stanford University.

Ballard, P. J. (2016). Longitudinal links between discrimination and civic development among Latino and Asian adolescents. *Journal of Research on Adolescence, 26*(4), 723–737. https://doi.org/10.1111/jora.12221.

Ballard, P. J., Malin, H., Porter, T. J., Colby, A., & Damon, W. (2015). Motivations for civic participation among diverse youth: More similarities than differences. *Research in Human Development, 12*(1–2), 63–83. https://doi.org/10.1080/15427609.2015.1010348.

Barajas-Gonzalez, R. G., Ayón, C., & Torres, F. (2018). Applying a community violence framework to understand the impact of immigration enforcement threat on Latino children. *Social Policy Report, 31*(3), 1–24. https://doi.org/10.1002 /sop2.1.

Batalova,J., Hanna, M., & Levesque, C. (2021, February 11). Frequently requested statistics on immigrants and immigration in the United States. Migration Policy Institute. www.migrationpolicy.org/article/frequently-requested-statistics-immigrants-and-immigration-united-states-2020.

Borjian, A. (2018). Academically successful Latino undocumented students in college: Resilience and civic engagement. *Hispanic Journal of Behavioral Sciences, 40*(1), 22–36. https://doi.org/10.1177/0739986317754299.

Branscombe, N. R., Schmitt, M. T., & Harvey, R. D. (1999). Perceiving pervasive discrimination among African Americans: Implications for group identification and well-being. *Journal of Personality and Social Psychology, 77*(1), 135–149. https://doi.org/10.1037/0022-3514.77.1.135.

Buckingham, S. L., Langhout, R. D., Rusch, D. et al. (2021). The roles of settings in supporting immigrants' resistance to injustice and oppression: A policy position statement by the society for community research and action. *American Journal of Community Psychology, 68*(3–4), 269–291. https://doi.org/10.1002/ajcp.12515.

Cadenas, G. A., Bernstein, B. L., & Tracey, T. J. G. (2018). Critical consciousness and intent to persist through college in DACA and US citizen students: The role of immigration status, race, and ethnicity. *Cultural Diversity and Ethnic Minority Psychology, 24*(4), 564–575. https://doi.org/10.1037/cdp0000200.

Cadenas, G. A., Liu, L., Li, K. M., & Beachy, S. (2021). Promoting critical consciousness, academic performance, and persistence among graduate students experiencing class-based oppression. *Journal of Diversity in Higher Education*, 15(1), 26–36. https://doi.org/10.1037/dhe0000250.

Cadenas, G. A., Lynn, N., Li, K. M. et al. (2020). Racial/ethnic minority community college students' critical consciousness and social cognitive career outcomes. *The Career Development Quarterly*, 68(4), 302–317. https://doi.org/10.1002/cdq.12238.

Chan, W. Y. (2011). An exploration of Asian American college students' civic engagement. *Asian American Journal of Psychology*, 2(3), 197–204. https://doi.org/10.1037/a0024675.

Chan, W. Y., & Latzman, R. D. (2015). Racial discrimination, multiple group identities, and civic beliefs among immigrant adolescents. *Cultural Diversity and Ethnic Minority Psychology*, 21(4), 527–532. https://doi.org/10.1037/cdp0000021.

Cherng, H.-Y. S., & Liu, J.-L. (2017). Academic social support and student expectations: The case of second-generation Asian Americans. *Asian American Journal of Psychology*, 8(1), 16–30. https://doi.org/10.1037/aap0000072.

Crookes, D. M., Stanhope, K. K., Kim, Y. J., Lummus, E., & Suglia, S. F. (2021). Federal, state, and local immigrant-related policies and child health outcomes: A systematic review. *Journal of Racial and Ethnic Health Disparities*, 9(2), 478–488. https://doi.org/10.1007/s40615-021-00978-w.

De Feyter, J. J., Parada, M. D., Hartman, S. C., Curby, T. W., & Winsler, A. (2020). The early academic resilience of children from low-income, immigrant families. *Early Childhood Research Quarterly*, 51, 446–461. https://doi.org/10.1016/j.ecresq.2020.01.001.

Diemer, M. A., McWhirter, E. H., Ozer, E. J., & Rapa, L. J. (2015). Advances in the conceptualization and measurement of critical consciousness. *The Urban Review*, 47(5), 809–823. https://doi.org/10.1007/s11256-015-0336-7.

Diemer, M. A., & Rapa, L. J. (2016). Unraveling the complexity of critical consciousness, political efficacy, and political action among marginalized adolescents. *Child Development*, 87(1), 221–238. https://doi.org/10.1111/cdev.12446.

Dixon, Z., Bessaha, M. L., & Post, M. (2018). Beyond the ballot: Immigrant integration through civic engagement and advocacy. *Race and Social Problems*, 10(4), 366–375. https://doi.org/10.1007/s12552-018-9237-1.

Dreby, J. (2010). *Divided by borders: Mexican migrants and their children*. University of California Press.

East, P. L. (2010). Children's provision of family caregiving: Benefit or burden? *Child Development Perspectives*, 4(1), 55–61. https://doi.org/10.1111/j.1750-8606.2009.00118.x.

Ekman, J., & Amnå, E. (2012). Political participation and civic engagement: Towards a new typology. *Human Affairs*, 22(3), 283–300. https://doi.org/10.2478/s13374-012-0024-1.

Ellis, S. J. (2004). Young people and political action: Who is taking responsibility for positive social change? *Journal of Youth Studies*, 7(1), 89–102. https://doi.org/10.1080/1367626042000209976.

Flanagan, C. A., Syvertsen, A. K., Gill, S., Gallay, L. S., & Cumsille, P. (2009). Ethnic awareness, prejudice, and civic commitments in four ethnic groups of American adolescents. *Journal of Youth and Adolescence, 38*(4), 500–518. https://doi-org.ezproxy.gsu.edu/10.1007/s10964-009-9394-z.

Forenza, B. (2018). Awareness, analysis, engagement: Critical consciousness through foster youth advisory board participation. *Child & Adolescent Social Work Journal, 35*(2), 119–126. https://doi.org/10.1007/s10560-017-0515-3.

Forenza, B., Rogers, B., & Lardier, D. T. (2017). What facilitates and supports political activism by, and for, undocumented students? *The Urban Review, 49*(4), 648–667. https://doi.org/10.1007/s11256-017-0413-1.

Freire, P. (1968). *Pedagogy of the oppressed.* Continuum

Fuligni, A. J., Hughes, D. L., & Way, N. (2009). Ethnicity and immigration. In R. M. Lerner & L. Steinberg (Eds.), *Handbook of adolescent psychology: Contextual influences on adolescent development* (pp. 527–569). John Wiley & Sons. https://doi.org/10.1002/9780470479193.adlpsy002016.

Fuligni, A. J., & Pedersen, S. (2002). Family obligation and the transition to young adulthood. *Developmental Psychology, 38*(5), 856–868. https://doi.org/10.1037/0012-1649.38.5.856.

Fuligni, A. J., Tseng, V., & Lam, M. (1999). Attitudes toward family obligations among American adolescents with Asian, Latin American, and European backgrounds. *Child Development, 70*(4), 1030–1044. https://doi.org/10.1111/1467-8624.00075.

George Mwangi, C. A., Daoud, N., Peralta, A., & Fries-Britt, S. (2019). Waking from the American dream: Conceptualizing racial activism and critical consciousness among Black immigrant college students. *Journal of College Student Development, 60*(4), 401–420. https://doi.org/10.1353/csd.2019.0037.

Ghavami, N., Katsiaficas, D., & Rogers, L. O. (2016). Toward an intersectional approach in developmental science: The role of race, gender, sexual orientation, and immigrant status. In S. S. Horn, M. D. Ruck, & L. S. Liben (Eds.), *Advances in child development and behavior: Vol. 50. Equity and justice in developmental science: Theoretical and methodological issues* (pp. 31–73). Elsevier Academic Press. https://doi.org/10.1016/bs.acdb.2015.12.001.

Godfrey, E. B., & Wolf, S. (2016). Developing critical consciousness or justifying the system? A qualitative analysis of attributions for poverty and wealth among low-income racial/ethnic minority and immigrant women. *Cultural Diversity and Ethnic Minority Psychology, 22*(1), 93–103. https://doi.org/10.1037/cdp0000048.

Greenfield, P. M., Keller, H., Fuligni, A., & Maynard, A. (2003). Cultural pathways through universal development. *Annual Review of Psychology, 54*(1), 461–490. https://doi.org/10.1146/annurev.psych.54.101601.145221.

Gutiérrez, L. A. (2014). Youth social justice engagement in the face of anti-Latina/o immigrant illegitimacy. *The Urban Review, 46*(2), 307–323. https://doi.org/10.1007/s11256-013-0269-y.

Harper, G. W., Jadwin-Cakmak, L., Cherenak, E., & Wilson, P. (2019). Critical consciousness-based HIV prevention interventions for Black gay and bisexual male youth. *American Journal of Sexuality Education, 14*(1), 109–133. https://doi.org/10.1080/15546128.2018.1479668.

Heberle, A. E., Rapa, L. J., & Farago, F. (2020). Critical consciousness in children and adolescents: A systematic review, critical assessment, and recommendations for future research. *Psychological Bulletin*, *146*(6), 525–551. https://doi.org/10.1037/bul0000230.

Jensen, L. A. (2008). Immigrants' cultural identities as sources of civic engagement. *Applied Developmental Science*, *12*(2), 74–83. https://doi.org/10.1080/10888690801997069.

Kao, G., & Tienda, M. (1995). Optimism and achievement: The educational performance of immigrant youth. *Social Science Quarterly*, *76*(1), 1–19. http://www.jstor.org/stable/44072586.

Katsiaficas, D. (2018). Infusing the study of social responsibilities with an intersectional approach. *New Directions for Child and Adolescent Development*, *2018*(161), 39–56. https://doi.org/10.1002/cad.20249.

Katsiaficas, D., Hernandez, E., Alcantar, C. M. et al. (2018). "We'll get through this together": Collective contribution in the lives of undocumented undergraduates. *Teachers College Record*, *120*(12), 1–48.

Katz, V. (2014). Shortchanging the immigrant bargain? In *Kids in the middle* (pp. 96–121). Rutgers University Press. https://doi.org/10.36019/9780813562209-008.

Kennedy, H., Matyasic, S., Schofield Clark, L. et al. (2020). Early adolescent critical consciousness development in the age of Trump. *Journal of Adolescent Research*, *35*(3), 279–308. https://doi.org/10.1177/0743558419852055.

Kiang, L., Christophe, N. K., & Stein, G. L. (2021). Differentiating pathways between ethnic-racial identity and critical consciousness. *Journal of Youth and Adolescence*, *50*(7), 1369–1383. https://doi.org/10.1007/s10964-021-01453-9.

Knight, M. G., & Watson, V. W. M. (2014). Toward participatory communal citizenship: Rendering visible the civic teaching, learning, and actions of African immigrant youth and young adults. *American Educational Research Journal*, *51*(3), 539–566. https://doi.org/10.3102/0002831213512517.

Kolano, L. Q., & Davila, L. T. (2019). Transformative learning of refugee girls within a community youth organization serving Southeast Asians in North Carolina. *Journal of Research in Childhood Education*, *33*(1), 119–133. https://doi.org/10.1080/02568543.2018.1531447.

Kuperminc, G. P., Jurkovic, G. J., & Casey, S. (2009). Relation of filial responsibility to the personal and social adjustment of Latino adolescents from immigrant families. *Journal of Family Psychology*, *23*(1), 14–22. https://doi.org/10.1037/a0014064.

Kuperminc, G. P., Wilkins, N. J., Jurkovic, G. J., & Perilla, J. L. (2013). Filial responsibility, perceived fairness, and psychological functioning of Latino youth from immigrant families. *Journal of Family Psychology*, *27*(2), 173–182. https://doi.org/10.1037/a0031880.

Kuperminc, G. P., Wilkins, N. J., Roche, C., & Alvarez-Jimenez, A. (2009). Risk, resilience, and positive development among Latino youth. In F. A. Villarruel, G. Carlo, J. M. Grau, et al. (Eds.), *Handbook of US Latino psychology: Developmental and community-based perspectives* (pp. 213–233). Sage Publications, Inc.

Louie, V. (2012). *Keeping the immigrant bargain: The costs and rewards of success in America*. Russell Sage Foundation.

Luginbuhl, P. J., McWhirter, E. H., & McWhirter, B. T. (2016). Sociopolitical development, autonomous motivation, and education outcomes: Implications for low-income Latina/o adolescents. *Journal of Latina/o Psychology*, 4(1), 43–59. https://doi.org/10.1037/lat0000041.

Martinez, C. R., Jr., McClure, H. H., & Eddy, J. M. (2009). Language brokering contexts and behavioral and emotional adjustment among Latino parents and adolescents. *The Journal of Early Adolescence*, 29(1), 71–98. https://doi.org/10.1177/0272431608324477.

Mathews, C. J., Medina, M. A., Bañales, J. et al. (2020). Mapping the intersections of adolescents' ethnic-racial identity and critical consciousness. *Adolescent Research Review*, 5, 363–379. https://doi.org/10.1007/s40894-019-00122-0.

McWhirter, E. H., Gomez, D., & Rau, E. D. (2019). "Never give up. Fight for what you believe in": Perceptions of how Latina/o adolescents can make a difference. *Cultural Diversity and Ethnic Minority Psychology*, 25(3), 403–412. https://doi.org/10.1037/cdp0000254.

McWhirter, E. H., & McWhirter, B. T. (2016). Critical consciousness and vocational development among Latina/o high school youth. *Journal of Career Assessment*, 24, 543–558. http://dx.doi.org/10.1177/1069072715599535

McWhirter, E. H., Rojas-Araúz, B. O., Ortega, R. et al. (2019). ALAS: An intervention to promote career development among Latina/o immigrant high school students. *Journal of Career Development*, 46(6), 608–622. https://doi.org/10.1177/0894845319828543.

Migration Policy Institute (2018). Children in US immigrant families. www.migrationpolicy.org/programs/data-hub/us-immigration-trends#children.

Moreno, O., Fuentes, L., Garcia-Rodriguez, I., Corona, R., & Cadenas, G. A. (2021). Psychological impact, strengths, and handling the uncertainty among Latinx DACA recipients. *The Counseling Psychologist*, 49(5), 728–753. https://doi.org/10.1177/00110000211006198.

Peterson, N. A., Peterson, C. H., Agre, L., Christens, B. D., & Morton, C. M. (2011). Measuring youth empowerment: Validation of a sociopolitical control scale for youth in an urban community context. *Journal of Community Psychology*, 39(5), 592–605. https://doi-org.ezproxy.gsu.edu/10.1002/jcop.20456.

Phinney, J. (2006). Ethnic identity exploration in emerging adulthood. In J. Arnett & J. L. Tanner (Eds.), *Coming of age in the 21st century: The lives and contexts of emerging adults* (pp. 117–134). American Psychological Association.

Pinedo, A., Durkee, M. I., Diemer, M. A., & Hope, E. C. (2021). Disentangling longitudinal trajectories of racial discrimination and critical action among Black and Latinx college students: What role do peers play? *Cultural Diversity and Ethnic Minority Psychology*, 27(3), 546–557. https://doi.org/10.1037/cdp0000434.

Pinetta, B. J., Blanco Martinez, S., Cross, F. L., & Rivas, D. D. (2020). Inherently political? Associations of parent ethnic–racial socialization and sociopolitical discussions with Latinx youths' emergent civic engagement. *American Journal of Community Psychology*, 66(1–2), 94–105. https://doi.org/10.1002/ajcp.12435.

Ramos, M. R., Cassidy, C., Reicher, S., & Haslam, S. A. (2012). A longitudinal investigation of the rejection-identification hypothesis. *The British Journal of Social Psychology*, 51(4), 642–660. https://doi.org/10.1111/j.2044-8309.2011.02029.x.

Rapa, L. J., Bolding, C. W., & Jamil, F. M. (2020). Development and initial validation of the short Critical Consciousness Scale (CCS-S). *Journal of Applied Developmental Psychology, 70*–101164. https://doi.org/10.1016/j.appdev.2020.101164.

Rubio-Hernandez, S. P., & Ayón, C. (2016). Pobrecitos los niños: The emotional impact of anti-immigration policies on Latino children. *Children and Youth Services Review, 60*, 20–26. https://doi.org/10.1016/j.childyouth.2015.11.013.

Sánchez-Jankowski, M. (2002). Minority youth and civic engagement: The impact of group relations. *Applied Developmental Science, 6*(4), 237–245. https://doi.org/10.1207/S1532480XADS0604_11.

Seider, S., Clark, S., & Graves, D. (2020). The development of critical consciousness and its relation to academic achievement in adolescents of color. *Child Development, 91*(2), e451–e474. https://doi.org/10.1111/cdev.13262.

Seider, S., Tamerat, J., Clark, S., & Soutter, M. (2017). Investigating adolescents' critical consciousness development through a character framework. *Journal of Youth and Adolescence, 46*(6), 1162–1178. https://doi.org/10.1007/s10964-017-0641-4.

Singh, S., Berezin, M. N., Wallach, L. N., B. Godfrey, E., & Javdani, S. (2021). Traumatic incidents and experiences of racism and sexism: Examining associations with components of critical consciousness for system-involved girls of color. *American Journal of Community Psychology, 67*(1–2), 64–75. https://doi.org/10.1002/ajcp.12479.

Stein, G. L., Cupito, A. M., Mendez, J. L. et al. (2014). Familism through a developmental lens. *Journal of Latina/o Psychology, 2*(4), 224–250. https://doi.org/10.1037/lat0000025.

Stepick, A., & Stepick, C. D. (2002). Becoming American, constructing ethnicity: Immigrant youth and civic engagement. *Applied Developmental Science, 6*(4), 246–257. https://doi.org/10.1207/S1532480XADS0604_12.

Stepick, A., Stepick, C. D., & Labissiere, Y. (2008). South Florida's immigrant youth and civic engagement: Major engagement: Minor differences. *Applied Developmental Science, 12*(2), 57–65. https://doi.org/10.1080/10888690801997036.

Suárez-Orozco, C., Hernández, M. G., & Casanova, S. (2015). "It's Sort of My Calling": The civic engagement and social responsibility of Latino immigrant-origin young adults. *Research in Human Development, 12*(1–2), 84–99. https://doi.org/10.1080/15427609.2015.1010350.

Suyemoto, K. L., Day, S. C., & Schwartz, S. (2015). Exploring effects of social justice youth programming on racial and ethnic identities and activism for Asian American youth. *Asian American Journal of Psychology, 6*(2), 125–135. https://doi.org/10.1037/aa0037789.

Sy, S. R., & Romero, J. (2008). Family responsibilities among Latina college students from immigrant families. *Journal of Hispanic Higher Education, 7*(3), 212–227. https://doi.org/10.1177/1538192708316208.

Tajfel, H. (1978). The achievement of inter-group differentiation. In H. Tajfel (Ed.), *Differentiation between social groups* (pp. 77–100). Academic Press.

Tajfel, H., & Turner, J. C. (1986). The social identity theory of intergroup behavior. In S. Worchel & W. G. Austin (Eds.), *Psychology of intergroup relations* (pp. 7–24). Nelson Hall.

Telzer, E. H., & Fuligni, A. J. (2009). Daily family assistance and the psychological well-being of adolescents from Latin American, Asian, and European backgrounds. *Developmental Psychology*, *45*(4), 1177–1189. https://doi.org/10.1037/a0014728.

Thomas, E. F., Zubielevitch, E., Sibley, C. G., & Osborne, D. (2020). Testing the social identity model of collective action longitudinally and across structurally disadvantaged and advantaged groups. *Personality and Social Psychology Bulletin*, *46*(6), 823–838. https://doi.org/10.1177/0146167219879111.

Tran, J., & Curtin, N. (2017). Not your model minority: Own-group activism among Asian Americans. *Cultural Diversity and Ethnic Minority Psychology*, *23*(4), 499–507. https://doi.org/10.1037/cdp0000145.

Turner, J. C., Hogg, M. A., Oakes, P. J., Reicher, S. D., & Wetherell, M. S. (1987). *Rediscovering the social group: A self-categorization theory*. Basil Blackwell.

Uriostegui, M., Roy, A. L., & Li-Grining, C. P. (2020). What drives you? Black and Latinx youth's critical consciousness, motivations, and academic and career activities. *Journal of Youth and Adolescence*, *50*, 58–74. https://doi.org/10.1007/s10964-020-01343-6.

van Zomeren, M., Postmes, T., & Spears, R. (2008). Toward an integrative social identity model of collective action: A quantitative research synthesis of three socio-psychological perspectives. *Psychological Bulletin*, *134*(4), 504–535. https://doi.org/10.1037/0033-2909.134.4.504.

Watts, R. J., Griffith, D. M., & Abdul-Adil, J. (1999). Sociopolitical development as an antidote for oppression: Theory and action. *American Journal of Community Psychology*, *27*(2), 255–271. https://doi-org.ezproxy.gsu.edu/10.1023/A:1022839818873.

Weisskirch, R. S. (2005). The relationship of language brokering to ethnic identity for Latino early adolescents. *Hispanic Journal of Behavioral Sciences*, *27*(3), 286–299. https://doi.org/10.1177/0739986305277931.

Wiley, S., Deaux, K., & Hagelskamp, C. (2012). Born in the USA: How immigrant generation shapes meritocracy and its relation to ethnic identity and collective action. *Cultural Diversity and Ethnic Minority Psychology*, *18*(2), 171–180. https://doi.org/10.1037/a0027661.

Wiley, S., Lawrence, D., Figueroa, J., & Percontino, R. (2013). Rejection-(dis)identification and ethnic political engagement among first-generation Latino immigrants to the United States. *Cultural Diversity and Ethnic Minority Psychology*, *19*(3), 310–319. https://doi.org/10.1037/a0031093.

Williams, C. D., Byrd, C. M., Quintana, S. M. et al. (2020). A lifespan model of ethnic-racial identity. *Research in Human Development*, *17*(2–3), 99–129. https://doi.org/10.1080/15427609.2020.1831882.

Wray-Lake, L., & Syvertsen, A. (2011). The developmental roots of social responsibility in childhood and adolescence. *New Directions for Child and Adolescent Development*, *2011*(134), 11–25. https://doi.org/10.1002/cd.308.

Wray-Lake, L., Wells, R., Alvis, L. et al. (2018). Being a Latinx adolescent under a Trump presidency: Analysis of Latinx youth's reactions to immigration politics. *Children and Youth Services Review*, *87*, 192–204. https://doi.org/10.1016/j.childyouth.2018.02.032.

Concluding Thoughts on the Role of Contexts and Settings in Youth Critical Consciousness Development

ERIN B. GODFREY AND LUKE J. RAPA

Youth today face a sociopolitical moment in which the systems of oppression that have long patterned American society are in bold relief (Bonilla-Silva, 1997, 2006). White supremacy, structural oppression, and systemic inequity are woven into the fabric of our society. They shape our present and future, as well as our past, and influence all aspects of our individual, social, and communal well-being. Developing critical consciousness (CC) (Freire, 1968/2000; Watts et al., 2011) – learning to critically "read" social conditions, feel motivated and empowered to change those conditions, and engage in action toward that goal – is fundamental to helping youth navigate and resist these oppressions, and in contributing to the fight for justice and liberation.

Through the contributions in this volume, we have endeavored to push scholarly and practical knowledge in this area by taking up core questions about how the contexts and settings youth inhabit inform their CC development. In so doing, we have sought to engage with Watts' and colleagues (1999) call to focus on the opportunity structures that shape youth's ability to critically read social conditions and take action to challenge oppression and inequity, and to respond to Heberle's and colleagues (2020) invitation to examine "critical consciousness as a characteristic of consciousness-raising systems" (p. 544). Accordingly, the chapters in this volume chart new conceptual and empirical terrain on the features of youth's everyday settings and contexts and their interplay with CC development. They do so in both nuanced and broadband ways, providing subtle yet important refinements to existing knowledge as well as introducing us to novel settings and perspectives.

Part I of the volume tackled pedagogical, curricular, and school-based contexts, showing that nuances in teacher practice can be as important as curricular features in creating consciousness-raising classrooms and schools and demonstrating that widely implemented curricula such as action civics programs can align with CC principles and promote its development even absent an explicit CC goal. Part II of the volume took up the question of extracurricular contexts programs, providing a novel theoretical integration of effective out-of-school practice with CC perspectives, and introducing us to conceptual and empirical evidence concerning the role of the arts and critical service learning in CC development. Finally, Part III of the volume broadened our perspective on key societal contexts of CC development, delineating and reconceptualizing how race, immigration, and documentation status function as distinct and unique societal contexts of CC development.

CONCLUDING THOUGHTS

The rich ideas theorized and evaluated in these pages open new doors of inquiry and suggest novel practical innovations to support youth's CC development. By way of conclusion, we leave you with a few thoughts and open questions about the contexts and settings of CC development that the scholarship in this volume, and elsewhere, raises for us. Our goal is to draw these thoughts and insights into the light for further scholarship and practice in the field to consider.

(M)Any Contexts and Settings Can be Consciousness Raising

It is easy to assume that promoting CC in youth requires a particular curriculum, set of activities, or assemblage of structured elements. While these certainly form the backbone of many consciousness-raising settings, they are not necessarily required, and may not even be the most important features of consciousness-raising settings. Indeed, scholars summarizing CC development across different contexts and settings, such as community organizing (e.g., Kirshner & Ginwright, 2012), intervention programs (e.g., Heberle et al., 2020), and schools (e.g., Seider & Graves, 2020), have noted that *how* this work is implemented is just as, if not more, important than *what* is implemented. The chapters shared in this volume reiterate and reinforce this idea. They illustrate the many different contexts and settings – from civic action programs, to arts and creative activities, to advocacy-based service learning, to everyday after school programs – that can function as consciousness-promoting contexts in youth's lives. Chapters 2, 3, 5, and 6 illustrate how widely different types of programming, implemented in different contexts, and focused on different substantive issues, can all play a role in the CC development of young people. What these settings have in common is a set of social processes (e.g., Tseng & Seidman, 2007) that bolster youth's CC development and allow them to serve as counterspaces to forces of oppression. Foundational social processes that characterize consciousness-promoting settings include: prioritization of critical thinking and questioning; engagement in open and respectful dialogue; connection of critical perspectives to lived experiences; encouragement of members to share their experiences and perspectives; presence of power-sharing and youth–adult partnerships; modeling of anti-oppressive stances and practices; emphasis on the importance of struggle and the need fight injustice; and identification of the many ways – both big and small – that youth can resist oppression in their everyday lives. Indeed, toward this goal, Chapter 4 aligns broad principles of effective out-of-school programs with many of these social processes to show how a variety of after-school programs, with varying content areas, can be leveraged toward CC goals. Chapter 1 powerfully demonstrates how even culturally relevant pedagogical tools attuned to social injustice can go awry when not implemented with attention to these social processes. We encourage the field to engage with these ideas and draw from the rich foundation of scholarship on setting-level processes, social regularities, and empowering contexts from our community psychology colleagues (e.g., Christens et al., 2016; Ibrahim et al., in prep; Rappaport, 1987; Seidman, 1988; Tseng & Seidman, 2007) in this endeavor.

Consciousness-Raising Settings Should Support the Skills That Support Critical Consciousness

Multiple contributors to this volume, and our companion volume *Critical Consciousness: Expanding Theory and Measurement* (Rapa & Godfrey, in press[b]), remind us that promoting CC involves more than supporting youth's ability to critically reflect on injustice, feel motivated to fight it, and take action to do so. It also involves supporting the underlying skills and capabilities that make such critical reflection, motivation, and action possible. It is evident across the chapters in this volume that the contexts and settings that foster critical consciousness do so both directly and indirectly, promoting CC itself as well as its underlying skills and capabilities. For example, Chapter 5 delineates how a seemingly unrelated competency – arts production – can foster fundamental critical thinking, perspective taking, self-expression, identity exploration, and social skills that serve as the foundation on which CC can be built. Similarly, the key features of quality out-of-school programming described in Chapter 4's integrated model support CC through the development of underlying skills such as goal setting, critical thinking, and leadership. Thus, it seems that settings effective at promoting CC also help youth develop their ability to effectively express themselves and their ideas, tolerate distress, feel empathy, take another's perspective, recognize social power, and identify concrete strategies for action.

Emotions Need to be Taken Into Account

To date, theory and empirical research on CC has focused primarily on the cognitive and behavioral components of its development, prioritizing what young people *think* and *do* as they navigate social inequity over how they *feel* about it. The chapters in this volume, along with other emerging work (e.g., Burson, 2021), point to emotions as an important and overlooked element in the CC process. This work suggests that, to promote CC, contexts and settings must hold space for the pain of oppression and marginalization to be acknowledged and felt, and they must resist the temptation to paint a rosy picture about the future or about the potential success of change efforts. Settings in which the pain and difficulty involved in fighting injustice is honored promote the growth of critical rather than false hope (Clay, 2019; Duncan-Andrade, 2009; Graves et al., Chapter 1 [this volume]). Chapter 1 is a powerful reminder of how the emotional pain of oppression needs to be recognized, validated, and honored in order to reach a place of true CC, for the adults in the setting as well as the youth. Consciousness-raising settings must also acknowledge the guilt and discomfort some may feel in facing their privileged status and their role in perpetuating the status quo (DiAngelo, 2018). Settings that provide skills to tolerate this distress and normalize these reactions can help people resist white savior models of coping with these uncomfortable feelings. In addition, the model of critical race consciousness presented in Chapter 7 reminds us that emotional reactions in response to racism (and other forms of systemic oppression) need to be more deeply considered in our developmental accounts of CC. Emotions such as pain, anger, outrage, frustration, guilt, and hopelessness figure in the reflection–motivation–action cycle in ways we are only beginning to delineate. These require our immediate attention if we are to achieve the goal of fostering greater CC development among youth.

Consciousness Raising Settings Can Start "Small"

The systems of oppression that pattern our society shape our everyday contexts and settings as well, and play out across all sectors of our lives and communities. An important takeaway from the chapters presented in this volume is that efforts to support CC development in youth do not have to tackle the largest-scale version of the problem to be effective. Instead, settings can provide opportunities for reflection, motivation, and action that are smaller in scale, focused on particular local issues, and specific to particular marginalizing institutions or forms of oppression. In fact, this kind of specificity can promote a deeper, more nuanced understanding of how social, historical, economic, and other structural forces underlie injustice, foster greater motivation to change these realities, and present many more varied opportunities to take action against injustice in smaller, more accessible, and more direct ways. For example, the action civics programs described in Chapters 2 and 3 and the critical service learning advocacy program described in Chapter 6 provided opportunities for youth to delve deeply into specific, localized issues of social injustice and use these as springboards for growth in CC writ large. In addition, as highlighted by Chapters 7, 8, 9, and 10, focusing on certain forms of marginalization or systems of oppression (e.g., racism, nativism) allows for a more refined understanding of CC and the opportunity to conceptualize how it interplays with youth's background, culture, experiences, and social positionality. Whether, and how, these specific forms of CC translate to a broader critical perspective is debated – and a fundamental area for further study (Diemer et al., 2016; Rapa & Godfrey, in press[a]) – but we suspect they might (e.g., Burson & Godfrey, 2020).

Positionality Matters

Scholars originally developed CC and sociopolitical development theories with populations experiencing marginalization firsthand in mind (Freire, 1968/2000; Watts et al., 2011). However, there is growing recognition of the importance of CC as developmental competency for more privileged youth as well, and increasing acknowledgment of the complex intersections between oppression and privilege (e.g., Godfrey & Burson, 2018). The chapters in this volume highlight the need to think deeply about youth's social and cultural positionality when considering the contexts and settings of their CC development (see also Johnson et al., in press). Longstanding developmental theory suggests that development occurs through rich transactions between the characteristics of individuals and those of the proximal and distal settings and contexts individuals inhabit (e.g., Bronfenbrenner & Morris, 1998; Garcia Coll et al., 1996; Spencer et al., 1997). Thus, the contexts and settings of CC development are likely to invoke different emotional, cognitive, and identity processes for youth with differing social and cultural positionalities, and youth are likely to bring different affordances and challenges to bear on those settings. Chapters 7, 8, 9, and 10 make compelling cases for how the realities of marginalization are experienced differently and processed differently by youth of color versus white youth, and Chapters 1 and 4 remind us that power and positionality are inherent in transactions about CC. As a field, we need to continue to incorporate this lens into our scholarship and practice in order to illuminate how the contexts and settings of CC similarly or differently inform its development for different youth.

Many Other Contexts and Settings Inform Critical Consciousness Development Too

The focus of this volume, and the scholarly literature in general, on pedagogical, curricular, and school-based contexts, extracurricular contexts, and specific societal contexts (e.g., racism and nativism) should not be taken to imply that these are the only, or even the most important, settings of CC development. There is a wealth of contexts relevant for CC development that we have not yet explored and that are ripe for further thinking. What other forms of family, peer, or school socialization (e.g., racial/ethnic socialization, achievement narratives, historical narratives) might be relevant settings of CC development (see Bañales et al., 2020 and Bañales et al., 2021 for emergent work in this area)? How do the features and characteristics of neighborhoods and communities contribute to CC development? What is the role of social media in the critical reflection–motivation–action cycle, and how does the social media context itself change how we conceptualize or operationalize these dimensions? How does CC develop in the context of other marginalizing forces and systems of oppression, such as heterosexism, homophobia, transphobia, ableism, and classism? These are just a few of the additional contexts and settings we hope this volume will inspire scholars and practitioners to explore.

Individual development and well-being is intimately interwoven with the familial, social, communal, institutional, and physical settings of our lives. We hope these concluding thoughts on the role of contexts and settings in youth CC development serve as helpful takeaways from the cutting-edge work presented in this volume, and that they provoke new ideas and avenues to support the critical consciousness development of youth. The field has come far, but the struggle to make this world a fairer, more loving, and more equitable place is ongoing.

REFERENCES

Bañales, J., Lozada, F. T., Channey, J., & Jagers, R. J. (2021). Relating through oppression: Longitudinal relations between parental racial socialization, school racial climate, oppressed minority ideology, and empathy in Black male adolescents' prosocial development. *American Journal of Community Psychology, 68*(1–2), 88–99.

Bañales, J., Marchand, A. D., Skinner, O. D. et al. (2020). Black adolescents' critical reflection development: Parents' racial socialization and attributions about race achievement gaps. *Journal of Research on Adolescence, 30,* 403–417.

Bonilla-Silva, E. (1997). Rethinking racism: Toward a structural interpretation. *American Sociological Review, 62,* 465–480. http://doi.org/10.2307/2657316.

Bonilla-Silva, E. (2006). *Racism without racists: Color-blind racism and the persistence of racial inequality in the United States.* Rowman & Littlefield Publishers.

Bronfenbrenner, U., & Morris, P. A. (1998). The ecology of developmental processes. In W. Damon & R. M. Lerner (Eds.), *Handbook of child psychology: Theoretical models of human development* (pp. 993–1028). John Wiley & Sons Inc.

Burson, E. (2021). *Critical consciousness and intraminority solidarity: A mixed methods dissertation* (Order No. 28545162). Available from ProQuest Dissertations & Theses Global.

Burson, E., & Godfrey, E. B. (2020). Intraminority solidarity: The role of critical consciousness. *European Journal of Social Psychology, 50*(6), 1362–1377.

Christens, B. D., Winn, L. T., & Duke, A. M. (2016). Empowerment and critical consciousness: A conceptual cross-fertilization. *Adolescent Research Review, 1*(1), 15–27.

Clay, K. L. (2019). "Despite the odds": Unpacking the politics of Black resilience neoliberalism. *American Educational Research Journal, 56*(1), 75–110. https://doi.org/10.3102/0002831218790214.

Coll, C. G., Crnic, K., Lamberty, G. et al. (1996). An integrative model for the study of developmental competencies in minority children. *Child Development, 67*(5), 1891–1914.

DiAngelo, R. (2018). *White fragility: Why it's so hard for white people to talk about racism.* Beacon Press.

Diemer, M. A., Rapa, L. J., Voight, A. M., & McWhirter, E. H. (2016). Critical consciousness: A developmental approach to addressing marginalization and oppression. *Child Development Perspectives, 10*(4), 216–221.

Duncan-Andrade, J. (2009). Note to educators: Hope required when growing roses in concrete. *Harvard Educational Review, 79*(2), 181–194. https://doi.org/10.17763.

Freire, P. (1968/2000). *Pedagogy of the oppressed.* Continuum.

Godfrey, E. B., & Burson, E. (2018). Interrogating the intersections: How intersectional perspectives can inform developmental scholarship on critical consciousness. *New Directions for Child and Adolescent Development, 2018* (161), 17–38.

Heberle, A. E., Rapa, L. J., & Farago, F. (2020). Critical consciousness in children and adolescents: A systematic review, critical assessment, and recommendations for future research. *Psychological Bulletin, 146*(6), 525–551. https://doi.org/10.1037/bul0000230.

Ibrahim, D., Godfrey, E. B., & Yoshikawa, H. (in prep). Understanding the Processes and Contextual Features of Arts Programming Conducive to Critical Consciousness for Youth: An Ecologically Informed Theory of Change.

Johnson, S. K., Gee, M., Diaz, A., & Hershberg, R. (in press). Measurement and analysis in quantitative critical consciousness research: Attending to the complexities of systems and selves. In L. J. Rapa and E. B. Godfrey (Eds). *Critical consciousness: Expanding theory and measurement.* Cambridge University Press.

Kirshner, B., & Ginwright, S. (2012). Youth organizing as a developmental context for African American and Latino adolescents. *Child Development Perspectives, 6*(3), 288–294.

Rapa, L. J., & Godfrey, E. B. (2023). Critical consciousness theory and measurement: Mapping the complex terrain. In L. J. Rapa and E. B. Godfrey (Eds), *Critical consciousness: Expanding theory and measurement.* Cambridge University Press.

Rapa, L. J., & Godfrey, E. B. (Eds.) (2023). *Critical consciousness: Expanding theory and measurement.* Cambridge University Press.

Rappaport, J. (1987). Terms of empowerment/exemplars of prevention: Toward a theory for community psychology. *American Journal of Community Psychology, 15*(2), 121–148.

Seider, S., & Graves, D. (2020). *Schooling for critical consciousness: Engaging Black and Latinx youth in analyzing, navigating, and challenging racial injustice.* Harvard Education Press.

Seidman, E. (1988). Back to the future, community psychology: Unfolding a theory of social intervention. *American Journal of Community Psychology, 16*(1), 3–24.

Spencer, M. B., Dupree, D., & Hartmann, T. (1997). A phenomenological variant of ecological systems theory (PVEST): A self-organization perspective in context. *Development and Psychopathology, 9*(4), 817–833.

Tseng, V., & Seidman, E. (2007). A systems framework for understanding social settings. *American Journal of Community Psychology, 39*(3), 217–228.

Watts, R. J., Diemer, M. A., & Voight, A. M. (2011). Critical consciousness: Current status and future directions. *New Directions for Child and Adolescent Development, 2011*(134), 43–57. https://doi.org/10.1002/cd.310.

Watts, R. J., Griffith, D. M., & Abdul-Adil, J. (1999). Sociopolitical development as an antidote for oppression: Theory and action. *American Journal of Community Psychology, 27*(2), 255–271.

INDEX

Ingram Content Group UK Ltd.
Milton Keynes UK
UKHW020739290523
422439UK00029B/227

9 781009 153829